James Madison's Constitution

James Madison's Constitution

A DOUBLE SECURITY AND A PARCHMENT BARRIER

Edited by Eric T. Kasper and Howard Schweber

The University of Georgia Press
ATHENS

The editors thank the University of Wisconsin–Eau Claire Menard Center for
Constitutional Studies for its contribution of funds to pay for the index.
© 2025 by the University of Georgia Press
Athens, Georgia 30602
www.ugapress.org
All rights reserved
Designed by Kaelin Chappell Broaddus
Set in 10.5/13.5 Garamond Premier Pro
Most University of Georgia Press titles are
available from popular e-book vendors.

Printed digitally
Library of Congress Cataloging-in-Publication Data
Names: Kasper, Eric T., editor. | Schweber, Howard H., editor.
Title: James Madison's Constitution : a double security and a parchment barrier / edited by Eric T.
Kasper and Howard Schweber.
Description: Athens : The University of Georgia Press, 2025. | Includes bibliographical references and
index.
Identifiers: LCCN 2024028288 | ISBN 9780820368009 (hardback) | ISBN 9780820368016 (paperback) |
ISBN 9780820368023 (epub) | ISBN 9780820368030 (pdf)
Subjects: LCSH: Constitutional history—United States. | Freedom of religion—United States. |
Madison, James, 1751–1836—Political and social views. | Federal government—United States—
History. | United States—Politics and government—1783–1809. | Republicanism.
Classification: LCC KF4541 .J345 2025 | DDC 342.7302/9—dc23/eng/20240719
LC record available at https://lccn.loc.gov/2024028288

CONTENTS

EDITORS' INTRODUCTION: JAMES MADISON'S
RELEVANCE TO THE CONSTITUTION TODAY
Eric T. Kasper and Howard Schweber

1

INTRODUCTION: JAMES MADISON, POLITICAL STRATEGIST
Jack N. Rakove

18

"FATHER OF THE CONSTITUTION"?
CAN MADISON PASS THE PATERNITY TEST?
Lynn Uzzell

38

REPUBLICANISM AND "GOOD GOVERNMENT":
MADISON'S COMPLEX CASE FOR "OUR COMPLICATED SYSTEM"
Alan R. Gibson

55

"GREAT AS THE EVIL IS":
MADISON, SLAVERY, AND THE CONSTITUTION
Quentin P. Taylor

84

THE PARADOX OF JUDICIAL REVIEW:
MADISON ON THE JUDICIARY
Michael P. Zuckert

107

"A FAULTLESS PLAN WAS NOT TO BE EXPECTED":
MADISON AND THE SEPARATION OF POWERS
David J. Siemers

123

"THE LAST HOPE OF TRUE LIBERTY": MADISON AND
THE EVOLUTION OF AMERICAN FEDERALISM
Jeff Broadwater

147

THE "STEPFATHER" OF THE BILL OF RIGHTS: MADISON
AND THE PROBLEM OF PARCHMENT BARRIERS
Paul Finkelman

165

"PRAY OF LIBERTY OF CONSCIENCE TO REVIVE AMONG
US": MADISON ON FREEDOM OF RELIGION
Howard Schweber

195

MADISON AND THE LOGIC OF REPUBLICAN GOVERNMENT
George Thomas

220

BEYOND MANDATE TALK: MADISONIAN
CONSTITUTIONALISM AND DEMOCRATIC DISCOURSE
Zachary K. German

237

CONTRIBUTORS

257

INDEX

261

James Madison's Constitution

EDITORS' INTRODUCTION

James Madison's Relevance to the Constitution Today

Eric T. Kasper and Howard Schweber

Alexis de Tocqueville famously said in *Democracy in America*, "There is virtually no political question in the United States that does not sooner or later resolve itself into a judicial question."[1] The reason, of course, is that American politics is legally bounded by the Constitution, and by the time Tocqueville was writing in the 1830s, the tradition was well established that questions of constitutional law should be decided by courts. He might equally well have said that there is virtually no question of constitutional law that does not resolve itself into a political question. The term "constitutional politics" describes how clashing theories of constitutionalism have become the basis for political ideologies and movements since the beginning of the American Republic. Among the founding generation no one was more involved in the creation, initial interpretation, and political contestation of the Constitution than James Madison. To be sure, Madison lost key battles, primarily with respect to the role of the federal government in relation to the states. On the other hand, his Virginia Plan provided a starting model, and after ratification he played an important role in working out the practice of American constitutionalism as a member of Congress, the main proponent of the Bill of Rights, secretary of state, and president. As a political theorist, his approach to what Gordon Wood calls the Americans' "new science of politics"—with its emphases on institutional designs of mixed government, electoral representation, and incorporation of both liberal and republican principles into a model of modern state capacity—remains a core element of American political and constitutional thinking.[2]

Madison's influence has extended far beyond his own lifetime. In the modern era, as conflicting views of constitutional law and constitutional politics have become the basis of increasingly stark divisions, it is striking to note the extent to which all sides attempt to claim Madison's mantle as their own. On the U.S. Supreme Court, James Madison has long been cited as an authority when the justices interpret provisions of the Constitution.[3] Among "originalists" who propose that modern courts are bound to enforce historical understandings that were prevalent when the text was adopted, there is no individual who is more prominently cited than Madison. But among "living constitutionalists" who insist that the meaning of the Constitution must evolve with the nation and its people, Madison is a touchstone too. To reference only a few examples: in separation of powers cases Madison has been cited both for the proposition that executive agencies must be subject to presidential control and that they may be given independent authority by Congress;[4] in First Amendment Establishment Clause cases Madison has been cited both for the proposition that public money must not be used to support religious education and that public money must be available for that purpose;[5] and Madison's most famous contributions to the *Federalist Papers*, Nos. 10 and 51, are cited for multiple positions in almost any discussion of federalism and separation of powers.[6]

These debates and usages of Madison extend well beyond the Supreme Court. Many Americans—including jurists, policymakers, journalists, academics, and the general public—still think what Madison thought matters today. And with a moniker like "Father of the Constitution," these continued references should not be surprising. In popular periodicals in recent years, his name has been mentioned as an authority or discussed in pieces interpreting what the Constitution means with regard to congressional subpoena power,[7] executive orders,[8] judicial review,[9] federalism,[10] government intervention in the economy,[11] the freedom of religion,[12] the freedom of speech,[13] the freedom of the press,[14] the right to keep and bear arms,[15] the right against unreasonable searches and seizures,[16] the right to a jury trial,[17] and issues related to slavery and race.[18] These appeals to Madison on constitutional questions come from across the political spectrum. They demonstrate that Madison remains squarely in conversations over current events and constitutional questions in the United States.

There is good reason for Madison to continue to be a part of these conversations. As Jack Rakove recently stated, Madison is "America's leading constitutional theorist."[19] Madison expressed many thoughts about the constitutional issues we continue to face today. In 1785 in his "Memorial and Remonstrance against Religious Assessments," Madison declared his thoughts about a right that eventually would be protected by the First Amendment: "The Religion . . . of every man must be left to the conviction and conscience of every man; and it is the right of every man to exercise it as these may dictate."[20] As an active member of the 1787 Constitutional Convention, Madison expressed his views on many questions of power and rights in helping formulate a new government for the United States, including making known his thoughts on the enduring constitutional question of the separation of powers: "If it be essential to the preservation of liberty that the Legisl: Execut: & Judiciary powers be separate, it is essential to a maintenance of the separation, that they should be independent of each other."[21] Madison helped secure ratification of the Constitution in New York, the nation's commercial center, by writing twenty-nine of the eighty-five *Federalist Papers*, which spanned a variety of subjects, including emphasizing how federalism and the separation of powers would provide "a double security ... to the rights of the people."[22] Madison then headed to Virginia to push for ratification of the Constitution in his home state, the most populous in the union.[23]

With the Constitution secured, the amendment process and the delicate balance between majority rule and minority rights were Madison's concerns in 1789 when, as a representative in the First Congress, he proposed the Bill of Rights. Even though he had previously complained of the "inefficacy of a bill of rights" due to "repeated violations of these parchment barriers," Madison proposed a list of freedoms in 1789 in part because "if they are incorporated into the constitution, independent tribunals of justice will consider themselves in a peculiar manner the guardians of those rights."[24] One of those rights—the freedom of speech—was at issue when Madison favored the rights of people joining Democratic-Republican Societies to express their views. In 1794, Madison exhorted to his congressional colleagues that "if we advert to the nature of republican government, we shall find that the censorial power is in the people over the government, and not in the government over the people."[25] In another famous appeal to protecting First Amendment rights, Madison defended the freedom of the press when he penned his "Report on the Alien and Sedition Acts" in 1800.[26] And his lived experience in the Congress he helped create was followed by sixteen years in the federal executive branch established by the Constitution, with Madison serving two terms as Jefferson's secretary of state and two terms as the fourth president.

Madison's key role at the Constitution's founding—and the ideas he expressed then and when serving in that new government during its first few decades—proved instrumental in forging the document into what it is and how it is understood today. And in many areas, today's Constitution still reflects Madison's conception and design. In other ways, however, the Constitution as it emerged in its final text, and as it has been amended and interpreted to the present day, does not conform to Madison's vision as he expressed it at the Constitutional Convention. Madison advocated for a Council of Revision, made up of the president and a group of judges, to have veto power over congressional legislation,[27] which would have provided us with a fundamentally different system of separation of powers. He wanted Congress to have the ability to negate state legislation,[28] something that would have produced a radically different federal framework. He thought both houses of Congress should be based on population,[29] a structural change that would have given us a much different Senate than the one we have. The list of convention defeats goes on. Finally, Madison—an enslaver himself—participated in convention compromises and signed his name to a document that permitted chattel slavery to continue, until a later generation would formally end the nefarious practice with the Civil War and the ratification of the Thirteenth Amendment.

Nevertheless, examining Madison's thinking across a range of constitutional issues has much to offer when contemplating our nation's primary governing document today. We offer this not to argue that Madison's vision of the Constitution *must* be adhered to in the twenty-first century. In fact, there are serious flaws with using Madison to try to score points in a political or legal debate. He lived in a different time and faced different obstacles. Furthermore, he was not the only person who was instrumental in producing the Constitution. Madison himself probably would have eschewed the very notion that we think of him that way, remarking the following toward the end of his life: "You give me a credit to which I have no claim, in calling me '*the* writer of the Constitution of the U.S.' This was not, like the fabled Goddess of Wisdom, the offspring of a single brain. It ought to be regarded as the work of many heads & many hands."[30] Still, regardless of one's preferred method of constitutional interpretation, having a better understanding of the historical origins of the document—and the thinking behind the document's text—can help inform what we think our Constitution means now. Madison's speeches, writings, and actions are useful reminders that debates over big issues such as the separation of powers, federalism, and individual rights have vexed and divided our leading political thinkers back to the time when the original Constitution took shape in the summer of 1787 and the Bill of Rights was drafted two years later. Indeed, the ongoing disagreements Americans have today remain a part of the national conversation about the Constitution's meaning that have been occurring since the country's founding. Those debates are encouraged and can take place, in part, because of the First Amendment's protection for free speech, a protection initiated by Madison himself.

It is surprising, therefore, that despite the voluminous literature on Madison, there is not a readily available contemporary volume that surveys his understanding of constitutional law and politics across all of these matters, as opposed to his thinking on one constitutional issue or his more general political philosophy.[31] The chapters in this book attempt to provide such a focused discussion. This volume illuminates Madison's thinking about key concepts and issues that arise in contemporary debates over questions of what the Constitution requires, permits, and prohibits and the background principles that are at stake in those debates. Intended for an interested reader or a teacher rather than an academic specialist, the chapters that follow provide several different perspectives on Madison's constitutional thought applied to various topics of significance. These chapters are written by some of the most preeminent scholars of Madison and the Constitution. The treatment of Madison's thought is both more legalistic—in the sense of addressing specific questions of constitutional doctrine—and more oriented toward the lessons to be drawn for present-day issues insofar as the same constitutional issues that troubled Madison continue to be subjects of legal and political controversy. The goal of this examination is not only to tease out the contours of Madison's sometimes ambiguous constitutional ideas, but also to clarify the context and development of Madison's thinking as a subject of historical study and to provide a basis for evaluating contemporary invocations of Madison's authority. While it would not be possible for one book-length collection to cover all the areas in which Madison's legacy is cited by writers and judges, each chapter addresses a major issue in Madison's constitutionalism.

Jack N. Rakove's introduction sets the tone for the volume by discussing the "grand themes" characterized by the treatment of Madison as the father of the Constitution and the Constitution as a fundamentally Madisonian document. Rakove adds an account of Madison's role as a constitutional statesman, focusing on the years between the First Congress and the Constitution and through the process of proposing, drafting, and adopting the Constitution. Specifically, Rakove explores Madison's express caution about too ready a resort to constituent power, rejecting Jefferson's idea of regular conventions. As Rakove tells it, Madison had to concede that such an idea was appropriate as a matter of republican theory but rejected it out of hand as a matter of "republican *politics*." The reminder calls our attention to the repeated appearance of elements of pragmatism, compromise, and development in Madison's constitutionalism. There is an old joke that describes an economist as "someone who says, when an idea works in practice, 'let's see if it works in theory.'" Rakove reminds us, as many of the succeeding chapters demonstrate, that Madison was not the kind of formalistic thinker portrayed in the economist's joke. That might be the most valuable lesson for modern American constitutionalism that the father of the Constitution can teach.

The first three chapters explore the contours and influence of Madison's constitutionalism in general terms. Lynn Uzzell begins the discussion by asking whether Madison truly deserves the sobriquet "father of the Constitution." Uzzell's provocative inquiry compels us to reconsider the propriety of invoking Madison as an authority on constitutional questions in the first place. Contrary to some recent arguments, Uzzell finds that Madison was unique among the founding generation of writers in the extent to which he developed a complete and coherent constitutional theory, and that Madison's understanding had a dominant influence over contemporaneous debates. Among other things, this confirms the basis of the book's project (which is fortunate) while drawing our attention to the way different elements of Madison's constitutional thinking fit together into a fully developed constitutional theory.

Alan R. Gibson continues to set the intellectual stage for an examination of Madison's constitutional ideas by reviewing arguments about the character of Madison's republicanism, with a particular focus on the question of democracy. How "democratic" was Madison's republican conception, and how does the answer to that question shade our understanding of his positions on constitutional controversies? Gibson calls our attention to the necessity of locating this discussion in an understanding of what we, today, mean by "democratic," a concept he expands to include "inclusiveness," "political equality," and "responsiveness"—formulations that emphasize the extent to which Madison's constitutional vision included a particular conception of politics. Gibson argues that Madison's famous treatment of the problem of faction and his insistence on virtuous representatives in *Federalist* No. 10 is only one illustration of a larger pattern that extended to his position in debates over qualifications for officeholding and voting, finding that in those debates Madison was "among the most liberal and cosmopolitan of his contemporaries," a location confirmed by Madison's support for population-based representation in the Senate.

Where Madison's commitment to equality failed, of course, was in his support for the Three-Fifths Clause. Additionally, Madison took no action attempting to limit state constitutional restrictions on political participation (thus failing to guarantee many Americans, including free Blacks and women, the right to vote). He took part in the construction of an Electoral College and amendment process that, after equal state representation was ensured in the Senate, augmented the power of slave states. Gibson concludes this had to do with Madison's concern to protect southern sectional interests against northern intrusion, an issue that initially arose in the unrelated context of debates over river navigation rights. Finally, Gibson explores Madison's "long leash" theory of democratic representation. Although Gibson does not go down this particular road, it is worth noting that this is a theme that takes us into the conflict among theories of representation characterized as "delegate" versus "trustee" in Hanna Pitkin's classic formulation, a distinction emphasized in Anti-Federalists' insistence on an "instruction" model of representation in which members of Congress would convey decisions of state legislatures.[32] As Gibson observes, Madison feared excessively tight connections between representatives and constituents, concerned that an *overly* responsive form of government would create opportunities for domination. Gibson comments that "Madison's complex case" for our complicated system has "too often been misinterpreted and misrepresented by scholars with a political axe to grind—whether it be defending and preserving or criticizing and reforming." He could equally have observed that modern Supreme Court justices, among others, fail to understand the complexity of Madison's approach to democratic representation when they invoke his ideas in debates over issues such as voting rights, campaign finances, and the role of the First Amendment in the practices of American politics.[33]

As noted, Gibson's treatment of Madison's constitutionalist conception of politics runs into a huge obstacle—a ship hitting an iceberg would not be an inappropriate analogy—when we reach Madison's support for the Three-Fifths Clause. Quentin P. Taylor explores Madison's constitutional thinking and its relation to his attitudes about slavery not only as a moral issue but as a problem for constitutional design. Taylor argues that Madison equated enslaved Blacks and Native Americans as two unassimilable populations that could never be incorporated into the national polity. With respect to Native Americans Madison's solution was removal; Taylor finds support for the idea that Madison's solution with respect to a population of freed ex-slaves would have been the same. Thus, Taylor concludes that in his writings Madison both opposed slavery and feared the presence of free Black citizens. In multiple writings, Madison declared that the institution of slavery was anathema to republican government—describing the southern states as "aristocracies"—but at the same time he refused to publicly challenge the practice, adopting what Taylor calls a "policy of avoidance" that involved willingness to accept almost any compromise to secure unity. And in his private life he hypocritically enslaved more than one hundred people and lived in luxury because of their labor. As Taylor shows, by the time of the Constitutional Convention Madison understood that slavery was the defining basis of political division in the country; some of the most controversially undemocratic aspects of modern American politics such as the Electoral College appear as desperate compromises necessary to preserve the interests of the slaveholding South and secure their agreement. Taylor's contribution is to show the key role Madison played in these compromises and the extent to which he was fully aware that he was abandoning his own core principles to secure his nation-building project. That heritage serves as a caution for those who would invoke these Madisonian compromises as expressions of Madison's constitutionalism.

These first three chapters lay the groundwork for understanding Madison's constitutional thinking. The next set of chapters focus on particular important elements of that thinking: judicial review, separation of powers, and federalism.

Next Michael P. Zuckert examines Madison's thinking on the crucial question of judicial review. Zuckert finds that on this critical subject Madison's views cannot be easily reconciled, constituting instead a "paradox." For Madison, says Zuckert, substantive judicial review was "never intended, and can never be proper," yet at the same time the judicial duty to expound the law of the land includes the Constitution. The paradox, for Zuckert, is that judicial "paramountcy" is a power correctly inferred from the constitutional design that is nonetheless illegitimate. Locating the discussion in terms of Madison's ideas about separation of powers—a principle in tension with checks and balances—Zuckert finds that for Madison the key role of courts was the imposition of punishments. The legislature was only to make general rules, the executive "was to bring the law home to individuals," but only the judiciary could impose punishments.

Yet at the same time Madison was not a departmentalist, as demonstrated by his proposal for a "Council of Revision" composed of executive and judicial officials, an exception to strict separation of powers principles that was needed to restrain "the legislative vortex." Madison's preferred model, in other words, was dialogic. In response to an inquiry about a proposed Kentucky state constitution, Madison came up with a truly elaborate plan under which bills would be separately sent to the executive and the judicial branches for review, either of which would have the power of veto subject to override by both legislative repassage and a subsequent election. That plan was unsurprisingly rejected, but Zuckert shows that in practice and as president, while Madison accepted the authority of the courts he continued to insist on a proper role for executives and legislators to debate and promote constitutional understandings, including criticisms of judicial determinations. Madison's famous reversal on the question of a national bank is particularly interesting, as in Madison's view it was essentially decided based on his proposed Kentucky procedures: a qualified veto overturned by a subsequent election and readoption. Ultimately, despite this and other reversals on particular questions, Zuckert finds that a coherent Madisonian view of judicial constitutional review emerges, one that does not encourage judicial activism but a dialogic relationship between courts and other branches at both state and federal levels. This is a conclusion that locates Madison's thinking outside of any of the usual positions for which he is cited in modern constitutional debates.

David J. Siemers continues the exploration of the critical role of separation of powers in Madisonian constitutionalism. This is yet another area in which Madison appears to present inconsistent or incomplete arguments. Siemers suggests that such ambiguities were inevitable, claiming of Madison that "we extend Madison too much credit for foresight and design in 1787, but too little for his understanding that the separation of powers is a matter of ongoing construction and negotiation within a working republic." Thus, in his advice on a constitutional design for Kentucky mentioned earlier, Madison embraced a proposal by Thomas Jefferson that any two branches should be able to call a convention to resolve a dispute with the third, a position that he repudiated in *Federalist* No. 49. More generally, Siemers finds that given repeated opportunities to add to his separation of powers theory, Madison frequently chose reticence. In Siemers's view Madison rejected "pure" theory of separation of powers from the beginning, so that the Council of Revision aimed at limiting the supremacy of the legislature was not an exception but rather an illustration of what for Madison was the rule. Siemers points out that Madison freely accepted the legislature's encroachment on the executive during the Confederation Congress as a matter of necessity. But crucial questions were left unanswered, as early debates over removal of officials and the Jay Treaty revealed unresolved questions that foreshadowed modern debates about the limits of executive authority. Ultimately, in Siemers's view, the question of whether Madison was consistent over time is irrelevant, as he "was engaged in constitutional learning that required refining his principles over time and an ongoing elucidation of constitutionalism that necessitated aligning the separation of powers with other political principles in complex and novel situations."

Jeff Broadwater considers another core element of Madison's constitutional design: federal-state relations, a problem that Madison called "the Gordian knot of the Constitution." In his Virginia Plan Madison described a clearly supreme national government; later, he adjusted his views to support "a system partly federal and partly consolidated" and recognized authority of courts to police the boundaries. What drove these adjustments was Madison's observations of the "shameful deficiency of some of the states" and, later, equally grave failures of Congress to secure critical national interests. To secure unity Madison was once again willing to sacrifice principle. *Federalist* No. 62 presented the Great Compromise as just that, a surrender of principles in the face of opposition for the sake of unity and stability, while *Federalist* No. 39 saw Madison extolling the federal character of the constitutional system, referring famously to states' "residuary and inviolable sovereignty." This formulation has been used in modern times to find a range of implicit privileges and immunities that attach to states as elements of an assumed background understanding of "sovereignty" at the time of ratification, a conception that is at odds with Madison's query in *Federalist* No. 45:

> [If] the Union be essential to the happiness of the people of America, is it not preposterous, to urge as an objection . . . that such a government may derogate from the importance of the governments of the individual States? Was, then, the American Revolution effected . . . not that the people of America should

enjoy peace, liberty, and safety, but that the government of the individual States, that particular municipal establishments, might enjoy a certain extent of power, and be arrayed with certain dignities and attributes of sovereignty?[34]

In the Virginia Resolutions Madison argued states could "interpose" themselves to thwart seemingly unconstitutional exercise of federal power, a term Broadwater argues was deliberately ambiguous; in the 1830s Madison rejected Calhoun's arguments for nullification.

Thus, Madison at different times distanced himself from his own early strong nationalist position and from proponents of the compact theory. Ultimately, Broadwater concludes, Madison depended on deference to the judiciary to preserve national supremacy, a "precarious balance" that depended on a court that shared his views. That conclusion has sweeping implications for the modern jurisprudence that is known as "the New Federalism," particularly since proponents of that jurisprudence inevitably cite Madison as an authority for their arguments. The special importance attached to courts also connects back to Zuckert's discussion of judicial review; the dialogic relationship that Zuckert found in the separation of powers context seems to be out of place in Madison's treatment of federalism issues. From a biographical standpoint, one cannot help wondering what Madison would make of the way his perhaps casual use of the term "residual sovereignty" has been turned into a set of constitutional doctrines that so sharply depart from what Siemers finds in Madison's thinking.

The next three chapters shift the focus away from questions of institutional structure (judicial review, federalism) and take up questions of rights and liberties. Paul Finkelman explores Madison's complex relationship to the Bill of Rights, while Howard Schweber focuses specifically on matters of religious liberty in Madison's constitutional vision, and George Thomas explores the significance of free expression for Madison's theory of a constitutional republic.

Finkelman suggests that we think of Madison as the "stepfather" of the Bill of Rights, a quasi-paternity that was "reluctant and unenthusiastic." The limits of Madison's affection for his alleged progeny were captured perfectly in his description of the proposed amendments as "neither improper nor altogether useless." Finkelman carefully traces Madison's maneuvers before and during the ratification process, describing the compromise reached in Massachusetts and Virginia that led to consideration of amendments, Madison's fear of a new convention and its potential consequences, and the challenges raised by Anti-Federalists. Some of these Anti-Federalist fears could be easily dismissed, such as their expressions of concern that someone who is Jewish or Muslim could someday become president, or that the Constitution would lead to the abolition of slavery (Finkelman points out that in *The Federalist Papers* Madison very noticeably made no mention of the Fugitive Slave Clause in his response to the Anti-Federalists). But the complaint about the absence of a bill of rights was harder to dismiss and had support even from well-meaning critics of the Constitution.

Madison had previously dismissed bills of rights as "parchment barriers" based on his observations of states; ineffective, unnecessary, redundant, dangerous in that rights not enumerated may be considered excluded, and contrary to republican principles as checks on the will of the people. Parsing the history of correspondence between Madison and Jefferson, Finkelman argues that, despite the claims of many scholars of a "Great Collaboration" between Madison and Jefferson, Madison's support for amendments was in fact not influenced by Jefferson: Madison was moving to support the Bill of Rights while Jefferson was in France, and his letters giving Madison advice always arrived well after Madison had changed his position. Finkelman demonstrates that Madison's acceptance of a bill of rights was a purely pragmatic compromise to secure the Constitution, which he had come to see as essential for the survival of the nation. And Madison recognized the possibility that a bill of rights might serve a kind of teaching function, as "political truths declared" in a "solemn manner" would "acquire by degrees the character of fundamental maxims of free Government." As for the danger of exclusion of rights by enumeration of others, that would be met by what becomes the Ninth Amendment.

An understanding of Madison's ambivalence and the crucial role he expected the Ninth Amendment to play is not of mere antiquarian value. Modern constitutional lawyers and judges frequently assert that rights not enumerated in the Bill of Rights therefore lack constitutional protection, and the Ninth Amendment is treated as a nullity—Robert Bork memorably called it "an ink blot"[35]— even as judges and political leaders call for a jurisprudence that recovers original understandings starting with those of Madison. As Finkelman says (quoting Jack Rakove), "glib calls to return to a 'jurisprudence of original intention'" emphasize the importance of recovering Madison's own concerns, especially about the dangers of enumeration. Madison's goal was to mollify critics of the Constitution, a political goal that rested uneasily with his constitutional commitments. This conclusion is as informative in thinking about constitutional rights protections as it is in thinking about questions of separation of powers or state sovereignty.

Howard Schweber turns his attention to a core element of Madison's conception of liberty secured by constitutionally guaranteed rights, the freedom of religion. In Schweber's reading, the most important conclusion to be drawn is that for Madison religious liberty was not just an example of freedom of conscience or expression. Rather, religion was a special case: specially precious, specially dangerous, and specially vulnerable. It is particularly noteworthy, by Schweber's argument, that Madison's concern to prevent political intrusion on religious ideas had no counterpart in political ideas.

Religious liberty provided a template for Madison's structuralist approach to the problem of factions, as his observation of the "multiplicity of sects" in Virginia gave rise to his theory of factions. But this was not because Madison viewed religion as an unmitigated blessing. In 1787 he wrote, "even in its coolest state [religion] has been much oftener a motive to oppression than a restraint from it," and he repeatedly pointed out that reliance on religious faith to secure political virtue would be fruitless. But Schweber finds copious evidence that Madison saw religion as a critical constitutional topic in ways that had no parallel in other areas of conscience or expression, including his repeated emphases on dangers of public financial support and even extending to practices such as thanksgiving declarations or maintenance of a congressional chaplain. These were practices that in Madison's view clearly violated the Establishment Clause even as he accepted their legitimacy as a matter of popular constitutional understanding (the same argument that he relied upon in eventually accepting the existence of a national bank). On the free exercise side of religious liberty Madison was unequivocal in insisting on complete freedom of worship and exemption from the responsibility of bearing arms, but he was almost equally completely ambiguous about other specific questions. "It may not be easy," he wrote, "in every possible case, to trace the line of separation between the rights of religion and the Civil authority with such distinctness to avoid collisions and doubts on unessential points." Regarding military service and freedom of worship he insisted on absolute rights guarantees. Regarding "unessential" issues he was willing to rely on democratic politics and popular constitutionalism.

Schweber traces the way these principles affect thinking about First Amendment issues in modern constitutional jurisprudence, reviewing current doctrines concerning the use of public funds to support religious activities, "endorsements" of religion, and claims of constitutional entitlement to religious exemption from the operation of antidiscrimination law. Time and again, Schweber finds today's Supreme Court justices departing from Madison's core principles even as they invoke his authority.

George Thomas turns to another set of First Amendment questions, this time concerning freedoms of speech and the press and their place in Madison's theory of representative democracy. Thomas locates Madison's increasing concern with freedom of expression with a shift in his thinking. From the "filter" model of elite representation by virtuous exemplars that he laid out in *Federalist* No. 10, Madison moved to a model of politics "out-of-doors" in which the populace, parties, and the press all played key roles in educating the public so that they could be active in holding representatives accountable.

In Thomas's reading, this was the change in understanding that underlay Madison's opposition to the Sedition Acts. The change in thinking is profound considering Madison's famous statement in *Federalist* No. 63 that the great innovation of American republican government was "the TOTAL EXCLUSION OF THE PEOPLE, IN THEIR COLLECTIVE CAPACITY, from any share" in government. As in most areas, however, Madison also kept his commitments to principles that were in tension with his emerging enthusiasm for popular participation. Thus, Thomas finds Madison insisting on "space" between representatives and constituents.

Nonetheless, after the 1790s, Thomas finds Madison emphasizing parties, the press, and the role of schools to shape the public mind so that citizens could assert control over their representatives. The Sedition Act controversy illustrates the connection to free speech, giving rise to mobilization of parties to protect the Constitution *against* representatives. "The right of freely examining public characters and measures" was essential to "the just exercise of [the peoples'] electoral rights." In his *Report on the Virginia Resolutions* Madison emphasized the relation between these rights and the American constitutional system: "The nature of governments elective, limited, and responsible, in all their branches, may well be supposed to require a greater freedom of animadversion than might be tolerated by the genius of such a government as that of Great Britain." From the outset Madison had proposed that protections of rights of the press and expression should apply to the states (a position that separated him from Jefferson). After the 1790s these arguments became couched in part as expressions of concern about the "popular arts" where the people might be "misled by the artful misrepresentations of interested men." This is a concern that surely remains relevant. Thomas's exploration of Madison's thinking reminds us of the key connection between rights of expression and a particular model of politics, a connection that receives scant attention in the tendency toward an interpretation of the First Amendment that treats freedoms of speech and the press as unconnected to any larger constitutional or political conception.

In the final chapter Zachary K. German concludes the body of the book with a continuation of the exploration begun by Thomas of the Constitution's implications for politics. Rather than focusing on a particular set of rights, however, German focuses on practices of political expression. Specifically, German is concerned with the modern tendency to engage in "mandate talk," arguing that this practice reflects a departure from the model of political discourse implied by Madison's constitutionalism. As German describes it, "mandate talk" is the habit of referring to an electoral victory as authorization to carry out a specific policy program. One of the unhealthy results of this way of thinking is that resistance to the presumed mandate appears as an illegitimate rejection of popular self-government. Both elements of this view, says German, are contrary to Madison's understanding. For Madison, defusing the dangers of majority faction meant preventing electoral agenda setting. He had observed how majority rule in the states had resulted in sacrificing the common good for partisan advantage of the winning faction and sought to create a model that would counter that tendency. In this view, mandate talk denies the complexity of a large republic. In addition, talk of mandates undermines constraints such as federalism, as the subject of a mandate is necessarily understood as something within the scope of the national agenda. And yet a third problem is that the idea of an electoral mandate conflicts with Madison's idea of fixed institutional mandates for the different branches, each pushing in different directions by design. Thus, the House is institutionally committed to protect republican liberty, the Senate to provide stability and wisdom, and the executive to be a source of energetic execution.

While German does not pursue this point, his discussion provides an excellent context for understanding Madison's opposition to the Anti-Federalists' "instruction" model of representation as described by Elbridge Gerry in 1789: "The power of instruction is in my opinion essential to check an administration which should be guilty of abuses.... To deny the people this right is to arrogate to ourselves more wisdom than the whole body of the people possesses ... our constituents have not only a right to instruct, but to bind this legislature."[36] The instruction model is the logical implication of mandate talk. For Madison, such a form of discourse would distract the people from paying attention to whether the branches were carrying out their institutional roles and thus keeping the government accountable for its constitutional functions as opposed to its success in achieving the policy goals of a majority faction. If we accept that premise, that modes of political discourse matter for how people think about political actors, then it should not need to be said that a Madisonian retreat from mandate talk might be a highly salutary change from the present state of American political discourse.

It is undeniable that Madison's ideas provide a lasting part of our constitutional *ethos*. Even as the Constitution continues to be reinterpreted, and even as new amendments are ratified in the future, Madison's writings and speeches will continue to be considered as sources of inspiration and authority. As with many questions, it is useful to reflect on where one has been before contemplating where one is going, and that contemplation is what our authors ask you to do in the pages that follow. Madison's writings and speeches tell us a major part of the constitutional story of where we have been. Where we go with the knowledge and understanding he tried to impart is up to us.

NOTES

1. Alexis de Tocqueville, *Democracy in America*, vol. 1 (New York: Library of America, 2004), 310.
2. Isaac Kramnick identifies four primary "idioms" of constitutional discourse in the founding era: liberalism, republicanism, a modern theory of state power, and "work ethic Protestantism." As Kramnick shows, each of these is demonstrated in Madison's thinking as well as that of other Federalist and Anti-Federalist writers. Isaac Kramnick, "The Great National Discussion: The Discourse of Politics in 1787," *William and Mary Quarterly* 45 (1988): 3–32; see also Richard Dagger, *Civic Virtues: Rights, Citizenship, and Republican Liberalism* (New York: Oxford University Press, 1997).
3. See Eric T. Kasper, *To Secure the Liberty of the People: James Madison's Bill of Rights and the Supreme Court's Interpretation* (DeKalb: Northern Illinois University Press, 2010).
4. Compare *Morrison v. Olson*, 487 U.S. 654, 694 (1988) (Rehnquist, C. J.) and id. at 697 (Scalia J., dissenting); see also *Seila Law v. Consumer Financial Protection Bureau* 140 S. Ct. 2183, 2197, 2202–3 (2020) (Roberts, C. J.).
5. Compare *Espinoza v. Montana Department of Revenue*, 140 S. Ct. 2246, 2258 n3 (2020) (Roberts, C. J.) with id. at 2284 (Breyer, dissenting), citing Madison for opposite conclusions.
6. See, e.g., *Arizona v. Mayorkas*, 143 S. Ct. 1312, 1316 n.25 (2023) (Statement of Gorsuch, J.) (citing *Federalist* No. 10); Seila Law, 140 S. Ct. at 2202 (citing *Federalist* No. 51); Trump v. Mazars USA, 140 S. Ct. 2019, 2026 (2020) (citing *Federalist* No. 51); Gamble v. United States, 139 S. Ct. 1960, 1991 (2019) (Ginsburg, J., dissenting) (citing *Federalist* No. 51); Evenwel v. Abbott, 578 U.S. 54, 81, 84 (2016) (Thomas, J., dissenting) (citing *Federalist* Nos. 10 and 51).
7. Robert Black, "The Court Got the Trump Subpoena Cases Exactly Backward," *The Atlantic*, July 18, 2020, https://www.theatlantic.com/ideas/archive/2020/07/court-got-trump-subpoena-cases-exactly-backward/614299/.
8. John Yoo, "Executive Non-Enforcement in the Era of the Trump Presidency," *Newsweek*, July 29, 2020, https://www.newsweek.com/executive-non-enforcement-era-trump-presidency-opinion-1521173.
9. Greg Weiner, "The Not-So-Supreme Court," *The Atlantic*, September 25, 2019, https://www.theatlantic.com/ideas/archive/2019/09/not-so-supreme-court/598633/.
10. David French, "Trump's Intervention in Portland Shows That the Republican Party Has Lost Its Way on States' Rights," *Time*, July 23, 2020, https://time.com/5870943/republicans-lost-states-rights/.
11. Bruce Bartlett, "Socialism Is as American as Apple Pie," *New Republic*, August 17, 2020, https://newrepublic.com/article/158921/socialism-american-pence-biden-sanders-2020-election.
12. Howard Slugh, "Score Another Victory for Religious Liberty at the Supreme Court,"

Newsweek, July 13, 2020, https://www.newsweek.com/score-another-victory-religious-liberty-supreme-court-opinion-1517252.

13. Nemo, "In Defense of Pen Names," *National Review*, August 8, 2020, https://www.nationalreview.com/2020/08/bring-back-pen-names/.
14. "The Freedom of the Press Is Yours," *The Atlantic*, August 15, 2018, https://www.theatlantic.com/ideas/archive/2018/08/the-freedom-of-the-press-is-yours/567655/.
15. Katie Scofield, "Myth: Second Amendment Protects Individual Liberties," *The Hill*, June 11, 2020, https://thehill.com/opinion/civil-rights/502253-myth-second-amendment-protects-individual-liberties.
16. Andrew Napolitano, "Government Is Spying on Us without Warrants, in Violation of Constitution," *Fox News*, February 13, 2020, https://www.foxnews.com/opinion/judge-andrew-napolitano-bulk-surveillance-privacy.
17. Matt Ford, "The Supreme Court's War over Jury Trials Could Change Everything," *New Republic*, April 21, 2020.
18. Noah Feldman, "James Madison's Lessons in Racism," *New York Times*, October 28, 2017, https://www.nytimes.com/2017/10/28/opinion/sunday/james-madison-racism.html.
19. Jack N. Rakove, *A Politician Thinking: The Creative Mind of James Madison* (Norman: University of Oklahoma Press, 2017), 5.
20. James Madison, "Memorial and Remonstrance against Religious Assessments," in *Madison: Writings*, ed. Jack N. Rakove (New York: Library of America, 1999), 30.
21. James Madison, *Notes of Debates in the Federal Convention of 1787* (New York: Norton, 1966), 311.
22. James Madison, "*Federalist* No. 51," in Alexander Hamilton, James Madison, and John Jay, *The Federalist Papers*, ed. Clinton Rossiter (New York: Mentor, 1961), 323 (subsequent citations are to this edition).
23. James Madison, "Speech in the Virginia Ratifying Convention in Defense of the Constitution," in *Madison: Writings*, 356.
24. James Madison, "Letter to Thomas Jefferson," October 17, 1788, in *Madison: Writings*, 420; James Madison, "Speech in Congress Proposing Constitutional Amendments," June 8, 1789, in *Madison: Writings*, 449.
25. James Madison, "Speech in Congress on 'Self-Created Societies,'" in *Madison: Writings*, 552.
26. James Madison, "Report on the Alien and Sedition Acts," in *Madison: Writings*, 647.
27. Madison, *Notes of Debates*, 66, 79.
28. Ibid., 304–5.
29. Ibid., 293–95.
30. James Madison, "Letter to William Cogswell," March 10, 1834, in *The Writings of James Madison*, ed. Galliard Hunt (New York: Putnam, 1910), 9:533.
31. Prior contributions include biographical studies, ranging from Irving Brant's magisterial six-volume study, *The Fourth President: A Life of James Madison* (Indianapolis: Bobbs-Merrill, 1970), to Jack Rakove's study of Madison's navigation of the constitutional system during his career as a politician, *A Politician Thinking: The Creative Mind of*

James Madison (Norman: University of Oklahoma Press, 2017), to Noah Feldman's intellectual biography, *The Three Lives of James Madison* (New York: Random House, 2017), just to name a few. A recent collection of essays edited by Samuel Kernell explores the thought of Madison as a political theorist and institutionalist, *James Madison: The Theory and Practice of Republican Government* (Stanford University Press 2003), while other recent works include Jeremy Bailey's study of how Madison thought the Constitution could survive changing circumstances, *James Madison and Constitutional Imperfection* (New York: Cambridge University Press, 2015); Carol Berkin's exploration of the politics behind Madison's ultimate support for the Bill of Rights, *The Bill of Rights: The Fight to Secure America's Liberties* (New York: Simon & Schuster, 2015); and Jeff Broadwater's study of the ways Madison's and Jefferson's constitutional ideas changed over time, *Jefferson, Madison, and the Making of the Constitution* (Chapel Hill: University of North Carolina Press, 2019).

32. Hanna Pitkin, *The Concept of Representation* (Berkeley: University of California Press, 1967).

33. For a specific critique of the late Justice Scalia's treatment of politics in contrast to that of Madison, see Howard Schweber, "Justice Scalia's Anti-Madisonian Theory of Politics," in *The Conservative Revolution of Antonin Scalia*, ed. David Schultz and Howard Schweber (Lanham, Md.: Lexington Books, 2018).

34. Madison, *Federalist* No. 45, 288–89.

35. See, e.g., Kurt T. Lash, "Inkblot: The Ninth Amendment as Textual Justification for Judicial Enforcement of the Right to Privacy," *University of Chicago Law Review Dialogue* 80, no. 1 (2017): 220, https://chicagounbound.uchicago.edu/cgi/viewcontent.cgi?article=1020&context=uclrev_online.

36. Debates in House of Representatives, September 3, 1789, *Annals of Congress* 1: 733–45.

INTRODUCTION

James Madison, Political Strategist

Jack N. Rakove

Two grand themes dominate our accounts of the life and legacy of James Madison. One involves his role as either the "Father of the Constitution," the familiar image that Lynn Uzzell deploys in her ingenious essay, or at least its "stepfather," as Paul Finkelman half-waggishly suggests. Whatever the degree of his paternity and however one measures his gains and losses at the Constitutional Convention, Madison appears as the most important author of the sacred charter, including both the text drafted at Philadelphia in 1787 and the amendments the First Federal Congress soon proposed. Give James Wilson and Gouverneur Morris their due; recognize the brilliance of Alexander Hamilton; admire the persistence of small-state leaders such as Roger Sherman, John Dickinson, and William Paterson: as constitutional architect Madison nevertheless stands *primus inter pares*, and perhaps a bit taller than that, too, even at 5'4".[1]

The second grand theme that dominates our view of Madison reflects the belief that Americans still inhabit a Madisonian Constitution and that the best guide to its original meaning is found in his writings, especially his seminal contributions to *The Federalist*. The celebrated arguments of *Federalist* Nos. 10 and 51 are subject to almost liturgical recital complemented by midrash-style commentaries on their meaning.[2] *Federalist* Nos. 39, 45, and 46 also merit close attention for their discussion of federalism, as do the four essays preceding *Federalist* No. 51 for articulating a broader conception of separated powers. Then, too, any scholar who overlooks the epistemological insights of *Federalist* No. 37 will never fully appreciate a Madisonian approach to constitutionalism writ large.[3]

Yet this emphasis on a single event, no matter how epochal, and a small number of concise essays may make it more difficult to measure Madison's significance fully. Of course, that single event was the adoption of the Constitution, an event we now understand even better with the publication of thirty-nine volumes compiling *The Documentary History of the Ratification of the Constitution*. This was an event of enormous significance, not only for the United States but for the global history of popular government. That alone is a reasonable basis for fame, and whether we treat Madison as father, stepfather, agenda setter, or original commentator, his role in the making of the Constitution will always be worth study.

Yet while this emphasis on Madison's dual role as constitution maker and commentator is wholly sensible, it also leaves open some broader problems with the interpretation of an active public career that spanned four continuous decades, from his election to Virginia's Fifth Provincial Convention in the independence spring of 1776 to his retirement from the presidency in March 1817. His career as constitutional commentator lasted until his death on June 28, 1836, when at breakfast, after his niece asked him if something was wrong, he replied, "Nothing more than a change of mind, my dear," and then quietly expired. (The biographer naturally wonders, what was his last thought?) The only real interruption in Madison's public career came in 1797–98, when he and Dolley returned to his family's Montpelier plantation outside Orange, Virginia. At that point, effective leadership of the nascent Republican party shifted to Vice President Thomas Jefferson. From then on, Jefferson's primacy in the friendship was evident, and Madison willingly deferred to Jefferson's status as party leader. Though it is foolish to follow Joseph Ellis in speculating that Jefferson was a father figure to Madison—they were only eight years apart in age, and James Senior and Junior had a harmonious relationship until the former's death in 1801—theirs arguably remains the most important friendship in American political history. Still, while we can plausibly speak of the "age of Jefferson," applying the same honorific to Madison would go a tribute or two too far. The idea of "father of the Constitution" and our conception of a Madisonian constitution are the best we can do.

As Eric T. Kasper and Howard Schweber observe in the editors' introduction, the underlying purpose of this volume is to "illuminate" Madison's thinking about key concepts and issues that arise in contemporary debates over questions of what the Constitution requires, permits, and prohibits." We might think of this endeavor as an effort to draw helpful lessons, insights, and applications from Madison, or even, in times of constitutional despair and disrepair—such as the present moment—a source of commitment to the American constitutional project. A similar concern animated another nicely titled volume that appeared in 2015: *What Would Madison Do?: The Father of the Constitution Meets Modern American Politics*.[4] Of course, if the notion of WWMD is not quite the constitutional equivalent of the tetragrammaton, it still sounds a potent theological echo in contemporary American culture, even though Madison was more a thinking politician and political thinker than a political prophet.

Many historians are skeptical that the real value of historical knowledge is to teach lessons for action. Rather than draw simplistic lessons based on shallow comparisons between past and present, history may be more valuable when it encourages us to distinguish the two and not conflate them. But having authoritative accounts of the origins of the Constitution and its particular clauses will always be valuable, whether one believes that the purported "original meaning" of the text should bind modern interpretation or that knowledge of these seminal debates provide useful points of departure for how one thinks critically about "the political system of the United States" (to borrow a key Madison phrase titling his famous pre–Constitutional Convention memorandum of April 1787, better known in the trade as "the vices").[5]

Still, given the "veneration" that Madison deemed beneficial to any constitutional regime, it is well worth asking which lessons have the greatest value, either for application or merely examination, and which problems still resonate most deeply. On this point the contributors to this volume offer an array of suggestions, some rather general, others more focused. Alan R. Gibson and George Thomas, for example, both consider one of the broadest problems of all: how to define and weigh the republican and democratic elements of Madison's political thinking, but to do so by measuring Madison's avowedly republican conceptions against modern norms of democratic governance. Another concern of equal importance was the great issue that Quentin P. Taylor examines in his essay on slavery. But unlike republicanism, slavery was a question about which Madison wrote relatively little—and when he did, as in the contrived voice of *Federalist* No. 54, his defense of the peculiar institution exposed at least a few misgivings. Yet we also know that Madison long understood how the concentrated presence or complete absence of slavery in particular regions threatened to undermine his theoretical system of the extended republic. And the fact that Madison was the original author of the three-fifths idea, as it appeared in the amendments to the Articles of Confederation that the Continental Congress proposed in April 1783, has more than symbolic significance.[6]

Other essays in this volume refer to classic problems in American constitutionalism: the authority of the judiciary, separation of powers, and federalism. Taking as his point of departure a famous paragraph in Madison's October 1788 observations on Jefferson's proposed revisions to the Virginia constitution, Michael Zuckert describes the apparent "paradox" in which Madison recognized, as a simple matter of law, that judges necessarily possessed the power to determine whether laws were constitutional, while simultaneously noting that the exercise of this power "was never intended, and can never be proper." The resolution of this paradox, Zuckert suggests, lies in a proper understanding of Madison's conception of the separation of powers, which he then goes on to elaborate. David J. Siemers pursues the same subject in his essay. Noting at the outset that many interpreters have placed greater emphasis on Madison's views of federalism, Siemers rightly suggests that his shifting perceptions about how the constitutional system of separated powers was functioning deserve equal attention. Here it is essential to track the "slippages between theory and practice" that are bound to occur, Siemers observes, "when someone acts as a theorist of politics and then a politician." It might also have been the case, though, that Madison acted first as a politician, then as a theorist.

Yet ultimately it was the resolution of conflicts within the federal system rather than interdepartmental quarrels that posed the greatest threat to the constitutional order. Madison's theory of the extended republic offered one heralded solution to the problem of federal instability by arguing that the majorities needed to govern nationally would prove less vulnerable to "the mischiefs of faction" than their counterparts in the states. But, as Jeff Broadwater explains in his essay, the belief that such majorities would continue to form within the states led Madison to propose his most radical measure: the congressional negative on state laws that, he ideally hoped, would enable the national government to protect itself against interfering laws enacted by the states while also empowering it to protect minorities within the states against unjust legislation. The rejection of this proposal in the immediate aftermath of the narrow decision of July 16, 1787, giving each state an equal vote in the Senate, marked an emotional low point for Madison. Over time, he gave greater importance to his passing observation in *Federalist* No. 39 that in controversies over the boundaries between the jurisdictions of national and state governments, "the decision is to be impartially made, according to the rules of the Constitution," by the Supreme Court.[7] But whether any judicial decision could surmount truly deep political conflicts remained highly problematic. The legacy of *Dred Scott* tells a different story.

Beyond his role in framing the Constitution, Madison's other great legacy lay in the adoption of the ten amendments that eventually came to be known as the Bill of Rights. Or perhaps we should say that this additional round of constitutional deliberations, which began in the House of Representatives with Madison's speech of June 6, 1789, and ended with Virginia's ratification of the amendments in December 1791, was the proper epilogue to the great debate of 1787–88. One could argue that the First Congress would have ignored the subject entirely, had Madison not insisted on fulfilling his Virginia campaign pledge to pursue the matter of amendments. Few Federalists in Congress shared Madison's enthusiasm for the project, and Anti-Federalist members, knowing they would never get the changes they wanted, were also indifferent to the cause. It therefore mattered that Madison, who had some experience framing legislative agendas, made that a top priority. One can speculate how American constitutional history would have developed had Madison not taken this commitment so seriously, literally forcing the "nauseous project" of amendments down the throats of his congressional colleagues. Perhaps he was something more than the "stepfather" whom Paul Finkelman identifies. Yet as Finkelman also persuasively argues, Madison never abandoned the qualms he originally expressed about the necessity of a bill of rights or even its utility. Those qualms remain just as intriguing as his rationale (or rationalizations) for supporting amendments.

Yet there was one right, one liberty, to which Madison was absolutely and unequivocally attached: the free exercise of religion by morally autonomous individuals, which would be best supported by a thorough disestablishment of any and all denominations. That was the first political commitment he forged as a youth, and a lasting achievement he celebrated until his death. Along with Jefferson's complementary writings on the subject, most famously the Virginia Statute of Religious Freedom, Madison's "Memorial and Remonstrance Against Religious Assessments" and other texts have long served as authoritative sources for the development of judicial doctrine on religious freedom. But as Howard Schweber notes in his essay on this topic, this has arguably become the one area in modern American law where Madison's modern legacy has become most vulnerable to an arguably "anti-Madisonian position" that fails to recognize the extent to which religion constituted a "special case" justifying its own distinctive treatment.

Taken together, these issues reflect the recurring concerns that have long dominated Madison scholarship. That scholarship, it must be confessed, lacks the diversity and range that we accord to the other members of the "big six" founding fathers (Franklin, Washington, Jefferson, John Adams, and Alexander Hamilton rounding out the group). Madison is simply a less engaging subject of biography, though some authors (Lynne Cheney, Richard Brookhiser, Michael Signer, and Noah Feldman) have recently given the effort the old trade-book try. In the end, though, it seems quite difficult to separate Madison from the Constitution, which is still perceived as his legacy.

Are there fresh questions for Madison scholarship that one could still propose? This is a question on which I have brooded for some time, having published a short biography more than three decades ago and a more recent interpretive work that distinguishes the creative activity of political thinking from the published thoughts we routinely study in our accounts of the Madisonian constitution.[8] Here, then, are a few thoughts of topics for future research or consideration.

We esteem Madison as a political theorist and constitutional architect, a "votary" of republicanism and a student of the institutions of representative government. But he was also a political strategist who began actively considering how the debilities (or later the "imbecility") of national government under the Articles of Confederation could be reformed or cured. Strategy in this sense means something other than the constitutional remedies that framed the Virginia Plan of May 1787. It was concerned instead with the political steps that reformers would have to take, either to repair the obvious weaknesses of the Continental Congress or to devise a method to replace the Articles of Confederation with a more efficacious charter of national government.

At first glance, Alexander Hamilton seems a better example of a political strategist. He was an *American Machiavelli*, as John Lamberton Harper's biography aptly called him, and arguably much more of a political adventurer and risk-taker than Madison. Until Madison drafted his "Vices of the Political System of the United States" in April 1787, the most astute assessment of the premises of the Articles of Confederation came in Hamilton's lengthy letter to James Duane of July 1780. When he and Madison served together in the Continental Congress in 1782–83, it was Hamilton who fomented the impression that the officers of the Continental Army, encamped at Newburgh, New York, could be mobilized to support the comprehensive program of Robert Morris, the superintendent of finance. Hamilton even tried to gull George Washington into leading this ploy and then waited nervously to learn how the commander-in-chief would respond to his maneuver. Similarly, around the time when Madison left the Continental Congress in October 1783—its first term-limited casualty!—Hamilton was drafting a resolution, never submitted, to summon a constitutional convention to replace the Articles of Confederation.

Yet in the end, Madison proved a superior constitutional *strategist* as well as *theorist*, and a satisfactory exploration of his political biography needs to take this into account. When Madison entered the Continental Congress in March 1780, he still had much to learn. With the British army roaming through the South, Congress no longer printing paper currency, and the Continental Army relying on a system of "specific supplies" from the states, Madison worried that the American military effort was teetering toward collapse. His first notion of how to get the states to comply with their federal responsibilities took a rather crude form. Delinquent states should be punished for their dereliction by having the navy anchor a frigate outside their main port, cutting off their commerce until they did their duty. But that was a formula for coercion, not persuasion or willing cooperation. Though Madison did not wholly abandon this impractical idea, experience and calculation carried his thinking in a different direction.

One significant example of this process occurred in the winter of 1783, when

Congress was wrestling with the program of financial reforms that Robert Morris was insisting it approve in its entirety. Within Congress, Morris had the active support of James Wilson and Hamilton, who was trying to foment enough unrest at Newburgh to advance the whole Morris program. But at a dinner held at the house of Thomas FitzSimons on February 20, 1783, after Hamilton bluntly described the unrest at Newburgh, Madison and a handful of other delegates rejected that effort and concluded instead that Congress must pursue a more tempered set of objectives. Over the next eight weeks, Madison became the leading architect of the three amendments to the Articles of Confederation that Congress submitted to the states on April 18, 1783. Those proposals rested on a candid assessment of the insuperable difficulties the Morris program would face in securing the approval of all thirteen state legislatures (the amendment rule under the Articles).[9] The critical vote in Congress was taken over the sole dissent of Rhode Island and the divided vote of New York, which was the result, Madison wrote Jefferson, of "the rigid adherence of Mr. Hamilton to a plan which he supposed more perfect."[10]

A year later Congress proposed two further amendments to the Confederation, seeking limited authority to regulate foreign commerce. Along with the revenue amendments of 1783, these proposals constituted the modest agenda of constitutional reform that supporters of a stronger federal union favored. Unlike the situation that confronted American resistance leaders in 1774, the dilemma of the Confederation did not require urgent action. Would-be reformers, such as Madison, had to wait patiently as the amendments made their way through the state legislatures, mindful of the awkward fact that a single rejection could doom the entire enterprise. Once individual amendments were adopted, they hoped, useful precedents would be set to further the cause of reform. But this was less a strategy of reform than a philosophy of patience, a default option that had to be pursued because other methods were unavailable.

For lack of any effective alternative, this remained Madison's position until the New Year of 1786 created a more sobering political logic. Instead of a philosophy of patience, one needed to devise an active strategy of reform. Four factors shaped this determination. First, the two sets of amendments that Congress had sent to the states in 1783 and 1784 remained unratified. Second, the perceived "imbecility" of Congress, and public indifference to its dealings, suggested that Congress could no longer fulfill its constitutional responsibility to propose amendments when they seemed necessary. Third, the divisions within Congress raised by the Jay-Gardoqui negotiations, particularly the dispute over American navigation rights on the Mississippi River, raised plausible fears that the Union could devolve into two or three regional confederacies. Finally, the unrest in

Massachusetts that led to Shays' Rebellion raised disturbing questions about the stability of America's republican constitutions.

The starting point for a reconsideration of political strategy came in January 1786, when the Virginia legislature invited other states to attend a conference to discuss the need to give Congress adequate powers over foreign commerce. Madison was not the original advocate of this measure, and he initially doubted it would succeed. But by mid-March 1786, he had changed his mind. When his friend and congressional correspondent James Monroe expressed his doubts about the meeting, Madison relayed his new calculations. Where Monroe thought the Virginia invitation did not go far enough, Madison argued that something had to be attempted *now*. Any amendment proposed by Congress seemed unlikely to succeed, he reasoned, and a success in this "first instance" could set a precedent for later reforms of a similar nature. That opinion was confirmed when Madison learned that Congress was considering either calling a general convention or proposing a new set of amendments. But Madison and Monroe now agreed that the conference set for Annapolis in September had become the best avenue for reform, not least because its results would indicate how far public opinion was prepared to go. Madison was aware, as he informed Jefferson, that "Many Gentlemen both within & without Congs. wish to make this meeting subservient to a Plenipotentiary Convention for amending the Confederation," a goal he also supported. Yet he still thought that the Annapolis meeting should focus on the commercial issue, and he remained pessimistic that even this goal could be accomplished.[11]

When the Annapolis delegates convened at Mann's Tavern, however, their numbers were too few to proceed to act. While a well-attended convention could have stolen a constitutional march, this rump gathering felt too diffident to pursue its agenda. But the dozen commissioners present included Madison, Hamilton, John Dickinson (the main author of the Articles of Confederation), Edmund Randolph, and Abraham Clark, a veteran New Jersey leader. Hamilton is usually given the credit for suggesting that the meeting exploit a clause in the commission of the New Jersey members to issue a call for a general convention, but the decision to take that step had to be consensual in nature: in for a constitutional penny, in for a constitutional pound.

Once the Annapolis convention issued its invitation, Madison became the dominant strategist in the proto-Federalist movement. He was not the sole leader to think in these terms. Dickinson and Charles Pinckney developed their own notions of how the Philadelphia convention should proceed, and as the late Pauline Maier demonstrated in her great book, *Ratification*, there is much to be said for viewing the convention from the vantage point of Mount Vernon. In his own way, George Washington, Virginia born and bred, was the greatest nationalist of the Revolutionary era, and Maier offers an intriguing contrast to the customary emphasis on Madison.[12] Yet in the final analysis, Madison's comprehensive strategy of constitutional revision, amply documented in his papers—especially his "Notes on Ancient and Modern Confederacies"; his pre-convention letters to Jefferson, Randolph, and Washington; and his working memorandum on the "Vices of the Political System of the United States," all culminating in the Virginia Plan—describe the evolution of his agenda.

The substance of this agenda and its fate are well known to all serious students of the origins of the Constitution and need not be detailed here. But some points deserve emphasis because their very familiarity obscures their significance. Having invested so much energy in solving the problems of republican government, Madison went to Philadelphia confident that he could convince others of the superior wisdom of his analysis. Instituting rules of proportional representation in both houses of a national legislature, Madison concluded, would be the precondition for deciding how powerful the new government would be. At the same time, his calculations suggested why this stratagem should succeed. Northern states would support it because they enjoyed the current advantage in population; southern states would do so because they expected future population growth would bring their region into parity with the North; and in the end small states would have to accede simply because they had no other place to go. When the Pennsylvania and Virginia delegations caucused in mid-May while they were awaiting the other delegations, Madison opposed the Pennsylvanians' proposal to deny the small states an equal vote in the convention itself. That would alarm them too much at the outset, Madison replied, but he remained confident that the small states could be compelled or convinced to yield the point as the deliberations proceeded.[13]

In pursuing these calculations, Madison became the casualty of his own intellectual passion. Although the basis on which the small states defended their right to an equal vote in one house of the new legislature often shifted, they never abandoned their claim. The argument on which Madison and his allies relied was one that remains as relevant today as it was in 1787. It held, quite simply and correctly, that the size of the population of a state would never define the political interests and preferences of its citizens—except, of course, when one was voting on rules of voting. The interests of the most populous states—that is, their underlying social, economic, and demographic characteristics—were hardly identical. One could not intelligently ask, what common interests would unite Virginia, Pennsylvania, and Massachusetts in one course of political action? Contrariwise, one could plausibly, indeed persuasively, argue that the presence or absence of slavery as the basis of a state's labor system would define one of the controlling interests that would dominate a state's politics. But that fundamental social fact had nothing to do with the size of a state's population.

Reliance on the force of these arguments and the presumption that the small states would ultimately concede were the guiding force in Madison's Constitutional Convention strategy. That strategy proved unavailing. Willpower rather than intellectual consistency was the principle on which the small states relied. In the end, the defection of Elbridge Gerry and Caleb Strong nullified the vote of the Massachusetts delegation, giving the small states a narrow victory on the equal state vote in the Senate that became a "compromise" only retrospectively. Madison betrayed his own bitter disappointment in his notes of debate for July 16–17. He noted, for example, how Edmund Randolph's suggestion for an overnight adjournment was "so readily & strangely misinterpreted" to be a proposal for the entire Convention to disband sine die. When the large state delegates caucused the next morning to contemplate their future course of action, Madison complained, "The time was wasted in vague conversation on the subject, without any specific proposition or agreement." Mary Bilder's incisive account of the composition of Madison's notes for this episode captures the depth of his feelings. "As far as Madison was concerned," she observes, "the compromise over the branches was theoretically incoherent and due to the weak resolve of others. He was furious and in no mood for conciliation."[14]

One result of this decision was the immediate rejection of Madison's pet proposal to give Congress a negative on state laws. His strategy for reform had effectively collapsed, and his notes of debates for this period now became, as Bilder traces their composition, "An Account of Failed Strategies." Bilder's account of this period is essentially a story of Madison lapsing into his own passions of frustration and disappointment. Those sentiments were still resonating even as the convention adjourned, as his well-known letters to Jefferson of September 6 and October 24, 1787, amply illustrate.[15] If one wants to push the question of constitutional paternity seriously, the extent of Madison's disappointment is a factor that one has to take into account.

Yet in the end, after taking a few deep breaths, the completion and ratification of the Constitution remained a defining commitment in Madison's political behavior, and a factor that continued to shape the Federalist strategy of ratification. That strategy involved decisions that transcended the specific arguments made in support of the Constitution or even the concessions, mostly over the matter of amendments, that became politically necessary. Indeed, because we take the fact of ratification too much for granted, or perhaps because we anachronistically bestow too much importance on the Bill of Rights, we either fail to appreciate just how artful Federalist strategy was, or else, like Michael Klarman, we complain that the adoption of the Constitution was deficient because it fell short of modern criteria of democratic legitimacy.[16] What these qualms fail to consider is the entire novelty of the entire process of ratification. This was a constitutional enterprise for which there was only one useful precedent, the example set by Massachusetts in 1780, after that state had spent four years disputing how a new charter of government should be adopted. Even after Massachusetts resolved this problem with the ideal solution of having a constitution framed by a special convention and then ratified by the people in their town meetings, questions remained about the exact nature of the latter's consent.

In framing the Federalist strategy for ratification, Madison merged important theoretical concerns with pressing political calculations. The theoretical concerns implicated a problem essential to American law: how does one distinguish a written constitution from other forms of law? Or to rephrase the question: if one wanted to treat a written constitution as fundamental law, superior in authority to all other lawful acts of government, how would that distinction be established? In pursuing that problem, Madison and others grasped the significance of the legal doctrine *quos leges posteriors priores, contrarias abrogant* (later laws contradicting earlier laws abrogate them). Whereas a constitution adopted legislatively was always open to revision by a later meeting of the same body—because one legislature cannot bind its successors—a constitution framed by a special convention and then approved by the people, whether by a referendum or in town meetings or in a popularly elected convention, would escape or transcend that constraint. Because the state constitutions adopted prior to Massachusetts were never ratified by the people at large, their legal authority was only statutory in nature, making them subject to legislative revision.[17]

The idea of having the Constitution ratified by specially elected conventions thus had a powerful substantive implication, and one that required abandoning the rule subjecting all amendments to the Articles of Confederation to state legislative approval. The accompanying *political* calculations extended this logic along a different axis. Here the starting point was the problematic case of Rhode Island, which had refused to attend the Constitutional Convention, and which would likely reject any changes it proposed, particularly if those were transformative in nature. Rather than allow this notoriously "anti-federal" state to thwart the entire enterprise of reform, it made sense to abandon the rule requiring amendments to the Articles of Confederation to be approved by all thirteen states. Nine states would do.

That still left open the question of what form this approval would take. The customary story of ratification credits both sides with securing a grand bargain in the national interest. The Federalists created an effective national government, while the Anti-Federalists insisted on the eventual addition of the Bill of Rights. That judgment, however, rests on a flawed assumption that elevates our understanding of modern constitutional history over the actual options the Federalists confronted or the real changes Anti-Federalists actually preferred. The modern jurisprudence of the Bill of Rights, as its numerous provisions have been applied to the states under the incorporation doctrine of the Fourteenth Amendment, dominates the teaching of constitutional law—or at least gains equal billing with "structural" issues such as federalism and separation of powers, the concerns that mattered far more in 1787–88.

Yet the choice facing the Federalists that Madison was anxious to solve demanded a different strategy. Their objectives were to ensure that the call for amendments did not produce any substantive changes in the Constitution proper, in either the structure of government or the powers it wielded. Arguably the proposals that mattered most were those that would drive the new government back to the underlying rules of the Confederation, under which Congress would rely on the good faith compliance of the states with national recommendations and requisitions before resorting to sterner measures. The refutation of this reigning principle of American federalism (in its 1.0 version under the Articles) was one of the leading discoveries driving Madison's approach to constitutional reform. Reviving this practice through the backdoor call for amendments was anathema to his strategy and the Federalist agenda.[18]

Rather than open a path to this discussion, Federalists insisted on imposing two constraints on the ratification conventions. First, the Constitution had to be accepted or rejected in its entirety. The sovereign voice of the people would speak, but it could utter only one of two words: yes or no. Second, once the Federalists did encounter threatening opposition within the state conventions—which began with Massachusetts, the seventh state to meet—space had to be given for amendments to be proposed. But these amendments could not be conditional in nature; they could not be permitted to modify or supplant the prior duty to accept or reject the Constitution in toto.

It is easy to fault this strategy on democratic grounds, as Michael Klarman has recently done at great length. The people out-of-doors had no prior knowledge of the agenda of the great convention, and no opportunity to engage in concerted activity to alter any of its clauses prior to its ratification. Although the proposal to hold a second general convention to consider all the alterations that the state conventions had proposed never attained critical mass, Federalists were desperately anxious to preclude this possibility. Madison justified this opposition in a detailed letter to his friend Edmund Randolph, who vigorously supported a second convention. In this revealing letter of January 10, 1788—which has strangely not received the attention it deserves—Madison laid bare his reasons for opposing Randolph's plan. "Were a second trial to be made," the supporters "of a good constitution for the Union would not only find themselves not a little differing from each other as to the proper amendments; but perplexed & frustrated by men who had objects totally different." A second convention would lack the unity of purpose that had worked so well in 1787. "But were the first difficulties overcome," Madison continued, "and the Constitution re-edited with amendments, the event would still be infinitely precarious."

Here Madison dropped the veil and rendered a bleak assessment of the judgment of ordinary citizens. "There are subjects to which the capacities of the bulk of mankind are unequal," he observed, and constitutional deliberation was one of them. Most citizens "must follow the judgment of others not their own." The adoption of a new constitutional government, he concluded, "must result from a fortunate coincidence of leading opinions, and a general confidence of the people in those who recommend it." A second convention would destroy both conditions "and give a loose to human opinions; which must be as various and irreconcilable concerning theories of Government, as doctrines of Religion." In the realm of religion, that diversity would produce beneficial results, ensuring religious liberty for all; but in the realm of constitutional politics, it would only "give opportunities to designing men which it might be impossible to counteract."[19]

Three weeks later, Madison refined this private argument in Federalist Nos. 49 and 50, two of his most intriguing essays. Here he criticized Jefferson's idea of having popularly elected conventions, meeting on an "occasional" or "periodic" basis, resolve constitutional controversies among the departments. As a matter of "republican theory," this proposal was wholly appropriate because "the people themselves" were "the only legitimate fountain of power." But as a matter of republican politics, the idea was vulnerable to telling objections. The first was the likelihood that because "every appeal to the people would carry an implication of some defect in the government, frequent appeals would in great measure deprive the government of that veneration which time bestows on every thing, and without which perhaps the wisest and freest governments would not possess the requisite stability." Veneration can only develop over time, so this first caution in *Federalist* No. 49 was a warning against long-term, cumulative consequences. In our own historical moment, following a catastrophic presidency that subjected so many constitutional norms to wanton violation, Madison's concern with veneration retains a grim relevance.[20]

But there was a more immediate lesson that Madison wished to apply, drawn both from the Philadelphia convention and recollections of his own political debut at the Fifth Provincial Convention of 1776, the body that had drafted the Virginia constitution that Jefferson had been criticizing. These two essays echo Federalist No. 37 in explaining why constitution making was an inherently difficult business, especially when the document in question had to receive popular approval. "Notwithstanding the success which has attended the revisions of our established forms of government," Madison wrote:

> it must be confessed that the experiments are of too ticklish a nature to be unnecessarily multiplied. We are to recollect that all the existing constitutions were formed in the midst of a danger which repressed the passions most unfriendly to order and concord; of an enthusiastic confidence of the people in their patriotic leaders, which stifled the ordinary diversity of opinions on great national questions; of a universal ardor for new and opposite forms, produced by a universal resentment and indignation against the ancient government; and whilst no spirit of party connected with the changes to be made, or the abuses to be reformed, could mingle its leaven in the operation.[21]

One could not count on these conditions prevailing in the future. In Madison's view of the process of constitution making, due attention had to be paid to the fortuitous circumstances that had contributed to success in 1776, and that would hopefully prevail again in 1788, if the situation was well managed. But one also had to be mindful of the many obstacles that could discourage reaching the necessary agreement, especially if a second convention assembled.

Madison offered one final set of reasons for his opposition to Jefferson's proposal and the underlying norm of popular sovereignty it embodied. This final criticism, which he deemed "the greatest objection of all," offered a more pointed analysis of the political dynamics that seemed most likely to prevail in interdepartmental controversies. The most likely disruptors of "the constitutional equilibrium of the government" would be found in the legislative branch, he predicted, that "impetuous vortex" of aggressive, usurping, encroaching "activity" that posed the greatest danger to the separation of powers. But in Madison's deeper analysis of republican politics, the political force driving legislative usurpations would come from the people at large, or rather, the dominant factions within the larger body politic. And that was exactly why a scheme of constitutional monitoring relying, as Jefferson would have it, on popularly elected conventions would never work. There could be no impartial judgment in this process, no balanced judgment rendered "on the true merits of the question."[22]

Weighed against our modern criteria and norms, Madison does not emerge as a hero of democratic theory. His blunt letter to Randolph strikes avowedly elitist and reactionary notes, and *Federalist* Nos. 49 and 50 imply that the people can rarely act as effective monitors of constitutional norms. Yet when one weighs the risks of permitting or even promoting constitutional dissensus against the democratic promise of continued deliberation, who is to say that Madison's political strategy of 1787–88 was defective? "The Framers' Coup" that Klarman alleges to have occurred was not even in his own analysis a seizure of power in the ordinary use of the term. It would after all be quite an unusual coup that depended, first, on the consent of popularly elected conventions, chosen by electorates that in eighteenth-century terms were quite broad (vastly outnumbering the contemporary British "political nation"), and then on peaceful elections held in the eleven states that had ratified the Constitution by July 1788. Nor were the dissident or secessionist states of Rhode Island and North Carolina to be punished or repressed for going their separate ways.

So the strategy of insisting that the state conventions unequivocally approve or reject the Constitution while preventing the call for amendments from becoming a contingent condition of ratification was a stroke of political genius. Perhaps Americans still owe the Anti-Federalists a great debt for adding the Bill of Rights to the Constitution. But that debt only began to be collected in the twentieth century, a near century and a half after the original articles were signed. Madison's real achievement was to pursue a strategy of constitutional reform that made a collective decision defying the existing rules for amending the Articles of Confederation wholly legitimate. His insistence on pursuing amendments in the First Congress, against the preferences of his colleagues, was a codicil to that strategy. Though his feelings about the positive value of rights-protecting amendments remained mixed, he believed that it was essential to accommodate moderate Anti-Federalists and thus contribute to the public conviction that the Constitution had indeed been fairly considered. Such a strategy would foster the conditions of veneration he had celebrated in *Federalist* No. 49 and thus would help promote the stability of the new political system.

In a book devoted in part to considering Madisonian lessons for our own time, much can thus be said for pondering how the great sage of Montpelier combined political activity and reflection. To think of Madison primarily as the great original theorist of the Constitution diminishes his actual contribution to its adoption. That appreciation may be more important while we are collectively living through a moment when the entire constitutional system is being sorely tested and indeed has arguably failed, as it did in the two Trump impeachments of 2020 and 2021.[23]

To appreciate his role, then, involves doing something more than debating the tired question of constitutional paternity, which in the end is not all that interesting a matter analytically. A better though more complicated problem involves the matter of how one weighs his legacy. The idea that Americans still live under a Madisonian constitution offers one obvious framework for assessing that problem. But that notion, too, seems so familiar that it offers little inspiration. If we push the study of Madison's ideas further, however, beyond the well-known statements about extended republics and counteracting ambitions in *Federalist* Nos. 10 and 51, some of his ideas remain relevant, for two reasons. First, they may provide valuable insights into aspects of contemporary political behavior and constitutional structure that remain revealing. Second, even when Madison's expectations appear deficient, they often identify useful baselines for understanding how the entire political system has evolved since his era.

Start, then, with what may be the best-known paragraph in his writings: the discussion of the sources of faction in *Federalist* No. 10. What loom largest in the scholarly interpretation of this essay are the concluding five sentences on the impact of economic interests on politics. These form "the most common and durable sources of faction," Madison observed. They also provided the theoretical foundation for the *Economic Interpretation of the Constitution* that Charles A. Beard erected eleven decades ago, which other Progressive and neo-Progressive scholars, such as Woody Holton and Michael Klarman, have echoed ever since. But in the light of recent events, the first half of the paragraph now seems equally interesting. The "latent causes of faction" had many sources, Madison wrote: "A zeal for different opinions concerning religion, concerning government, and many other points, as well of speculation as of practice; an attachment to different leaders ambitiously contending for pre-eminence and power; or to persons of other descriptions whose fortunes have been interesting to the human passions": these were all sources of factious behavior and "violent conflicts."[24] As a general description of American politics today, these observations remain timely.

Yet what *Federalist* No. 10 omits is the deeper comparative analysis on which these judgments rested. The point of the essay was to explain why an extended national republic would better resist factious politics than the states, but not to discuss why the states hereafter would remain vulnerable to these evils. Because his critique of the vices of state politics was tied to his lost proposal for a congressional negative on state laws, Madison (as Publius) had no reason to reprise the devastating analysis of state politics that permeated his April 1787 memorandum on the vices of the political system. Elements of that critique did appear discreetly in individual essays, but *The Federalist* had other agendas to pursue.

The underlying analysis of state politics and the comparative assessment of the relative failings and dangers of state versus national governance remain as valid today as they were in 1787. The logic of Madison's position rested, in part, on a simple arithmetical presumption (call it an axiom). The smaller the entity of governance, the easier it is for skewed or "factious" majorities to form, producing ruling alliances that would not elevate the public good or private rights above their self-interested concerns. At the national level, the multiplicity of interests will make this process more difficult; at the state level, those restraints ordinarily will be fewer and weaker. It does not take a jaundiced view of American politics in the 2020s to say that this analysis still provides a valuable framework for assessing many of the issues currently vexing the polity, where questions involving voter suppression, abortion, and the status of the LGBTQ community are agitated predominantly at the state level.

The composition of the two parties arguably reinforces this analysis. The modern Democratic Party—which Madison and Jefferson cofounded as the Republican party of the 1790s that evolved into the post-Jacksonian Democratic Party—has become much more of a pluralist coalition than its Republican opponents: multiracial, multidenominational, and divided between its moderate and progressive wings. By contrast, the modern Republican Party represents more homogeneous communities: primarily old-stock white Americans and individuals who affiliate with evangelical Protestantism (though the depth of their religiosity has been called into question). Given the marked social asymmetry between the two parties, the Madisonian framework remains germane. And if one regards the degeneration of the Republican Party as the single most important factor affecting our current political system, explaining the character of its current factiousness is essential.

Where this model breaks down, however, is in accounting for the specific political practices that reinforce the factious characteristics of party politics. There is no eighteenth-century equivalent for the modern party primary, which is arguably the one procedure that works most powerfully to maintain factious enthusiasm and discipline. Because only the most highly mobilized or engaged voters regularly turn out for party primaries, the cost of deviating from party ideology and orthodoxy has grown quite high for incumbent lawmakers. The fear of being "primaried" in safe-seat districts that favor one's own party is now a pervasive concern among incumbent Republican lawmakers. That fear has in turn worked to drive the current Republican Party ever further to the right, to the point where many observers believes that there is no longer any bloc of legislators who could legitimately be called moderates.

Yet important as primary elections have become in the selection of lawmakers, their modern invention and the decisive influence they exercise do not represent the most significant departure from Madison's original expectations. As a politician whose skills had been nurtured in deliberative bodies, Madison would have welcomed the idea of improving the performance of national and state governments by recruiting and retaining veteran lawmakers. But the world Madison inhabited was one where legislative politics was less a career that one pursued than an avocation and a duty one accepted. Today, any analytical model of congressional behavior would make the desire for reelection the dominant independent variable. By contrast, Madison correctly assumed that most members in any given session of Congress would be newcomers who would serve a term or two and then rotate home, perhaps seeking another, less burdensome office close to family and property. Under this model of behavior, every Congress would create its own learning cycle, with members' knowledge of both issues and colleagues developing from one seasonal session to the next.

In part because Madison rightly anticipated that this ongoing process of rotation would long characterize the House of Representatives, he continued to believe that a well-constituted Senate was necessary to create "wisdom and stability" in legislative deliberation. He held to that belief even after the Federal Convention narrowly approved the misnamed Great Compromise giving each state an equal vote in the Senate. That was as bitter a defeat as the rejection of the congressional negative on state laws, and Madison explicitly refused to defend it on principle. The opening passage of *Federalist* No. 62 makes this point abundantly clear. Rather than apply the various arguments that the delegates from the small states had used to defend the equal state vote, Madison simply concluded that "it is superfluous to try, by the standard of theory, a part of the Constitution which is allowed on all hands to be the result, not of theory, but [quoting George Washington's post-Convention letter to the Continental Congress] 'of a spirit of amity, and that mutual deference and concession which the peculiarity of our situation renders indispensable.'"[25] When Madison evoked "the standard of theory," he was describing the principle that the people should be represented proportionally in *both* houses of the new Congress. In Madison's deeply held view, the idea that the smallest states deserved an equal state vote in at least one house of Congress, merely because they were less populous than their neighbors, was specious. The size of a state's population was wholly irrelevant to the true political interests of its citizens.[26]

Among all the propositions that one can extract from Madison's political thinking, this is the one that arguably remains most salient to the American constitutional system today. The interests of voters in small states are not substantively or qualitatively different from citizens in larger states. No one, in either the electorate or Congress, ever votes on that basis. Yet the consequences of that decision continue to resonate politically in both the composition of the Senate and the allocation of presidential electors among the states (due to the "senatorial bump"). This distortion of majority rule and the injury it inflicts on the one-person, one-vote norm constitute, as they potentially always have, an impairment of democratic principles.

Having spent the past half century thinking and writing about Madison, I find that the complexities and nuances of his political thinking and the genuine insights they convey remain fascinating still, and perhaps never more so than at this unexpectedly perilous moment in the history of the nation he did so much to fashion.

NOTES

1. For a quite different conception of his role as "Father of the Constitution," see David S. Schwartz and John Mikhail, "The Other Madison Problem," *Fordham Law Review* 89 (2021), 2033–83; and Akhil Amar, "Founding Myths," in *Myth America: Historians Take on the Biggest Legends and Lies about Our Past*, ed. Kevin Kruse and Julian E. Zelizer (New York: Basic Books, 2023). For my response, see Jack N. Rakove, "A MARvel of Constitutional Demythologizing," *Journal of American Constitutional History* 1 (2023): 287–311, https://doi.org/10.59015/jach.MTYZ9289.

2. I sometimes think it would be fun to present at least the major *Federalist* essays in a Talmudic page format, with leading commentaries arrayed around the main text.

3. For the most recent sustained discussion of *The Federalist*, see the essays collected in *The Cambridge Companion to "The Federalist,"* ed. Jack N. Rakove and Colleen Sheehan (New York: Cambridge University Press, 2020);and for a brilliant reassessment of *Federalist* No. 37, see Todd Estes, "The Emergence and Centrality of James Madison's *Federalist* 37: Historians, Political Theorists, and the Recentering of Meaning in *The Federalist*," *American Political Thought*, 12 (2023), 424–52.

4. Benjamin Wittes and Pietro Nivola, eds., *What Would Madison Do?: The Father of the Constitution Meets Modern American Politics* (Washington, D.C.: Brookings Institution Press, 2015).

5. Madison, "Vices of the Political System of the United States," April 1787, *Papers of James Madison*, ed. William T. Hutchinson et al., Congressional series, 9:345–58, https://founders.archives.gov/documents/Madison/01-09-02-0187. Madison's use of the phrase "political system" deserves further conceptual analysis. On the eighteenth-century conception of a "political system," see the intriguing comments of the great diplomatic historian Felix Gilbert, *To the Farewell Address: Ideas of Early American Foreign Policy* (Princeton: Princeton University Press, 1961), 100–104.

6. Howard Ohline, "Republicanism and Slavery: Origins of the Three-Fifths Clause in the United States Constitution," *William and Mary Quarterly* 28 (1971): 563–84.

7. Madison, *Federalist* No. 39, in Alexander Hamilton, James Madison, and John Jay, *The Federalist*, ed. Jacob E. Cooke (Middletown Conn.: Wesleyan University Press, 1961), 256.(Subsequent citations are to this edition.)

8. Jack N. Rakove, *James Madison and the Creation of the American Republic*, 3rd ed. (New York: Longman, 2007); Jack N. Rakove, *A Politician Thinking: The Creative Mind of James Madison* (Norman: University of Oklahoma Press, 2017).

9. Madison, Notes of Debates, February 20 and 21, 1783, *Papers of James Madison*, 6:265–66,

270–74; Jack N. Rakove, *The Beginnings of National Politics: An Interpretive History of the Continental Congress* (New York: Alfred A. Knopf, 1979), 307–24.

10. Madison to Jefferson, April 22, 1783, *Papers of Madison*, 6:481.

11. Rakove, *Beginnings of National Politics*, 368–74; Madison to Monroe, March 14 and 19, 1786, *Papers of Madison*, 8:497–98, 505–6; Madison to Jefferson, August 12, 1786, ibid., 9:95–97.

12. Pauline Maier, *Ratification: The People Debate the Constitution, 1787-1788* (New York: Simon and Schuster, 2010), 1–26.

13. Madison to Washington, April 16, 1787, *Papers of Madison*, 9:383–84; Max Farrand, ed., *Records of the Federal Convention* (New Haven: Yale University Press, 1913, 1966), 1:10–11n*; Jack N. Rakove, *Original Meanings: Politics and Ideas in the Making of the Constitution* (New York: Alfred Knopf, 1996), 58–60.

14. Farrand, *Records of the Federal Convention*, 2:17–20; Mary Bilder, *Madison's Hand: Revising the Constitutional Convention* (Cambridge, Mass.: Harvard University Press, 2015), 108–15 (quotation at 113). For my extensive review of her book, see Jack Rakove, "A Biography of Madison's Notes of Debates," *Constitutional Commentary* 31 (2016): 317–49.

15. *Papers of Madison*, 10:163–64, 206–19.

16. Michael Klarman, *The Framers' Coup: The Making of the United States Constitution* (New York: Oxford University Press, 2016); for my criticisms of Klarman's argument, see Rakove, "The Real Motives behind the Constitution: The Endless Quest," *Reviews in American History* 48 (2020): 216–28.

17. For a more elaborate discussion, see Gordon S. Wood, *The Creation of the American Republic, 1776–1787* (Chapel Hill: University of North Carolina Press, 1969), 306–43; Rakove, *Original Meanings*, 94–130.

18. Rakove, *Politician Thinking*, 45–53.

19. Madison to Edmund Randolph, January 10, 1788, *Papers of Madison*, 10:354–56.

20. For a more skeptical assessment of Madison's attachment to the norm of veneration, see Jeremy D. Bailey, *James Madison and Constitutional Imperfection* (New York: Cambridge University Press, 2015), 15–37.

21. Madison, *Federalist* No. 37, 340–41.

22. Ibid., 341–43.

23. Jack N. Rakove, "Impeachment, Responsibility, and Constitutional Failure: From Watergate to January 6," in *British Origins and American Practice of Impeachment*, ed. Matthew Flinders and Chris Monaghan (London: Routledge, 2024), 206–37.

24. Madison, *Federalist* No, 10, 58–59.

25. Madison, *Federalist* No. 62, 416–17.

26. See Jack N. Rakove, "A Model for Deliberation or Obstruction: Madison's Thoughts about the Senate," in Wittes and Nivola, *What Would Madison Do?*, 111–28.

"Father of the Constitution"?

Can Madison Pass the Paternity Test?

LYNN UZZELL

James Madison does not loom large in America's popular imagination. He was no military hero like George Washington, nor a wit and bon vivant like Benjamin Franklin, and he lacked the rhetorical flair of Thomas Jefferson. Unlike John Adams or Alexander Hamilton, his life hasn't been featured in an HBO miniseries or (an even surer road to immortality) a smash hit Broadway musical. For most people, Madison's contributions to the American legacy may seem a bit obscure; his life and personality have been overshadowed by the company he kept. Nevertheless, if Americans know only one thing about Madison, it is his constitutional paternity; he is popularly known as "The Father of the Constitution."

The scholarly appreciation of Madison's legacy could not be more different than the popular one. Among political theorists and intellectual historians, in particular, Madison has long been considered a rock star of the American founding. Even when Madison stands alongside the "assembly of demigods" of this elite generation, few have even pretended to rival the depth and breadth of his thinking on constitutional topics. Nevertheless, scholars have been more skeptical about the facile description that he fathered the founding charter. After all, it is the job of the bookish class to question popular assumptions and to skewer sacred cows.

Is it true, though, that Madison's title cannot survive a more serious and scholarly examination? In other words, if Madison were to be given a constitutional paternity test, would he pass it? The idea of "fathering" a constitution is obviously a metaphor, an analogy, a poetic figure of speech. And it might seem at first glance to be a rather frivolous exercise to defend the legitimacy of a mere figure of speech. Perhaps it would be, were it not for the extraordinary energies that have already been expended trying either to defend or (more commonly) to debunk this title. Moreover, such an inquiry is not as frivolous as it might at first appear. The proper use of metaphor does not merely adorn language, like bedecking a woman in shiny baubles. As Richard Weaver has shown, metaphor is one of the primary ways that the human mind gropes for understanding when confronting obscure or unfamiliar subjects. Socrates, for instance, "believed that some things are best told by parable and some perhaps discoverable only by parable. Real investigation goes forward with the help of analogy." Even the use of language to convey meaning is, at bottom, metaphorical.[1]

We begin our present investigation, then, with an abstract question that defies easy answers: What is the relationship between James Madison and the United States Constitution? Even before Madison's death, people sought to elucidate this obscurity by drawing parallels between the more abstract association and one that was more immediate and familiar: Madison is to the Constitution what a father is to his child. For about 150 years, this analogy was largely accepted as an apt way to capture the essence of the connection between the two subjects. In recent decades, however, the analogy has come under increasing fire from scholars who claim that calling Madison Father of the Constitution misleads more than illumines our understanding. Nevertheless, a more rigorous examination into the history of the title will demonstrate that the original metaphor remains apt, but only if it is understood with the meaning it was originally meant to convey.

THE GROWING SCHOLARLY MOMENTUM
AGAINST THE TITLE

Scholars used to be less jaded than today's crop, and at one time Madison's title was accepted uncritically. Charles Warren, writing in 1928, said that Madison "has been termed, without dissent, the 'Father of the Constitution.'" By the Freudian fifties, however, Edward S. Corwin seemed embarrassed that anyone should feel the need "to gratify the father complex of the American people." Still, he grudgingly acknowledged that "Madison was probably the most eligible candidate," if that urge must be gratified. Clinton Rossiter, writing less than a decade later, said with only a touch of circumspection that "few historians begrudge Madison the title 'Father of the Constitution.'" But Rossiter was writing in what was still a relatively innocent year of 1961, before historians began in earnest their grudge match against Madison's paternity. By the 1980s, Christopher and James Lincoln Collier were still conceding that "most historians would accept" that title, but they also made it abundantly clear that these two authors should not be counted among their ranks. Forrest McDonald unceremoniously dismissed the title outright as a "myth," and he lamented, at the same time, that it was such a "deeply rooted" one. Probably no one to this day has done more than McDonald to demythologize Madison's paternity.[2]

Although some authors have sought to question or debunk the title, others—with more or less charity toward Madison—have sought alternative monikers for him. Richard Brookhiser suggested, no doubt trying to be charitable, that "If [Madison] was not quite the Father of the Constitution . . . he was its midwife."

Greg Weiner, striving for a more dignified image, suggested Madison was "better understood as the attending physician at its birth—and, later, as its tutor." Kevin R. C. Gutzman was both less charitable and less dignified: "Far from being the 'father of the Constitution,'... Madison was an unhappy witness at its C-section birth. Perhaps he might be more appropriately called an attending nurse." And Bruce G. Kauffmann prefers the title "Godfather of the Constitution."[3] (In all likelihood, Kauffmann intended by this metaphor to evoke images of our infant Constitution at the baptismal font, and a benignant Madison on hand with swaddling clothes ready to confer his blessing. Nevertheless, the consumer of American pop culture can't help but read into that title more sinister connotations. If Madison was "Godfather of the Constitution," one cannot help wondering: which Anti-Federalist might be waking up next to a horse's head?)

Not all skeptics have tried to obliterate or replace the title altogether; some are keen to retain the idea of the Constitution's father, but they wish to confer it on rival claimants. More than one scholar believes that a good case can be made that James Wilson of Pennsylvania was at least as deserving as Madison of the honorific. Richard Brookhiser thinks another Pennsylvanian, Gouverneur Morris, deserves at least "a share of the paternity," especially for his role in composing the final draft of the Constitution.[4] But the sons of South Carolina are determined not to be outdone by Pennsylvania.

The very first rival claimant for the title appears to be Charles Pinckney. And the very first person to make the case for Pinckney's paternity appears to be his grandnephew. According to William S. Elliott, writing in 1864, Pinckney "has always been considered as entitled to the high and honorable designation of 'The Father of the Constitution.'" Most people did not take that claim seriously until almost a century later, when Sidney Ulmer, who was almost as zealous about inflating Charles Pinckney's reputation as Charles Pinckney was about inflating his own reputation, wrote an entire article defending Pinckney's right to that name. But another South Carolinian, John Rutledge, has also been found worthy of being called the Constitution's father. In 1942, Richard Barry, Rutledge's quirky biographer, subtly accused Madison of attempting to misappropriate the title for himself, in "a masterpiece of suggestion," by drafting his *Notes of the Convention* in such a way as to give himself credit for writing the Constitution. Barry had a different tale to tell. He claimed that when Alexis de Tocqueville was touring the country before writing *Democracy in America*, he was incredulous to hear that "the Constitution had been written by 'The Founding Fathers.'" Instead, he believed that such an ingenious document "can have but *one* authentic father. Who was he?'" After poring over the surviving records, including Madison's *Notes*, he concluded: "There is no mystery about it—the authorship of the Constitution is quite clear—a man named John Rutledge wrote it." Barry's story is pure fiction, but the tall tale was nonetheless engraved on Rutledge's tombstone in the mid-twentieth century and can be seen there today.[5] This flight of fancy is some indication of the lengths to which some historians will go to wrest paternity claims from Madison and bestow them elsewhere.

Other writers, impatient with this nickel-and-diming approach of choosing just one father for the Constitution, have suggested sharing paternity much more broadly. William Lee Miller protests the "singleness of the metaphor," pointing out that "victory has a hundred fathers." Richard Brookhiser further minimizes Madison's paternity claims by multiplying Lee's progenitors by ten: "success has a thousand fathers." And John R. Vile has effectively multiplied that number at least a thousandfold again, by conferring the honorific on every American citizen. He notes that the only source capable of bestowing authority on our republican Constitution is the people who ratified its text and subsequent amendments; therefore, only the great body of American citizens have the ultimate claim to be "fathers and mothers" of the Constitution. Nevertheless, Vile does not wish to diminish Madison's claims to pure insignificance. He concedes that Madison may still at least be described as "first among equals" in this new, more inclusive, poli-patristic image of fatherhood.[6]

The current state of scholarship on this question is perhaps best encapsulated in a recent exchange in *Starting Points Journal*. Sanford V. Levinson, calling for "a DNA Test to Determine Paternity of the Constitution," alleged that certain "inflated claims" about Madison are responsible for "One of the hoariest cliches of American constitutional history." In his "Reply to Levinson," Alan Gibson insisted at the outset: "I have no intention of arguing that Madison was the 'Father of the Constitution'"; nevertheless, Madison "has a lot to teach us about the Constitution."[7] When the scholarly "debate" on this topic has been reduced to quibbling over the *degree* of the metaphor's unsuitability, we can pronounce with confidence that, insofar as scholars are concerned, the analogy is dead. Where once there was a near-universal consensus in favor of the title, there is now a near-universal consensus against it.

THE CASE AGAINST MADISON'S PATERNITY

Three serious objections have been lodged against Madison's claims to paternity. First, numerous writers have argued that we should reject the title because Madison rejected it. Responding to a correspondent's attempts to saddle him with that honorific (the story goes), he objected that the Constitution "was not, like the fabled Goddess of Wisdom, the offspring of a single brain. It ought to be regarded as the work of many heads & many hands." Those words are indeed Madison's; however, he was not rejecting the title "Father of the Constitution" at the time he wrote them. He was responding to William Cogswell in 1834, who had referred to him as "The writer of the Constitution." The term "writer" is notably different from the term "father." There is no metaphorical meaning when calling someone the "writer" of a document, and its literal meaning is obviously false. Since no single person can plausibly claim sole authorship to the Constitution, Madison was unquestionably correct when he rejected that title out of hand. However, those debunkers who have claimed that Madison explicitly denied being "Father of the Constitution" in this letter (and numerous authors have advanced iterations of this argument) are simply mistaken in the facts.[8] The Cogswell letter gets us nowhere when addressing the present question: Would it be fair to describe Madison as Father of the Constitution?

Scholars have also cited, as a second reason for jettisoning the title, Madison's deep sense of disappointment and pessimism at the close of the Constitutional Convention. Writing to his friend Jefferson less than two weeks before the convention adjourned, Madison privately expressed his opinion that this new Constitution, "should it be adopted[,] will neither effectually answer its national object nor prevent the local mischiefs which every where excite disgusts ag[ain]st the state governments." Some writers consider his disappointment and pessimism to be convincing evidence that Madison could not be the Constitution's father.[9] Once again, the words quoted are Madison's, but these circumstances are an unsatisfactory paternity test. For if a father's occasional disappointment and frustration with his offspring were sufficient to delegitimize them, such a test would make bastards of half the world's population, at least.

So far, we have breezily dispensed with two objections, but the most formidable one is yet to come. Forrest McDonald, who deliberately set out to debunk the "myth" of Madison's paternity, has argued that the constitution Madison set out to achieve when he arrived in Philadelphia in 1787 "bears limited resemblance to the document that was drafted by the convention." But the failure to find a resemblance doesn't end there; McDonald also tallies up Madison's pitiable score during the convention's debates: "of seventy-one specific proposals that Madison moved, seconded, or spoke unequivocally in regard to, he was on the losing side forty times." These facts seem to pose a daunting challenge to the paternity narrative, and nearly every writer who has since taken a firm stance against awarding that title to Madison cites McDonald's arguments. Some of them go on to add that many of Madison's losses at the convention were his most cherished or distinctive proposals, such as proportional representation in both houses of Congress, the federal veto, and the council of revision. While it is true that the basic structure that Madison wanted to see in the Constitution—its three branches and its bicameral legislature—is reflected in the Constitution that was ratified, it must be acknowledged that such ideas of government were hardly unique; as Madison himself acknowledged, these structural foundations of government were "generally taken" among the many delegates professing a wish to substitute a "regular Government" for the old Articles of Confederation.[10]

The purpose of a modern-day DNA test is to locate the distinctive biological material that could come from one set of parents and from no other individuals. And even before we reached this degree of technological sophistication, an informal paternity test would seek to discover distinctive features in the child—the curve of a lip or the shape of the eye—that could come from that child's father and no other. If it is true, as indeed it seems to be, that "Madison's Constitution"—meaning, the one that he had wanted or defended before and during the Constitutional Convention—bears little resemblance to the one that was actually born on September 17, 1787, then it appears that Madison has failed the constitutional DNA test. His claims to fatherhood, on this showing, would seem to be annihilated.

But not so fast. Before we shut the files on this paternity suit and stamp it with a resounding "case closed," we should pause first to parse the meaning of this phrase more carefully than either its defenders or its detractors have ever done. The word "father," after all, has two distinct definitions. Only one of those definitions relates to the mere biological act of begetting offspring—the sort of paternity that man shares with all the animals. Another distinct meaning of the word, and the more distinctively human meaning, is that of rearing, protecting, nurturing, and forming the character of a child from infancy to maturity. Of the two definitions of "father," the second one, after all, is generally regarded as the more meaningful. For those of us who purchase cards for Fathers' Day, most likely we are not gratefully acknowledging one man's single encounter with our mother, no matter how exquisite, but rather the years of sacrifice and care that came after. And if we applied this meaning of "fatherhood" to Madison's relationship to the Constitution, would he be able to pass that paternity test?

Skeptics and naysayers are apt to cry foul at this point, alleging that, by drawing this distinction between the different meanings of the word "father," I'm trying to pull a dirty swindle. Since McDonald and others have given compelling reasons to reject Madison's claims to something like biological fatherhood, they might accuse me of attempting to substitute an alternative meaning as a retroactive attempt to salvage Madison's title in the face of consummate defeat. The skeptics and naysayers would be mistaken. The case I'm making—that we need to shift our focus from the biological to the more meaningful and distinctively human definition of fatherhood—is not a retroactive bait and switch; it is a retrospective revival of the metaphor's original meaning. In fact, those who believe that "Father of the Constitution" is supposed to evoke the biological act of begetting have grossly misunderstood the analogy, and they have been perpetuating this misunderstanding for generations. If we intend to finally take this metaphor seriously, and to question in all earnestness whether Madison deserves it, the first step is to recover its original and authentic meaning. A proper investigation requires revisiting the evening when the honorific was first bestowed.

THE ORIGIN STORY OF "THE FATHER OF THE CONSTITUTION"

On November 3, 1827, the Pennsylvania Society for the Encouragement of Manufactures hosted a dinner for one Professor Friedrich List (a man whose laurels, along with his "Letters on Political Economy," have since receded into the mists of historic insignificance). Perhaps owing to a dearth of news in Greater Philadelphia that week, details of this dinner were covered at length in the papers. Apparently, fifteen toasts were offered in quick succession, and that was before the opportunity for lengthier toasts and speeches got underway. Judging by the number of times guests were invited to raise their glasses that evening, the reports that "glee and repeated bursts of applause" greeted each speech were probably not exaggerated. But the only speech of lasting significance was the longest toast of all. It was offered by Charles Jared Ingersoll, then vice president of the society. He raised a glass to "the health and happiness of James Madison, the father and guardian of the constitution."[11]

Ingersoll's moniker stuck, at least the "father" part, and it was not long before it gained widespread acceptance. But if we attend to the rest of the speech, it becomes obvious that Ingersoll did not intend to evoke anything like biological parentage. He began:

> If Washington was the Father of our Country, Mr. Madison is entitled to be considered the Father of that Constitution, by which it has accomplished eminent prosperity and power. Without ever appealing to the passions, but always addressing the reason of his fellow citizens, this illustrious Patriarch, through a long career of public functions, as a member of Congress before the present Constitution, of the Convention which formed it, of Congress afterwards, of the Legislature of Virginia, when his resolutions of 1798 were adopted, as Secretary of State, and as President of the United States, impressed as much, if not

more of his mind, than that of any other on our now well defined and established Institutions.[12]

Ingersoll does include Madison's services within the Federal Convention among his many contributions on behalf of the Constitution, but he lays no special emphasis on the circumstances of the Constitution's birth. Indeed, if Ingersoll's speech privileges any one period in Madison's life over all the others, it was his presidency and retirement years, not the years surrounding the Constitutional Convention.

A week after that evening's revels, *Poulson's American Daily Advertiser* published an article that "substantially contained" Ingersoll's speech (and it would later be republished in other newspapers across the country). The toastmaster wasted no time clipping the article and sending it to Madison. Ingersoll wanted to tell the object of his homage about the specific circumstances that had elicited these words of "reverence and regard" for Madison's "character and public life." He was particularly moved to draft this speech because of his mentor's most recent intervention on behalf of his progeny: Madison had lately written a public letter defending what he believed to be the proper interpretation of the Constitution.[13]

Madison responded to Ingersoll in his usual self-effacing way. He was indebted to the author for both the gracious letter and the newspaper clipping, "and not less so," he added, "that in weighing my public services, the friendly hand unconsciously favored that end of the beam" (the "beam," in this context, referring to the crossbar of a balance). We therefore find that Madison did gently protest that Ingersoll had amiably though inadvertently put his thumb on the scale when weighing his merits. But we know of no instance, either then or later, in which Madison repudiated or quarreled with the title that Ingersoll had bestowed on him in his toast. And among Madison's contemporaries, the "Father of the Constitution" metaphor appears to have been understood with the meaning that Ingersoll had given to it. In 1832, Elisha Smith urged Madison to break his silence once again and defend the Constitution's true meaning. Patriotism demanded that he make this sacrifice, he said, seeing as how the retired president was "considerd the father of the Constitution."[14] When Smith made this appeal to Madison's paternal feelings, the Constitution was then approaching its forty-fifth birthday, and its putative "father" was already in his eighties! Thus we find that Madison's generation did not believe that the duties of fatherhood ceased once a successful birth was assured.

We should not be surprised that Madison's contemporaries did not focus on his potency at the Constitutional Convention when considering him to be Father of the Constitution. Recall that at this time, the only complete and reliable record of what took place in those secret proceedings in Philadelphia were in Madison's possession, and these records would not be published until after his death. Ingersoll, being the son of one of the framers, may have heard some stories from his father about Madison's prowess when he served at the convention. But he could not have had any detailed knowledge about Madison's personal involvement in the Constitution's conception and birth. Scholars today have access to much better records of this episode in our history than even the best-informed men and women living in the last decade of Madison's life.

In one sense, the scholarly consensus against the title is justified. If the meaning of "fathering" a constitution is reduced to one exquisite moment of constitutional conception (and the more immaculate the better), or even if its meaning were slightly expanded to encompass a father's role in ensuring that his infant would not be stillborn, then the strained analogy to biological parentage would be an exaggeration of Madison's (admittedly significant) deeds in 1787 and 1788. But the emerging scholarly consensus against the title has been based, all along, on a misunderstanding of its authentic meaning. To be fair, the misunderstanding of the metaphor does not appear to have originated with its debunkers. Indeed, it seems to have begun shortly after Madison's death. In John Quincy Adams's eulogy of Madison, he claimed that it was Virginia's ratification of the Constitution that "affixed the seal of James Madison as the Father of the Constitution."[15]

Even as this distorted meaning took hold, his claims to the moniker went virtually undisputed for years, simply because no other claimant ever seriously rivaled Madison's importance among constitutional scholars. Increasingly, however, the honorific was conferred under false pretenses. John Vile is probably correct when he speculates that it is no coincidence that in the 1940s and 1950s, repetitions of the title "Father of the Constitution" proliferated simultaneously with increased scholarly attention to the framing of the Constitution. It is certainly true that, if we today review the uses of the phrase over the last century—whether by Madison's defenders or his detractors—we find that they almost universally refer to the Constitution's conception and birth (whether the period of birth is confined to the Constitutional Convention alone or extended to the ratification, and perhaps even to the adoption of the Bill of Rights).[16] And by confining Madison's fatherhood of the Constitution within these narrow functions, even his champions, though undoubtedly well intentioned, were unwittingly laying the groundwork for legitimate questions to be raised by others. McDonald was right to debunk the "myth" of Madison's paternity. But the myth was not inherent in the title as it was originally bestowed; the image of biological fatherhood was a mythology that developed later and supplanted the only meaning that could possibly be defended. It was the unfortunate distortion of the metaphor that inexorably led to its debunking: the scholarly equivalent of Madison's epaulettes being publicly snipped from his shoulders.

ASKING THE QUESTION ANEW

It's time to start anew. If Madison is seriously to be subjected to a constitutional "paternity test," it ought to be the test appropriate to discovering the kind of paternity that the phrase "Father of the Constitution" was meant to convey. We are not to ask, then: Can we discover Madison's DNA, and only his DNA, in the text of our Constitution? But rather: When Fathers' Day rolls around, does James Madison deserve a card, and perhaps a new cravat? However, before that question can be answered, we must finish parsing the metaphor. Not only do we need to reconsider the gist of the word "father"; we also need to recover the authentic meaning of the word "constitution."

It is largely owing to the success of the American experiment that, when we think of "The Constitution," we think of a document—the one that was signed by its framers on September 17, 1787, that was ratified the following year, and that now sits under hermetically sealed glass in the National Archives. But we must remember that the word "constitution" had a robust meaning long before it referred to a written document. It meant the way that the government was constituted—how political power was distributed and, above all, how it was controlled. And that older meaning of constitution was still very much alive when Madison was still alive and when his title was conferred. That Ingersoll was at least partly, if not primarily, operating under that older meaning of constitution is clear if we attend, once again, to his defense of Madison as its father: "Without ever appealing to the passions, but always addressing the reason of his fellow citizens, this illustrious Patriarch, through a long career of public functions, . . . impressed as much, if not more of his mind, than that of any other on our now well-defined and established Institutions."[17]

According to Ingersoll, Madison's role as Father of the Constitution did not only (did not even primarily) mean fathering the document born of the Convention of 1787; rather, Madison formed our constitutional institutions in accordance with that document. Impressing his mind onto the political conflicts of his day, he reared America's institutions from their indeterminate infancy into their matured, "established" character. And, even more important, he did so by cultivating "the reason of his fellow citizens." For if every constitution refers to the distribution and control of powers within a given form of government, then a central feature of a republican government will be the powers that are exercised by the citizenry; therefore, controlling power within republican institutions requires, above all, the citizens' ability to control themselves. And Madison, according to Ingersoll, was more instrumental than any of his contemporaries not only in shaping the formal institutions of political life but also in cultivating the reason of his fellow citizens. The written document, after all, only recommends how the institutions should be formed. It is the will of the citizenry—whether proceeding from their reason or their passions—that shall, more than any other force, give shape to those institutions. Or, to state Ingersoll's proposition more simply, he was saying that Madison deserves more credit than anyone else for forming Americans into a constitutional people.

Now that we finally understand the real history and proper meaning of the phrase "Father of the Constitution," is Madison deserving of it? Unfortunately, once the question is understood in its proper signification, we see immediately that no single chapter could do justice to Madison's contributions toward guarding our constitutional institutions and cultivating Americans into a constitutional people. To appreciate why Madison deserves that title would require a careful analysis of more than sixty years' worth of Madison's writings, speeches, and public service. The entirety of the present volume—which touches on Madison's unique contributions to America's notions of its presidency, judiciary, federalism, religious liberty, and representative democracy, among other topics—is still only a partial account of all the constitutional topics that could be covered.

Indeed, if the fecundity of a political theorist can be known by his fruits, then Madison's legacy is secured. The number and variety of superb essays and books about Madison's life and political thought are staggering. Scholars seem drawn to Madison in the same way that gold miners were drawn to California in 1848. His political and constitutional writings are a rich vein that seems almost inexhaustible. Even episodes that currently get scant attention from scholars are worth further investigation. For instance, although some theorists have explored Madison's thinking about executive power, his own presidency is often treated as if it were the nadir of his political career. It is therefore striking to contrast today's judgments to those of his peers. Ingersoll was not an outlier among his generation when he proclaimed Madison's presidency to be "the most constitutional and the most glorious period of our national existence." Even John Adams, who is typically safe from the accusation that he praised Madison too effusively, and who is generally even less guilty of speaking too modestly about himself, had this to say about Madison's presidency: "notwithstand[ing] a thousand Faults and blunders, his Administration has acquired more glory, and established more

Union, than all his three Predecessors Washington Adams and Jefferson put together."[18]

To fully understand why Madison's generation regarded him as the "Father of the Constitution," we would have to understand better why they saw his presidency as "the most constitutional," or why they regarded his administration as one that "established more Union," than any other. Such an exploration, alas, falls well beyond the scope of this chapter. Nevertheless, by finally placing the meaning of this metaphor in the proper light, we have opened the way for a much richer and more interesting exploration of Madison's paternity than continuing to defend or debunk the simplistic trope that Madison personally sired the U.S. Constitution in 1787.

CONSTITUTIONAL GENERATIONS: LATER FATHERS?

Now that we can see that Ingersoll's judgment is a defensible proposition—that Madison deserves more credit for rearing America's political institutions than any other person—it raises another interesting question. Even if we grant that Madison *was* rightly considered Father of the Constitution while he lived, should he still be regarded in that light today? Or would it only be proper to employ the moniker in the past tense: "Madison was the Father of the Constitution"? It can hardly be denied that not only have many generations passed away since Madison lived, but the Constitution has also gone through several generations, and each constitutional generation has been superintended by statesmen who may plausibly claim to be its progenitor.[19] Arguably the first and most important heir in the Constitution's line of succession was the one conceived by Abraham Lincoln.

Prior to the Civil War, Lincoln described slavery as a "wen or a cancer" that the framers of the Constitution could not immediately remove without killing the patient, so they hid it from view within the text of the Constitution until the body politic was strong enough to excise it. The experience of waging a bloody Civil War, however, altered Lincoln's political diagnosis. Slavery, he believed, was a congenital defect in the Constitution, a potentially fatal one, and nothing less than a rebirth was needed. In the words of the Gettysburg Address: although the nation was "conceived in Liberty," it required from the present generation "a new birth of freedom."[20] The Reconstruction Amendments (Thirteenth, Fourteenth, and Fifteenth) constituted that rebirth: in many ways the Constitution was transformed into something new by the addition of those three amendments. Employing Ingersoll's understanding of both "father" and "constitution," Lincoln is rightly deemed the father of this new constitution.

But the evolution of the Constitution did not end there. According to Darwinian theory, evolution usually takes hundreds, if not thousands, of generations for an organism to meaningfully change. But Woodrow Wilson's constitutional theories sped up that process. He believed that the Constitution should be regarded as "a living thing" and interpreted "according to the Darwinian principle" of evolution.[21] In this way, the Constitution would be continually evolving, even if the words of the document remained the same. This understanding of the Constitution is in many ways antithetical to Madison's thinking. Nevertheless, it is undeniable that Wilson impressed his own mind on our political institutions. These days students arrive at college not only believing that we are today governed by a "living constitution," but they generally believe that the framers intended the Constitution to be interpreted in this way. That shift in constitutional thinking means that Wilson must also be deemed a "Father of the Constitution," if we follow Ingersoll's meaning of that title.

Franklin Delano Roosevelt must also be deemed a father. He argued that the Bill of Rights, while sufficient for its day, no longer met the country's needs. He proposed a new "Economic Bill of Rights." Although his suggested amendments were never formally adopted into the Constitution, our federal institutions are interpreted as if they had been. Michael Lind even cautions liberals against embracing Madison's title of "Father of the Constitution," since his understanding of "the federal constitution was intended to prevent anything like the New Deal from occurring."[22] Once again, the Constitution—whether understood as our interpretations of a written document or the modern political institutions that are designed in conformity to it—bears little resemblance to the one Madison defended in his lifetime.

The list of the Constitution's possible fathers might go on. But the closer we approach our own time, the more likely it is that scholars will disagree over father figures. And if we were to question whether these later fathers reared their progeny as well as their forebears, even more forceful disagreements will likely be sparked. But the foregoing consideration of constitutional generations raises one final important question. If Madison's status as "Father of the Constitution" was specific to an era in our past, yet other fathers have emerged since then, is his title simply irrelevant to us today? His ancient paternity may be regarded as a historical curiosity, perhaps, but would it be true to say that his fathering of our Constitution, some two centuries ago, no longer has any lingering importance?

No, Madison's paternity is still important, because he was the Constitution's first father, and he remains its leading patriarch. And being a patriarch is nothing to sneeze at; just ask the followers of any one of the three Abrahamic religions. It may be that few of the faithful, if any, practice exactly the same religion that Abraham did. But for Jews, Christians, and Muslims, Abraham is the point of departure, a touchstone, for all pious believers, even if an unconscious one. Indeed, Abraham's influence might be even more significant because it is unconscious and simply taken for granted among the faithful. In the same way, Madison looms large over our political discourse today, even if unconsciously, and even if modern political parties depart from his beliefs in different ways and to different degrees.

For instance, it is not uncommon for members of both major parties to accuse their adversaries of precipitating a constitutional crisis. They mean that their opponents are threatening, by their actions, to undermine the established constitutional order. These are fighting words, to be sure. But in many ways the shared commitments that unite these parties are more important than their differences. All agree that we are bound by a common superior that restrains our own will. True, each party is always more apt to recognize these constitutional restraints when applied to their opponents than to themselves (it has become cliché that whichever party captures the White House soon discovers a revived appreciation for executive prerogative). But to the extent that we all still appeal to a common authority, we agree, in principle, to be bound by those same restraints under like circumstances. We are acknowledging that the Constitution is superior to individual will, and even superior to majority will. That is a Madisonian understanding of constitutionalism, and its predominance today must be seen as his triumph. For it was not a foregone conclusion—even after the successful conception and birth of the United States Constitution—that we would eventually mature into a constitutional people.

With that thought in mind, I can think of no better way to conclude this chapter than to quote the closing words of Ingersoll's toast:

> Suffer me to add a wish which doubtless is that of Mr. Madison, that party may spare at least the pillars of our political mansion, that in the strife of the politics of place, the *principles*, the *resources*, and the institutions of our country may, like its religion, be held sacred by all. I offer for your acceptance, Gentlemen, as a sentiment becoming this meeting,
>
> The health and happiness of James Madison, the father and guardian of the constitution.[23]

NOTES

1. Richard M. Weaver, *The Ethics of Rhetoric* (Chicago: H. Regnery, 1965), 5; see also 203–4.
2. Charles Warren, *The Making of the Constitution* (Boston: Little, Brown, 1928), 57; Edward S. Corwin, "James Madison: Layman, Publicist and Exegete," *New York University Law Review* 27, no. 2 (April 1952): 298; Clinton Rossiter, introduction to Alexander Hamilton, James Madison, and John Jay, *The Federalist Papers*, ed. Rossiter (New York: Penguin, 1961), x; Christopher Collier and James Lincoln Collier, *Decision in Philadelphia: The Constitutional Convention of 1787* (New York: Random House/Reader's Digest, 1986), 25; Forrest McDonald, *Novus Ordo Seclorum: The Intellectual Origins of the Constitution* (Lawrence: University Press of Kansas, 1985), 205.
3. Richard Brookhiser, *James Madison* (New York: Basic Books, 2011), 84; Greg Weiner, *Madison's Metronome: The Constitution, Majority Rule, and the Tempo of American Politics* (Lawrence: University Press of Kansas, 2012), xi; Kevin R. C. Gutzman, *James Madison and the Making of America* (New York: St. Martin's Press, 2012), 136; Bruce G. Kauffmann, "James Madison 'Godfather of the Constitution,'" *Early American Review* (blog), Summer 1997, https://www.varsitytutors.com/earlyamerica/early-america-review/volume-2/james-madison-godfather-constitution.
4. For a defense of Wilson's paternity, see Pierre Gooding, "James Wilson, Legislative Authority, & Section 1501 of the Patient Protection and Affordable Care Act," *Seton Hall Legislative Journal* 36, no. 1 (February 17, 2012): 32; and Nicholas Pederson, "The Lost Founder: James Wilson in American Memory—PDF," *Yale Journal of Law & the Humanities* 22, no. 2 (2010): 269, 311, 316–17, 326, 328, 333–36; for Morris's defense, see Richard Brookhiser, *Gentleman Revolutionary: Gouverneur Morris, the Rake Who Wrote the Constitution* (New York: Free Press, 2004), xv.
5. Pinckney's champions include William S. Elliott, "Honorable Charles Pinckney, LL.D., of South Carolina," *De Bow's Review*, August 1864, 63; and Sidney Ulmer, "Charles Pinckney: Father of the Constitution?," *South Carolina Law Quarterly* 10 (1958): 225–47; for Rutledge's advocates, see Richard Barry, *Mr. Rutledge of South Carolina* (New York: Duell, Sloan and Pearce, 1942), 337, 365; see also Lawrence Goldstone, *Dark Bargain: Slavery, Profits, and the Struggle for the Constitution* (New York: Walker, 2005), 222–23 (likewise naming Rutledge as Father of the Constitution, for completely different reasons). To name just one telltale error that Barry makes when fabricating his story, he claims that Tocqueville was "referred to the archives" when seeking the Constitution's author. There he pored over all the records that were "then available," including Madison's *Notes*. However, when Tocqueville made his journey through America in 1831, Madison's *Notes* were not available in any archive; they were still at his home in Montpelier (where Tocqueville never visited). These records would not be purchased by Congress until 1837, and they would not be published until 1840. Rutledge's tombstone is found at St. Michael's Episcopal Church in Charleston, South Carolina.
6. William Lee Miller, *The Business of May Next: James Madison and the Founding* (Charlottesville: University of Virginia Press, 1992), 141; Brookhiser, *James Madison*, 84; John R. Vile, "James Madison and Constitutional Paternity," in *James Madison: Philosopher, Founder, and Statesman*, ed. John R. Vile, William D Pederson, and Frank J. Williams (Athens: Ohio University Press, 2008), 42–44, 48–52.
7. Sanford V. Levinson, "It's Time for a DNA Test to Determine Paternity of the Constitu-

tion," *Starting Points*, November 1, 2021, https://startingpointsjournal.com/its-time-for-a-dna-test-to-determine-paternity-of-the-constitution/; Alan Gibson, "Madison and the Constitution: A Reply to Levinson," *Starting Points*, November 3, 2021, https://startingpointsjournal.com/madison-and-the-constitution-a-reply-to-levinson/.

8. James Madison to William Cogswell, March 10, 1834, in *The Records of the Federal Convention of 1787*, ed. Max Farrand, rev. ed, vol. 3 (New Haven: Yale University Press, 1937), 532; for just one example of an author confusing both circumstances and dates when using this letter to debunk Madison's title, see Miller, *Business of May Next*, 147.

9. James Madison to Thomas Jefferson, September 6, 1787, in *The Papers of James Madison Digital Edition*, ed. J. C. A. Stagg (Charlottesville: University of Virginia Press, Rotunda, 2010), https://rotunda.upress.virginia.edu/founders/JSMN-01-10-02-0115; for examples of authors using Madison's disappointment to cast doubt on his constitutional paternity, see William Ewald, "James Wilson and the Drafting of the Constitution," *University of Pennsylvania Journal of Constitutional Law* 10, no. 5 (June 2008): 919–20n44; and Gordon S. Wood, "Is There a 'James Madison Problem'?," in *Liberty and American Experience in the Eighteenth Century*, ed. David Womersley (Indianapolis: Liberty Fund, 2006), http://oll.libertyfund.org/titles/womersely-liberty-and-american-experience-in-the-eighteenth-century.

10. McDonald, *Novus Ordo Seclorum*, 205–6, 208–9; Madison to Jared Sparks, November 25, 1831, in Farrand, *Records of the Federal Convention*, 3:515.

11. "Dinner to Professor List," *Poulson's American Daily Advertiser*, November 9, 1827; Irving Brant, *James Madison: Commander in Chief: 1812–36*, vol. 6 (Indianapolis: Bobbs-Merrill, 1961), 471.

12. "Dinner to Professor List."

13. Charles J. Ingersoll to James Madison, November 9, 1827, with clippings, Manuscript/Mixed Material, https://www.loc.gov/item/mjm022828/. The clipping that Ingersoll sent to Madison is still stored with the letter in the Library of Congress, but it lacks a masthead (and a small portion of the toast is also missing). But the identical article was published in *Poulson's American Daily Advertiser* on the same day that Ingersoll wrote to Madison.

14. James Madison to Charles J. Ingersoll, November 17, 1827; Elisha Smith to James Madison, May 1, 1832, in *Founders Online*, National Archives, accessed September 29, 2019, https://founders.archives.gov/documents/Madison/04-04-02-0562, and https://founders.archives.gov/documents/Madison/99-02-02-2563.

15. John Quincy Adams, *An Eulogy on the Life and Character of James Madison* (Boston: American Stationers' Company, 1836), 84.

16. Vile, "Constitutional Paternity," 53n7. In addition to the authors already cited, numerous others could be added—both among the title's defenders and detractors—who likewise confine its meaning to the Constitution's conception and birth. The two that come closest to broadening the meaning of the title from its usual formula are Harold C. Schultz, "James Madison: Father of the Constitution?," *Quarterly Journal of the Library of Congress* 37, no. 2 (Spring 1980): 222; and Lance Banning, "'To Secure These Rights': Patrick Henry, James Madison, and the Revolutionary Legitimacy of the Constitution," in *To*

Secure the Blessings of Liberty: First Principles of the Constitution, ed. Sarah Baumgartner Thurow (Lanham, Md.: University Press of America, 1988), 291.

17. "Dinner to Professor List."
18. Charles J. Ingersoll to James Madison, November 9, 1827, Manuscript/Mixed Material, https://www.loc.gov/item/mjm022828/; John Adams to Thomas Jefferson, February 2, 1817, in *The Papers of Thomas Jefferson Digital Edition*, ed. James P. McClure and J. Jefferson Looney (Charlottesville: University of Virginia Press, Rotunda, 2008), https://rotunda.upress.virginia.edu/founders/TSJN-03-11-02-0033.
19. Vile, "Constitutional Paternity," 49.
20. Speech at Peoria, Illinois, October 16, 1854, and Gettysburg Address, November 19, 1863, in Abraham Lincoln, *Selected Speeches and Writings* (New York: Vintage Books, 1992), 96–97, 405.
21. Woodrow Wilson and William Bayard Hale, *The New Freedom: A Call for the Emancipation of the Generous Energies of a People* (Garden City, N.Y.: Doubleday, Page, 1921), 48.
22. State of the Union Address, January 11, 1944, in Franklin Delano Roosevelt, *The War Messages of Franklin D. Roosevelt, December 8, 1941 to April 13, 1945* ([Washington, D.C.: Government Printing Office?], 1945), 109; Michael Lind, *The Next American Nation: The New Nationalism and the Fourth American Revolution* (New York: Free Press, 1995), 91n.
23. "Dinner to Professor List."

Republicanism and "Good Government"

Madison's Complex Case for "Our Complicated System"

ALAN R. GIBSON

This essay returns to two foundational questions: Is Madisonian republicanism democratic? How democratic was the Madisonian political system formed by the original or Founders' Constitution?[1] These closely related questions have a long and boisterous history that can be traced back to the ratification debates of 1787–88, raise complex and intractable interpretive problems, and have generated a sprawling body of commentary. They are important not only because they inform how we view the statesman often considered the chief architect of the Constitution but also because they speak to the fundamental character and legitimacy of the American political system. They are intractable because "republicanism" was a deeply contested concept at the founding, and "democracy" has subsequently become even more so. With no common definition or standard in place for assessing either republicanism or democracy, scholars frequently argue past each other.

If this is not enough, the transformation of democracy from a technical description of rule by a segment of society during the founding to a diffuse term of praise and a designation of legitimacy today has meant that analysis of the Madisonian political system has become inextricably linked with debates about the legitimacy of the Constitution and the propriety of constitutional reform.[2] Defenders of Madison, the Founders' Constitution, and the original Madisonian political system signal their support by labeling it democratic. Scholars who argue that it was undemocratic lodge an indictment, challenge the legitimacy of the Constitution, and hope to pave a path for reform.[3]

The scholars, politicians, and activists who have most relentlessly lodged that indictment are the Progressives. Originally formulated in the late nineteenth century by James Allen Smith and Charles Beard, the Progressive interpretation combined empirical analysis of the framers' economic holdings with criticism of the Constitution as antidemocratic. Madison and the framers, Beard and his early allies argued, championed state property qualifications to disenfranchise voters without significant property holdings, transferred powers over currency and commercial regulation to the national government, and relied upon an extended republic, judicial review, and a complex system of checks and balances to "break the force of majority rule," protect the economic interests of the creditor class, and allow Congress to pursue policies advantageous to those same interests.[4]

Recent Progressives have set forth more complex and nuanced variations of the antidemocratic interpretation that eschew the reductionist readings of their intellectual ancestors. Two claims have been important. First, neo-Progressives have observed that Indigenous peoples, women, enslaved persons, and free Blacks were almost totally excluded from the political process in 1787. The "salient fact" about the original Constitution, according to Rogers Smith, is that it "left intact the state constitutions that denied women [and, in some states, free Blacks] the franchise and other legal and political privileges." "While political participation in the new regime was possible for virtually any man," Smith continues, state suffrage restrictions based on race, gender, and property holdings meant that "significant participation would be confined to a relative few."[5]

Second, neo-Progressives such as Woody Holton and Jennifer Nedelsky have argued that "some of the heftiest restraints the framers placed on popular power," especially the election of representatives from large districts, "were also the least visible."[6] Madison and his Federalist allies, according to Holton, knew that the "size of the [electoral] districts that sent men to the statehouse helped determine what sort of policies came out of it."[7] They thus reduced the number of representatives who would serve under the Constitution compared to the state legislatures. The original House of Representatives had only sixty-five members—far fewer per capita than any of the state legislatures in 1787. Elections from vast electoral districts, Nedelsky added, were a form of "wealth-based inequality of access to political power."[8] They tilted elections, both Holton and Nedelsky have claimed, in favor of cosmopolitan elites with greater wealth, education, refinement, connections, social status, and broader reputations over "middling" politicians, demagogues, and local men likely to indulge their constituents with paper money and other forms of debtor relief legislation.

A no less formidable group of scholars, however, has argued that Madisonian republicanism and the Founders' Constitution were genuinely democratic. The scholar most closely associated with this interpretation is Martin Diamond, who formulated it in 1959 in direct response to Progressive, Marxist, and New Left criticisms of the Constitution.[9] Madison, Diamond acknowledged, was never a champion of a "democracy of enthusiastic egalitarianism."[10] Nevertheless, he favored a "decent, even though democratic" political system that featured a large, commercial republic where a diversity of interests would block schemes of oppression by majority factions and promote the formation of moderate majorities formed by coalitions. The extended republic, according to Diamond, was the framers' method of averting a class struggle while preserving democracy.[11]

The democratic interpretation has subsequently been given a variety of twists, most prominently in the scholarship of Lance Banning, Colleen Sheehan, and Akhil Reed Amar. For his part, Banning rejected Diamond's commercial republican interpretation of the extended republic but still claimed that Madison championed the "people's active and continuous participation in the [political] system." Like Diamond, Banning did not ignore Madison's concerns about the threats of majority rule to individual rights. Instead, he held that Madison's signature contribution was to reconcile the protection of rights and negative liberty with democracy and positive liberty.[12] For her part, Sheehan contends that Madison's commitment to a profoundly democratic system is illustrated in the robust politics of public opinion in his political writings, especially of the 1790s. Like Diamond and Banning, she acknowledges that the Madisonian political system qualified and conditioned majority rule—in her account through a comprehensive system of civic education designed to ennoble democracy. Employing an early modern form of *paideia* or moral pedagogy, Madison, Sheehan maintains, created a political system in which representatives refined public opinion, written declarations of rights educated citizens about the character and importance of rights, and the extended republic created a "commerce of ideas" in which the sovereignty of public opinion would be modified until it was consistent with the regime's first principles.[13]

Finally, Akhil Reed Amar has boldly proclaimed that in 1787 the American Constitution was "the most democratic deed the world had ever seen." In direct opposition to more recent Progressives, Amar argues that the most salient characteristic of the original Constitution, when placed within its historical context, is its remarkable inclusiveness. This holds true, he maintains, even for the ostensibly restrictive barriers in it including age requirements for holding office and the "natural born citizen requirement" for serving as president. Age requirements were democratic because they allowed young men without substantial means time to acquire the skills, resources, and reputation necessary to compete for political office. Meanwhile, the natural-born citizen requirement "represented a considerable liberalization of eighteenth-century English practice." Overall, the size of the electorate in revolutionary America, the absence of formal barriers to holding political office, and the anti-dynastic features of the Founders' Constitution, according to Amar, invited political participation from an unprecedentedly broad swath of citizens.[14]

This essay employs two strategies in pursuit of some much-needed distance from the politics and entrenched terms of this debate. The first addresses the intractable problem of establishing a common definition of democracy against which the Founders' Constitution can be judged by extrapolating three essential characteristics of republicanism from Madison's writings. These include inclusiveness (who is eligible to vote and run for office?), political equality (does the political system give everyone equal political weight?), and responsiveness (does the system facilitate majority rule and promote the transfer of public opinion into public policies?). The primary goal here is less to create a scorecard based on these fundamental characteristics of democratic political systems than to gain an overview of the character of the original Constitution. Working from the commonsense proposition that a political system is more democratic to the degree that it is inclusive, is responsive, and institutionalizes political equality provides common standards, drawn from the founding, for evaluating the character of the Founders' Constitution and Madisonian republicanism. It thereby serves as a prophylactic against anachronistic judgments, allows us to compare the claims of scholars who have commonly argued past each other, and prevents scholars from focusing only on the features of the Founders' Constitution that support their preferred interpretation.

The second strategy for gaining a more exacting and less politicized account on this foundational issue involves exploring Madison's assumptions about the capabilities of the electorate and the tension he observed between popular government and the "valuable ingredients" of "good Government," including stability, energy, impartiality, and the protection of rights.[15] An exploration of these issues provides insight into *why* Madison favored an elitist and meritocratic conception of republicanism and the justifications he gave for the anti-majoritarian features of the Founders' Constitution. Together, these strategies bring into view a complex Madisonian understanding of republicanism—indeed a Madisonian *apologia* for what he called "our complicated system."[16] Madison's understanding and defense of this system, I conclude, provides a better guide for assessing its character than either the exaggerated claims of his enthusiastic defenders or the wrongheaded criticisms of his detractors. The contemporary relevance of Madison's apologia for the Constitution lies in the role it can play in our interpretations of the character of the American political system and debates about the propriety and focus of constitutional reform.

INCLUSIVENESS: WHO VOTES AND HOLDS OFFICE?

To rehearse fundamentals, the Founders' Constitution stipulated that voting for members of the House of Representatives be set to the qualifications each state adopted for electing the legislators in the most numerous branch of that state's legislature.[17] Conversely, the framers did not create a national standard of citizenship or provide uniform national requirements for voting and thus did not attempt to create a national political community. This decision, in turn, divorced citizenship and naturalization requirements (to be determined by Congress) from voting and thereby created a broad class of nonvoting citizens who were not guaranteed the right of suffrage by the Constitution until much later. Deceptively simple on its face, the federal character of suffrage requirements in the Constitution has created confusion and contention since 1787, especially about the framers' motives for this provision. The Founders' Constitution did not, as is widely believed, *formally* exclude free Black Americans or women from voting or stipulate property qualifications. Conversely, however, it also did not *guarantee* women or free Blacks the right to vote or overturn property qualifications for voting in place in the states in 1787.

This much ought to be uncontroversial. Scholars disagree, however, about the framers' motives for leaving existing state qualifications in place and the effect of this decision on the character of the original political system. Much of this disagreement springs from competing speculations and inferences from the short and unrevealing debates at the Constitutional Convention and during ratification. The historical sources provide support for only a few responsible generalizations. Most obviously, the framers' decision not to create uniform national requirements for voting sprang from the impracticality of establishing such standards in the face of the diversity of existing state laws and practices and the belief, among some, that the states were a better judge of proper voting qualifications for their citizens than the national government.[18] It also seems likely that most of the delegates at the Constitutional Convention did not view creating a uniform national standard for voting as part of the charge of their appointment and were unwilling to hazard the risk that a uniform standard might pose for ratification.[19]

Contrary to the accounts of the original Progressives, the available evidence does not support the claim that the framers believed that state property qualifications in place in the states in 1787 would severely restrict the adult white male electorate. Indeed, the debates at the Constitutional Convention point in the opposite direction—toward a preponderance of delegates who believed that most white males in the states were eligible to vote under existing state laws and that little could or should be done at that point to restrict suffrage in the states.[20] The only exceptions to this were the sprinkling of delegates, led by Gouverneur Morris, who believed that voting in the states was too extensive and thus favored a national freehold requirement and the even smaller subset who wanted to create a uniform residency requirement in the states for electing members of the House.[21] In observing that most white males voted in the states in 1787, convention delegates took note of what later historical investigations have confirmed. Although estimates vary, most historians now believe that from 60 percent to

70 percent of the adult white male population in the early republic were able to meet the property qualifications set by the states.[22] Even these minimal qualifications were often not enforced. These observations are the source of the common claim that the Founders' Constitution set the contours of a political class that "was of a proportion that had no precedent in a modern state, constituting for practical purposes the entire adult white male public."[23] Although accurate, this claim points to the nascent character of democracy in the world more than its robust development in the United States. Great Britain and France, we should remember, were the only other political societies in the world in the late eighteenth century with a plausible claim to be even developing democracies. Other nations at this time were ruled by sultans, monarchs, or some other authoritarian figure.

To get a fairer portrait of the breath of the electorate in revolutionary America under the Founders' Constitution, we also need a general portrait of those excluded. First, constituting about 18 percent of the population, the 694,280 enslaved peoples in the United States in 1790 were designated as property by law in the states where they lived and excluded from political society.[24] At the same time, free Blacks were "tacitly enfranchised" in at least six states in 1787 and explicitly prohibited from voting in only three: Georgia, South Carolina, and Virginia.[25] For their part, Native Americans were referred to as "Indians not taxed" in the clause apportioning representatives among the states. This cryptic language indicated that most Indians were outside of the jurisdiction of the federal government and the political communities created by the states, could not be taxed, and thus should not be counted for purposes of apportionment.[26]

Under the Founders' Constitution, women were included in the population determining the apportionment of representatives among the states (white and free Black women on a one-to-one basis and enslaved Black women using the three-fifths formula), even though they had not been counted for purposes of allocating representation in the revolutionary state constitutions.[27] Their voting status depended upon state law. Famously, some number of women, probably never more than a few hundred, voted in elections in New Jersey from 1790 to 1807.[28] With only a few exceptions, women voting in New Jersey during this window were widows or unmarried because coverture laws made it extremely difficult for married women to own enough property to meet the state's property qualification for voting. More broadly, white women in revolutionary America were among those best described as nonvoting citizens but, unlike enslaved peoples and Native Americans, were also members of the political community. They performed several informal political functions, including acting as republican mothers, electioneers, and deal brokers, and were conventionally held to be "virtually" represented by their husbands and fathers.[29]

Putting all of this together suggests that, however expansive voting in the United States in the Revolutionary era was in comparison with other nations, at least 70 percent of the United States population in 1787 were rendered ineligible for voting by slavery, exclusionary state laws, or informal practice.[30] Perhaps most importantly, the Founders' Constitution did not create a single national political community. The "We the People" of the Constitution's preamble was instead a "We the Peoples" composed of thirteen political communities constituted by the laws and constitutions of the states. Each state's political community could be expanded or contracted by that state's legislature or by a constitutional amendment or judicial ruling imposed on that state. In 1787, the political communities of the thirteen states were exclusionary to varying degrees, but unsurprisingly none approached contemporary multicultural standards of inclusiveness. With this said, once again, they were also, independently, the most inclusive democracies in the world in 1787, giving the United States collectively that same status. While these conflicting observations are often used for partisan purposes and set against each other, both are true and essential for grasping the contours of revolutionary America as a nascent democracy.

If we turn from the qualifications of electors to the qualifications of the elected, then the Founders' Constitution was also inclusive for the time in which it was adopted.[31] It required that representatives be twenty-five years old, citizens of the United States for seven years, and inhabitants of the state they represented "when elected"; senators had only to be thirty years old, nine years a citizen of the United States, and inhabitants of the state they represented. The president had to be thirty-five years old, a "natural born" citizen, and a resident within the United States for fourteen years prior to his election.[32] As with suffrage, the Founders' Constitution contained no *formal* race or gender qualifications for any office of the United States. Indeed, it included no formal requirements, including age or citizenship requirements, for any federal judge, including Supreme Court justices. The most unorthodox and progressive feature of the Founders' Constitution from the perspective of 1787, however, was the prohibition of any religious test oaths for office.[33] Twelve of the fourteen state constitutions adopted before 1787 required religious test oaths for office, and five of those constitutions had prohibitions against clergy holding office.[34] Finally, national officers were paid from money in the national treasury—thus effectively extending the opportunity to hold elective office beyond the leisured class and established families.[35] The major exception to the formal openness of the Constitution for office holders was the requirement that the president be a "natural born" citizen.[36] This provision was seen by several of the delegates at the Constitutional Convention as necessary to guard against a foreign conspiracy to capture the presidency.[37]

What requirements for voting and holding office did Madison favor? Put briefly, he was among the most liberal and cosmopolitan of his contemporaries but also was captured by the limitations of the eighteenth century. At the convention, he stated flatly that "a Republic may be converted into an aristocracy or oligarchy as well by limiting the number capable of being elected, as the number authorised to elect."[38] As Publius, Madison added that "the definition of the right of suffrage is very justly regarded as a fundamental article of republican government."[39] Most famously, he wrote in *Federalist* No. 57:

> Who are to be the electors of the federal representatives? Not the rich, more than the poor; not the learned, more than the ignorant; not the haughty heirs of distinguished names, more than the humble sons of obscurity and unpropitious fortune. The electors are to be the great body of the people of the United States. They are to be the same who exercise the right in every State of electing the corresponding branch of the legislature of the State.
>
> Who are to be the objects of popular choice? Every citizen whose merit may recommend him to the esteem and confidence of his country. No qualification of wealth, of birth, of religious faith, or of civil profession, is permitted to fetter the judgment or disappoint the inclination of the people.[40]

These observations fortify Madison's earlier claims from *Federalist* Nos. 14 and 39 that the political system created by the constitution was "wholly popular" and "strictly republican." They also give texture to his famous multidimensional definition of a republic as "a government which derives all its powers directly or indirectly from the great body of the people," contains no self-appointed or hereditary offices, and is "derived from the great body of the society, not from an inconsiderable proportion, or a favored class of it."[41]

In his private notes and writings, however, Madison was franker and more skeptical. In 1791, he observed that "nearly half the free inhabitants" of the commonwealth of Virginia were disenfranchised by property qualifications, making it difficult to call the commonwealth a republic. He also observed that "in proportion as slavery prevails in a State, the Government, however democratic in name, must be aristocratic in fact." "The Southern States of America," Madison concluded, "are on the same principle aristocracies."[42] Despite the clarity and moral force of these judgments, however, Madison did not, for a variety of complex reasons, publicize these observations or set forth proposals for freeing enslaved peoples within the United States, let alone give them the right to vote or hold office.

Otherwise, the only other important exception to Madison's preference for full *formal* openness for voting and holding office came for his qualified and short-lived support for what the Founders called a "freehold" or property-holding requirement for voting for members of the House of Representatives. Such a requirement, Madison argued at the convention, was appropriate on the "merits alone" because "the freeholders of the Country would be the safest repositories of Republican liberty." Nevertheless, Madison quickly qualified his support for a freehold requirement depending upon its probable reception in the states where "citizens of every description" already voted. Even if it was desirable, the time had passed, Madison seemed to conclude, when a freehold requirement might have been implemented.[43]

What about Nedelsky's and Holton's claims that large electoral districts were favored by established elites and were a means of funneling members of the creditor class into the House? To be sure, limiting the number of representatives had the effect of establishing a context for House elections that favored elite statesmen. As Anti-Federalists pointed out in 1787 and numerous scholars have subsequently observed, the sixty-five national representatives called into service under the Constitution of 1787 was substantially fewer than the 1,600 to 1,700 total legislators in the states selected by the same electorate.[44] Forcing an intense competition for office, Madison hoped, would be a partial cure to the "defect of adequate Statesmen" that he had identified with both state and national representatives.[45] As a member of the ruling elite, Madison doubtlessly considered the possession of property, education, a high level of social status, and a diffusive reputation evidence that a candidate was a member of the small subset of men deserving of consideration for office. Clearly, candidates with these advantages would be more likely to win elections, especially in large districts.

Nevertheless, like other important scholars, Nedelsky and Holton exaggerate the significance of expanded electoral districts in the Founders' Constitution and Madisonian republicanism and misconstrue the kind of sieve they created.[46] Remarkably enough considering the emphasis scholars have given to it, there is little evidence that elections from large districts played an important role in Madison's thinking about constitutional reform. Before and after the convention, this electoral mechanism was a secondary point in Madison's argument for controlling factionalism.[47] Even when he did defend it, Madison was, as Holton concedes, a "relative moderate" in his advocacy.[48] At the Constitutional Convention, he twice supported doubling the number of national representatives.[49] As Publius, Madison repeatedly defended the "smallness of the number [of representatives], as a temporary regulation" and pledged that the number would be increased shortly after the adoption of the Constitution. Absent that supposition, Madison observed, the criticism that there were too few representatives would have "very great weight indeed."⁵⁰ In the First Congress, he then supported several measures to secure an immediate increase in the number of representatives and subsequent periodic increases as the population of the United States increased.⁵¹

Even these proposals, however, would not have brought federal representation into line with representation in the state legislatures—a goal that Madison would never have supported in the first place. Indeed, Madison's central point in emphasizing the "sufficiency of a moderate number of representatives" was that there would not and should not be as many national representatives per capita as state legislators.⁵² Only if the number of representatives was kept at a moderate number would elections "extract from the mass of the Society the purest and noblest characters which it contains."⁵³ The best summation of his position on this procedure is that he held standard Federalist views of its benefits, but he was a moderate among Federalists and always kept his eye on establishing a mean or moderate number of representatives. He also kept in mind that political science had not yet advanced to the point where an exact number could be determined and that errors in either direction brought distinct problems. For now, Madison concluded that the lessons of experience were not exact but pointed to the value of a mean number—large enough to promote a fair hearing for the claims of every interest and to "guard against the cabals of a few," but also small enough to prevent the House from experiencing the "confusion of the multitude," the vicissitudes that had plagued the state legislatures during the mid-1780s, and the paradoxical centralization of decision-making that Madison held took place in legislative bodies with too many members.⁵⁴

If Nedelsky and Holton exaggerate the importance of expanded electoral districts for Madison, Holton compounds that error by suggesting that Madison carried water for the creditor class and favored elections from large districts to secure the election of members of that class or their spokesmen to defend their interests. To be sure, the republic had no more vehement opponent of the "rage for paper money, for an abolition of debts, [or] for an equal division of property" than Madison.⁵⁵ Madison believed that violating the rights of property of creditors or any other group was not only foundationally unjust but stifled economic prosperity. Unjust and fluctuating policies that had violated property rights, Madison held in 1787–88, was the central source of the "prevailing and increasing distrust of public engagements" that had caused economic hardship in the 1780s. It made creditors less likely to lend and diminished the industry of ordinary Americans. "The evils issuing from these sources," Madison maintained, "contributed more to that uneasiness which produced the Convention, and prepared the public mind for a general [constitutional] reform, than those which accrued to our national character and interest from the inadequacy of the Confederation to its immediate objects."[56]

With this said, Madison's opposition to popular appeals for abrogating contracts and defrauding creditors did not mean that he equated the common good with the policies creditors favored or envisioned them or their spokesmen as the likely or proper winners of contests from large districts. In 1787 and indeed throughout his long political career, Madison combined his intense opposition to factional schemes for debtor relief with an equally strong contempt for self-interested, self-dealing politicians. This later group included "land mongers" who speculated in public lands, men who had gone into debt and then secured public office to pass paper money legislation and debtor relief policies to reduce their debts, and wealthy speculators and interested politicians who profited from insider information.[57] In contrast, the "impartial" or disinterested men that Madison hoped would be elected from large districts would fight a two-front battle against the impulsive many and the calculating few. In Madison's eyes, both groups were guilty of self-dealing in violation of the fundamental axiom that no group or man "is allowed to be a judge in his own cause."[58] Elite, disinterested representatives elected from large districts, however, would "hold the balance" between the nation's many interests and sections, protecting the rights of each and advancing the prosperity of all. Such men were a part, but only a part, of the solution to the puzzle of constructing a just government that "*impartially* secures to every man, whatever is his *own*."[59]

POLITICAL EQUALITY: PROPORTIONAL AND DEFENSIVE REPRESENTATION

In addition to inclusiveness, a second standard against which Madisonian republicanism and the Founders' Constitution should be measured is political equality. At minimum, a constitutional system based on perfect political equality would give every citizen equal weight in the selection of public officials and the power-sharing arrangements created by the constitutional system. Political equality was evident in the Founders' Constitution mostly in the apportionment of representatives among the states according to population in the House of Representatives, but even here, incompletely. The Founders' Constitution does not explicitly stipulate that representatives be elected from the same number of citizens or indeed explicitly recognize malapportionment as a problem or injustice.[60]

Two provisions in the original Founders' Constitution—the three-fifths clause and equal representation for each state in the Senate—fundamentally compromise the democratic principle of political equality and its concomitant, majority rule. Under the original Constitution, representatives were apportioned *among the states* based upon the whole number of free inhabitants and three-fifths of the enslaved persons within each state. The three-fifths clause significantly enhanced the political power of southern or slave states. As Akhil Reed Amar has observed, its practical effect was to guarantee that South Carolina received two more representatives in the House in 1790 because of its hundred thousand enslaved persons than New Hampshire, even though both had roughly the same number of free citizens. Even more dramatically, Massachusetts had a significantly larger population of free inhabitants than Virginia, but the "Old Dominion" received five more seats in the House because of its nearly three hundred thousand enslaved persons.[61] Moreover, since the number of electoral votes for president for each state was calculated by adding the number of representatives and senators and since amendments to the Constitution must typically pass through the House, slave states also received substantially greater power in the selection of the president and the amendment process than was warranted by calculations based on their free populations.

The inequity created by equal representation in the Senate was also substantial. In 1790, the two senators from the largest state (Virginia) represented 747,550 citizens or almost thirteen times the number represented by the two senators from the smallest state (Delaware), who represented 59,096 citizens. If enslaved persons are removed from this calculation, Virginia's two senators represented roughly nine times as many free individuals as Delaware's. The total population of the four largest states in the nation in 1790—Virginia, Pennsylvania, North Carolina, and Massachusetts—was 1,954,772. The total population of the remaining nine states was 1,683,491. Thus, eight senators represented roughly 54 percent of the population and the remaining eighteen about 46 percent.[62] Perhaps most remarkably, a majority in the United States Senate in 1790 (fourteen votes) could be gathered from senators representing seven states with about 28 percent of the total population.[63] Like the inequity created by the three-fifths clause, the inequity created by equal representation in the Senate was institutionalized in the Electoral College and the amendment process.

For his part, Madison did not favor the exclusive use of single member geographically defined districts with virtually identical numbers of electors electing representatives—the most common method we think of today for securing "one person, one vote." Instead, he advocated experimentation with several methods of electing representatives at both the state and national levels, including elections from single-member districts, at-large elections, and hybrid methods. Nevertheless, he seems to have favored proportional representation no matter what the method of election or level of government and expressed concern for malapportionment resulting from disproportionate population increases in different districts. At the state level at least, he favored increasing the number of representatives in districts with population increases as the proper remedy for this problem rather than redrawing county or district lines.[64]

At the Constitutional Convention, he remarked that representatives "ought to vote in the same proportion in which their citizens would do, if the people of all the States were collectively met."[65] Consistent with this principle, he was the convention's most relentless advocate of proportional representation based on state population and conversely the most penetrating critic of equal representation in the Senate. Equal representation, he insisted, was unjust, unnecessary, and destructive. It was unjust because it would allow a minority of the people to "give law to the whole."[66] It was unnecessary because small states had no interests resulting from their size alone and nothing to fear from a coalition of the large ones who shared no common interests. Thus, they did not need or deserve a boost of representation.[67] Finally, equal representation in the Senate would be destructive, Madison presciently predicted, because it would allow the majority of *states* to obstruct policies the majority of the *people* favored, small states to extort the large states for policies advantageous to themselves, and small states to pass policies unimpeded in areas where the Senate had exclusive powers.[68]

In sharp contrast, however, Madison's supported the three-fifths clause because it boosted the representation of Virginia and other southern states, even though this "slave bonus" was as much a breach of proportional equality and majority rule as equal representation in the Senate and had the same potential to allow the obstruction, extortion, and imposition of policies on the majority. Why this difference in Madison's thinking? Scholars frequently conclude that Madison was simply trying to protect the institution of slavery and advance the interests of slaveholders. To be sure, the three-fifths clause constitutionalized slavery and protected the interests of slaveholders. A more generous and exacting interpretation of Madison's motives, however, is that he supported the three-fifths clause as part of an effort to forge a coalition of small southern slave states and large states in favor of proportional representation in both branches of Congress and because he was concerned to protect the sectional interests of the South from encroachments by northern states. During his service in the Confederation Congress, he had witnessed several efforts by northern delegates to sacrifice the interests of southern states. Indeed, Madison's most eloquent, moralistic, and angry rebuke of the consequences of majority tyranny came, not in decrying the abuses of paper money or sounding the alarm about the threat of a majority religious sect to religious liberty, but in response to the northern states' plan to barter navigation rights on the Mississippi for a favorable trade agreement with Spain.[69]

Such threats, Madison concluded, could be averted if every interest and section in the nation had a defensive power against the others.[70] Madison's preferred "defensive power" for southern states to resist northern encroachments was to apportion one branch of the national legislature on the basis of its free inhabitants and the second on its comprehensive population of enslaved and free inhabitants.[71] Nevertheless, he settled upon the adoption of the three-fifths clause as an adequate alternative. Madison's critics, today and at the founding, have rightly shaken their heads at Madison's support for this provision. It is best understood, though not justified, by recalling Madison's uncompromising commitment to southern rights for free navigation on the Mississippi River and the place of that right in his vision of American nationality. Northern politicians, he feared, would sell out the South again if given the chance. In the end, then, the difference between the three-fifths clause and equal representation in the Senate, in Madison's view, was that the three-fifths clause protected real interests from a real threat. Equal representation did not.[72]

RESPONSIVENESS: LONG LEASHES AND THE EXTENDED REPUBLIC

Finally, how responsive was the Founders' Constitution, and how responsive did Madison want it to be? Again, it is necessary to rehearse fundamentals. The Founders' Constitution created only one popularly elected branch: the House of Representatives. Members of the House served two-year terms. As previously noted, only sixty-five representatives were elected under the original Constitution. In most states, state representatives and senators were elected from districts that included a few thousand constituents and, Madison estimated, about five or six hundred voters. Under the new Constitution, in contrast, representatives could not be elected from districts that contained fewer than thirty thousand inhabitants. There were approximately forty-five to fifty thousand inhabitants in each of the electoral districts that selected the sixty-five representatives to the First Congress. These representatives, Madison estimated, would be elected by five or six thousand voters.[73]

Additionally, the original Constitution provided for six-year terms for senators who were elected by the state legislatures in a staggered cycle in which one-third faced reelection every two years. This election cycle prevented the whole Senate from being reconstituted in a single election. The president was elected through the Electoral College, served four-year terms, and was eligible for perpetual reelection. The most indirect modes of appointment under this scheme of successive filtrations and the longest terms of office were given to federal judges who were nominated by the president, confirmed by the Senate, and served terms of "good behavior."[74]

Madison and his Federalist colleagues viewed the legislative branch generally and the House of Representatives specifically as the most powerful, passionate, and aggressive branch. It was, Madison concluded, an "impetuous vortex" that "necessarily predominates" in republican governments.[75] They therefore created a system of separation of powers to control its ability to encroach on the constitutional powers of the other branches. This goal was achieved by electing the president, Senate, and judiciary from separate constituencies, giving them long terms of office, properly intermixing powers among the branches, giving each independent powers, and providing each with specific checks upon the House, including the presidential veto, judicial review, but especially the bicameral or senatorial check. Overall, the goal was to enhance the independence of the less popular branches and to provide them with the proper means and motives for blocking factious legislation and preventing encroachments by the more powerful and passionate House. This system of controlling the government was, in turn, employed in an extended republic designed to control the governed. The creation of an extended republic, Madison famously argued, would splinter majority factions across the republic and create a number of obstacles—including distance, a diversity of interests, and a large number of individuals—to prevent the concert of factious majorities and block them from ever gaining control of the House in the first place.[76]

Madison characterized this system as an "extended" or "extensive," "unmixed," "federal" republic and argued that it was consistent with the republican form that he famously defined in *The Federalist* No. 39 as a system deriving "all of its powers directly or indirectly from the great body of the people."[77] Broadly speaking, the scheme of direct elections from expanded electoral districts, staggered elections and appointments for members of the other branches, and long terms of office in the Founders' Constitution is best described following Michael Zuckert as a system of long leash or "gappy" republicanism in contrast to the "short leash" republicanism institutionalized in the Articles of Confederation and the revolutionary state constitutions.[78] As Publius, Madison suggested that there were only minimal differences between the longer terms of office and the moderate number of representatives in the political system formed by the Constitution and the shorter terms and greater number of officials serving in the states. This misleading analysis was designed to blunt the Anti-Federalist criticism that the proposed Constitution provided inadequate representation and would thus create an aristocratic political system or at least a system likely to transform into one.[79]

The long terms of offices and moderate number of representatives featured in Madisonian "long leash" republicanism were coupled with, indeed further constituted by, the elitist conception of representation Madison and his Federalist colleagues espoused. In this conception, representatives were given an initial independence from their constituents by the sheer breath of the extended republic. Conceived as "disinterested" or impartial arbiters of factional conflicts, they were charged to "refine and enlarge the public views" rather than merely reflect them.[80] As is well known, this conception of representation was deliberately opposed to the mirror, mandate, or instruction model of representation championed by many Anti-Federalists and also to the Anti-Federalist proposition that representation was only effective if members of various occupations and social groups were represented by members of their own group or, at minimum, a substantial number of representatives came from the "middling" class.[81]

Scholars have written voluminously on these differing conceptions of representation and the corresponding character of the so-called Madisonian model. They have, however, less frequently compared the "long leash" Madisonian system with the "short leash" one embedded in the revolutionary state constitutions. For their part, neither Madison's contemporary defenders nor Madison himself convincingly counters the observation that the Founders' Constitution set up a political system that was markedly less responsive to public views than the contemporaneous state governments. Twelve of the fourteen state constitutions adopted between 1776 and 1787 had annual elections for members of the lower house, four for the state senate, and ten for the state's chief executive. The lower houses were directly elected in all of the fourteen state constitutions, upper houses in eight states, and governors in five states, with nine states featuring the legislative election of their state's chief executive.[82]

Both the federal Constitution and the state constitutions rested on the premise that "in republican government the legislative authority, necessarily, predominates." Nevertheless, the federal Constitution took the endemic responsiveness, imperious character, and predominance of the legislative branch in republican governments to be an "inconveniency" to be mitigated, not a quality to be strengthened by constitutional design.[83] In contrast, the state governments rested on a scheme of separation of powers designed to control the executive rather than the legislative branch. Thus, the state constitutions checked the power of the states' chief executives and held them on tight leashes. In addition to annual elections, governors were subject to requirements for rotation in office in seven states. Furthermore, the revolutionary state constitutions withheld powers from governors and state judges (especially a qualified veto and judicial review) that were given to the president and the judiciary in the United States Constitution to control the legislature. Finally, whereas the state constitutions allowed amendments to be passed by the legislature or did not specify an amending procedure, the Constitution created an amendment process based on a cumbersome system that, under most circumstances, required congressional and state cooperation.[84]

Broadly speaking, the state governments institutionalized direct popular sovereignty and were confined within a relatively small geographic compass. For example, a majority of states wrote written guarantees for the right of the people to instruct their representatives into their state declarations of rights. In contrast, Madison and his colleagues prevented such a guarantee from being included in the federal Bill of Rights.[85] The relative proximity of the people to each other made collective action among the people a reality in many states. Indeed, even the largest states had regular practices in colonial and revolutionary America of submitting petitions for legislation to the people for their consideration and basing decisions on their response. In contrast, the obstacles established in the extended republic to the concert of majority factions—especially the greater distance, greater diversity of interests, and greater number of individuals—made it much more difficult for citizens to coordinate collective action among themselves and to communicate with and control their specific representatives than had been the case when the most important public policies were decided within the states.

Defenders of the democratic interpretation of the Founders' Constitution and Madisonian republicanism have often countered the criticism that extent of territory made the system unresponsive and undemocratic by suggesting that the obstacles in the extended republic mitigated majority factions but somehow nevertheless facilitated majority rule. Unfortunately for their case, proponents of this claim have never been able to show how neutral barriers to communication and collective action—distance or space, a greater number of individuals, and a greater diversity of interests—facilitate the formation of "good" majorities but prevent "bad" ones—even if it is possible to agree about which are which.[86] Furthermore, Madison did not defend extent of territory merely as a means of transforming the character of majorities that were formed, but also for its ability to *mask* the presence of *any* majority, good or bad. In "Vices of the Political System of the United States," he wrote:

> If an enlargement of the sphere is found to lessen the insecurity of private rights, *it is not because the impulse of a common interest or passion is less predominant in*

this case with the majority; but because a common interest or passion is less apt to be felt and the requisite combinations less easy to be formed by a great than by a small number. The Society becomes broken into a greater variety of interests, of pursuits, of passions, which check each other, whilst those who may feel a common sentiment have less opportunity of communication and concert.[87]

What is important here is that Madison clearly recognizes the presence of a majority that either will not know it is a majority or will be unable to act upon this knowledge. In the end, if extent of territory prevents the formation of majority factions but somehow magically facilitates non-factious ones, this can only take place *within Congress*. A congressional solution, however, substitutes the rule of legislative majorities for popular ones or, perhaps more precisely, assumes that legislative majorities reflect popular ones.

To be sure, the claim that the Founders' Constitution and Madisonian republicanism made the national government less responsive than that of the states is not the same as saying, as some Progressives do, that it was or was intended to be unresponsive. Such an interpretation can easily be carried too far. Madison spoke of the "practicable sphere of republican administration" and was careful to point out that the extended republic needed to be confined to a "sphere of a mean extent" so that the people could throw the rascals out of office in a "defensive concert" if necessary.[88] He knew that there were limits to how long the leashes between the representatives and their constituents could be and how few representatives an assembly could contain if the government was to retain its republican character. Moreover, he championed long terms of office, moderate representation, and an extended republic to contain, not nullify, the force of public opinion on the national government. Finally, as previously noted, he did not believe that increasing the number of representatives beyond a number "sufficient" to secure safety, provide local information, and represent the whole society would make Congress operate more democratically. The "countenance" of a large deliberative assembly, he observed, might be more democratic, but the soul that animated it would be more oligarchic than in a moderate-size assembly because decision-making within the large assembly would be highly centralized.[89]

Nevertheless, proponents of the democratic interpretation cannot reasonably deny that Madison was among the most enthusiastic supporters of long leashes in the movement for constitutional reform. In a famous pre–Constitutional Convention letter to Jefferson outlining his preliminary thoughts on constitutional reform, he exposed his Hamiltonian side in observing that the mortal diseases of the current confederation "challenge from the votaries of liberty *every concession* in favor of stable Government not infringing fundamental principles."[90]

At the Constitutional Convention, he proposed or spoke in favor of three-year terms for representatives,[91] nine-year terms for senators,[92] and, most dramatically, a "fair hearing & discussion" of a term of life for the president unless a better means could be determined for securing executive independence.[93] The Virginia Plan, which generally expressed Madison's initial preferences for constitutional reform, called for the indirect election of the Senate by the lower house.[94] Even Madison's defense of the "practical sphere" of the republic should be understood within the context of the ratification debate where Federalists had to shield the Constitution against the Anti-Federalists' charge that the republic was too vast and would consolidate into a unitary republic. This is why Madison insisted that the extended republic would be confined to a "practicable sphere" in one context, but he described it as "large republic" and observed that the "practicable sphere may be carried to a very great extent" in another. Most decisively, Madison never denied that the extended republic formed from the union of the states created by the Constitution was one of unprecedented size.[95]

ON THE COMPLEXITY AND CHARACTER OF MADISONIAN REPUBLICANISM

The Founders' Constitution created a political system that was formally inclusive by the standards of 1787, contained two important structural features (equal representation of the states in the Senate and the three-fifths clause) that institutionalized political inequality, and featured long leashes—including long terms of office and the creation of an extended republic—to distance the people from the government. But why this familiar, but peculiar, mix of attributes? The answer to this question, and with it, further insight into the character of Madisonian republicanism, can be found in Madison's basic assumptions about the capacities and limitations of people for self-government and his understanding of the features of constitutional design necessary to promote the essential qualities of "good Government."[96]

Although a full exploration of this line of analysis is impossible here, three points about Madison's views of the capabilities of the people for self-government are relevant. First, following standard assumptions within mixed government theory about democracy, Madison held that the people were honest and always intended their own good, but were impetuous and likely to be duped by demagogues who might then violate their interests. The people, he observed, "never willfully betray their own interests," but were likely to fall into "temporary errors and delusions" regarding them.[97] Second, Madison was deeply concerned in 1787 with the threat of majority factions. These concerns arose from his observations that the rule of majority factions was simply an instance of the rule of force as a measure of right, that majority factions could work their mischiefs "under the forms of the Constitution," and that factions, especially large ones, were animated by passion and distinguished by collective irrationality.[98]

Third, despite these concerns, Madison held a more favorable but complex view of the capabilities of ordinary voters when they were acting as individuals outside of factions. The people, he announced at the Virginia ratifying convention, would have the "virtue and intelligence to select men of virtue and wisdom."[99] Unlike many of his contemporary Progressive critics, however, he never suggested that ordinary Americans were prepared for the kind of complex decision-making necessary to formulate public policies. In a revealing letter to Edmund Randolph in 1788, Madison observed that "there can be no doubt that there are subjects to which the capacities of the bulk of mankind are unequal, and on which they must and will be governed by those with whom they happen to have acquaintance and confidence."[100]

Most important for our purposes, these assumptions informed the peculiar character and contours of Madisonian republicanism and Madison's defense of the Founders' Constitution. Madison's belief that the people had the intelligence and virtue to select wise and virtuous rulers supported his foundational belief that the election of at least one branch of the government directly by the people was a "clear principle of a free Gov[ernmen]t."[101] Such a system did not rely upon formal exclusions of either voters or candidates because such exclusions were contrary to the nature of republican government and unnecessary in a properly designed one. The extended republic—including both the election of representatives from large districts and extent of territory—provides the best case in point. Designed on the assumptions that voters would be drawn to candidates with broad reputations and that a broad reputation was synonymous with a virtuous character, elections from large districts are best understood as an early exercise of what contemporary economists and political scientists call "choice architecture"—the structuring of decision-making to "nudge" individuals toward the choice the designer believes are in their best interest without otherwise restricting their choice.[102] Whereas a small electoral district might not contain an enlightened statesman, large districts were more likely to have one or even several. Given a choice between such candidates and "middling" men of local reputation and limited qualifications, voters would be drawn, like planetary bodies pulled by gravity, Madison suggested in *Federalist* No. 10, toward the candidates "who possess the most attractive merit, and the most diffusive and established characters."[103]

Similarly, extent of territory structures the decision-making and behavior of the people without denying their right to self-government or creating hereditary or self-appointed offices.[104] In "pure" democracies and short leash republics such as the states in 1787, the people, Federalists held, would readily know and easily communicate their preferences and passions to each other and their representatives. Kindled by the "sympathy of the multitude," individuals within large factions would join in acts they would find revolting if presented to them in private. Through coordinated impulsive actions, they would gain control of the legislature, elect men to execute their factious schemes, and successfully execute "improper or wicked project[s]."[105]

In the extended republic, however, the transfer of decision-making from the states to the national government and the obstacles in the extended republic posed by greater distance, diversity, and a greater number of individuals mask and diffuse the passions animating majority factions. No longer caught up in the passions of others, they are bought to repose. Meanwhile, the elite leaders they have elected to office would be placed hundreds of miles away in a three-mile-per-hour society, charged with making decisions, and only periodically answerable to their constituents. Informed by but independent of their constituents, these national representatives would act as impartial umpires in factional disputes, wise guardians of the common interest, and just arbiters in questions that required the distribution of scarce resources. Impartial legislative majorities would be formed by enlightened statesmen qualified by their personal character and the circumstances of their office to deliberate, compromise, and formulate public policies consistent with the public interest.

In addition to diffusing and refining the sovereign will of the people, the modes of selection and "long leash" features of the Founders' Constitution would also enhance the institutional capacity of the national government to achieve the panoply of "valuable ingredients" necessary for the conduct of "good Government," including impartiality, stability, and energy.[106] Extent of territory and elections from large districts solve "the great desideratum in Government" or the problem of reconciling popular control by the people over their government with impartial administration of factional disputes.[107] Elections by the people promote popular control of the government, but its "long leash" features break the force of majority factions without violating the principle of majority rule and infuse the monarchical attribute of impartiality—"the vital principle of the Administration"—into the republican institutions created by the Constitution.[108]

Stability and energy are infused into the new government by the Senate and president—the more permanent branches of the national government. These qualities of "good Government" could only be achieved, Madison acknowledged, at the expense of the responsiveness and accountability of public officials.

> The genius of Republican liberty, seems to demand on one side, not only that all power should be derived from the people; but, that those entrusted with it should be kept in dependence on the people, by a short duration of their appointments; and, that, even during this short period, the trust should be placed not in a few, but a number of hands. Stability, on the contrary, requires, that the hands in which power is lodged, should continue for a length of time, the same. A frequent change of men will result from a frequent return of electors, and a frequent change of measures, from a frequent change of men: whilst energy in government requires not only a certain duration of power, but the execution of it by a single hand.[109]

Specifically, Madison held that the Senate would serve as the central check on the popular and impetuous House of Representatives and act as a guardian of the nation's reputation by first acting as a bulwark against fluctuating public policies. Whereas a state legislator in Rhode Island was unlikely to care how foolish and fluctuating policies would be perceived by other nations, senators would be sagacious and impartial men concerned to cultivate the reputation of the nation alongside their own.[110] Serving long terms of office and chosen in staggered elections, senators would prevent the passage of impetuous public policies that would diminish the United States in the eyes of the world. Overall, the Senate would supply wisdom and stability to the constitutional system as "the great anchor of the Government."[111]

Finally, a republican president would supply "energy" to the government. Like the monarch in mixed governments, the single person selected as the nation's republican executive would be peculiarly situated to act with secrecy and dispatch in defending the republic against foreign enemies and domestic threats and in executing the laws in a timely and salutary manner.[112] Unlike a monarch, however, the chief executive in the Founders' Constitution would be a republican executive restrained by a republican legislature capable of impeaching him and chosen by and accountable to the people. Although Madison had initially hoped that the president would be selected in a direct election, he eventually approved of the indirect method (the Electoral College) stipulated in the Founders' Constitution.[113]

"Our Complicated System" and Madison's complex case for it have too often been misinterpreted and misrepresented by scholars with a political axe to grind—whether it be defending and preserving or criticizing and reforming. For their part, Madison's enthusiastic defenders have erred by suggesting that Madison was committed to conserving the "most profoundly revolutionary institutions and convictions of his time."[114] Celebrating the formal inclusiveness of the Founders' Constitution for its time, they have been unwilling to acknowledge its elitist character and counter-majoritarian features. With few exceptions, they have also ignored Madison's role in constitutionalizing slavery and his conclusions about the limitations of ordinary men for self-government.

In contrast, Progressives have been too eager to criticize Madison. To them, his vision of an impartial republic is not a noble ideal, imperfectly executed, but a farce that illustrates the partiality of those claiming to want to institutionalize impartiality. Conversely, they have been unwilling to acknowledge the more democratic aspects of the Founders' Constitution, especially its basic commitment to formal inclusiveness. They have also been unwilling to credit the most egalitarian aspects of Madisonian republicanism, including Madison's majoritarian defense of proportional representation in both branches of Congress and the underlying principle of proportional equality and proportional justice on which it rests.

Most broadly, they have given reductionistic interpretations of his justifications for the long leash and counter-majoritarian features of the Founders' Constitution or ignored them altogether. As we have seen, Madison's defense of longer terms of office and indirect elections rested on the claim that the attributes of "good Government" can only be achieved in a political system that significantly distances the people from their leaders.[115] In failing to confront this claim, Progressives end up judging a constitutional system meant to achieve several goals entirely by its ability to achieve one. In the end, Progressives conclude where they ought to begin. A meaningful confrontation with Madisonian republicanism and a convincing case for the necessity of constitutional reform needs not only to call attention to its elitist and counter-majoritarian features but also provide a convincing case that the multiple institutional goals we ask government to serve can be achieved by a more democratic one.

For our part, at this moment when American political institutions are profoundly unpopular and widely judged to be ineffective and illegitimate, we would be well served to acknowledge that, whether the goal is a convincing apologia or mature and effective criticism of the American political system, the path forward begins by taking Madison's complex case for "our complicated system" seriously.[116] Madison remains our best source for understanding the Constitution.

NOTES

The author would like to thank Eric Kasper, Howard Schweber, and Michael Zuckert for their helpful suggestions on this essay.

1. I use the term "Founders' Constitution" in this essay to refer to the political system created in the Constitution of 1787–88. "Madisonian republicanism" refers to the interpretation and defense that Madison gave to this system but also features of it he initially opposed.
2. Douglass Adair, *Fame and the Founding Fathers: Essays by Douglass Adair*, ed. Trevor Colbourn (New York: W. W. Norton, 1974), 121–23.
3. Scholarship on this debate is voluminous, necessitating the analysis and citation of only the most representative works. For a sampling of additional examples see *How Democratic Is the Constitution?*, ed. Robert A. Goldwin and William A. Schambra (Washington, D.C.: American Enterprise Institute, 1980).
4. James Allen Smith, *The Spirit of American Government* (Cambridge, Mass.: Belknap Press of Harvard University Press, 1965), 37–39, 42–43, 205–7; Charles A. Beard, *An Economic Interpretation of the Constitution of the United States* (New York: Free Press, 1913, 1986), 152–83, quote from 154.
5. Rogers Smith, *Civic Ideals: Conflicting Visions of Citizenship in U.S. History* (New Haven: Yale University Press, 1997), 115–36; quotes from 131, 121.
6. Woody Holton, *UnRuly Americans and the Origins of the Constitution* (New York: Hill and Wang, 2007), 179–212, quote from 199; Holton, "'Divide et Impera': *Federalist* 10 in a Wider Sphere," *William and Mary Quarterly* 62 (April 2005): 175–212; Jennifer Nedelsky, *Private Property and the Limits of American Constitutionalism: The Madisonian Framework and Its Legacy* (Chicago: University of Chicago Press, 1990), esp. 49–55.
7. Holton, *UnRuly Americans*, 171.
8. Nedelsky, *Private Property*, 2.
9. Martin Diamond, "Democracy and *The Federalist*: A Reconsideration of the Framers' Intent," *American Political Science Review* 53 (1959): 52–68. For the political motives underlying Diamond's interpretation see Alan Gibson, "The Commercial Republic and the Pluralist Critique of Marxism: An Analysis of Martin Diamond's Interpretation of the Tenth *Federalist* Paper," Polity 25 (Summer 1993), 497–528.
10. Martin Diamond, "The American Idea of Equality: The View from the Founding," *Review of Politics* 37 (July 1976), 313–31, quote from 328.
11. Martin Diamond, *The Founding of the Democratic Republic* (Itasca, Ill.: F. E. Peacock, 1981), 9–10, 61–98, quote from 9; Diamond, "Democracy and The Federalist," 52–68.
12. Lance Banning, *The Sacred Fire of Liberty: James Madison and the Founding of the Federal Republic* (Ithaca: Cornell University Press, 1995), 9.
13. Colleen Sheehan, *James Madison and the Spirit of Republican Self-Government* (Cambridge: Cambridge University Press, 2009).
14. Ahkil Reed Amar, *America's Constitution: A Biography* (New York: Random House, 2005), 5–7, 14–16, 18, 41, 44, 48, 51, 57, 69–70, 73, 88, 100, 103, 136, 139, 151–54, 159, 164–66, 170, 276–77, 279, 459, quotes from 5, 164.
15. *Federalist* No. 37, in Alexander Hamilton, James Madison, and John Jay, *The Federalist*,

ed. Jacob E. Cooke (Middletown, Conn.: Wesleyan University Press, 1961), 233 (subsequent citations are to this edition).
16. "Consolidation," December 3, 1791, *The Papers of James Madison*, ed. William T. Hutchinson et al. (vols. 1–10, Chicago: University of Chicago Press; volumes 11–17, Charlottesville: University Press of Virginia, 1962–), 14: 139. Hereafter cited as PJM.
17. United States Constitution, Article 1, Section 2.
18. Speeches of James Wilson and Oliver Ellsworth, August 7, *Notes of Debates in the Federal Convention of 1787 Reported by James Madison*, ed. Adrienne Koch (New York: W. W. Norton, 1987), 401; Federalist No. 52, 354.
19. Alexander Keyssar, *The Right to Vote: The Contest History of Democracy in the United States* (New York; Basic Books, 2000), 21–24.
20. Speeches by George Mason and Madison, August 7, in Koch, *Notes of Debates*, 401, 403.
21. Speeches of August 7 and 8, in ibid., 401–7.
22. Donald Lutz, "Political Participation in Eighteenth-Century America," *Albany Law Review* 53 (Winter 1989): 331, 333–35. See also Keyssar, *Right to Vote*, 24.
23. Stanley Elkins and Eric McKitrick, *The Age of Federalism* (New York: Oxford University Press, 1993), 717.
24. "1790 Census: Return of the Whole Number of Persons within the Several Districts of the United States," United States Census Bureau, https://www.census.gov/library/publications/1793/dec/number-of-persons.html.
25. Keyssar, *Right to Vote*, 20, 340–41, quote from 20.
26. See Smith, *Civic Ideals*, 131–32.
27. Jan Lewis, "'Of Every Age Sex & Condition': The Representation of Women in the Constitution," *Journal of the Early Republic* 15 (Autumn 1995): 359–87.
28. Rosemarie Zagarri, *Revolutionary Backlash: Women and Politics in the Early Republic* (Philadelphia: University of Pennsylvania Press, 2007), 30–37; Jennifer Schuessler, "On the Trail of America's First Women to Vote," New York Times, February 24, 2020, https://www.nytimes.com/2020/02/24/arts/first-women-voters-new-jersey.html.
29. Gretchen Ritter, *The Constitution as Social Design: Gender and Civic Membership in the American Constitutional Order* (Stanford, Calif.: Stanford University Press, 2006), 2–3. See also Catherine Allgor, *Parlor Politics: In Which the Ladies of Washington Help Build a City and a Government* (Charlottesville: University of Virginia Press, 2000); Linda Kerber, "The Republican Mother: Women and the Enlightenment—An American Perspective," *American Quarterly* 28 (Summer, 1976): 187–205; Linda Kerber, *Women of the Republic: Intellect and Ideology in Revolutionary America* (Chapel Hill: University of North Carolina Press, 1980).
30. Based on rough calculations from the 1790 Census, this figure is, if anything, a substantial underestimation of those ineligible to vote. It is determined by adding 70 percent of the free white males both over and under sixteen, 200 women voters, and everyone listed under the category "all other free persons." This gives us 1,178,971 individuals or about 30 percent of the total 1790 population of 3,893,635. If the estimate for free Blacks eligible to vote is reduced to the much more likely figure of at most a few thousand, the Native American population is included, or white men under sixteen (those disenfranchised by

age) are subtracted, then the total number and the percentage of eligible voters is precipitously reduced. "1790 Census."

31. Amar, *America's Constitution*, 66–76.
32. United States Constitution, Article 1, Section 2, Clause 2; Article 1, Section 3, Clause 3; Article II, Section 1, Clause 5.
33. United States Constitution, Article 6, paragraph 3.
34. Marc Kruman, *Between Authority and Liberty: State Constitution Making in Revolutionary America* (Chapel Hill: University of North Carolina Press, 1997), 96–97.
35. Amar, *America's Constitution*, 72–74.
36. Smith, *Civic Ideals*, 128–29. Cf. Amar, *America's Constitution*, 164–66, who defends this requirement as a liberalization of eighteenth-century English practice.
37. Amar, *America's Constitution*, 165.
38. Speech of August 10, Koch, *Notes of Debates*, 427.
39. *Federalist* No. 52, 354.
40. *Federalist* No. 57, 385. Regarding officeholding see also Federalist No. 52, 354–55.
41. *Federalist* No. 14, 84; *Federalist* No. 39, 250–53.
42. "Notes for the *National Gazette Essays*," *PJM*, 14:163–64. Madison's observation about slavery appeared in an adumbrated form earlier in "Vices of the Political System of the United States," *PJM*, 9:351.
43. Speech of August 7, Koch, *Notes of Debates*, 403–4.
44. *The Documentary History of the Ratification of the Constitution*, ed. Merrill Peterson et al (Madison: State Historical Society of Wisconsin, 1976–), 3:392n8. For the most sophisticated Anti-Federalist critique of inadequate representation in the Constitution see "Speeches by Melancton Smith in New York's State Convention" in David Siemers, T*he Antifederalists: Men of Great Faith and Forbearance* (Lanham, Md.: Rowman & Littlefield, 2003), 137–47.
45. Madison to Jefferson, March 27, 1780, *PJM*, 2:6. See also Madison to Edmund Randolph, May 27, 1783, *PJM*, 7:89.
46. Other leading scholars who make this error include Gordon Wood, *The Creation of the American Republic, 1776–1787* (Chapel Hill: University of North Carolina Press, 1969, 1998), 469–518; and Garry Wills, *Explaining America: The Federalist* (Garden City, N.Y.: Doubleday, 1981).
47. This electoral scheme appears in "Vices" but is not mentioned in any of the three letters Madison wrote in the spring of 1786 outline of what he later called the "first shoot in his thoughts of a plan of Federal Government." Douglass G. Adair, ed., "James Madison's Autobiography," *William and Mary Quarterly* 2 (April 1945), 202. "Vices," PJM, 9:357; Madison to George Washington, April 16, 1787, PJM, 9:383–85; Madison to Thomas Jefferson, March 19, 1787, PJM, 9:318–19; Madison to Edmund Randolph, April 8, 1787, PJM, 9:369–70.
48. Holton, "Divide et Impera," 177.
49. Speeches of July 10 and September 8, in Koch, *Notes of Debates*, 263, 608.
50. *Federalist* No. 55, 375; *Federalist* No. 58, 391–97.

51. In 1789, Madison proposed a constitutional amendment to coordinate increases in representation with increases in national population. In 1791, he proposed a standard of one representative for every thirty thousand inhabitants—the maximum number allowed under the Constitution—in the debates on apportionment pursuant to the census of 1790. See "Amendments to the Constitution," June 8, 1789, *PJM*, 12:200, 336–37; "Proportional Representation," *PJM*, 14:127; Madison to Edmund Pendleton, December 18, 1791, *PJM*, 14:156–57.
52. *Federalist* No. 56, 381.
53. "Vices," *PJM*, 9:357.
54. *Federalist* No. 10, 63. For Madison on the dynamics of large legislative bodies see *Federalist* No. 55, 373–74; *Federalist* No. 58, 395–96.
55. *Federalist* No. 10, 65.
56. *Federalist* No. 10, 65, 57; Federalist No. 62, 421–22; Madison to Jefferson, October 24, 1787, PJM, 10:212.
57. See Madison to Joseph Jones, October 17, 1780, *PJM*, 2:137; Speech of July 26, in Koch, *Notes of Debates*, 375; *Federalist* No. 62, 421–22; Alan Gibson, "Madison's 'Great Desideratum': Impartial Administration and the Extended Republic," *American Political Thought: A Journal of Ideas, Institutions, and Culture* 1 (Fall 2012): 181–207.
58. *Federalist* No. 10, 59. In 1791, Madison wrote that the speculative frenzy unleashed by Hamilton's economic program made it unclear "whether the system of the old paper under a bad Government, or of the new under a good one, be chargeable with the greater substantial injustice. The true difference seems to be that by the former the few were the victims to the many; by the latter the many to the few." Madison to Jefferson, August 8, 1791, *PJM*, 11:69.
59. *Federalist* No. 10, 60; "Property," *PJM*, 14:266.
60. The concept of district malapportionment is a twentieth-century constitutional construction of the equal protection clause of the Fourteenth Amendment (issued by the judiciary). Like the election of representatives from single member geographically defined districts, it is a constitutional construction, not an explicit mandate set forth in the text.
61. Amar, *America's Constitution*, 91.
62. Frances E. Lee and Bruce I. Oppenheimer, *Sizing Up the Senate: The Unequal Consequences of Equal Representation* (Chicago: University of Chicago Press, 1999), 35.
63. These calculations were conducted using census data from the Geospatial Statistical Data Center, University of Virginia Library, available at http://fisher.lib.virginia.edu/.
64. Madison to Caleb Wallace, August 23, 1785, *PJM*, 8:354; Madison to Jefferson, October 8, 1788, PJM, 11:276.
65. Speech of July 9, in Koch, *Notes of Debates*, 259.
66. Speech of June 19, in ibid., 148.
67. Speech of June 28, in ibid., 205–6.
68. Speech of June 30, in ibid., 223–25. For the best analysis and defense of Madison's case against equal representation see Jack Rakove, "The Great Compromise: Ideas, Interests, and the Politics of Constitution Making," *William and Mary Quarterly* 44 (1987): 424–57; Rakove, "A MARvel of Constitutional Demythologizing," *Journal of American*

Constitutional History 1 (Spring 2023), 303–6. For the prescience of Madison's predictions see Lee and Oppenheimer, *Sizing Up the Senate*.

69. "Editorial Note," *PJM*, 8:100–102; Banning, *Sacred Fire of Liberty*, 19, 58–70, 255–57, 268–69, 306–7; Madison to James Monroe, October 5, 1786, PJM, 9:141.
70. Speech of June 30, in Koch, *Notes of Debates*, 224.
71. Speech of June 30 and Speech of July 9, in ibid., 223, 259.
72. For a forceful statement of this thesis see Rakove, "MARvel of Constitutional Demythologizing," 303–6.
73. *Federalist* No. 57, 388.
74. United States Constitution, Article 3, Section 1.
75. See especially *Federalist* No. 48, 333–34; *Federalist* No. 51, 350.
76. See Alan Gibson, "Madison's Republican Remedy: The Tenth *Federalist* and the Creation of an Impartial Republic," in *The Cambridge Companion to "The Federalist,"* ed. Jack N. Rakove and Colleen A. Sheehan (Cambridge: Cambridge University Press, 2020): 263–301, esp. 279–93.
77. *Federalist* No. 10, 62; *Federalist* No. 14, 84, 88; *Federalist* No. 51, 353; *Federalist* No. 39, 253.
78. Michael Zuckert, "The Political Science of James Madison," in *History of American Political Thought*, ed. Bryan-Paul Frost and Jeffrey Sikkenga (Lanham, Md.: Lexington Books, 2003), 155–65, quotes from 159–60.
79. *Federalist* No. 53, 360; *Federalist* Nos. 55–58, 372–97.
80. *Federalist* No. 10, 62.
81. Terence Ball, "'A Republic—If You Can Keep It,'" in *Conceptual Change and the Constitution*, ed. Terence Ball and J. G. A. Pocock (Lawrence: University Press of Kansas, 1988), 137–64.
82. Alan Gibson, *Understanding the Founding: The Crucial Questions*, 2nd ed. (Lawrence: University Press of Kansas, 2010), 80–82}.
83. *Federalist* No. 51, 350. See also Federalist No. 48, 334.
84. Gibson, *Understanding the Founding*, 72-73.
85. "Amendments to the Constitution," August 15, 1789, *PJM*, 12:340–41.
86. The "good" majorities—'bad" majorities problem was first set forth by Robert Dahl. See Dahl, *A Preface to Democratic Theory* (Chicago: University of Chicago Press, 1956), 29–30.
87. "Vices," *PJM*, 9:356–57 (emphasis added).
88. *Federalist* No. 14, 83; Madison to Jefferson, October 24, 1787, *PJM*, 10:214. See also *Federalist* No. 51, 353.
89. *Federalist* No. 58, 395–96, quotes from 396. See also *Federalist* No. 55, 373–74.
90. Madison to Jefferson, March 19, 1787, *PJM*, 9:318 (emphasis added).
91. Speeches of June 12 and June 21, in Koch, *Notes of Debates*, 106, 169.
92. Speech of June 26, in ibid., 195. Earlier Madison had supported seven-year terms for senators. Speech of June 12, in ibid., 110–11 (emphasis added).

93. Speech of July 17, in ibid., 311–13, quote from 312; *PJM*, 10:104n1.
94. "Virginia Plan," May 29, 1787, *PJM*, 10:16.
95. *Federalist* No. 14, 83; Federalist No. 10, 64; Federalist No. 51, 64.
96. *Federalist* No. 37, 233–34.
97. *Federalist* No. 63, 426, 425.
98. *Federalist* No. 10, 60. See also Gibson, "Madison's Republican Remedy," 271–74.
99. Speech of June 10, 1788, Virginia Ratifying Convention, *PJM*, 11:163.
100. Madison to Edmund Randolph, January 10, 1788, *PJM*, 10:355. See also Madison to Benjamin Rush, March 7, 1790, *PJM*, 13:93–94; and the analysis of Madison's letter to Randolph in Jack Rakove, *A Politician Thinking: The Creative Mind of James Madison* (Norman: University of Oklahoma Press, 2017), 98–102.
101. Speech of June 6, in Koch, *Notes of Debates*, 75.
102. Richard H. Thaler, Cass R. Sunstein, and John P. Balz, "Choice Architecture," in *The Behavioral Foundations of Public Policy*, ed. Shafir Eldar (Princeton: Princeton University Press, 2013), 428–39.
103. *Federalist* No. 10, 63.
104. *Federalist* No. 51, 351.
105. "Vices," *PJM*, 9:356–57; *Federalist* No. 10, 63.
106. *Federalist* No. 37:233–34.
107. "Vices," *PJM*, 9:357.
108. Madison to Edmund Pendleton, October 20, 1788, *PJM*, 11:307; Gibson, "Madison's Republican Remedy," 279–93.
109. *Federalist* No. 37, 234.
110. "Vices," *PJM*, 9:355–56.
111. Madison to Jefferson, October 24, 1787, *PJM*, 10:209.
112. *Federalist* No. 37, 233–34.
113. See Rakove, "MARvel of Constitutional Demythologizing," 306–7, for Madison's initial support of the direct election of the president.
114. Banning, *Sacred Fire of Liberty*, 372.
115. *Federalist* No. 37, 233–34.
116. "Consolidation," December 3, 1791, *PJM*, 13:139.

"Great as the Evil Is"

Madison, Slavery, and the Constitution

QUENTIN P. TAYLOR

"Next to the case of the black race within our bosom, that of the red man on our borders is the problem most baffling to the policy of our country."[1] So wrote James Madison in 1826 as the nation approached the fiftieth anniversary of American independence. The political battles fought since the adoption of the Constitution—over banks, tariffs, trade, and war—had strained but not broken the system Madison had touted during the ratification contest as best suited to accommodate the inevitable clash of interests in a republic. The problems presented by the tribes and slavery, however, were of a wholly different order. Tribal Indians and enslaved Africans were not mere policies or programs over which partisan strife could be managed within existing institutions, but were entire classes of people widely regarded as foreign elements within the body politic. If not altogether outside the system—for both were acknowledged by federal and state law—they were anomalies within it.

By 1826 neither Madison nor a majority of his countrymen believed assimilation of these peoples into the broader (white) society was possible or even desirable. Attempts at assimilation of the Indians had almost entirely failed, and the tribal way of life was wholly at odds with an aggressively expansive, commercial society. Conversely, free Blacks were unwelcome in the South and largely outcasts in the North, the victims of racial prejudice that few could ever hope to overcome. These stark facts left Madison and the new nation in a "baffling" predicament. If neither the mass of Natives nor emancipated persons could be incorporated into the body politic, what was to be done with them? For Madison logic and necessity pointed to but one solution: removal. As he confided to former attorney general William Wirt in 1830, "It is evident that they can never be tranquil or happy within the bounds of a State, either in a separate or subject character, that a remove to another home, if a good one can be found, may well be the wish of their best friends."[2]

Although Madison was referring to American Indians, his words were no less applicable to African Americans. More than forty years earlier he had drafted a memorandum in which he proposed the "experiment" of relocating emancipated persons to Africa "or some other foreign situation" to facilitate the "abolition of slavery in America." The Indians, who occupied the "borders" of the nation, might be conveniently removed to the expanding frontier. Yet Black enslaved persons, nestled in the very "bosom" of society and subject to "the prejudice of the Whites," could not be freed and remain safely within it.[3]

At the time the Constitution was adopted, Vermont and Massachusetts had ended slavery, and Pennsylvania, Connecticut, and New Hampshire had adopted plans for gradual emancipation. Other states, including Virginia, had liberalized their manumission laws, while New York and New Jersey had done little to emancipate enslaved persons. When the delegates met in Philadelphia, the trend appeared to be in favor of freedom, but the pattern was erratic. In all states free Blacks still faced discrimination and disabilities—de jure and de facto—and the South's resistance to manumitting enslaved persons during the Revolutionary War exposed the limits of the era's libertarian impulses. Even the emancipation plan of the liberty-loving, slavery-hating Jefferson was contingent upon removal, preferably to Africa. It is likely that Madison adopted the same solution based on Jefferson's observations in *Notes on the State of Virginia* (1785).[4] Their shared experience as Old Dominion elites convinced them that large numbers of freed Blacks could not coexist on any basis of equality or safety with free whites. Only strict separation could shield formerly enslaved persons from white prejudice and offer their posterity the hope of an independent and dignified existence. Of course, it would also remove what the Virginia oligarchy feared most: a dependent, obnoxious, and dangerous caste of racial outsiders.[5]

As a young man Madison had concluded that slavery was a moral and political evil inconsistent with the natural law principles of the American Revolution, and in the early 1780s he welcomed a statute that permitted Virginians to manumit their enslaved persons. Yet by mid-decade he feared that hostility toward the expanding free Black population was threatening to overturn the policy. The impulse that led Virginians to emancipate thousands of enslaved persons in the aftermath of the Revolutionary War had been blunted by the "ill effects suffered from freedmen who retain the vices and habits of slaves."[6] Moreover, voluntary manumission had been opposed by many Virginians, and in 1785 a bill was introduced to repeal the Act of 1782. Madison, a delegate in the Virginia assembly, opposed the repeal as a "retrograde step with regard to an emancipation [that] will not only dishonor us extremely but hasten the event which is dreaded," that is, abolition without removal.[7] Like many antislavery Virginians, Madison thought it unwise to adopt a plan of general emancipation until freed enslaved persons could be permanently removed from the United States. Well before the memorandum of 1789, Madison had arrived at the conclusion that emancipation must be tied to relocation. It was a conviction he would retain for the remainder of his life.[8]

That life began as the son of the largest landowner in the Piedmont region of Virginia. Growing up on the family plantation, young James lived and played among the dozens of enslaved persons who populated his father's estate. One of these bondsman, Swaney, would accompany him to attend college at Princeton (1769–71), while another, Billey, would journey to Philadelphia where Madison took his seat in the Confederation Congress (1780–83).[9] In the interim, war had broken out between Britain and the colonies, and Congress had declared independence. That a war for American "rights" and "liberties" was pregnant with ramifications for slavery was evident to combatants on both sides. Six months prior to the Declaration of Independence, Lord Dunmore, the royal governor of Virginia, issued a proclamation offering freedom to all enslaved persons who would bear arms for the British. Madison, who had expressed his fear of this very stratagem a year earlier, identified the incitement of enslaved persons as the ill-concealed "secret" that would doom Virginia to "fall like Achilles" in an armed conflict.[10] While hundreds of enslaved persons would flee to the British lines (or otherwise escape), Dunmore's "Ethiopian Regiment" failed to develop into a viable force. Yet fears of a British-inspired slave insurrection were keenly felt in Virginia for the remainder of the war and delayed legalized manumission until after the surrender at Yorktown.[11]

Free Blacks had fought in the patriot ranks from the beginning of hostilities and would serve in the Continental army as well as the state militias for the duration of the war. Several northern states offered enslaved persons their freedom on condition of such service. Most of the southern states, however, balked at arming enslaved persons. A plan proposed by Congress to recruit enslaved persons in the Deep South was summarily dismissed by the Georgia and South Carolina legislatures. As an alternative, the Virginia Assembly proposed awarding white recruits an enslaved person as a bounty for enlisting. When Joseph Jones, a former Virginia congressman, expressed an interest in the plan, Madison demurred: "Would it not be as well to liberate and make soldiers at once of the blacks themselves as to make them instruments for enlisting white Soldiers? It wd. certainly be more consonant to the principles of liberty which ought never to be lost sight of in a contest for liberty."[12]

While military necessity had prompted calls to recruit enslaved persons, Madison linked the policy to "the principles of liberty" for which Americans were fighting. Like Hamilton, he would give enslaved persons their "freedom with their muskets." Yet few of his fellow Virginians agreed, including General Washington, who feared it would lead to an "arms race" with the British and threaten to destabilize the South's slave-based society. Madison did not share these fears but would not pursue the matter after it was rejected. Moreover, without a plan to remove freed persons from the nation, his antislavery principles would go no further than voluntary manumission.

Yet even this cautious approach would prove problematic. The thousands of enslaved persons liberated in Virginia in the decade following the Act of 1782 created the very reaction Madison would oppose in 1785 and warn against thereafter. Due to the ingrained habits of servitude and the intractability of white prejudice, "it is [now] found in fact that neither the good of the Society, nor the happiness of the individuals restored to freedom is promoted by a change in [the enslaved person's] condition."[13] In response, Virginia would impose a series of restrictions on emancipated persons culminating in an 1806 statute that required them to leave the state within a year or face re-enslavement. Madison left no record of his views of these laws, but the measures taken to control and limit the free Black population could have hardly come as a surprise.[14]

Then as before, Madison's preoccupation was not with slavery but with nation building. As a member of Congress he was among the nationalists who worked tirelessly—if in vain—to strengthen the hapless Articles of Confederation. For an amendment granting Congress the power to tax the states based on population, southern delegates hoped to exempt enslaved persons from the count. When northern delegates proved intransigent, various ratios were proposed (and rejected) until Madison's three-fifths motion gained approval. (Four years later the same "federal ratio" would be adopted at the Philadelphia Convention for assigning representation in the lower house.) Returning to the Virginia legislature in 1784, Madison continued to press for reform at both the state and national levels. Along with Hamilton, he used the occasion of the failed Annapolis Convention (1786) to call for a meeting of the states to affect a general reform of the Articles.

Madison's extensive preparation for the subsequent gathering in Philadelphia included compiling a list of "Vices of the Political System of the United States." Among these was the ability of the minority to thwart the will of the majority under the state sovereignty provision of the Articles. If this contradicted a leading tenet of "Republican Theory"—that power and right rested with the majority—an appeal to "fact and experience" confirmed the contradiction among the states themselves, which restricted the franchise to a minority of property owners. If this practice undermined the majoritarian basis of republicanism among white males, the presence of chattel slavery rendered it nearly meaningless. As Madison wrote, "Where slavery exists the republican Theory becomes still more fallacious."[15]

This was a remarkable admission for the man who would shortly become America's foremost theorist of republican government. It indicates a stark recognition that the grand experiment in popular rule was compromised from the start: first, by denying the vote to a significant portion of adult white males, and second, by the widespread practice of Black enslavement. Dubious in theory, the practical implications of such apparent violations of republican principles were potentially far worse.[16] If the farmers led by Daniel Shays were willing to pick up arms in redress of grievances, what might other marginalized whites—not to mention enslaved Blacks—be capable of? For Madison, the question was far from rhetorical and the answer far from comforting. "For obvious reasons [such aggrieved persons] will be more likely to join the standard of sedition than that of the established Government."[17]

Madison could reasonably expect the "vice" of state equality to be ameliorated in the Constitutional Convention, but he could not anticipate the removal of other deviations from republican theory. In the first instance, he received half a loaf: representation in the lower house would be based on population. Power to restrict voting rights and control over slavery, however, would remain with the states. In tacit recognition of the dangers of an unduly restricted franchise and a system of forced labor, the Constitution's framers granted the central government the power to "suppress Insurrections" and defend the states "against domestic Violence." The Constitution's guarantee of a "Republican Form of Government" for each state provided an additional safeguard. Yet for Madison the states were not, strictly speaking, republics at all. Paradoxically, the Constitution empowered the central government to suppress the very "Insurrections" and acts of "domestic Violence" that might aim to bring republican practice into closer conformity with republican ideals. In the convention Madison would stop short of explicitly drawing this unsettling conclusion (although it would be drawn by some northern delegates). He did, however, repeat verbatim his remarks in the "Vices" on the anomalous existence of both enslaved persons and quasi-citizens within a "republic." His aim was not to expose the state governments as the oligarchies they in fact were, but to demonstrate that only a government that could act directly on the states through an independent source of power could defend these oligarchies from the dangers inherent in their social and political composition. It was never Madison's intention to create a frame of government that would ensure the dominance of the few over the many. Yet as long as the states denied a large number of their inhabitants full citizenship or basic liberty, the prospect of civil unrest would remain a palpable threat to the "internal tranquility of the States."[18] This was a threat that might require the armed intervention of a federal force.

Writing as Publius, Madison would identify "the extent and proper structure of the Union" as "a Republican remedy for the diseases most incident to Republican government."[19] The diseases were "faction" and "majority tyranny," while the prescribed remedy was "representation" and an "extensive republic." This resolution of the riddle of sustaining a popular government over a large territory is rightly celebrated as a seminal expression of American political thought. Yet for all its brilliance and originality, Madison's "Republican remedy" had not quite squared the circle, for it sidestepped a paradox that he recognized: the existence of quasi-citizenship and especially chattel slavery within a modern republic. This "Madisonian moment" would necessarily remain concealed from public view.[20] As a national statesman who believed the promise of republicanism could only be realized through a "more perfect Union" of imperfect states, Madison had nothing to gain by exposing discrepancies between theory and practice, words and deeds. Madison was a Virginia enslaver whose political efficacy depended upon the good opinion of his fellow oligarchs, so his ability to continue in the role of nation builder was incumbent upon his discretion. Behind closed doors he might decry the enslavement of Africans as "the most oppressive dominion ever exercised by man over man," but in public he remained conspicuously silent on the subject.[21]

Doing so required little effort. Madison rarely wrote for the public and then either anonymously or under a neoclassical pseudonym. In the notes he would draw upon for a series of articles in the *National Gazette* (1791–92), he expanded on the startling admission in the "Vices" he had shared under the rule of secrecy in the Convention.

> In proportion as slavery prevails in a State, the Government, however democratic in name, must be aristocratic in fact. The power lies in a part instead of the whole; in the hands of property, not in numbers. . . . The Southern states of America, are on the same principle aristocracies. In Virginia the aristocratic character is increased by the rule of suffrage, which requiring a freehold in land excludes nearly half the free inhabitants, and must exclude a greater proportion, as the population increases. At present slaves and non-freeholders amount to nearly ¾ of the State. The power is therefore in about ¼. Were the slaves freed and the right of suffrage extended to all, the operation of the Government might be very different. The slavery of the Southern States, throws the power much more into the hands of property, than in the Northern States. Hence the people in the former are much more contented with their establishd. Governments, than the people of property in the latter.[22]

Madison would not include these jarring thoughts in any of the nineteen articles he published in the *National Gazette*.[23] Madison was a scholar who plumbed the depths of political theory to unlock the secrets of republican regimes, and his confrontation with slavery—ancient and modern—was highly relevant. It made little sense for Madison, as a politician from Virginia whose life's work was the establishment and preservation of a federal republic, to draw attention to the unrepublican realities embedded in the states that comprised it. At a time when he was moving toward breaking with the Federalist administration and organizing a political party—and not long after the explosive debates in the House of Representatives over the introduction of antislavery petitions—Madison had abundant reasons for keeping these unseasonable thoughts concealed. Among these was not giving political opponents—whether northern Federalists or abolition groups—a cudgel with which to strike at the Virginia-led South.

All these considerations moved Madison to decline a request by a prominent Virginia abolitionist to introduce a petition in Congress aimed at abating the slave trade, as well as submit a plan of abolition to the Virginia legislature. The petitioner, Robert Pleasants, had freed over eighty enslaved persons, hired them as laborers, and provided for their instruction. Madison candidly explained that it would hardly become his place to give "a public wound" to "those from whom I derive my public station"—his slaveholding constituents—by introducing a measure designed to "lessen the value" of "that species of property" "on which they set so great a value." Moreover, such a measure was "likely to do harm rather than good" and might even hasten the repeal of voluntary manumission or result in a law requiring former enslaved persons to leave the state.[24] With this refusal Madison's views on abolition had reached an impasse. His political calculations would prove correct with respect to Virginia, but he had broader reasons for avoiding a confrontation over slavery.

Madison's policy of avoidance—the subordination of slavery to reasons of state—had been a hallmark of his performance at the Constitutional Convention. For an issue that had not been on the agenda, slavery played a conspicuous, and often contentious, role in the deliberations there.[25] From the outset slavery was implicated in the vital matter of representation. Madison and others were determined to replace the rule of state equality under the Articles of Confederation with a proportional system based on population or wealth. Oddly, the Virginia Plan's provision for popular representation was limited to "the number of free inhabitants." When Hamilton moved to adopt the measure, the Virginia delegation realized it had made a mistake, and quickly moved to postpone the matter. Madison considered it essential to establish the *principle* of proportional representation before the issue of *whom* would be represented was determined.[26] Yet if popular representation was to prevail, none of the five largest slaveholding states could ever be expected to confederate based on their "free inhabitants" alone. This led some southern delegates to propose *wealth* as the basis of representation, a measure that would include the full value of their enslaved persons, or alternatively to count enslaved persons *equally* with their free white population. Both were unacceptable to some northern delegates, who decried the inclusion of enslaved persons for either purpose—if enslaved persons were *persons* they should not be counted as *property*, and if property they should not be counted as persons. The convention agreed to provisionally count enslaved persons as three-fifths of a person for representation in the lower house and moved on to other business.

Madison did not enter into these debates but was singularly focused on establishing proportional representation in both the lower *and* upper houses of the national legislature. In an effort to overcome the opposition of the small states, who feared domination by their larger neighbors, Madison recast the conflict in terms of the "Northern & Southern" states, whose "different interests . . . resulted . . . principally from their having or not having slaves." This divergence had created a "peculiar interest" among a "class of citizens" that "ought to be secured as far as possible" from the "danger of attack" by a "constitutional power of defence." Accordingly, Madison proposed "counting the slaves as free" for representation in the House and "free inhabitants only" for the Senate. He admitted his reluctance to propose such a measure: it not only complicated the task of assigning different powers to each body but highlighted the real source of conflict.[27]

Was this an oblique ploy to persuade small states such as Delaware, New Jersey, and Maryland, which had significant populations of enslaved persons, to abandon state equality in the Senate in exchange for power to block northern attacks on their "property" in the House?[28] If so, it failed miserably. Undeterred, Madison later revived the proposal, this time making the Senate, "which had for one of its primary objects the guardianship of property," the repository of enslaved person representation. This too was ignored.[29]

On the eve of the final vote over representation, Madison made a last desperate bid to block state equality in the Senate. His objections included "the perpetuity it would give to the preponderance of the Northn. agst. the Southn." states; a daunting prospect for it "now seemed to be pretty well understood that the real difference of interest lay, not between the large & small but between the N. & Southn. States." More specifically, "the institution of slavery & its consequences formed the line of demarcation."[30] This veiled warning to southern delegates would prove no more effective than a Greek chorus. In the end the convention would compromise: representation in the House (and the apportionment of direct taxes) would be based on the number of free inhabitants and "three-fifths of all other Persons," and state equality would prevail in the Senate.

What Madison identified as a threat to the southern interest would in time prove a bulwark of its defense.[31] For the next sixty years, parity would prevail in the number of senators from free and slave states, with the balance of power tilting toward the South. The Great Compromise would further bolster the slave interest once the convention adopted the Electoral College for selecting the president. Before the compromise, the convention had considered various modes, with election by Congress having the most support. After the compromise, popular election of the president was revived but now faced an additional objection on sectional grounds. As Hugh Williamson of North Carolina observed, the South would be disadvantaged under such a system, for "slaves will have no suffrage." Madison, who favored popular election in principle, agreed that the "Southern states... could have no influence in the election on the score of the Negroes."[32] As such, he endorsed the use of presidential electors as the best solution to this objection and other difficulties.

That Madison had yet to see the advantage of a system of electors when linked to the three-fifths clause is clear from his reversal a week later, when he argued on behalf of popular election. Although it would initially place the slave states at a disadvantage, the expansion of the franchise "under the influence of the Republican laws" and the "more rapid increase in their population" would soon narrow the gap. For the good of the whole, he pledged himself—as a man of the South—"willing to make the sacrifice."[33]

Madison's fellow southerners, however, were not. More than a month later the Constitutional Convention was no nearer to a solution. The committee assigned to review the matter issued a report that proposed presidential selection by electors chosen by the state legislatures and equal in number to each state's representatives and senators. If any of the delegates perceived the advantage this would give states with large populations of enslaved persons, it is not reflected in the convention records: the provision was adopted without debate. Yet it is doubtful that such astute politicians were unaware of the direct link between the formula for assigning electors and the ratio for representing enslaved persons. A handful of northern delegates were prepared to repudiate the three-fifths compromise after the Committee of Detail produced a report that barred interference with the importation of enslaved persons and exempted these—and the exports their labor produced—from taxation. Rufus King and Gouverneur Morris denounced the report as a betrayal of the spirit that had animated their acquiescence to a partial representation of enslaved persons, whose unrestrained importation would swell the political power of the South and increase its vulnerability to foreign attack and domestic rebellion. Morris's final effort to overturn the three-fifths clause received but one state's vote. Any effort to delink the "federal number" from the Electoral College would have met the same fate. This—not ignorance of the connection—accounts for the silence.[34]

Opposition to the slave trade itself had broader support, but Lower South delegates would not agree to restrictions without concessions in return. Virginia had prohibited the trade in 1778, and its delegation was now solidly behind its speedy termination. George Mason virulently denounced the "nefarious traffic," but his diatribe failed to move the flinty hearts of Deep South delegates, who proposed the slave trade remain exempt from restriction for twenty years. Such an extension, Madison predicted, "will produce all the mischief that can be apprehended from the liberty to import slaves," as well as dishonor "the National character . . . [and] the Constitution."[35] The motion to extend the date from 1800 to 1808 was passed with the votes of the three New England states that had already begun to end slavery. Madison, who served on the committee that brokered the deal, later claimed that Yankee support was given in exchange for abandonment of the two-thirds requirement for laying taxes of imports.[36] This "dirty compromise" was a victory for those delegates (both northern and southern) who favored funding the new government through a reliable (and indirect) source of revenue and a concession by those (primarily southerners) who feared an unfair tax burden.[37] Since every state but Georgia had virtually banned the slave trade, exempting it from federal regulation for an additional eight years did not trouble the consciences of Connecticut's Oliver Ellsworth and Roger Sherman, who blithely (and mistakenly) assured their colleagues that slavery itself was on the path to extinction.

Sherman was, however, troubled by the proposal to tax the importation of enslaved persons, for it "implied that they were property" in the eyes of the Constitution. Earlier he had acquiesced in counting enslaved persons as three-fifths of a person for direct federal taxes. The lack of a census had complicated the Constitutional Convention's task of establishing an equitable basis for taxation, as well as distributing House seats among the states. Madison, who had proposed the three-fifths figure in Congress four years before, now warmly approved it for taxation and representation "because it tended to moderate the views both of the opponents & advocates for rating very high, the negroes."[38] Ironically, the delegate who first proposed linking taxation to representation, Gouverneur Morris, now denounced the compromise as a fraud. The impracticality of extracting direct taxes assured that the southern states would receive all the benefits and incur none of the burdens of the three-fifths compromise. The North had sold out enslaved persons for a mess of political pottage.

Morris's blistering remarks had been provoked by the Committee of Detail's report that exempted the slave trade from congressional power over foreign commerce. When the subject was revived two weeks later, Luther Martin of Maryland proposed "a prohibition or tax on the importation of slaves" in order to forestall the dangerous effects of proliferation that Morris and King had previously decried.[39] Sherman would reiterate his objection to "acknowledging men as property" through a tax directed at generating revenue, "not the discouragement of the importation."[40] Madison also "thought it wrong to admit in the Constitution the idea that there could be property in men," but not for the same reasons. If he shared the moral and political concerns of Morris, King, and Sherman, he would not express them here.[41] Rather, enslaved persons were not suitable for import duties because they were "not like merchandise, consumed."[42] Aside from the fact that enslaved persons were bought, sold, and consumed like merchandise, Madison's aversion to formally acknowledge the presence of slavery in the Constitution could not conceal its presence throughout the Union.[43] Nor could it prevent the motion from being adopted without opposition.

Three days later the South Carolina delegation moved "to require fugitive slaves and servants to be delivered up like criminals."[44] The Articles of Confederation contained no such provision, although a few northern states had passed laws to accommodate southern enslavers. In mid-July, a day after the convention adopted the three-fifths compromise, the Congress sitting in New York passed the Northwest Ordinance, providing for the establishment of government in the territories north of the Ohio River. The Ordinance also prohibited slavery but provided for the return of any fugitive "from whom labor or service is lawfully claimed." The delegates in Philadelphia soon learned of these provisions, and the Carolinians, who demanded security for the persons they enslaved, moved to have similar language inserted into the Constitution. James Wilson and Roger Sherman objected to implicating the state governments in the enforcement of such a measure. The motion was temporarily withdrawn, reworded, and introduced on the following day.[45] It was adopted without debate or opposition.[46]

On September 10, just one week before the convention adjourned, a Committee of Style and Arrangement was appointed to give the Constitution its final form. Earlier that day, John Rutledge of South Carolina rose to insert a measure into the text that would exempt the slave trade clause from amendment until 1808. Rutledge had remained silent when Morris had railed against "so nefarious a practice" and denounced "domestic slavery" as bringing "the curse of heaven on the States where it prevailed."[47] He had, however, been attentively listening. The antislavery spirit of Morris and a few others, as well as the abolitionist trend in the North, led Rutledge and Deep South delegates to insist on protections for slavery where it was most threatened: "by the States not interested in that property and prejudiced against it."[48] They usually got their way: the slave trade exemption, like the fugitive slave clause, was adopted without comment.

Madison was disappointed in certain features of the Constitution, but the compromises over slavery were not chief among them. Like Hamilton, he would lay aside his objections, sign the document, and campaign sedulously on behalf of its adoption by the states. To this end, he joined Hamilton and Jay in the *Federalist* project, whose principal aim was to explain, defend, and support the Constitution's ratification in New York. Although slavery would not assume a prominent place in any of the ratification debates, Madison—in the guise of Publius—felt compelled to address the issue.[49] The first reference appears as the last item in a litany of comparisons between the Articles of Confederation and the proposed Constitution in the form of a catechism: "Is the importation of slaves permitted by the new Constitution for twenty years? By the old, it is permitted forever."[50]

With a word Madison appeared to have dispatched the odious vestige of a heretical creed. In New York, where the slave trade had terminated in 1774, it was a moot point, and only in Georgia did it survive unrestricted. And yet the permission to practice this "unnatural traffic" for two more decades left a stain on the Constitution that no incantation could erase. Madison's revival of the issue in a subsequent essay suggests as much. Here he expressed his regret (as he had in the convention) that the trade had not been subject to earlier, indeed, to "immediate" termination. On the other hand, it was "a great point gained in favor of humanity" that the Constitution did (after 1807) authorize Congress to abolish the trade completely. In the interim, "it will receive a considerable discouragement" by the disapprobation of the federal government and the example of the vast majority of states. Madison's disapprobation of the slave trade, "a traffic which has so long and so loudly upbraided the barbarism of modern policy," was unequivocal. As Publius he could eagerly anticipate the day when not only the slave trade, but slavery itself was abolished, when "the unfortunate Africans ... [were] redeemed from the oppressions of their European brethren!"[51] For the master of Montpelier and point man for the Virginia-led South, that day would progressively recede until it was but a flicker in the imagination of the last of the founding fathers. When the day finally dawned—thirty years after his death—it appeared among the smoldering wreckage of the very Union Madison had made the sine qua non of American felicity.

Preserving that Union included vesting the federal government with the authority to "guarantee to every state . . . a Republican form of Government" and "to protect each of them . . . against domestic violence." The essence of the first part of what would become Article IV, section 4 of the Constitution was among the fifteen items of the Virginia Plan and likely the work of Madison. The domestic violence clause was tacked on, adopted by the Committee of Detail, and given its final gloss by the Committee of Style. Earlier in the convention, Madison had faulted the New Jersey Plan (a strengthened version of the Articles) for failing to provide for the suppression of uprisings such as Shays' Rebellion. It was here that Madison repeated his strictures from the "Vices" on republican government and the tyranny of the minority, concluding that "where slavery exists, the Republican Theory becomes still more fallacious." Now writing as Publius, Madison needed to sanitize his republican doctrine.

By early 1788, critics of the Constitution had charged that it deviated from the republican standard embodied in the state constitutions and, as such, should be rejected. Madison answered the critics in *Federalist* No. 39, a tour de force of clear, compact political reasoning that established the classic definition of a republic. Historically, the name "republic" had been bestowed on governments as diverse in composition as those of Holland, Venice, Poland, and England. The Constitution created a government far more republican than any of these—"a government which derives all its powers directly or indirectly from the people; and is administered by persons holding their offices during pleasure, for a limited period, or during good behavior." As the state constitutions contained such provisions—indirect election, life tenure—these could provide no grounds for objections to the federal charter. Moreover, the Constitution's ban on titles of nobility and "its express guarantee of the republican form" to each state were "decisive" in demonstrating the "republican complexion of this system."

If Madison's definition of a republic was minimalist, it had the virtue of logic and simplicity. And if it elided over the un-republican features in the state governments, it was arguably not his task—as an advocate for a Constitution that tolerated these features—to address them.[52] On the contrary, the interventionist power granted under Article IV (and fear of its abuse) prompted Madison to assure state residents that their current governments were republican in nature.[53] It was "against aristocratic or monarchical innovations" (not existing oligarchies based on a restricted franchise and/or servile labor) that the republican guarantee was directed, and it was "emergencies" like Shays' Rebellion (not revolts of enslaved persons) that the domestic violence clause encompassed. (Madison did not include these parenthetical remarks but they may be reasonably inferred.)

Still, he could not entirely escape reality on the ground, which once more expressed itself in a fear of a tyrannical minority augmented by the ranks of the devious, discontented, and dispossessed. "May it not happen in fine that the minority of CITIZENS may become a majority of PERSONS, by the accession of alien residents, of a casual concourse of adventurers, or of those whom the Constitution of the States has not admitted to the rights of suffrage?"[54]

Neither in the Convention nor in his subsequent "Notes on Government" did Madison explicitly countenance the role enslaved persons might play in such a scenario.[55] Not since Bacon's Rebellion a century prior to American independence had a group of disenfranchised whites led by an "adventurer" made common cause with enslaved and indentured Blacks. Yet a chilling passage from the *Federalist* indicates that he still considered it a possibility: "I take no notice of an unhappy species of population abounding in some of the States, who during the calm of regular government are sunk below the level of men; but who in the tempestuous scenes of civil violence may merge into the human character, and give a superiority of strength to any party with which they may associate themselves."[56]

In a few short years such scenes would be acted out in Saint Domingue and freeze the blood of every Virginia enslaver. It did not, however, lead them to seriously consider emancipation, but to further restrict it. Nor did it move the slavocracy to expand the suffrage or make representation more equitable among free whites. In defining a republic, Madison had declared it "*essential* to such a government, that it be derived from the great body of the society, not from an inconsiderable proportion, or a favored class of it." In his private notes he would deny that Virginia (and other southern states) met this criterion. Were the political leaders of these states merely aristocrats masquerading as republicans under pseudo-republican governments? Strictly speaking, the answer was "yes." However, Madison, a notable player in this masquerade, always saw "more harm than good"—for himself, Virginia, and the nation—arising from efforts to unmask the imposture. In the guise of Publius, however, he would lower his guard to reveal a personal distaste for slavery and its inconsistency with republicanism. On occasion it was subliminal, as when he contrasts a truly republican government with "a handful of tyrannical nobles, exercising their oppressions by a delegation of their powers, [who] might aspire to the rank of republicans, and claim for their government the honorable title of republic." (Could this not pass for a less than charitable description of the Virginia oligarchy?) Elsewhere he writes in a vein that, taken out of context, might be mistaken for a mid-nineteenth-century antislavery constitutionalist. "The more intimate the nature of such a Union may be, the greater interest have the members in the political institutions of each other; and the greater right to insist that the forms of government under which the compact was entered into, should be *substantially* maintained."⁵⁷

The oddly equivocal nature of Madison's remarks on slavery in the *Federalist* culminates with his attempt to unpack and defend the three-fifths clause. Having declared the use of the ratio the "least exceptionable" practical rule for assessing taxes, he proceeds to address objections to its use for representation. If enslaved persons are property subject to taxation, why should they be counted as persons entitled to representation? In providing an answer, Madison—writing northerners—assumes the persona of "one of our southern brethren" to distance himself from the argument. As such, he establishes the plain fact that by law and custom enslaved persons "partake of both these qualities": they are at once property and persons.⁵⁸ In the process, however, he does something remarkable as his cold logic turns to bitter irony. "In being compelled to labor not for himself, but for a master; in being vendible by one master to another; and in being subject at all times to be restrained in his liberty, and chastised in his body, by the capricious will of another, the slave may appear to be degraded from the human rank, and classed those with irrational animals, which fall under the legal denomination of property."⁵⁹

While ostensibly defending the three-fifths compromise, Madison captures the inhumanity and repulsive degradation upon which it was based. This is what treating men like property looked like. In contrast, when viewed as persons, those enslaved were "protected ... against the violence of all others, even the master of his labor and his liberty"; he was "punishable himself for all violence against others" and, as such, was "regarded by the law as a member of society; not as a part of the irrational creation; as a moral person, not as a mere article of property." This is what it meant to treat men as persons, as fully human. Only the law, not nature, had taken away his "rights" and "transformed the negroes into property." And "if the laws were to restore these rights ... the negroes could no longer be refused an equal share of representation with the other inhabitants."

Despite Madison's dispassionate tone, this was antislavery with a vengeance.⁶⁰ Slavery was a degrading, inhumane convention in direct violation of natural right, a "barbarous policy of considering as property a part of their human brethren." As a northerner, Publius had called the southern enslaver his "brethren" and then directed a terse but unmistakable indictment at the "barbarous policy" of slavery, which could never be justified under the forms of law. Even in their degraded condition, "the unfortunate race" of enslaved Africans were equal members of the family of man, the "human brethren" of slaveholders and abolitionists alike.

Here Madison did square the circle. The solution to the problem of slavery lay in the recognition of a common humanity, which he clearly recognized. The slave-hating enslaver of *Federalist* No. 54 was Madison himself, who could condemn slavery unequivocally and yet temporize its existence in the belief that it would one day be eradicated. Slavery was a tragic reality, and the status of enslaved persons "a peculiar one," particularly in a representative republic. Although "debased by servitude below the equal level of free inhabitants," those enslaved were still persons. Let them count, then, as three-fifths of a person, having been "divested of two fifths of the man."

Such frank reasoning has led some observers to pan Madison's performance in *Federalist* No. 54 as "embarrassing," "weird," even "perverse."[61] Others have found "a *constitutional* basis for the emancipation of slaves" in his remarks as Publius.[62] The greater significance lies in the Virginian's willingness to confront the crime of slavery and embrace its eventual abolition in the very process of building a consensus for a Constitution that tolerated it. *Federalist* No. 54 was not so much "a remarkable act of ventriloquism" as the covert confession of a troubled statesman whose personal and political fortunes were entailed to the very institution he despised.[63] This was Madison's triumph and tragedy.

After completing his final contribution to the *Federalist*, Madison set out for Virginia, where he would attend the state's ratifying convention. By June 1788, eight states had ratified the Constitution, one short of the number required for adoption. When the delegates assembled in Richmond, Madison and the supporters of ratification were a minority. Opponents included George Mason, who had refused to sign the Constitution, and Patrick Henry, who had refused to attend the convention. Both men's objections to the document were fundamental and went well beyond its treatment of slavery. In time, however, the status of slavery in the Constitution and its implications for Virginia gave rise to some sharp exchanges on the convention floor.

Mason's objections epitomized the moral confusion that characterized much of the Virginia slavocracy. Repeating his performance in Philadelphia, he denounced the slave trade as "diabolical in itself, and disgraceful to mankind," and yet decried the absence of constitutional protections for enslaved persons currently held. Moreover, he feared the "fatal... dangers" arising from the continued importation of enslaved persons, on the one hand, and the threat of coerced manumission through punitive taxation of enslaved persons, on the other. A wiser Constitution would have provided for the elimination of the slave trade and the security of enslavers.

Madison rose the following day to answer Mason and drove straight to the point: the protection of the slave trade was the price of Union. The Deep South delegates had made it clear that Georgia and Carolina planters would refuse to confederate on any other terms. These planters' investments required access to foreign slave markets, and they would not agree to a ban, only to purchase surplus enslaved persons in Virginia at inflated prices. On the positive side, Virginia could continue to bar the importation of enslaved persons and help secure abolition altogether in twenty years' time. Whatever taxes might be levied on enslaved persons could never amount to a prohibition of the trade or result in the manumission of the enslaved. Moreover, the Constitution's fugitive slave provision was "a better security than any that now exists" for the recovery of runaways. Yes, the continuation of the slave trade was a great evil, but it could not have been terminated "without encountering greater evils." These were the evils of *disunion* that Publius had exhaustively chronicled in the first volume of the *Federalist*. Here Madison lists but one of the "dreadful" consequences—foreign intervention—that might follow.[64]

The "dirty compromise" that preserved the slave trade and the "covenant with death" that preserved slavery were for Madison the price of preserving a political experiment whose failure would not only doom America but permanently tarnish the transcendent cause—liberty through self-government—for which it stood. Slavery was an acknowledged curse in direct conflict with the universalist principles of that cause, which was a strong point in favor of its eventual termination. For Madison, the curse of disunion had nothing in its favor, not even an amelioration in the condition of enslaved persons, and would therefore be a tragedy on even a greater scale than the obscenity of slavery. It was upon this Faustian calculus that Madison—the planter, the statesman, the man—staked all: "Great as the evil is, a dismemberment of the union would be worse."[65]

The dreaded evil would be dodged when Virginia and the remaining states ratified the Constitution. After a decade marked by war and political drift the Union had been secured. For the next thirty years, Madison would occupy center stage in the unfolding drama of the young Republic. Slavery, the "witch at the christening," would occasionally rap a bony knuckle on the doors of Congress, but before the Missouri Crisis (1819) was effectively barred entrance into the national councils. This, of course, did not prevent the growth and expansion of slavery: a development that increasingly bedeviled Madison after he left the White House in 1817. While his work as a nation builder was complete, his struggle with slavery—"the dreadful calamity which has so long afflicted our country and filled so many with despair"[66]—would only end in the silence of the grave.

NOTES

1. James Madison (JM) to Thomas L. McKinney, February 10, 1826, in *The Papers of James Madison* (hereafter PJM), Retirement series, vol. 3, ed. David B. Mattern et al. (Charlottesville: University of Virginia Press, 2016), 684–86.
2. JM to William Wirt, October 12, 1830, Founders Online, National Archives, https://founders.archives.gov/documents/Madison/99-02-02-2184.
3. Madison, "Memorandum on an African Colony for Freed Slaves," ca. October 20, 1789, *PJM*, Congressional series, vol. 12, ed. Charles F. Hobson and Robert A. Rutland, 1979, 437–38.
4. Jefferson sent Madison a copy of the *Notes on Virginia* in May 1785, which summarized the former's rationale and plan for gradual emancipation and removal. Donald L. Robinson, *Slavery in the Structure of American Politics, 1765–1820* (New York: Harcourt, Brace, Jovanovich, 1971), 95.
5. For background details on slavery in Madison's Virginia, see Eva Sheppard Wolf, *Race and Liberty in the New Nation: Emancipation in Virginia from the Revolution to Nat Turner's Rebellion* (Baton Rouge: Louisiana State University Press, 2006); Robert McColley, *Slavery and Jeffersonian Virginia*, 2nd ed. (Urbana: University of Illinois Press, 1973); and John C. Miller, *The Wolf by the Ears: Thomas Jefferson and Slavery* (New York: Free Press, 1977).
6. Madison, "Memorandum on an African Colony," *PJM*, Congressional series, 12:437.
7. JM to Ambrose Madison, December 15, 1785, PJM, Congressional series, vol. 8, ed. Robert A. Rutland and William M. E. Rachal (Chicago: University of Chicago Press, 1973), 442.
8. Madison's views on slavery and emancipation remained remarkably consistent over the course of a long life. He acknowledged privately that slavery was a "moral, political, and economic" evil, embraced the idea of gradual, compensated emancipation, supported efforts to remove and colonize freed enslaved persons, and drew up a plan in retirement to fund emancipation and removal through sales of the national domain. His latter-day reflections on slavery, however, did him little credit. For an outstanding account, see Drew R. McCoy, *The Last of the Fathers: James Madison and the Republican Legacy* (Cambridge: Cambridge University Press, 1989), 253–322.
9. Swaney and Billey were two of nine enslaved persons Madison owned before the death of his father in 1801, when he inherited over one hundred more. Many years earlier he had expressed a desire "to depend as little as possible on the labour of slaves." JM to Edmund Randolph, July 26, 1785, PJM, Congressional series, 8:328. Despite encouragement from his protégé Edward Coles, who freed persons he enslaved, the aged and insolvent Madison failed to do so.
10. JM to William Bradford, June 16, 1775, PJM, Congressional series, vol. 1, ed. William T. Hutchison and William M. E. Rachal (Chicago: University of Chicago Press, 1962), 151–54.
11. The standard source on slavery remains Duncan J. MacLeod, *Slavery, Race, and the American Revolution* (Cambridge: Cambridge University Press, 1974).
12. JM to Joseph Jones, November 28, 1780, PJM, Congressional series, vol. 2, ed. Hutchison and Rachal, 209.

13. Madison, "Memorandum on an African Colony," JM, Congressional series, 12:438.
14. Indeed, in the margin of the letter in which he had warned Robert Pleasants that strident efforts at emancipation in Virginia would lead to further restrictions, Madison later wrote: "it so happened." JM to Robert Pleasants, October 30, 1791, PJM, Congressional series, vol. 14, ed. Robert A. Rutland and Thomas A. Mason (Charlottesville: University of Virginia Press, 1983), 91–92.
15. Madison, "Vices of the Political System of the United States," April 1787, *PJM*, Congressional series, vol. 9, ed. Robert A. Rutland and William M. E. Rachal, 351. Put quite simply, slavery created a "tension in [Madison's] political theory that he was never able to reconcile." Scott J. Kester, *The Haunted Philosophe: James Madison, Republicanism, and Slavery* (Lanham, Md.: Lexington Books, 2008), 99. Kester's study is one of the very few to include a detailed discussion of Madison's views on slavery.
16. Just what qualified as a "republic" or "republicanism" was unclear and contested at the time of the founding. Both ancient and modern "republics" excluded women, bondsmen, and the property-less from full citizenship, without apparent contradiction. The natural right principles of the American Revolution, however, raised troubling questions about the status of at least some of these excluded groups. As Forrest McDonald observes, attempts to skirt the issue by the Founders were not entirely successful, for republicanism "carried with it a number of implications that were not entirely consonant with most Americans' ideas about liberty and property." Forrest McDonald, *Novos Ordo Seclorum: The Intellectual Origins of the Constitution* (Lawrence: University Press of Kansas, 1985), 5.
17. Madison, "Vices of the Political System," *PJM*, Congressional series, 9:351.
18. Max Farrand, ed., *The Records of the Federal Convention* (New Haven: Yale University Press, 1966), 1:318.
19. James Madison, *Federalist* No. 10, in Alexander Hamilton, James Madison, and John Jay, *The Federalist Papers*, ed. Clinton Rossiter (New York: Mentor, 1961), 84 (subsequent citations are to this edition).
20. This "Madisonian moment" should not be confused with the one popularized by Jack Rakove in his prizewinning *Original Meanings: Politics and Ideas in the Making of the Constitution* (New York: Vintage, 1997). For Rakove, Madison faced a moment in time when the fate of republican government hung in the balance. The reading here compounds Madison's task, for slavery presented a practical and theoretical difficulty that not even Machiavelli or the English republicans had to face.
21. Farrand, *Records of the Federal Convention*, 1:135.
22. Madison, "Notes for the National Gazette Essays," ca. December 1791—March 1792, *PJM*, Congressional series, 14:163–64.
23. As Richard K. Matthews writes, "That he elected not to incorporate his thoughts into his public essays can be readily appreciated since he comprehended fully the obvious contradictions." Matthews, *If Men Were Angels: James Madison and the Heartless Empire of Reason* (Lawrence: University Press of Kansas, 1995), 167–68. Prior to Colleen A. Sheehan's study of the "Notes on Government," this critical passage had received little attention from Madison scholars. Sheehan, *The Mind of James Madison: The Legacy of Classical Republicanism* (Cambridge: Cambridge University Press, 2015). A notable ex-

ception is W. B. Allen, who cites the entire passage to illustrate "the specific way in which the Constitution had a liberalizing tendency [in Virginia], apart from constitutional provisions." Allen's curious illustration is worth quoting at length: "To be precise, to the extent that Virginia ceased to be an independent nation and came to be integrated in a national republic, a republic verging dramatically less toward aristocracy than Virginia, Virginia itself would come to participate more in republicanism without effecting so much as a single change in its domestic institutions. The dynamics of democracy, more than any direct provisions of the Constitution, were the source of the antislavery implications of the founding. In that way the political accomplishment of the Constitution of 1787 was to deepen the influence and authority of the Declaration of Independence." Allen, "A New Birth of Freedom: Fulfillment or Derailment?," in *Slavery and Its Consequences: The Constitution, Equality, and Race*, ed., Robert A. Goldwin and Art Kaufman (Washington, D.C.: American Enterprise Institute, 1988), 65–66. In view of Virginia's actual history from the adoption of the Constitution to Madison's death and beyond, this dreamy tableau is pure fantasy.

24. JM to Robert Pleasants, October 30, 1791, *PJM*, Congressional series, 14:91–92.

25. The subject of slavery was notably absent from the key documents that led to the Philadelphia Convention. Neither the call for a convention from Annapolis, the resolution approved by Congress, nor the resolutions of twelve states to attend ever mentioned it. David O. Steward, *The Summer of 1787: The Men Who Invented the Constitution* (New York: Simon & Schuster, 2017), 68. This silence is deceptive, however, for slavery was almost universally understood as a matter left to the states, and once the plan for a strong central government was adopted at the outset of the Convention its status was contested. This made slavery "for the most part . . . a collateral rather than a primary theme" of the proceedings in Philadelphia. Don E. Fehrenbacher, "Slavery, the Framers, and the Living Constitution," in Goldwin and Kaufman, *Slavery and Its Consequences*, 7.

26. Farrand, *Records of the Federal Convention*, 1:35–36.

27. Ibid., 1:486–87.

28. David Brion Davis has suggested as much. "If Madison aimed his arguments against proposals for state equality in the Senate, his tactics presupposed that Southerners would agree that state sovereignty was insignificant compared to Constitutional protections for slavery." Davis, *The Problem of Slavery in the Age of Revolution, 1770–1823* (New York: Oxford University Press, 1999), 106.

29. Farrand, *Records of the Federal Convention*, 1:562.

30. Ibid.,, 2:9–10.

31. Not only Madison "but other southern spokesmen expected that the Senate would be the legislative bastion of the North rather than the South." Leonard L. Richards, *The Slave Power: The Free North and Southern Domination, 1780–1860* (Baton Rouge: Louisiana State University Press, 2000), 46.

32. Farrand, *Records of the Federal Convention*, 2:32, 57.

33. Ibid., 2:111.

34. Paul Finkelman finds "an immediate connection between slavery and the electoral college" in the three-fifths clause but fails to provide any real evidence for it. Finkelman, "The Proslavery Origins of the Electoral College," *Cardozo Law Review* 23 (2002): 1146–

47. Sean Wilentz has called the Electoral College perhaps "the most decisive triumph on behalf of slavery of the entire convention" and credited Madison with the victory. Wilentz, *No Property in Man: Slavery and Antislavery at the Nation's Founding* (Cambridge, Mass.: Harvard University Press, 2018), 70. On further consideration, however, Wilentz found "no evidence to suggest that slavery had anything to do with it." Wilentz, "The Electoral College Was Not a Pro-Slavery Ploy," *New York Times*, April 4, 2019. In either case, Madison and the delegates were undoubtedly aware of the intimate connection between electoral votes and the states' populations of enslaved persons.

35. Farrand, *Records of the Federal Convention*, 2:415. Mary Sarah Bilder argues that this sentence was among those Madison inserted into his notes after the convention to improve his image. If so, it remains consistent with his considered thoughts on slavery. Bilder, *Madison's Hand: Revising the Constitutional Convention* (Cambridge, Mass.: Harvard University Press, 2005), 188–89.

36. JM to Robert Walsh Jr., November 27, 1819, in PJM, Retirement series, vol. 1, ed. David B. Mattern et al. (2009), 548–49.

37. The "dirty compromise" was coined by Paul Finkelman to underscore the sordid nature of the bargain. Finkelman, *Slavery and the Founders: Race and Liberty in the Age of Jefferson* (Armonk, N.Y.: M. E. Sharpe, 1996), 19–29.

38. Farrand, *Records of the Federal Convention*, 1:602.

39. Ibid., 2:364. Martin also opposed the slave trade as "inconsistent with the principles of the revolution and dishonourable to the American character to have such a feature in the Constitution." Madison agreed but would accept its temporary continuation as the price for its termination under the Constitution.

40. Farrand, *Records of the Federal Convention*, 2:416–17.

41. Sean Wilentz has adopted Madison's notion of "no property in men" to rehabilitate those framers who worked to keep references to slavery or its legality out of the Constitution, but he fails to note the dubious basis of Madison's objection to the tax on enslaved persons. Wilentz, *No Property in Man*, xii.

42. Farrand, Records of the Federal Convention, 2: 417.

43. Indeed, "for all the talk of slavery's incongruence with republican principles, and even despite the baby steps being taken in some of the northern states to gradually end the practice, slavery was a national institution woven into the warp and woof of American life. Slavery and slave trading were being practiced almost everywhere in the United States." Patrick Rael, *Eighty-Eight Years: The Long Death of Slavery in the United States, 1777–1865* (Athens: University of Georgia Press, 2015), 76.

44. Farrand, *Records of the Federal Convention*, 2: 443.

45. Madison, who sat on the five-member Committee of Style, may have contributed to the changes in wording that "made it impossible to infer from the passage that the Constitution itself legally sanctioned slavery." Don E. Fehrenbacher, *The Slaveholding Republic: An Account of the United States Government's Relations to Slavery* (New York: Oxford University Press, 2001), 44. The Fugitive Slave Act passed by Congress in 1793, however, would make the inference explicit.

46. Given the earlier clashes over slavery, Paul Finkelman finds "the paucity of debate over the fugitive slave clause . . . remarkable." The lack of opposition may reflect the delegates

fatigue or, "more likely," their failure "to appreciate the legal problems and moral dilemmas" that the measure would pose. Finkelman, *Slavery and the Founders*, 82. Michael J. Klarman, in a thorough account of "Slavery and the Constitutional Convention," considers it "possible that northern delegates regarded the Fugitive Slave Clause as an additional part of the bargain over the foreign slave trade and Congress's power to enact navigation laws." Klarman, *The Framers' Coup: The Making of the United States Constitution* (New York: Oxford University Press, 2016), 293.

47. Farrand, *Records of the Federal Convention*, 2:221.

48. Ibid., 2:559.

49. "It appears that most of the participants in the ratification debates," notes Matthew Mason, "made up their minds about the Constitution independent of the issue of slavery, then used its slavery clauses to attack or defend it." Mason, *Slavery and Politics in the Early American Republic* (Chapel Hill: University of North Carolina Press, 2006), 33.

50. Madison, *Federalist* No. 38, 238.

51. Madison, *Federalist* No. 42, 266.

52. As Forrest McDonald shrewdly observes, "Madison, who had inherited the status of freeman amidst slavery and whose blacks had inherited their status as slaves, preferred a definition that would avoid the sticky question of status and merely considered as republican any system in which the governmental power derived from the consent of the 'public.'" McDonald, *Novus Ordo Seclorum*, 5.

53. Madison, *Federalist* No. 43.

54. Ibid., 277.

55. Rufus King, however, had. After the Committee of Detail's report—which left the slave trade unrestricted and added the domestic violence clause—the Massachusetts delegate wondered if the northern states would be called upon to help put down revolts of enslaved persons in the South. Apparently, "the importance of this observation for the guarantee clause, when King linked it to the possibility of slave insurrections, escaped the notice of the delegates." William M. Wiecek, *The Guarantee Clause of the U.S. Constitution* (Ithaca: Cornell University Press, 1972), 62.

56. Madison, *Federalist* No. 43, 277. Elsewhere William M. Wiecek reads Madison to embrace the domestic violence clause "not only to suppress insurrections, but to repress *nonviolent, extralegal attempts by blacks to secure political power for themselves*" (emphasis added). Wiecek, *The Sources of Antislavery Constitutionalism in American, 1760–1848* (Ithaca: Cornell University Press, 1977), 81. This reading, however, is neither supported by the text nor American experience. For Publius it is only "in the tempestuous scenes of civil violence" (such as Bacon's Rebellion) that enslaved persons assume a role in the balance of forces. See Winthrop D. Jordon, *White over Black: American Attitudes toward the Negro: 1550–1812*, 2nd ed. (Chapel Hill: University of North Carolina Press, 1968), 123.

57. Madison, *Federalist* No. 43, 274.

58. Madison, *Federalist* No. 54, 337.

59. Ibid.

60. Malick W. Ghachem, in an otherwise notable work of creative scholarship, elides over

the antislavery gravamen in this passage to find only a "guarded illusion to the moral lapse that slavery represented." Ghachem, "The Slave's Two Bodies: The Life on an American Fiction," *William and Mary Quarterly*, 3rd ser., 60 (2003): 838.

61. David O. Stewart, *Madison's Gift: Five Partnerships That Built America* (New York: Simon & Shuster, 2015), 53; William Lee Miler, A*rguing about Slavery: The Great Battle in the United States Congress* (New York: Alfred A. Knopf, 1996), 260; Noah Feldman, *The Three Lives of James Madison: Genius, Partisan, President* (New York: Random House, 2017), 214.

62. Andrew Burstein and Nancy Isenberg, *Madison and Jefferson* (New York: Radom House, 2010), 177 (emphasis in original).

63. David Waldstreicher, *Slavery's Constitution: From Revolution to Ratification* (New York: Hill and Wang, 2009), 138.

64. Madison, "Slave Trade and Slave Holders' Rights," June 17, 1788, *PJM*, Congressional series, vol. 11, ed. Robert A. Rutland and Charles F. Hobson (Charlottesville: University Press of Virginia, 1977), 150–51.

65. Ibid., 151.

66. JM to Rev. R. R. Gurley, December 29, 1831, *Founders Online*, National Archives, https://founders.archives.gov/documents/Madison/99-02-02-2495.

The Paradox of Judicial Review

Madison on the Judiciary

MICHAEL P. ZUCKERT

James Madison earned many titles in his long career of public service, including congressman, secretary of state, and president, but never was he chief justice, nor even Judge Madison. Despite having legal training he never was a member of the bar.[1] Nonetheless, he engaged in a remarkable quantity of constitutional interpretation, not only as the chief author of the plan that formed the baseline scheme for the Constitution, not only as the leading member of the Constitutional Convention, but most especially in his career under the new Constitution when, as a member of Congress, as president, and finally as elder statesman he regularly engaged in the kind of constitutional reasoning we now tend to associate almost exclusively with courts, and in doing so he developed a recognizable approach to the Constitution we can plausibly call a jurisprudence.[2] His interpretative activity stretched across the full range of issues raised by the new Constitution—the powers of Congress and president under Articles I and II and the limitations on these powers in the Bill of Rights and elsewhere. Of greatest interest probably is his opinion regarding the power of the courts to settle constitutional issues under Article III.

Philip Hamburger in his comprehensive study, *Law and Judicial Duty*, states the strongest argument I know of for the rootedness of something like judicial review in Anglo-American legal history. Hamburger's chief claim was that what we think of as judicial review was not so much of an innovation and certainly was not a usurpation as it has often been said to be. Rather, judicial duty in English common law courts mandated that judges consider and apply the totality of relevant law in any given case before them. This duty implied as part of normal judicial activity that judges consider the bearing of constitutional principles along with other relevant law to their decisions. In effect, then, Hamburger argues, a power of judicial review was always part of judicial duty in Anglo-American law. This practice, according to Hamburger, was a matter of "judicial ideals," that is, of standard norms governing the practice of judging. He recognizes Madison as something of a dissenter from the story of judicial duty that he tells. Madison spoke "from [a different] perspective ... far above legal ideals rather than situated within them." Madison's position was "drawn as much from political theory as from law." No one, according to Hamburger, "more vigorously espoused" an alternative view, "challenging to [the] traditional ideas of judicial authority" on which Hamburger builds his case, "than James Madison."[3] My goal in this chapter is to look in some detail at this seeming outlier, James Madison on constitutional review. Perhaps paradoxically, I make the case that Madison is both strongly in agreement with that traditional notion of judicial duty but at the same time poses a yet deeper and stronger challenge to that conception of duty.

MADISON'S PARADOX

Madison is among the greatest supporters of Hamburger's thesis about courts and constitutional interpretation. Madison is among the greatest opponents of Hamburger's thesis about courts and constitutional interpretation.

This paradoxical formulation is not mine but was provided, in advance so to speak, by Madison himself. In 1788, a year after the close of the Constitutional Convention, an old Princeton friend, now settled in Kentucky, wrote to Madison seeking advice on a plan for a constitution for the soon-to-be new state of Kentucky. He most particularly sought Madison's advice on the constitutional plan Thomas Jefferson had drafted for Virginia in 1783 and had published with his *Notes on the State of Virginia*. In his reply Madison systematically went through Jefferson's plan, criticizing much of it as unwise and unsuitable.[4] In the course of his comments, Madison came on the topic of constitutional interpretation, or the power to settle disagreements about constitutional meaning among different actors within the constitutional system. In both the federal and state systems, Madison affirmed, "it results to . . . the Courts" to make the "final" judgment on "such questions."[5] That is to say, the power we now call judicial review does indeed belong to courts. He is not among those who believe courts somehow invented their own power of judicial review.[6] Yet Madison also said that this power (or its result) "was never intended, and can never be proper."[7] Madison seems to line up both for and against judicial review. His positions can easily be partially reconciled by noting that he affirms the power as a descriptive matter—the Constitution as it is does provide for it—but he rejects it as a normative matter. But he also rejects it as "never intended" despite granting courts the "final" judgment on constitutional matters.

So far as Madison affirms the power as present in the various American constitutions, he does not mean to say that it is explicitly provided for in so many words. His position appears to be exactly what Hamburger called our attention to as the dominant historical understanding of judicial duty, that is, a recognized "duty of judges to decide in accord with the law of the land."[8] According to Hamburger, "if constitutions willed by the people were part of the law of the land, and if judges had a duty to decide in accord with the law of the land, American judges, like their English predecessors, had no choice but to decide the constitutionality of governmental acts."[9] Thus no special empowerment was needed; what we call judicial review followed as a matter of course from ordinary judicial duty. Madison, a frequent critic of judicial review, nonetheless approaches the issue in close conformity with this paradigm. The power of constitutional review accrues to the courts via their ordinary business of deciding cases under the law. They have a duty, along with other constitutional actors, to consult and take account of the Constitution. They have a special authority on matters of constitutional interpretation because they have the "last say": "as the courts are generally the last in making their decision it results to them, by refusing or not refusing to execute a law, to stamp it with its final character."[10]

Yet Madison has serious reservations about the constitutional role of courts. When the judiciary has the "final say," "this makes the Judiciary Department paramount in fact to the Legislature, which was never intended, and can never be proper."[11] Hamburger notes Madison's dissent from the standard legal position, to his taking a political view, from the "perspective" of "balance of power" among the branches, rather than a legal view.[12]

Although Hamburger is correct so far as he goes, I do not believe he brings out sufficiently the grounds for Madison's hesitations about judicial review, largely because he does not appreciate "Madison's Paradox," that the judicial duty to expound the law of the land includes the Constitution and thus leads more or less automatically to judicial review, but yet that result "can never be proper." Madison's paradox raises two urgent questions: First, how can he say that it "was never intended"? Second, why does he say that it "can never be proper"?

In rejecting constitutional review as "never intended," Madison puzzles us, for he had in this very context just presented an account of how the power derives to courts from the logic of the Constitution, if not from explicit intent. Perhaps that is what he means to say: judicial review per se was not so much intended as that it is an implication of other constitutional principles and structures that were intended.

More likely, however, what Madison has in mind as "never intended" is judicial supremacy over the legislature. That is to say, judicial review may have been implicit in the logic or even explicit in the minds of constitution makers, but whichever it was, judicial "paramountcy" was not intended.[13] Madison is saying that judicial review is a legitimate power of the courts, that is, a power correctly inferred from the constitutional text and structure. It is, however, in a deeper sense, illegitimate. That is the paradox of Madison's position on judicial review.

Its illegitimacy comes to view when the practice is viewed not from the perspective of balance of powers, as Hamburger would have it, but from the now largely forgotten perspective of the original theory of separation of powers. The Supreme Court's special role as most authoritative interpreter of the Constitution derives from its place in the separation of powers scheme, but that role at the same time counters the logic of separation of powers. The courts do not have in themselves a special claim to custody over the Constitution. All branches of the government derive their powers from the Constitution, and all are both empowered by and obliged to consult the Constitution in the course of attempting to discharge their duties. Just as courts are to decide cases according to the law of the land, so the executive is to enforce the law of the land, including the Constitution. Moreover, Congress too derives its powers from the Constitution, and it too is to take its bearings by the Constitution.

Moreover, the three branches are all held to be independent, more or less, and equal. "It is evident that each department should have a will of its own; and consequently should be so constituted, that the members of each should have as little agency as possible in the appointment of the members of the others."[14] None is to have authority over the others such that the separation of powers is overcome. So far as the branches share power it is for the sake of maintaining the separation. Separation of powers theory mandates that the government not be able to act upon citizens in a punitive way without acting through the judiciary. The judiciary is to have the last say, in that it is to determine how the array of laws, including the Constitution, bears on a given case or situation. Separation of powers theory mandates that so far as the other branches (especially the executive) act on or even touch a case decided by the courts, they follow the mandates established by the courts. Nor can the legislature revise the judgments of courts. That is both a violation of the nature of the legislative power, to make general rules and not decide particular cases, and a violation of the judiciary's place in the separation of powers scheme. One of the leading complaints against the constitutional system of the United States that led to the movement for a new constitution in 1787 was the tendency by state legislatures to reverse or revise state court determinations. This practice was understood to be violative of separation of powers principles. In *Federalist* No. 47 Madison quoted "the celebrated Montesquieu" on the evils of legislative intrusion on the judicial function: "were the power of judging joined with the legislative, the life and liberty of the subject would be exposed to arbitrary control, for the judge would then be the legislator."[15] Wielding a power that it has no more than the other branches, the courts thus came, almost by accident—certainly this was not the intent—to have a supremacy over, not an equality with, the other branches by virtue of their having the final say on constitutional matters. These constitutional matters concern not only its own powers, as some commentators have suggested, but all the powers and rights implicated in cases that come before it.

So Madison's paradox comes down to the view that the practice we think of as judicial review is both an implication and a violation of the logic of separation of powers. To appreciate properly Madison's unhappiness at judicial review, one must understand the logic of separation of powers as he did. Contrary to the textbook version of that system, Madison did not understand the system of separation as being for the sake of checks and balances. Indeed, the reverse was the case: checks and balances, requiring a limited and controlled blending of powers, existed to maintain the separation of powers, as his argument in *Federalist* No. 51 makes clear.[16] In brief, the point of having and maintaining the separation of powers, as Madison learned from Montesquieu, was to guarantee, so far as possible, the rule of law in the strong sense of law ruling. The separation of powers was meant to ensure that a properly constructed body, a legislature, would govern only through enacting general rules, which applied to all, including themselves, their friends, and families. The legislature would have to do only with these general rules; so far as the law touched individuals it would do so via the agency of the other two branches. The executive, possessor of the organized or legitimate force of the community, was to bring the law home to individuals through its efforts to enforce or execute the general rules and policies laid down by the legislature. But the executive is limited in what it may do by the requirement that it may act to deprive individuals of life, liberty, or property only via the agency of the judiciary. Thus, if the separation of powers is working properly, the coercive authority of government is applied to members of society only according to the general rules in the law and not arbitrarily. The result, as both Montesquieu and Madison see it, is "liberty," or a sense of security in the citizen body.

Montesquieu's theory of separation of powers is in turn an adaptation of the somewhat more primitive but nonetheless recognizable form of the doctrine that appeared in Locke's *Second Treatise*. The point of the institution in Locke is even clearer than in Montesquieu, although I believe the ultimate point is the same in both. As Locke so insistently says, the aim of government is the securing of the natural rights to life, liberty, and property (or pursuit of happiness, in Jefferson's amended form).[17] The institutional separation of powers is the constitutional means whereby that security in rights is thought most likely to occur.

In the classic Montesquieuean version of separation of powers, to say nothing of in Locke's version, the judiciary has nothing like the power of judicial review. By standing between the citizens and the agents of governance, it casts the protection of law around the citizen and thus fulfills its function. Checking and balancing occurs via the bicameral legislature and the executive veto. Other than its own power to apply the law to individual cases, the judiciary has no separate checking function. It most definitely does not have the power to dictate their powers to the other branches.

In order to fulfill its function within the classic separation of powers scheme, the judiciary must indeed have the last say, but the power of judicial review, as Madison sees it, transcends its proper traditional role of standing between government and citizen, thereby guaranteeing rule of law. Instead, it becomes part of the governing or rule-making structure, indeed in a sense the supreme part. This is not what it should be. So, to conclude this part of the discussion: Madison's paradox turns on the way judicial review both fulfills and violates the logic of separation of powers. His final judgment on it is that it is more illegitimate than legitimate, that is, that its violation of the logic of separation of powers is more important than its fulfillment of that logic. Since the separation is ultimately in the service of securing natural rights, our first conclusion is that, according to Madison, judicial review as we know it is "improper" because of the natural rights aspect of the natural rights republic.

MADISON'S PREFERRED ALTERNATIVE

When we come to Madison's preferred alternative to judicial review, we come to see that its impropriety also arises from its violation of the republican aspect of the natural rights republic. Although often thought to be, Madison was not a partisan of the position known as departmentalism, that is, the view that each branch has the right to judge of its own powers (and often, by implication, of the powers of other branches) with no branch or agency having power to adjudicate or have the final say, for he granted the judiciary the "last say." Madison's alternative to departmentalism was complex. Although departmentalism was in accord with the logic of separation of powers as Madison understood that logic, nonetheless he had two countervailing ideas. First, he was concerned that departmentalism would lead to a disorderly situation where constitutional claims and counterclaims could lead to harmful conflict among the branches and perhaps to stalemate. Secondly, he recognized that although the branches were all equal under the theory of separation of powers, in actuality they were not. The legislature, by virtue of its power of legislation and because of its intimate connections with the people in the republican form of government, had an immensely greater power than the other two branches. Thus, Madison's well-known fears of "the legislative vortex," which could suck into itself the other powers and thereby overcome the separation of powers and endanger liberty.[18] As he frequently said, every form of regime has its own special dangers, and the dangers facing democratic republics come from the legislature, not the executive, as many of his fellow Americans and his friend Thomas Jefferson continued to believe. "Wherever the real power in a government lies, there is the danger of oppression."[19] Where the danger of oppression lies, there safeguards must be constructed.

Madison's preferred safeguard against the dangers deriving from the legislature lay in the construction of a Council of Revision, to be composed of the executive head and some number of the judges. The council was to have a "qualified negative" on acts of the legislature, that is, a veto that could be overridden by a special legislative majority.[20] The council would be empowered to exercise its negative in order to guard against the full range of evils that the legislature might commit. Thus it could act to control unconstitutional acts, but it could also act to control unwise or unjust but not unconstitutional acts. The powers of the Council of Revision were thus thoroughly political powers and not judicial. The council would possess such powers not as an instantiation of the logic of separation of powers or of judicial duty, as with judicial review, but as a positively granted, consciously constructed institution of checking and balancing. In this regard it is on an identical footing with the executive veto that is part of the Constitution as adopted.

Madison proposed his Council of Revision at the Constitutional Convention on many different occasions, failing to persuade the assembly every time. Among the frequently made objections to the proposal was the observation that it violated the logic of separation of powers. It did so in two related ways. First, it would give to judges a power not part of the judicial function, the power to share in making the laws. Secondly, it would compromise the judges in the exercise of the power they did have, the power to expound laws they did not make.[21] The latter point was especially important for delegates who pointed to the courts' possession of the power of judicial review. It would be particularly inappropriate for the judges to whom would accrue the power to determine the constitutionality of legislative acts to have had a hand in making the laws.

Despite these objections, with which he must have had some sympathy, for they appeal to an understanding of the logic of separation of powers like his own, Madison persisted in his advocacy of the Council of Revision. He must have had strong reason to do so. His main reason was that there had to be a check against the "legislative vortex," and this Council of Revision was, in his opinion, the only one that could effectively act this part. At the convention Madison "observed that the great difficulty . . . arose from the nature of republican government, which would not give to an individual citizen that settled pre-eminence in the eyes of the rest, that weight of property, that personal interest agst. betraying the

National interest, which appertain to an hereditary magistrate.... His firmness therefore wd. need support."[22] He thought the judges should be joined to the executive because neither branch alone could stand up to the legislature. The revisionary council would "also enable the Judiciary Department the better to defend itself agst. Legislative encroachment."[23] Moreover, the judges could bring special competences to the examination of the laws. They could supply a voice for clear draftsmanship and consistency of new law with already existing law. They could bring a special sensitivity to justice and rights, developed in the course of their legal training and judicial service. Although Madison understood that his Council of Revision broke with the internal logic of separation of powers, he accepted as a general necessity the need to breach the lines established by that logic from time to time in order to achieve specific goals, chief among them checks and balances to preserve the larger system of separation of powers. Thus, he famously viewed the constitutional mandate that the Senate share with the president the power of appointment to executive office to be a specially carved-out piece of what is in its nature an executive power.[24]

The delegates at the convention were able to accept the principle that sharing of powers was at times necessary, but they could not accept the particular version of shared powers embodied in Madison's proposal for a Council of Revision. The aspect that seems to have been especially problematic to them was the conflict between this institution and its involvement of the judiciary in making law with the power of judicial review that followed from the logic of judicial duty in a constitutional system like this one. Elbridge Gerry of Massachusetts, for example, opposed the joint executive-judicial Council of Revision on the ground that the "Judiciary... will have a sufficient check agst. encroachments... by their exposition of the laws, which involved a power of deciding on their Constitutionality."[25] For one of the few times at the convention, Madison had no reply to objections to one of his favored institutions.

By the time he came to give his advice on the Kentucky constitution a year later he had come up with a response. One of the shortcomings of Jefferson's "draught constitution" is that it contained no provision for a Council of Revision, and Madison considered it essential that a council be included in the planned new constitution for Kentucky. "A revisionary power is meant as a check to precipitate, to unjust, and to unconstitutional laws."[26] He came up with an elaborate scheme for structuring this revisionary power:

> These important ends would... be more effectually secured, without disarming the Legislature of its requisite authority, by requiring bills to be separately communicated to the Executive and Judiciary departments. If either of these object,

let ⅔, if both ¾ of each House be necessary to overrule the objection; and if either or both protest against a bill as violating the Constitution, let it moreover be suspended, notwithstanding the overruling proposition of the Assembly, until there shall have been a subsequent election of the H[ouse] of D[elegate]s and a repassage of bill by ⅔ or ¾ of both Houses, as the case may be. It s[houl]d not be allowed the Judges or the Ex[ecutive] to pronounce a law thus enacted, unconstitu[tional] and invalid.[27]

Madison's elaborate scheme thus has two defining elements. First, he includes a solution to the problem that had eluded him at the convention. The judges are to be explicitly denied the power that would derive from "judicial duty" to pronounce laws unconstitutional when the laws have been vetted by the Council of Revision. The judges will not pass twice on the same laws with regard to their constitutionality. The second feature of his ornate plan is the clear affirmation that the executive/judicial veto can ultimately be overridden by the legislature, with the approval of the people. The legislature and the people represented therein cannot be shunted aside in a republic. As Madison said in his well-known definition of a republic in *Federalist* No. 39: "It is *essential* to such a government, that it be derived from the great body of the society, not from an inconsiderable proportion, or a favored class of it."[28] Although Madison's definition of republic leaves room for much indirect governance via institutions derived at one or two steps removed from the people and only responsible to them indirectly, nonetheless he affirms that ultimate control over the meaning of the Constitution must remain with the constituent body (the people) and the institution best embodying their presence (the legislature), even if trammeled by the super-majority requirement. As with his thinking about separation of powers and rights, Madison is engaged in a delicate balancing act in attempting to provide properly for the republican aspect of the natural rights republic. Madison's central point, then, is that republicanism too speaks against the practice of judicial review as the Constitution embodies it and as we know it.

MADISON'S ACCOMMODATION TO JUDICIAL REVIEW AS PRACTICED

Madison's idea of an executive/judicial conditional revisionary power found no place in the Constitution. Instead, we have the practice of judicial review operating originally more or less according to the logic of judicial duty as explained by Hamburger. Given this imperfection in the Constitution, what did Madison do? Probably the most prominent feature of his attempt to work with the Constitution we have is the development of what George Thomas has called the "Madisonian Constitution," a constitution in which all parts of the constitutional order not only have a right but possess a duty to "expound the Constitution, yielding multiple and conflicting views of the Constitution as an inherent . . . part of the constitutional order."[29]

All through his congressional career Madison provoked and engaged in extended constitutional debates. He regularly resisted those who said it was inappropriate for Congress to take up these issues since the Supreme Court was the proper body to make judgments about constitutional meaning.[30] Although Madison never denied that the courts had the last word in any given case, as the official theory of separation of powers held, he never accepted the broader claim that it was the business of only the courts to interpret the Constitution. This was his way of coping with the impropriety of the "Judiciary Department" being "paramount in fact to the Legislature." As president, he continued to engage in constitutional interpretation, producing some of his most important constitutional expositions.

To explore Madison as a constitutional interpreter would indeed be a major enterprise, well beyond the scope of this chapter. But I do wish to explore two of the best-known and puzzling moments of Madison's post-1788 constitutionalism, for I think the above discussion of his stance toward judicial review helps make good sense of both. The first is his doctrine of state interposition as asserted in the 1798 Virginia Resolutions and defended in the Virginia Report of the following year. The other is his reversal of himself on the constitutionality of a national bank in 1816 as defended at some length in 1831.

A few preliminary comments are necessary before we consider Madison's approach to constitutional interpretation in his Virginia Resolutions and Report. First, a reminder of the context. In 1798 the Federalist Party controlling Congress passed a series of laws, the Alien and Sedition Acts, aimed at controlling the democratic unrest surrounding the French Revolution and the war between France and most of the other European powers, into which, willy-nilly, the United States was threatened to be pulled. Madison, Jefferson, and other leaders of the Republican Party considered these laws thoroughly unconstitutional but had little hope of having their view underwritten in any branch of the general government, all of which were at the time in the hands of the ranks-closing Federalist Party. As part of their campaign against these laws, Madison and Jefferson turned to the states, with the former drafting a set of resolutions against the acts for the Virginia legislature and the latter drafting resolutions adopted in Kentucky.

My second preliminary comment: under no circumstances should we treat the two sets of resolutions as identical with each other or attribute to Madison any sentiments in Jefferson's draft that Madison does not himself endorse. Most revealing for present purposes is the response of the other state legislatures to which Kentucky and Virginia sent their resolutions, hoping to rally them to the cause of opposition to the Alien and Sedition Acts. The other legislatures for the most part failed to side with the protesting states and, most to the point, even hesitated to engage the claims of unconstitutionality raised in the resolutions. Thus the Rhode Island legislature replied: "*Resolved*, that in the opinion of this legislature, the second section of the third article of the Constitution of the United States . . . vests in the Federal Courts, exclusively, and in the Supreme Court of the United States, ultimately, the authority of deciding on constitutionality of any act or law of the Congress of the United States."[31] Rhode Island's second resolution went on to draw the conclusion: it is illegitimate for a state legislature to do what Virginia and Kentucky's had done, to pronounce on the constitutionality of congressional legislation.[32]

The issue became, if it was not from the first, whether the two states had the right and power to do what they purported to do in the resolutions. In the Virginian Resolutions Madison had defended the power of the states to pronounce on constitutionality in terms of a theory of the union that in later times was to become notorious for its connection to the secessionist movement. Most significant in this respect was the third Virginia Resolution:

> That this Assembly doth explicitly and peremptorily declare that it views the powers of the Federal government as resulting from the compact to which the states are parties, as limited by the plain sense and intention of the instrument constituting that compact; as no further valid than they are authorized by the grants enumerated in the compact; and that in case of a deliberate, palpable and dangerous exercise of other powers not granted by the said compact, the states, who are parties thereto, have the right to interpose for arresting the evil, and for maintaining within their respective limits the authorities, rights, and liberties appertaining to them.[33]

Three items in Resolution 3 are particularly noteworthy. First, Madison endorses a theory of the states as the parties to the "compact" that made the union and the Constitution. Second, he affirms a right of the states as compactors to judge the bounds of the constitutional authority of the general government. And third, he affirms a power of state interposition, "for arresting the progress of the evil."

All three of these elements played a role in the later conflict leading up to the Civil War. But just as one cannot identify Madison's position with Jefferson's, so one may not, without more ado, identify it with John C. Calhoun's either. Madison denied later that his Virginia Resolutions and Report were a foundation for

Calhounian doctrines such as state sovereignty within the union, or the right of nullification, or the right of secession. Although a full-scale treatment of all these themes is beyond the scope of this chapter, I do wish to express my view that Madison is correct in his claim, and I attempt to show that so far as I can within the bounds set by my topic.[34]

It is sometimes said that in claiming that "the powers of the Federal government . . . [result] from a compact to which the states are parties," Madison had changed his mind, under the influence of Jefferson or of political developments of the 1790s from what he had believed at the time of the making of the Constitution. This is not a viable claim, as is clear from Madison's account of the juridical bases of the Constitution in *Federalist* No. 39: "it appears . . . that the Constitution is to be founded on the assent and ratification of the people of America, given by deputies elected for the special purpose; but . . . this assent and ratification is to be given by the people, not as individuals composing one entire nation; but as composing the distinct and independent states to which they respectively belong. It is to be the supreme authority in each state, the authority of the people themselves."[35] Madison would defend his interpretation of the origin of the union by pointing to the fact that a majority of the delegates to ratifying conventions, summed over the whole nation, could not commit the United States as a whole to the new Constitution, but that only each state, state by state, could commit to the Constitution. Madison did not believe that the states as original parties to the union thereby had a power or right to leave the union as they had entered it, nor even a right to disregard, that is, nullify, the laws made by Congress. He was careful to say that states had a right to "interpose," without carefully defining what this meant. His later testimony denies that interposition is equivalent to nullification, and in 1800, in his defense of the third Virginia Resolution, he is careful not to specify in too great detail what he means by this opaque term. He leaves open a range of interpretation of what state interposition might involve. It is certainly at least what the two states were attempting to do in the Resolutions: to sound the alarm and attempt to rally opinion in other states against the offending laws. Madison does not endorse, but he does not explicitly reject, stronger measures. Thus, one could read something like nullification into it, but more likely what Madison actually had in mind, as he described it later, was the role of the states in passing amendments or, if all else fails, the "extra and ultra right" to exercise the natural right of revolution.[36]

Whatever other points Madison had in mind, it is valuable to locate the Virginia Resolutions in the context of Madison's reservations about judicial review as expressed in his comments on Jefferson's "draught constitution." In that comment he raised objections to judicial supremacy on both separation of powers and on republicanism grounds. One response is to encourage constitutional reflection and assertion in all parts of the general government. Almost strictly parallel is his effort to foster constitutional reflection and assertion in the states as well. Madison's in-advance reply to those who say the states have no right to engage in constitutional interpretation is his emphasis on the states as parties to the compact; they are parties in the sense that they are the original source of the powers of the general government, and they remain as the bearers of the powers they did not give up. As such they have a right, as integral members of the total constitutional system, to judge their own and, by implication, the constitutional powers of Congress. Their claims in this regard are not radically different from those of Congress or the president. In what he actually says, apart from ambiguities that may hint at more, Madison does not grant the states any more powers of constitutional interpretation than he does Congress or the president. The final say in any given case remains with the federal judiciary, but this fact does not foreclose continued constitutional activity by the states, as well as by the other federal branches. This activity prevents constitutional issues from becoming the exclusive preserve and specialization of the courts and at least moves toward shoring up the republican bona fides of constitutional interpretation in the system as a whole.

A related puzzle in Madison's constitutional understanding can also be clarified by considering his reservations and ideal solution to the problem posed by judicial review. In 1791 when Hamilton first proposed that Congress charter a national bank, Madison delivered a strong statement in Congress holding the bill to be beyond the powers of Congress. But in 1816, as president, he signed a bill reauthorizing the bank. How could he do both? In 1831, in response to just that query, Madison wrote an extensive defense of his acceptance of the bank in 1816. The key part of that defense was this:

> The act originally establishing a bank had undergone ample discussion in its passage through the several branches of the government. It had been carried into execution throughout a period of twenty years with annual legislative recognition; in one instance, with a positive ramification of it into a new state; and with the entire acquiescence of all the local authorities, as well as of the nation at large; to all of which may be added, a decreasing prospect of any change in public opinion adverse to the constitutionality of such an institution. A veto from the Executive, under these circumstances ... would have been a defiance of all the obligations derived from a course of precedents amounting to the requisite evidence of the national judgment and intention.[37]

Madison's rationale for signing the bank bill is very close to the arrangement he looked to in a more "proper" constitutional system for constitutional interpretation. He proposed, it will be recalled, a conditional constitutional negative, a negative that could be overridden by a special majority where an election intervened between the original decision to override and the final decision to do so. Such an arrangement, he believed, would be more consonant with the requisites of republicanism, such that the deliberate democratic will of the people ultimately prevailed. The details differ in the actual case from Madison's ideal solution, but Madison showed the way to a practice within the Constitution that is a step toward the constitution that should be.

Contrary to many of the usual views of Madison, I think I have shown what rhyme and reason there was to what seems to have been his wavering and changeable views on the judiciary and constitutional review over the course of his career. It should also be clear that Madison would not be a supporter of those who invoke his authority on behalf of an enthusiastic endorsement of judicial activism.[38] His reservations against majority tyranny and the legislative vortex did not extend to favoring the strong empowerment of an activist and independent judiciary.

NOTES

1. Mary Sarah Bilder, "James Madison, Law Student and Demi-Lawyer," *Law and History Review*, 28 (2010): 389–449.
2. See, e.g., Michael Zuckert, "The Sound of the Third Hand Clapping," in *McCulloch v. Maryland at 200*, ed. Gary Schmitt and Rebecca Burgess (Washington, D.C.: AEI, 2020), 39–50.
3. Philip Hamburger, *Law and Judicial Duty* (Cambridge, Mass.: Harvard University Press, 2008), 550.
4. For contextual information, see Marvin Meyers, ed., *The Mind of the Founder: Sources of the Political Thought of James Madison*, rev. ed. (Hanover, N.H.: University Press of New England, 1981), 34.
5. James Madison, "Observations on the 'Draught of a Constitution for Virginia,' c. October 15, 1788," in *James Madison: Writings*, ed. Jack N. Rakove (New York: Library of America, 1999), 417.
6. See, for instance, Hamburger, *Law and Judicial Duty*, 1–2.
7. Madison, "Observations on the 'Draught,'" 417.
8. Hamburger, *Law and Judicial Duty*, 2.
9. Ibid., 612.
10. Madison, "Observations on the 'Draught,'" 417.
11. Ibid.

12. Ibid., 550–51.
13. That judicial review was consciously intended by the framers is clear from the reaction by delegates to Madison's proposal for a Council of Revision, For details, see Michael Zuckert, "Judicial Review and the Incomplete Constitution: A Madisonian Perspective on the Supreme Court and the Idea of Constitutionalism," in *The Supreme Court and the Idea of Constitutionalism,* ed. Steven Kautz, Arthur Melzer, Jerry Weinberger, and M. Richard Zinman (Philadelphia: University of Pennsylvania Press, 2009) 64–69. Also see Jack Rakove, "James Madison and the Judicial Power," National Constitution Center, https://constitutioncenter.org/debate/special-projects/a-madisonian-constitution-for-all/essay-series/james-madison-and-the-judicial-power, 6–7, 9.
14. *Federalist* No. 51, in Alexander Hamilton, James Madison, and John Jay, *The Federalist,* ed. Jacob Cooke (Middletown, Conn.: Wesleyan University Press, 1961), 348 (subsequent citations are to this edition). In general, see Madison's analysis in Federalist Nos. 47–51.
15. *Federalist* No. 47, 326.
16. For more on this topic, see "Judicial Review and the Incomplete Constitution," in Kautz et al., *Supreme Court and the Idea,* 58–60.
17. John Locke, *Two Treatises on Government* (Cambridge: Cambridge University Press, 1992, 2.3, 123.
18. See James Madison, *Federalist* No. 48, 256–57; Rakove, "James Madison and the Judicial Power," 2.
19. James Madison to Thomas Jefferson, October 17, 1788, in Rakove, *James Madison: Writings,* 421.
20. Max Farrand, *The Records of the Federal Convention of 1787* (New Haven: Yale University Press, 1966), 1:21.
21. For more on this, see "Judicial Review and the Incomplete Constitution," in Kautz et. al., *Supreme Court and the Idea,* 65–69.
22. Farrand, *Records of the Federal Convention,* 1:138.
23. Ibid.
24. See James Madison, "Speech in Congress on Presidential Removal Power, June 16, 17, 1789," in Rakove, *James Madison: Writings,* 456.
25. Farrand, *Records of the Federal Convention,* 1:97.
26. Madison, "Observations on the 'Draught,'" 417.
27. Ibid.
28. James Madison, *Federalist* No. 39, 194 (emphasis in original).
29. George Thomas, *The Madisonian Constitution* (Baltimore: Johns Hopkins University Press, 2008), 15.
30. Consider "Report on the Alien and Sedition Acts," in Rakove, *James Madison: Writings,* 608–62.
31. See Henry Steele Commager, ed., *Documents of American History,* vol. 1, *To 1898,* 7th ed. (New York: Appleton-Century-Crofts, 1963), 184.

32. Ibid.
33. James Madison, "Virginia Resolutions against the Alien and Sedition Acts, December 21, 1798," in Rakove, *James Madison: Writings*, 589.
34. For Madison's later views on these matters, see James Madison to Edward Everett, August 28, 1830, in Rakove, *James Madison: Writings*, 842–52; and "Notes on Nullification, 1835–1836," in Meyers, *Mind of the Founder*, 417–42.
35. Madison, *Federalist* No. 39, 196. For nearly identical language, see Madison, "Report on the Alien and Sedition Acts, January 7, 1800," in Rakove, *James Madison: Writings*, 610.
36. Madison to Everett, August 28, 1830, 848.
37. James Madison to Charles Jared Ingersoll, June 25, 1831, in Meyers, *Mind of the Founder*, 393.
38. E.g., Rakove, "James Madison," 13.

"A Faultless Plan Was Not to Be Expected"
Madison and the Separation of Powers

DAVID J. SIEMERS

Was James Madison principled and consistent in his approach to politics, or was he more calculating and opportunistic? This question has prompted much scholarly work, but it has centered primarily around Madison's approach to the federal relationship. A recent historiographical summary notes that the evidence in this regard does "not inspire confidence in Madison's credibility, and . . . raise[s] real questions about consistency-thesis advocates who hang so much on Madison's" own claims of fidelity to his ideals.[1] Alan R. Gibson disagrees in his summary of scholars who "establish . . . broad threads of consistency within Madison's political thought that unify his goals and commitments."[2] Gordon S. Wood adds an essential coda to this scholarly dispute. Many *want* to find James Madison consistent, but that would have required significantly more foresight than anyone could possibly have.[3] The unpredictable twists and turns of practical politics force even those with great insight to think and act innovatively and even inconsistently when confronted with new situations. This warning applies to those emphasizing Madison's inconsistency as well as to those touting his consistency. The very nature of politics requires anyone involved in it for long periods of time to adapt, adjust, and evolve.

Notably absent from the "threads of consistency" Gibson describes is the separation of powers. It challenged Madison through the years. Assessing Madison's consistency or inconsistency concerning the separation of powers is as important as figuring out how he approached federalism, because his work in this area was influential and innovative.

Recent writing has elucidated key points in Madison's thinking. Michael Zuckert points out that Madison understood the work of each branch as an essential competency of government, to be safeguarded and preserved. Thus, "checks and balances are for the sake of separation of powers," preserving the distinctive work of each branch instead of the powers being "separated for the sake of checking and balancing" government activity.[4] George Thomas stresses the "agonistic" nature of the "Madisonian Constitution." Constitutional contests between institutions are not a nuisance in the Madisonian system; they are a purposeful, vital, and a welcome part of the Constitution's institutional design.

The nation's functional constitutionalism is shaped by these dynamics and had to be shaped by it, as no written constitution can be implemented without figuring out practical matters on the fly.[5] Jeremy D. Bailey writes that we are misled by the ratification era into thinking that Madison wanted each branch to mediate and tame the public will. Later developments show Madison being at least as committed to energy in government and popular rule as he was in stability, with profound implications for the political branches. Bailey concludes that Madison was thus much more comfortable with presidential leadership and coordination between the political branches than we typically give him credit for.[6]

These are admiring views, as are, typically, textbooks, which credit the "Madisonian system" of checks and balances for preserving the American government and preventing tyranny. Popular works tout Madison's separation of powers prowess. William F. Connelly Jr. provocatively argues that "James Madison Rules America" in large part because of the Madisonian Constitution's institutional flexibility. The "history of the separation of powers consists of frequent pendulum swings between the executive and legislative branch" that preserve the system of government while addressing the nation's challenges.[7] Madison is described by Lynne Cheney as the political equivalent of a Mozart or an Einstein in 1787, and Richard Brookhiser describes Madison as having "invented" politics as we know it.[8] But if he could not have been so prescient regarding federalism, could he have been regarding the separation of powers?

In this chapter I argue that we extend Madison too much credit for foresight and design in 1787, but too little for his understanding that the separation of powers is a matter of ongoing construction and negotiation within a working republic. Practical politics challenged and altered Madison's original understanding of the separation of powers. There are bound to be slippages between theory and practice when someone acts as a theorist of politics and then as a politician. This should not prompt cynicism or despair. It is an indication that separation of powers issues are complex, inevitably responsive to a variety of inputs and part of a web of competing political values.

This chapter opens by examining Madison's long-term hopes for the separation of powers juxtaposed against the broad scope of American practice. Madison's goal for the three "tectonic plates" of government, the legislative, executive, and judicial branches, was to not have any of them move over and subsume another. This required enabling each to preserve its own designated function. But this macro-level understanding of separation of powers dynamics was significantly underinformed, as later developments demonstrate.

Madison also thought very seriously about micro-level causes of how the separation of powers might shift or be undermined in the conduct of everyday politics. Three separation-of-powers challenges identified in The *Federalist* are covered in a second section: the conceptual fuzziness of the three divisions of power, practical political necessities that would prompt departures from separation-of-powers norms, and partisan zeal, which might also limit dedication to the more abstract principle of separating powers. Each may warp the desired power relations within a republican government.

Madison the political practitioner would be tested himself in each of these three areas, and the rest of this chapter focuses on one example of each type of challenge from Madison's subsequent political career. Already in the First Congress Madison confused his House colleagues about who could control government officers. He bowed to political necessity as secretary of state, temporarily putting aside separation-of-powers concerns in the initial administration of the Louisiana Territory. And his zeal for American sovereignty led him to undermine the Jay Treaty, even as many of his co-partisans abandoned their opposition. Madison the embedded politician did not remain fully faithful to the understandings and standards set forth by Madison the constitutional theorist of 1787. But that was, to a large degree, inevitable. He continued to learn how the separation of powers worked, and he balanced its requirements with other important political values in a pragmatic ongoing constitutionalism.

SUCKED INTO THE LEGISLATIVE VORTEX

Madison's ratification-era approach to the separation of powers was animated by a very specific problem: power migrating across branches of republics. In his understanding, legislatures were almost exclusively to blame, as they consistently encroached on executive and judicial functions. So in the Philadelphia Convention he noted to his fellow delegates that "experience in *all the states* had evinced a powerful tendency in the Legislature *to absorb all power* into its vortex."[9] His April 1787 "Vices of the Political System" memo written in preparation for the Philadelphia Convention concentrates mainly on the deficiencies of the Confederation, but when it turns to problems within the states, it settles blame exclusively on legislative assemblies. The state legislatures passed too many laws, the laws were changed too often, and they were frequently unjust.[10] Citizens in monarchies were rightly fearful of executive power; however, the fresh experiences of the American states showed that the primary danger in republics came from overbearing legislatures.[11]

The placement of power among institutions would have to be altered. Madison came to the Philadelphia Convention with "a strong bias in favor of an enumeration and definition of the powers necessary to be exercised by the national

Legislature" to prevent it from going beyond its stated powers.[12] Critically, he also favored provisions that would fortify the executive and judicial branches. Other priorities, like bicameralism, would check the legislature internally.

This was a self-conscious, theory-based correction to the American response to the Revolution, during which states had erected strong legislatures and weak executives to avoid any semblance of monarchism. It was also a rejection of a particular kind of separation-of-powers thinking that M. J. C. Vile calls the "pure doctrine of the separation of powers": the legislature should have the exclusive right to legislate, the executive should be exclusively responsible for executing the laws and no more, and the judiciary would only adjudicate legal controversies within courts of law. This was the most prevalent view of this concept until ratification.[13]

Experience informed Madison that attempts to enact this doctrinal view failed in two ways. First, to the extent that the powers could be separated in this way, the legislative branch would have such stark advantages that it would come to predominate.[14] Second, practical adjustments to the "pure doctrine" of the separation of powers were inevitable. No state's practices actually conformed to it. In fact, there was "not a single instance in which the several departments of power have been kept absolutely separate and distinct."[15] Nor did Montesquieu, endlessly cited by the Anti-Federalists in their favor, envision such a formulaic separation either.[16]

So Madison worked to develop a different understanding of the separation of powers, one that would effectively safeguard the ability of each branch to wield primary responsibility for its distinctive function. No branch was to fundamentally shape or control a major function of government other than its own. On this understanding select powers could thus be moved by constitutional rule or even shared between branches. In fact, this would *have to be done* to preserve the particular role of each branch.

Given this understanding, the U.S. Constitution did not violate separation of powers expectations. Rather, it fulfilled them, in that it granted each branch sufficient defensive power to fend off interbranch challenges to their own distinctive work. In this way, the Constitution anticipated the panoply of descriptions offered about institutional dynamics in the American system: Edward S. Corwin's "invitation to struggle," Richard E. Neustadt's "system of separated institutions sharing powers," James A. Thurber describing Congress and president as "rivals for power," and George Thomas describing an "agonistic" institutional system.[17]

It is hard to overestimate the extent to which Madison intended the specific checks written into the Constitution to be directed at the legislative branch. Since the legislative branch "necessarily predominates" in a republic, devising effective measures to keep it from overstepping its constitutional bounds was essential.[18] Bicameralism, staggered elections, different constituencies, and the ability of each chamber to make its own rules were all in service of keeping the legislature in its proper lane.[19] The veto and the independent presidential selection process would enable the chief executive to resist congressional encroachments on executing the law.[20] He triumphantly observed that the convention "so contrive[ed] the interior structure of the government as that its several constituent parts may, by their mutual relations, be the means of keeping each other *in their proper places.*"[21]

In retrospect, it would be hard to conclude that Madison was right about the legislature "necessarily" predominating. Institutional power ebbs and flows, subject to a wide array of contextual factors, as well as human agency. There have been times in American political history where Congress has appeared predominant, but others where Congress has clearly subordinated itself to presidential leadership. Charles O. Jones suggests that these eras of dominance are exceptions and that a "tandem institutions" model, with presidency and Congress working as rough equals, is a better overall explanation of institutional power.[22] Predominance and equality are very different descriptors of interbranch power, of course.

The last hundred years of American history demonstrate that executive power, at least in a developed nation with a large administrative apparatus, is far more resilient, adaptable, and encompassing than Madison believed it would be in 1787.[23] Presidents have invented and exploited numerous mechanisms to make unilateral decisions, from executive orders and executive agreements to signing statements and declarations of emergency. To a great degree Congress has acquiesced, willingly delegating a great deal of its decision-making authority to the "administrative state," headed by the president. This administrative state is powerful because, quite simply, there is a great deal to administer. The judiciary, too, has grown significantly in stature, particularly in recent decades, as it has asserted for itself the role of the definitive arbiter of the Constitution and status as (at least) a "coequal branch."[24] Scholars have discerned a tendency toward judicialization, in which governmental decisions in longstanding democracies become more and more prone to judicial settlement, with the United States being a case in point.[25] Likewise, we are now more familiar with the collective action problems that generally plague legislatures far more than any other branch, seeming to limit their effectiveness and proactivity.

In short, there was a great deal more to be known about how government institutions in republics worked than what had been discerned by 1787. There was also a great deal yet to be discovered about how the institutions of the American national government would work. Madison's Vices Memo lamented that the state legislatures were too active—they made too many laws. Madison idealistically thought that a more functional republic would make fewer laws, but that was not to be. Decade by decade there would be more laws and more complicated laws to administer, which meant ever greater activity and discretion for the executive. There would also be more foreign policy, also requiring more executive activity. The Senate and, especially, the House of Representatives would grow, exacerbating their collective action challenges.

Unsurprisingly, Madison's thinking in 1787 did not encompass the full set of factors that alter institutional power in separated systems. He also could not possibly have foreseen the depth of the collective action problems that plague large legislatures, as the state legislatures were quite small at the time. All this means that there are substantial separation-of-powers dynamics that escaped his grasp when he helped formulate the Constitution and argued in favor of ratification. At the time of the Philadelphia Convention Madison possessed an epistemic certainty about power dynamics in a republic that was too high. This certainty was informed by just twelve years of experience in a single subcontinental setting with polities that were substantially similar to each other. This was not a malicious error, but it did require course correction, prompting a change in tactics and the formation of an opposition political party. Madison could remain normatively dedicated to a legislature-centered polity through his life, but after the early 1790s he knew this was not a descriptive inevitability, reversing one of the things he was most sure about in 1787.

THREE SEPARATION OF POWERS CHALLENGES IN THE FEDERALIST

Madison's ratification-era rethinking and rearguing of norms occurred at the macro-level: how did those tectonic plates of the legislative, executive, and judicial departments move over time? How could they be made to grind against each other, without overlapping? What constitutional arrangements would reliably preserve the ability of each branch to do its own work? He also engaged in micro-level analysis about the nature of separation-of-powers challenges. Much of his institutional thinking in *The Federalist* is dedicated to why those in positions of public trust make decisions that eventuate in the migration of power across branches, and it is here where Madison displayed much greater insight than he did about the macro-level tendencies of the three departments of republican government.

By 1787 Madison had learned from his experiences that separation-of-powers standards were compromised by the fuzziness of the conceptual divisions of power themselves (*Federalist* No. 37), by exigencies of the public good that required action out of step with constitutional divisions of power (*Federalist* Nos. 38 and 42), and by "partisan zeal" (*Federalist* No. 50). Each of these three was part of Madison's lived experience, but they were worth distinguishing because the motives involved differed, as did their justifications and effects.

Madison hinted at the conceptual fuzziness of the separation of powers in his letter to Thomas Jefferson outlining the results of the Philadelphia Convention. The main point of the letter was to lament that the national government's sovereignty would likely be compromised by the states. This prompted Madison to discuss several matters that were distinct in theory, but not in practice. His last example was the separation of powers. He wrote to his political ally that "even the boundaries between the Executive, Legislative & Judiciary powers, though in general so strongly marked in themselves, consist in many instances of mere shades of difference."[26]

Federalist No. 37 raises the same issue. As Madison began his major series of twenty-two essays, he embedded his observation within more general comments, counseling readers not to expect perfection in government. He couched his comments within a discussion of epistemology and the science of perception: "no skill in the science of government has yet been able to discriminate and define, with sufficient certainty, its great three provinces—the legislative, executive, and judiciary . . . questions daily occur in the course of practice, which prove the obscurity which reigns in these subjects, and which puzzle the greatest adepts in political science."[27] This "political science" was different from hard science. Madison noted that taxonomists made errors solely because they lacked the ability to see the fine distinctions that nature had made, which were "perfectly accurate." The concepts of government were, by their nature, less than perfectly distinct. In "the institutions of man . . . the obscurity arises as well from the object itself [in addition to] the organ by which it is contemplated."[28] Even with a well-crafted constitution, separation-of-powers dilemmas would be frequent. Their particular shape cannot be anticipated until politics is actually practiced under it. Human imperfection will always make the separation of powers a work in progress. The inevitable shape of human things, as opposed to natural things, is to be somewhat imprecise.

Of the three challenges outlined by Madison, this is the least problematic. Novel situations routinely and innocently crop up that defy the easy application of prior standards. The very fuzziness of these divisions allows for a variety of resolutions and for realistic justifications of what might be decided upon.

Federalist No. 38 raises a second reason why interbranch boundaries are transgressed: political exigency and the public good. The lack of power in the central government had often forced the Confederation Congress to exceed the terms of the Articles of Confederation in practice. The legislature expanded its own powers unilaterally and created new executive powers where none were authorized. The example Madison turned to in *The Federalist* was the disposition of western lands. With the conclusion of the Revolutionary War, the nation's boundaries had become clear. Congress prevailed upon states with claims of land beyond the Appalachian Mountains to cede them to the national government. This effort was largely successful. Congress then formed territorial boundaries, erected governments in them, and populated them with the necessary officials. It also set out the conditions under which these territories could become states. "All this has been done," Madison noted, "without the least color of constitutional authority."[29]

Instead of blaming the Confederation Congress for its work, or expressing qualms about it, Madison voiced unequivocal support. In taking this stance he was supporting himself, of course, as he had been directly involved. His discussion concluded by observing, "I am sensible they could not have done otherwise. The public interest, the necessity of the case, imposed upon them the task of overleaping their constitutional limits."[30] Madison, often thought to be among the most constitutionally scrupulous of American politicians, was ready to engage in a kind of legislative prerogative. An inadequate constitution might place the legislature in the position of defining its own authority. Under these conditions a legislature could act in the public good outside of the bounds of a constitution.

This was far from Madison's first choice. He was among those who designed amendments to grant the national government greater authority "that would empower Congress to use military and economic sanctions against recalcitrant states."[31] Most of these amendments never came up for a vote, because it was clear they would fail the required unanimous endorsement of the states. But exceeding the constitutional powers of the Articles hardly seemed like a last resort for Madison either. The Confederation Congress had also exceeded its authority in regulating commerce and conducting diplomacy.[32] Heads of departments—those entrusted with executing legislative directives—had gone beyond lawful bounds as well, and Madison often supported them.[33] Madison observed in *Federalist* No. 42 that "a list of the cases in which Congress have been betrayed, or forced by the defects of the Confederation, into violations of their chartered authorities, would not a little surprise those who have paid no attention to the subject."[34]

The Confederation's primary problem was a lack of central power. This created the necessity of a legislature expanding its own authority. It also fostered separation-of-functions tensions, despite (or maybe due to) the fact that there was no independent executive or judicial branch. Where the separation of functions was clearly defective, political actors were justified in defining their own powers to meet the public good. What is much less clear is how quickly, or under what precise conditions, James Madison would fly to such an expedient under a better constitution. By definition, such a move would have to be justified by the pursuit of the public good, but it would also be highly problematic, especially under a good constitution, because it would violate what he called the "sacred principle" of the separation of powers and create a precedent for ignoring constitutional strictures.[35]

A third reason that the separation of functions was vulnerable was much more problematic. The views of partisans were often so ardent that they would not heed constitutional barriers if given the chance to overrun them. His primary example in *The Federalist* was Pennsylvania's "Council of Censors," which convened in 1783–84 to determine if the state constitution had been violated and to right any wrongs that may have occurred. In theory, charging a special body with examining the state's fidelity to its constitution was a good idea. In practice, Madison stressed that it produced a worse result than doing nothing.

Madison argued in *Federalist* No. 50 that if constitutional controversies were submitted to citizens for a decision, it would inflame public passions, fail to solve the underlying problem, and degrade the constitution's standing among the public. It was clear that Pennsylvania's "constitution had been flagrantly violated by the legislature in a variety of important instances."[36] If independent, knowledgeable, well-meaning individuals would populate the Council of Censors, then these problems might have been fixed. But that did not happen, because the same individuals who had violated the state constitution in the first place were selected to serve on the council, and they ardently continued their prior fight in this new venue. Madison stressed that the selection of interested parties was probably inevitable, preventing such a plan from working.[37] His illustration of the inability of "the people" to solve constitutional controversies becomes a story about how hardened political parties are often unable to remain faithful to the constitutional separation of functions between branches.

This last cause of separation-of-functions failures was far more worrisome than disputes over minor boundary issues. It was not a result of innocent confusion, nor of practical necessity, but of an ardent spirit and even willful malice toward constitutional boundaries. Partisans often elevate their programmatic wishes over separation-of-powers rules and norms. Madison hoped that the extended republic might help solve this problem because it required majorities at the national level to be diverse coalitions. This presumably made them less ardent about any specific policy. However, he would find out, and very quickly, that even in the extended republic party politics was able to produce majorities that threatened the separation of powers.

"SEPARATE AND DISTINCT" OR INSTITUTIONS SHARING POWERS?

Among the first tests for the Constitution's separation of powers was the "removal" debate of June 1789. Some of Madison's fellow House members believed that the president should not have the power to remove officers from their positions unilaterally. They reasoned that if the Senate had a hand in approving cabinet officers, the Senate should have an equal say in relieving them of their duties. Some argued that the impeachment mechanism should be employed. Madison, hoping to build an effective national government, argued vehemently that removal should be a unilateral executive power: personnel in the executive branch should be subject to presidential removal without the requirement that Congress act. Otherwise incompetent or corrupt officials supported by members of Congress could remain in their jobs.

In the case of the Constitution not being explicit, there was an easy decision rule for Madison: "We must suppose that [the branches] were intended to be kept separate in all cases in which they are not [explicitly] blended."[38] Shared powers were to be spelled out, otherwise "the three great departments of Government [should] be kept separate and distinct."[39] Opponents violated this logic at the cost of liberty and effective government. It was during this debate that Madison suggested to his colleagues that "if there was a principle in our Constitution, more sacred than another, it is that which separates the legislative, executive, and judicial powers.[40]

True to Madison's prediction in *The Federalist*, perplexing issues about the boundaries between the branches cropped up readily. The debate over the removal of executive officers occurred during the House discussion about the Department of "Foreign Affairs" (not yet called the Department of State). That conversation concluded on June 22, 1789. Madison turned heads just one week later, when the House took up a bill to establish the Department of the Treasury. The committee that drafted the legislation had done so "without making any provision respecting the tenure by which the Comptroller is to hold his office."[41] This position was to be given the responsibility of determining whether the claims of individuals against the U.S. Treasury were authorized for payout, such as benefits for Revolutionary War soldiers. Madison stated that this work made the position "not purely of an executive nature."[42] Determining whether claimants qualified for benefits "partakes strongly of the judicial character." The comptroller would serve as a kind of "arbitrator" between the public and claimants.

Motivated by republican frugality and historical knowledge of how parliaments reined in kingly excess, Madison wanted to tie the position closer to Congress. This would "make him [more] responsible to the public," a better guardian of the people's money.[43] So Madison suggested that the appointment be made for a set number of years and that Congress should be able to adjust the comptroller's salary within that span as an inducement to proper service. The president could still remove someone from the job, but Congress would retain controls over the behavior of the person appointed.

This proposal was met with shock. Theodore Sedgwick of Massachusetts noted that this officer would be executing the law, and thus there was no reason to consider the work to be judicial or to grant Congress greater control than over other executive officers. Egbert Benson of New York believed that Madison's line of thinking would reopen the removal debate that had just been painstakingly concluded. He objected by citing a familiar separation-of-powers worry that Madison had repeatedly voiced, including in the previous week: this would be a step toward the legislative branch "overthrow[ing] the Executive power."[44] Maryland's Michael Jenifer Stone declared the proposal "perfectly novel" and noted that claimants could use the courts if they were wrongly denied.

Through a seeming inconsistency, Madison had confused many of his colleagues. His rejoinder to these criticisms was that "if gentlemen will consult the true spirit and scope of the constitution, they will perhaps find my propositions not so obnoxious as some seem to think."[45] But his fellow representatives had not drawn the same lessons, especially not from one who had just lectured them about proper execution of law requiring exclusive presidential control of executive branch workers. Some stressed that Madison's proposal violated the idea that exceptions to the separation of branches would have to be explicitly mentioned in the Constitution. Nevertheless, Madison asked the committee that brought in the bill to consider his proposal. Not finding support, the next day he withdrew the motion.[46]

In Madison's view, this was surely an honest (and relatively minor) separation-of-functions boundary quarrel, the kind of constitutional disagreement that he had described in *Federalist* No. 37. His motivation was not to oppose the Washington administration; he was a staunch supporter at the time. Nor did he wish to set a precedent of excessive legislative meddling in executive affairs. Why Madison did not foresee the confusion and resistance his stance would provoke is harder to discern, particularly given his arguments of the previous week.

He did have other choices. Even if he thought of the comptroller's work as somewhat judicial in nature, he could have let the matter pass without comment. He could have suggested that members of the judiciary make these determinations. This would have created an unexpected job for federal judges, but if that would best preserve the separation of functions in republican government, then why not? Alternatively, he could have concluded that the work of all those in the executive branch is inherently executive in nature, and any legislative qualifiers would be problematic. Instead, he justified his position by arguing that the specific work done by an officer should determine who should control that officer. This approach threatened to provoke many more boundary skirmishes in the future, with every government job being scrutinized for the nature of its particular work. This is a much more complicated way of effecting the separation of powers than what might otherwise have been done.

Madison's proposal foreshadows a good deal of future congressional action. Congress has created independent agencies, government corporations, mechanisms of prosecutorial independence, inspectors general, and set terms for certain appointees regardless of presidential will. These are now commonplace features of the federal government. They are not recent inventions, and they have stood the test of time. Officials and agencies whose roles are not considered exclusively executive do not prevent the United States government from working. At the same time, they are part of the thickened and complex governmental environment famously described by Neustadt as "separated institutions sharing powers."[47]

Thus, Madison's post-ratification position helped put a particular kind of flesh on the Constitution's bones that was unanticipated in 1787, at least by many. In the Philadelphia Convention the checks Madison endorsed seemed broad, selective, and intentional, so that the predominant work of execution remained with the president, the work of adjudicating stayed in the federal courts, and the Congress was responsible for legislating. Madison was not embracing gridlock.[48] The comptroller debate indicates that the Constitution might (and eventually did) feature a robust intertwining of institutional activity and the need for substantial ongoing interbranch cooperation. It could have been far different. Madison's stated goal in *The Federalist* was to produce a government that was stable and effective, one with "energy," and characterized by a "prompt and salutary execution of [just] laws."[49] There is tension between this vision for government, with its emphasis on effectiveness and efficiency, and the complex interbranch environment produced by the robust sharing of control over government personnel and policy. Madison did not comment on this tension in 1787, but as the United States government has aged it has become increasingly apparent. This is why Neustadt's pithy characterization of the American institutional setting has been so popular. And it is the reason why current U.S. politics features frequent executive attempts to circumvent the complicated intertwining of institutional prerogatives. That Madison came to endorse this intertwined constitutional structure suggests that in 1787 he did not acknowledge or was not explicit about the full extent or complexity of government operations in a functioning republic. What he did do is react to governing realities as they developed in a defensible but far from inevitable manner, arguing for an arrangement that has become a feature of American constitutional practice.

THE STRANGE SILENCE SURROUNDING LOUISIANA

One of the more curious aspects about the Louisiana Purchase is that we know relatively little about what James Madison, the cabinet member most responsible for the annexation of territory, was thinking, other than being strongly in favor of the acquisition. President Jefferson asked his cabinet officers to weigh in on whether a constitutional amendment was advisable. Madison did not write a response, though he seems to have been consulted by Albert Gallatin, who did.[50] Madison apparently disagreed with Jefferson, thinking that the annexation of land by treaty was an inherent right of nations—a position with some logical force, but one that was still controversial. In the end, the president acquiesced to that view. Proposed amendments were written to address this matter, including one by Madison himself, but the Jefferson administration considered it sufficient to have the Senate ratify the treaty and to have Congress enact enabling legislation.[51] As Ralph Ketcham notes of Madison at this time, "He was generally silent or vague."[52]

The primary constitutional issue that had worried Jefferson concerned the extent of federal power. There was a less-noted but second constitutional concern that probably should have bothered Madison: could the newly acquired land be administered without squarely violating the separation of powers? The purchase was made in haste, with Congress called into special session by the president to conduct the necessary business. Legislative language initially offered in the House caused great controversy. It read: "Until Congress shall have made provision for the temporary government of the said Territories, all the military, civil, and judicial powers exercised by the officers of the existing government of the same, shall be vested in such person or persons, and shall be exercised in such manner, as the President of the United States shall direct."[53]

These words raised several different constitutional issues. Could Congress enable President Jefferson to administer the territory without giving him specific instructions? Would this language allow the president to wield powers that were legislative and judicial in nature, as well as those that were executive? Would this open-ended authorization allow the president such latitude that he could violate the Constitution's provisions within the newly acquired lands, either innocently, by spending money or creating offices without congressional authorization, or in a more sinister manner, governing the territory tyrannically or capriciously?

Once the Senate ratified a treaty, was the Congress obligated to enact legislation to implement it? Each of these arguments was made during the debate over the Louisiana Purchase.[54] James Elliot of Vermont spoke for a vocal group when he pledged "never [to] consent to delegate, for a single moment, such extensive powers to the President, even over a Territory. Such a delegation of power is unconstitutional."[55] These critics were objecting to language that other legislators had written in consultation with Secretary Madison.[56]

Madison's fellow Virginian, John Randolph, moved to soften criticism by adding a sentence to the bill that constrained the president to "maintaining and protecting the inhabitants of Louisiana in the full enjoyment of their liberty, property, and religion."[57] This would be a rough guide that might safeguard constitutional rights, but it did not directly address most of the constitutional concerns that had been aired. The resolution, with Randolph's amendment, passed easily, 89–23. Most in the substantial Jeffersonian majority took the view of Massachusetts' Jacob Crowninshield. To gain so much land at such a cheap price, erecting a barrier against the encroachment of European powers on the South and the West and making these lands available to millions of American homesteaders, was too good of a situation to pass up.[58]

As president, Madison meticulously reasoned out a means of validating the national bank's constitutionality. He did not do something similar for the Louisiana Purchase. Nor did he explain his constitutional position publicly. Privately he thought much like Representative Crowninshield, that the huge amount of good this annexation promised outweighed any technical qualms about its constitutionality.[59] As Ralph Ketcham notes, "When Senator John Quincy Adams asked him if the administration intended to submit an amendment, Madison submitted that the Constitution didn't cover the case of the Louisiana Purchase, but that it was necessary to remember 'the magnitude of the object,' and to trust 'the candor of the country' to approve the deed."[60] While this particular comment was about the federal government's authority to purchase new lands, Madison presumably thought similarly about the separation-of-powers issues raised by the purchase as well. Congress could replace the bare bones delegation with laws and an administrative structure of its own choosing as quickly as it could act. In the meantime, the Jefferson administration would move to protect and superintend the new U.S. territory.

Madison understood he was creating a temporary autocracy in Louisiana. To the newly appointed territorial governor William C. C. Claiborne he wrote that he was "vesting in you alone the power necessary for the immediate Government of the ceded territory."[61] While early territorial governments tended to be rough-

and-ready establishments, this one was particularly loosely constructed. Claiborne himself, far from enjoying the power offered by his commission, chafed under the "great latitude of powers with which I am temporarily entrusted." He hoped that Congress would "soon relieve me from that difficulty," by enacting a more regular form of government.[62] Claiborne used his authority to make judicial decisions, created offices, appointed officers to these posts, determined what to do about the slave trade in the territory, and chartered a territorial bank. He apologized for taking some of these actions, defending himself by observing that he had received virtually no guidance from Madison.[63] Claiborne acknowledged that it was up to him to "introduce[e] the principles of the American Government into this province." He thought that he could succeed in erecting a benign and just administration, but that subsequent governors would have much more to do in this regard, particularly in establishing a working republican government.[64] Congress passed legislation that created a full territorial government in late March 1804, scheduled to begin its work in October. The bill made provision for an independent judiciary and a legislative council, relieving Claiborne of the work of these other branches. Thus ended Claiborne's run as the sole governmental authority of the Louisiana Territory, something which had clearly bothered him but had not perturbed Secretary of State Madison.

The immediate aftermath of the Louisiana Purchase demonstrated that Madison's commitment to the separation of powers was still, to an extent, situational. Given a particular context, pursuit of the public good could override regular commitments to the separation of powers. For a time, William Claiborne, and by extension Madison himself, had served as the executive, legislative, and judicial power in Louisiana. This was the "very definition of tyranny" that Madison had described in *Federalist* No. 47. But in Madison's view the administration would be temporary, benign, and immensely beneficial to the United States. Though he did not bother to say so, Madison could have made this into another of his constitutionalizing rules, like the one formulated about the National Bank: *for a very large public benefit, typical separation of powers requirements might be temporarily set aside when this involves very little hazard and when not doing so would jeopardize the benefit*. This was like a highly circumscribed form of Locke's prerogative power, a surprising development given the concerns expressed by Madison in 1787. It applied only in a territory, affecting very few citizens. Like Locke's prerogative, use of it required acting in the public good. Yet spelling this out would likely have done more harm than good. It would seem to give license to set aside the separation of powers, because of the frequent temptations to bypass it to achieve programmatic goals. Better to simply bask in the glow of this great national triumph.

COMPROMISE IN THE PUBLIC GOOD, OR NOT

Madison's opponents had a model in arguing that implementing the Louisiana Purchase would require the approval of Congress as a whole—James Madison himself. During his final term in Congress Madison was aghast at the poor terms of the Jay Treaty. The treaty allowed Britons entry into the Northwest Territory to trade and travel but forbade American entry to the West Indies. The British received full navigation rights on the Mississippi while American trade abroad would be restricted, contrary to what Madison believed to be the law of nations. There was no guarantee that the Americans' standing grievances about interdiction at sea would be favorably addressed, yet most-favored-nation status was extended to Britain. In short, Madison thought that Britain gained much from the Jay Treaty, while the United States lost, with its very sovereign status being called into question.[65] As a tacit rejection of a close U.S. relationship with France, it also offended his view that republics should be allies. The proposed treaty was unworthy of adoption in his mind, and very bad policy.

Seeing things differently, the more Anglophilic Federalist majority in the Senate ratified the treaty, with just one modification. George Washington and George III both accepted this decision, granting the treaty legal status. Thinking American nationhood and republican principles at stake, Madison did not end his opposition. The House of Representatives first voted to request documents pertaining to the negotiation, some of which might embarrass the administration, and then proceeded to engage in a months-long discussion of whether it should refuse to enact legislation required to implement the treaty.

This was a constitutional gray area. The Senate and the president had the constitutional right to conclude a treaty without input from the House, but the House was also clearly within its constitutional right not to enact legislation. Nothing in the Constitution could resolve this clash of legitimate but contradictory powers. President Washington refused to deliver confidential papers to the House and objected to its resistance, citing a vote at the Philadelphia Convention.

During the House debate Madison attempted to formulate a general answer to such intractable disputes. "If the difference [between institutions] cannot be adjusted by friendly conference and mutual concession," then three factors should be considered: the public will, guidance provided by ratifying conventions, and, if satisfaction was not to be had by either of these, amending the Constitution.⁶⁶ The public outcry against the treaty had been significant, justifying the House's resistance, in Madison's view. But his continued opposition ignored the fact that the public had warmed to the treaty considerably, especially after it had President Washington's endorsement and the imprimatur of law.⁶⁷

Madison pointed out that several ratifying conventions had discussed an amendment to the Constitution acknowledging that "in a free Government . . . no power could supersede a law without the consent of the people in the Legislature."⁶⁸ This language might be used to place laws ahead of treaties, suggesting that if the House refused to pass enabling legislation a treaty could not be enacted. Yet Madison's argument here was uncharacteristically weak, because the language he cited had not been legally adopted. President Washington suggesting that the House was required to support the newly concluded treaty was not any better, as it was also unsupported by any explicit constitutional provision.⁶⁹ By definition, a ratified treaty supersedes prior statutes and is law, yet the House still possesses independent power to legislate or refrain from legislating to enable it. Madison acknowledged the constitutional dilemma but insisted that the treaty power did not give the president and Senate a backdoor means of regulating commerce, appropriating money, or defining the nature of the armed forces, all things that implementation of the treaty required. Upon this basis he insisted that the House's determination on this matter would be definitive.

There was, seemingly, no optimal solution. If the House accepted that treaties were binding on it, that would put an end to the controversy but set a problematic precedent by limiting its legislative independence. If it rejected implementation of the treaty, that would also put an end to the controversy but yield the awkwardness of having binding treaties potentially undermined immediately upon adoption, as well as leaving the nation in diplomatic limbo.⁷⁰ The House cleverly split the difference, insisting that it was free not to enact enabling legislation but then actually passing the necessary legislation by the narrowest of margins. Speaker Frederick Augustus Muhlenberg cast the decisive vote. Many members of Madison's party defected from their earlier opposition, a bitter disappointment to him.⁷¹ But what if they had not defected? The tussle between the Federalists and the Jeffersonian Republicans exposed a constitutional dilemma. The situation was made acute by the emergence of strong political parties that viewed each other with grave suspicion. The different representational schemes of the House and Senate produced very different preferences in the two chambers that had made the clash intractable—at least for a while.

James Madison consistently decried "partisan zeal." There has been much written about his insistence on the cool control of elites and deliberate institutions instead of zealous partisanship.⁷² He continued to complain about the evils of partisanship long after he left the national stage. For instance, an 1827 letter to Charles Ingersoll notes that "the attempts of party zeal when pursuing its favorite object, to break into the domain of the Constitution, cannot be too much deplored."[73] Madison would not ever have described himself as a party zealot. In his own mind he was defending what was nonnegotiable—American sovereignty—but from the outside looking in on the Jay Treaty controversy, his ability to escape this charge is less than fully clear. In the words of Stanley Elkins and Eric McKitrick, "Opposition to the treaty had become a party commitment and had taken on a life of its own, in some degree independent of the ebb and flow of popular sentiment."[74]

Strongly committed to the theory of the equality of nations, Madison refused to acknowledge how vulnerable the United States was in practice—something that recommended coming to agreement with Britain, even one that favored Britain. Wedded to an electoral coalition that was strongest in the American West, he fought adamantly for the interests of the western settlers who had the most to lose from the Jay Treaty. Inside the national legislature he did his best to rally his troops to retroactively invalidate the treaty; outside of it he worked to shape public opinion against the treaty. In the end he turned out to be more partisan than many of his colleagues, who voted for a more pragmatic approach, preserving the right of the House to legislate and the viability of the treaty power, all while confirming peace with a potentially dangerous adversary. Madison believed so fervently that he was right about the nation's need to establish itself as an equal in the community of nations and to resist Britain's monarchism and its mercantile foreign policy that he worked to undermine the constitutionally valid means of concluding international agreements. This precedent would have significantly complicated the conduct of American foreign policy.

The American system of robust, intertwined checks and balances frequently requires concession among its actors and institutions to work effectively. Madison has frequently been praised for pointing us toward a politics of moderation and compromise. Ironically, this same necessity produces pitched political battles that often favor highly recalcitrant actors. If one party or institution wishes to stop legislation (or a treaty), they are often in an immensely favored position to do so, Madison's loss in the case of the Jay Treaty notwithstanding. Madison himself was no naive actor. He knew that "enlightened statesmen will not *always* be at the helm."[75] But enlightened statesmen do need to be at the helm *sometimes* for a Madisonian-style separated system to work well. In the end, this necessity may have been better provided for by the sober acceptance of the Jeffersonians who acquiesced to the treaty, rather than by Madison's more zealous opposition.

CONCLUSION: ONGOING CONSTITUTIONALISM

Though Madison called the separation of powers "sacred," his thinking about it was also a moving target. In dispensing advice on a state constitution for Kentucky in 1785, he endorsed an enthusiasm of Thomas Jefferson—any two branches should be able to call a convention to resolve a constitutional dispute with the remaining branch.[76] In *Federalist* No. 49 he repudiated that very solution. Less than three years had elapsed.

Madison helped construct and explain the innovative institutional structure set up in the Constitution. It contained a new distribution of powers and interinstitutional checks informed by experience, intended to prevent usurpation. If successful, no branch would be able to do the work of any other. He and his compatriots did sufficiently well at this theory-driven exercise that we are still using the Constitution and thinking about its interbranch power dynamics well over two hundred years later. Madison deserves credit as an innovative and pragmatic separation-of-powers thinker. But his innovative and pragmatic tendencies did not stop with ratification. As a prominent political actor for three decades after ratification Madison worked to add to, adjust, and refine the separation of powers in practice. The turns of actual politics prompted learning and necessitated some compromise to what had been worked out in 1787. There was never a point in time where Madison was in full possession of all the knowledge required to produce a foolproof separation-of-powers system. The reason for this is simple—there is no perfect, static solution to how the three branches exercise their powers and interact. Ongoing constitutional construction is necessary, for reasons that Madison identified in The *Federalist*: new, novel situations crop up, the public good sometimes requires imperfect separation-of-powers scrupulousness, and political actors possess strong views that tend to undermine this more abstract political commitment.

In *Federalist* No. 51 Madison wrote that legislatures "predominate" in republics. This was both an empirical understanding and a normative hope. Madison believed that legislatures should set the direction of the polity; the question was whether they could predominate without dominating. Authorizing special congressional oversight mechanisms for the comptroller was one way to reinforce legislative predominance in one area of policy. The early years of the republic surprised Madison, as the executive proved to be stronger and the legislative branch weaker than he had imagined they would be. This prompted him to organize a political party with like-minded politicians that could coordinate opposition to the executive-centric politics of the Federalists within Congress. Madison was rethinking and adjusting on the fly. It took hard work to establish and maintain Congress's central role in governance.

During the Jay Treaty controversy, he worked to have the most popular branch effectively cancel the constitutionally sanctioned work of the president and Senate. Because of his perception that its undermining of U.S. sovereignty was an existential matter, he was willing to forego negotiation and exploit to the full an unresolved (and still unresolved) conundrum in how legislation and treaties relate. In the case of Louisiana, Madison was part of the executive branch and supporting administrative latitude for it. This was justified to achieve a once-in-a-lifetime opportunity to double the size of the nation. The compromise made was temporary, benign (in his view), and approved by Congress. This was not usurpation; it was necessary stewardship of the public good.

A crucial debate over Madison's political behavior is whether or not he was consistent. This framing is instructive, but only to a point. It suggests two possibilities, both of which assume that Madison's political principles were clearly stated at a point in time and relatively static. The difference between these views is an assessment of whether he remained faithful to those principles or whether he knowingly violated them in the pursuit of his perceived interests. A third option is suggested by the episodes discussed in this chapter. Madison was engaged in constitutional learning that required refining his principles over time and an ongoing elucidation of constitutionalism that necessitated aligning the separation of powers with other political principles in complex and novel situations. We may want to find Madison consistent in regard to the separation of powers, but that would require more forethought than anyone could possibly have had.

NOTES

The title is drawn from *Federalist* No. 37, in Alexander Hamilton, James Madison, and John Jay, *The Federalist*, ed. Jacob E. Cooke (Cleveland: World, 1961), 232. This was Madison's initial argument about the Constitution in his long series of twenty-two *Federalist* essays (Nos. 37 through 58) that I apply here to his approach to the separation of powers. Subsequent citations to the *Federalist* are to this edition.

1. Peter Daniel Haworth, "James Madison and James Monroe Historiography: A Tale of Two Divergent Bodies of Scholarship," in *A Companion to James Madison and James Monroe*, ed. Stuart Leibiger (Oxford: Wiley-Blackwell, 2013), 527.
2. Alan Gibson, "The Madisonian Madison and the Question of Consistency: The Significance and Challenge of Recent Research," in *Review of Politics* 64, no. 2 (2002): 311–38, quote on 335.
3. Gordon S. Wood, *Revolutionary Characters: What Made the Founders Different* (New York: Penguin, 2006), 155.
4. Michael Zuckert, "James Madison in *The Federalist*: Elucidating 'The Particular Struc-

ture of This Government,'" in *A Companion to James Madison and James Monroe*, ed. Stuart Leibiger (Malden, Mass.: Wiley-Blackwell, 2013), 103.

5. George Thomas, *The Madisonian Constitution* (Baltimore: Johns Hopkins University Press, 2008).

6. Jeremy D. Bailey, *James Madison and Constitutional Imperfection* (New York: Cambridge University Press, 2015).

7. William F. Connelly Jr., *James Madison Rules America: The Constitutional Origins of Congressional Partisanship* (Lanham, Md.: Rowman & Littlefield, 2010), 235.

8. Lynne Cheney, *James Madison: A Life Reconsidered* (New York: Viking Books, 2014), 7; Richard Brookhiser, *James Madison* (New York: Viking, 2014), 7; Brookhiser, "James Madison: Father of Politics," Alpheus T. Mason speech on Constitutional Law and Political Thought, October 10, 2011, Princeton, N.J.

9. Max Farrand, ed., *Records of the Federal Convention of 1787*, vol. 2 (New Haven: Yale University Press, 1966), 74 (emphasis added).

10. James Madison, *The Papers of James Madison* (hereafter PJM), Congressional series, ed. William T. Hutchinson et al., 17 vols., (Chicago and Charlottesville: University of Chicago Press and University of Virginia Press, 1962–91), 9:345–58. These are vices number 9 through number 11. Vice number 12 was headed "impotence of the law of the states." Madison did not offer any commentary on this vice, but it is logical to conclude that this was also a criticism of legislatures, because legislatures actively intruded upon executive affairs, preventing them from effectively carrying out the laws.

11. *Federalist* No. 48, in Alexander Hamilton, James Madison, and John Jay, *The Federalist*, ed. Jacob Cooke (Middletown, Conn.: Wesleyan University Press, 1961), 333–34.

12. Farrand, *Records of the Federal Convention*, 1:53.

13. M. J. C. Vile, *Constitutionalism and the Separation of Powers* (Indianapolis: Liberty Fund, 1998), 14 and chap. 6. Anti-Federalists relied heavily on this idea, stressing that "the legislative, executive, and judicial powers [must] be kept separate," and objecting that the proposed Constitution violated this requirement in several ways. David Siemers, *The Antifederalists: Men of Great Faith and Foresight* (Lanham, Md.: Rowman & Littlefield, 2003), 96.

14. *Federalist* No. 48, 334. Madison described legislative power as "more extensive and less susceptible to precise limits" in *Federalist* No. 48, while executive power was naturally "restrained within a narrower compass."

15. *Federalist* No. 47, 327.

16. Ibid., 326–27.

17. Edwin S. Corwin, *The President, Office and Powers, 1787–1957: History and Analysis of Practice and Opinion*, 4th rev. ed. (1957; repr., New York: New York University Press, 1990), 171; Richard E. Neustadt, *Presidential Power and the Modern Presidents: The Politics of Leadership from Roosevelt to Reagan* (New York: Free Press, 1991), 29; James A. Thurber and Jordan Tama, eds., *Rivals for Power: Presidential-Congressional Relations* (Lanham, Md.: Rowman & Littlefield, 2017); Thomas, *Madisonian Constitution*, 2–6.

18. *Federalist* No. 51, 350.

19. Madison himself would have happily gone farther than the convention in checking legis-

lative power. He had repeatedly attempted to get his fellow delegates to adopt a "Council of Revision," composed of the president and Supreme Court justices that would examine congressional bills for constitutionality and desirability before they became law. Farrand, *Records of the Federal Convention*, 1:74.

20. The fact that this is not how the veto power is used today and does not well describe the president's substantial legislative role demonstrates my point. Madison was thinking more "defensively" about presidential power than "offensively."

21. *Federalist* No. 51, 347–48.

22. Charles O. Jones, *Separate but Equal Branches: Congress and the Presidency* (New York: Chatham House, 1999), 8–13.

23. Arthur M. Schlesinger Jr., *The Imperial Presidency* (Boston: Houghton, Mifflin, 1973); Andrew Rudalevige, *The New Imperial Presidency: Renewing Presidential Power after Watergate* (Ann Arbor: University of Michigan Press, 2005).

24. Mark A. Lemley, "The Imperial Judiciary," *Harvard Law Review* 136, no. 1 (2002): 97–118; David J. Siemers, *The Myth of Coequal Branches: Restoring the Constitution's Separation of Functions* (Columbia: University of Missouri Press, 2018), chap. 5.

25. Martin Shapiro, "Judicialization of Politics in the United States," *International Political Science Review* 15, no. 2 (1994): 101–12.

26. Madison to Thomas Jefferson of October 24, 1787, *PJM*, Congressional series, 10:205–20.

27. *Federalist* No. 37, 235.

28. Ibid.

29. *Federalist* No. 38, 248.

30. Ibid., 249.

31. Richard P. McCormick, "Ambiguous Authority: The Ordinances of the Confederation Congress, 1781–1789," *American Journal of Legal History* 41, no. 4 (1997): 414. Also see PJM, Congressional series, 3:17–20.

32. *Federalist* No. 42, 279–80.

33. To finance the Revolutionary War, Finance Secretary Robert Morris engaged in activities that struck many in Congress as unauthorized. However, if a radically defective constitution justified extraconstitutional laws for the public good, then why would it not authorize such activities from its executive agents? Madison routinely sided with Morris during these controversies. Just how conflicted Madison was about going beyond constitutional bounds is a matter of scholarly dispute. Ralph Ketcham describes Madison's response to the failure of amendments as bold and unequivocal, while Lance Banning describes a more reluctant Madison. Ketcham, *James Madison: A Biography* (Charlottesville: University of Virginia Press, 1990), 114; Banning, *The Sacred Fire of Liberty: James Madison and the Founding of the Federal Republic* (Ithaca, N.Y.: Cornell University Press, 1995), 26.

34. *Federalist* No. 42, 280.

35. *Annals of Congress* (Washington, D.C.: Gales & Seaton, 1834), 1:604.

36. *Federalist* No. 50, 336.

37. Ibid., 345–46.

38. *Annals of Congress,* 1:517.
39. Ibid., 1:516.
40. Ibid., 1:604.
41. Ibid., 1:635.
42. Ibid., 1:635.
43. Ibid., 1:636.
44. Ibid., 1:638.
45. Ibid., 1:638–39.
46. Ibid., 1:639.
47. Neustadt, *Presidential Power,* 29.
48. It is Richard Brookhiser's contention that Madison embraced gridlock in his approach to constitutionalism. See Brookhiser, "James Madison: Father of ... Government Gridlock," *Philadelphia Inquirer,* October 10, 2011.
49. *Federalist* No. 37, 233.
50. Ketcham, *James Madison,* 421.
51. *PJM,* Secretary of State series, ed. David B. Mattern et al, 5:156.
52. Ketcham, *James Madison,* 422.
53. *Annals of Congress,* 8th Congress, 1st session, 13:498.
54. Ibid. These four arguments were made in turn by Roger Griswold (Connecticut), 499, 500–501, Thomas Griffin (Virginia), 442, Samuel W. Dana (Connecticut), 504–5, John Jackson (Virginia), 510.
55. Ibid., 499.
56. The issue was even more fraught because of possible Spanish resistance. Spain had controlled New Orleans for forty years and had recently closed the city to Americans and their goods. The possibility that the secretary of state and president would lead the United States into war with Spain to take its new possession was very real. Those sent to receive the Louisiana Territory at New Orleans were instructed to take New Orleans by force, if necessary. Madison had been adamant in his Helvidius letters that republican nations would not be drawn into war by their executives, but here Madison was demonstrating that a republican foreign policy was not necessarily so peaceful or as legislatively led as had been hoped. JM to William C. C. Claiborne, October 31, 1803, *PJM,* Secretary of State series, 5:589–92; JM to Robert Livingston, November 9, 1803, ibid., Secretary of State series, 6:24–26.
57. *Annals of Congress,* 8th Congress, 1st session, 13:514.
58. Ibid., 13:548.
59. There were negatives, most notably enlarging territory into which slaves might be introduced, potentially exacerbating sectional tensions. David Brion Davis, *Inhuman Bondage: The Rise and Fall of Slavery in the New World* (Oxford: Oxford University Press, 2006), chap. 14.
60. Ketcham, *James Madison,* 422.
61. *PJM,* Secretary of State series, 5:589–90.

62. Ibid., Secretary of State series, 6:274.
63. E.g., ibid., Secretary of State series, 5:497, 574. Claiborne complained to Madison that "since my arrival here I have not received a single letter from the Department of State. In the exercise of my present great discretionary power, it would be a great relief to me to learn from time to time, the views and wishes of the Executive in relation to this Province" (ibid., 6:331). In Claiborne's first four months on the job, he received a single personal communication from Secretary Madison.
64. *PJM*, Secretary of State series, 7:36.
65. Ketcham, *James Madison*, 357.
66. *Annals of Congress*, House, 4th Congress, 1st session, 5:772.
67. Stanley Elkins and Eric McKitrick, *The Age of Federalism* (Oxford: Oxford University Press, 1993), 441.
68. *Annals of Congress*, House, 4th Congress, 1st session, 5:778.
69. This idea was brought up at the Philadelphia Convention, but it was only supported by two states, North Carolina and Virginia, so Washington was essentially suggesting that an idea rejected by the Philadelphia Convention was binding constitutional practice. *The Papers of George Washington*, Presidential series, ed. David R. Hoth (Charlottesville: University of Virginia Press, 2016), 19:635–39.
70. *Annals of Congress*, House, 4th Congress, 1st session, 5:780.
71. Elkins and McKitrick, *Age of Federalism*, 449.
72. E.g., Richard K. Mathews describes Madison as a cold and calculating Malthusian in *If Men Were Angels* (Lawrence: University Press of Kansas, 1995), and Greg Weiner stresses Madison's commitment to majoritarian decision-making in *Madison's Metronome* (Lawrence: University Press of Kansas, 2012).
73. Madison to Charles J. Ingersoll, November 17, 1827, Founders Online, National Archives, https://founders.archives.gov/documents/Madison/04-04-02-0562.
74. Elkins and McKitrick, *Age of Federalism*, 441–42.
75. *Federalist* No. 10, 60.
76. Madison to Caleb Wallace, August 23, 1785, in *PJM*, Congressional series, 8:350–58.

"The Last Hope of True Liberty"
Madison and the Evolution of American Federalism

JEFF BROADWATER

Shortly after the Constitutional Convention of 1787, James Madison wrote Thomas Jefferson that, of all the tasks facing the delegates, allocating authority between the national and state governments "was perhaps ... the most nice and difficult." Writing in 1792, he observed that separating the powers of the federal government's executive, legislative, and judicial branches proved easier than dividing power between the federal and state governments. Although it was difficult to distinguish one class of legislative, executive, or judicial powers from another, the "boundaries" between powers of a similar type "are more obscure and run more into each other." After leaving the White House, Madison confided to the Virginia jurist Spencer Roane his view that "the Gordian Knot of the Constitution seems to lie in the problem of collision between the federal & State powers."[1]

Madison had initially hoped to make the national government clearly dominant, with authority to overrule capricious state laws. Faced with opposition at the Philadelphia Convention and during the ratification debates, he assumed a more nuanced position: federal power would be supreme, largely preempting the states, when Congress acted pursuant to its enumerated powers, and perhaps certain implied powers, but the states remained sovereign regarding those functions reserved to them. Madison eventually came to see "a System partly federal and partly consolidated" as so essential to "individual rights, public order, and external safety" that its critics, he believed, threatened "the last hope of true Liberty on the face of the Earth." Critical as it was, however, federalism was only one of several means to an end: a stable Union based on the consent of the governed.[2]

Probably no American of Madison's generation gave more thought to the issue of federalism. Despite the difficulty of dividing power between different levels of government, Madison believed a balance had to be struck. In 1787, Madison's thinking about how to strike that balance reflected over a decade of reading and research, as well as practical experience. He had served in Congress and in the Virginia House of Delegates and found the national legislature wanting in authority and the state legislature lacking in wisdom. His experience convinced him that a weak central government would invite "schism" and disunion, but the "consolidation" of all authority at the national level represented, Madison later wrote, "the high road to monarchy."[3]

Under the Articles of Confederation, Congress, lacking the power to tax, had to requisition funds from the states. They rarely complied in full, which left Congress unable to adequately support the Continental Army during the Revolution or to pay the nation's war debts after the fighting stopped. By April 1781, Madison had decided "the shameful deficiency of some of the states" justified "arming Congress with coercive powers." He also supported an amendment to the Articles empowering Congress to collect duties and an impost on imported goods. By February 1783, Madison had concluded that "many of the most respectable people of America" believed "the preservation of the Confederacy" depended on giving Congress a reliable source of revenue. Amendments, however, had to be approved by all the states, and unanimity proved elusive.[4]

An impost amendment would have gone a long way toward solving another of Congress's problems—its inability to regulate trade. Madison complained repeatedly about British discrimination against American ships and goods, but Congress had no legal way to retaliate, and state regulations proved ineffective.[5]

Congress did manage to negotiate cessions to the national government of trans-Appalachian lands claimed by Virginia and other states and to pass ordinances for their governance. Otherwise, its ability to promote westward expansion seemed suspect. In 1784, Congress essentially stood by as Spain, which controlled Louisiana, closed the Mississippi River to American traffic. Congress's inability to enforce the Treaty of Paris of 1783, which ended the Revolutionary War, created additional anxieties in frontier regions. The treaty had recognized the right of British merchants to collect prewar debts from American debtors. Some states refused to open their courts to such suits and gave the British an excuse to renege on one of their treaty commitments: to evacuate their forts in the American West.[6]

The years Madison spent in the Virginia Assembly left him equally frustrated. Virginia's lawmakers routinely failed to satisfy the state's congressional requisitions or to impose taxes sufficient to meet the state's own needs, and they continued to block the recovery of British debts. Madison enjoyed some victories, including the passage of Jefferson's Bill for Establishing Religious Freedom. On other issues, progress came slowly. In the fall 1786 session, Madison handily defeated a resolution endorsing paper money, which he considered inflationary, but he ranked "the general rage for paper money" in other states as the worst of many examples of dubious state policies.[7]

In February 1787, in the wake of Shays' Rebellion in Massachusetts, Madison found himself predicting the imminent collapse of "the federal authority" if reforms were not soon forthcoming. As an alternative, "some leading minds" had "a propensity toward Monarchy." Most people, Madison believed, would prefer the creation of separate New England, mid-Atlantic, and southern confederacies.[8]

In December 1786, the Virginia Assembly had selected Madison as one of the state's delegates to the Constitutional Convention to be held the following May. Anticipating his new assignment, Madison began to organize his thoughts in a memorandum he titled "Vices of the Political System of the United States." It was a twelve-point indictment of government in America. Eight of the twelve vices belonged to the states. They had failed to comply with congressional requisitions; they had violated the Articles of Confederation by making compacts and treaties without the consent of Congress; they had violated U.S. treaties with other nations; and they had issued paper money and passed debtor-relief laws to the detriment of citizens in other states. Madison criticized the "multiplicity" and "mutability" of state legislation and charged that its "injustice" had called "into question the fundamental principle of republican Government, that the majority who rule in such Governments, are the safest Guardians both of public Good and of private rights."[9]

To Madison, America's political structure made its vices inevitable. "From the number of Legislatures, the sphere of life from which most of their members are taken, and the circumstances under which their legislative business is carried on, irregularities . . . must frequently happen." Every act of Congress weighed more heavily on some states than others; ambitious politicians would be tempted to exaggerate their state's burden in order to win popularity. States might refuse to comply with a "general act" if they feared other states would not submit. Because the Articles had not been ratified by voters within the individual states, it could plausibly be argued that state law ought to prevail where a conflict with federal authority arose. Lawmakers could be self-aggrandizing or civic-minded, but Madison argued ambition and personal interest usually prevailed over the public good. Human nature being what it was, the most ambitious politicians were often the "most industrious" and could sometimes dupe "the honest but unenlightened representative."[10]

Notwithstanding all the faulty policies attributable to the vices of their representatives, Madison wrote, "a still more fatal if not more frequent cause lies in the people themselves." Societies divided into "factions," and when a faction within a state constituted a majority, it was apt to oppress the minority. Concern for one's character or reputation or for public opinion out of state would not check a majority faction. Religion, which would presumably appeal to a people's more generous instincts, could instead become a source of oppression.[11]

Madison's solution was to enlarge the political sphere to encompass "a greater variety of interests." They would "check each other, whilst those who may feel a common sentiment would have less opportunity of communication and concert." In other words, even if a prospective majority faction existed in an extended sphere, it would be difficult to assemble. Madison hoped to create a government independent of factions and therefore able to prevent one faction from "invading the rights of another." This would be Madison's rationale for dramatically enhancing the power of the central government, and his plan offered "an auxiliary desideratum": elections to a rejuvenated Congress would attract a community's "purest and noblest characters." Madison was defying conventional wisdom, exemplified in the writings of Montesquieu, that republics had to be small and relatively homogenous so citizens could feel they shared a common interest.[12]

In letters to Thomas Jefferson, Edmund Randolph, and George Washington, Madison expanded on the reforms he envisioned. Writing Jefferson in March 1787, Madison argued that the new government should be ratified by the people "of the several States" to make it "clearly paramount to their Legislative authorities." In addition to regulating trade and other areas where uniformity was needed, "the federal head" should have "a negative *in all cases whatsoever* on the local Legislatures." That "negative," which Madison later refined into a congressional veto, was necessary, he believed, to protect federal jurisdiction from state encroachment, to protect states from one another, and to protect minorities within a state.[13]

Madison seems not to have anticipated the controversy his congressional veto would provoke, an odd oversight given its origins. He took the idea from the British Privy Council, which had wielded the power to veto acts of the colonial assemblies, and the phrase "in all cases whatsoever" echoed the hated Declaratory Act of 1766, which asserted Parliament's right to make laws for the colonies "in all cases whatsoever."[14]

Madison told Randolph and Washington he hoped to find "a middle ground" that would provide "a due supremacy of national authority" while leaving "local authorities" in place "so far as they can be subordinately useful." He declared the "consolidation" of all authority "into one simple republic" to be "unattainable" and "inexpedient," but his federal negative gave the national government ultimate sovereignty. "I hold it for a fundamental point that an individual independence of the States, is utterly irreconcilable with the idea of an aggregate sovereignty." Madison believed "no material sacrifices ought to be made to local or temporary prejudices."[15]

Madison's plans to rein in the states encountered opposition from the start of the Philadelphia Convention. The Virginia Plan, which the Virginia delegation put forward as a tentative outline of a constitution in the first days of the convention, proposed giving Congress the power to veto state laws "contravening in the opinion of the National Legislature the articles of Union." While still formidable, it was not as sweeping as Madison had originally intended, but he considered a legislative negative of some sort "as absolutely necessary to a perfect system." In a series of votes, the delegates rejected both the more limited negative and the broader veto he preferred. They seemed generally unimpressed with his argument that in an "extended republic" such a power could be safely vested in the general government. Most of the state delegations embraced the approach taken in the New Jersey Plan of June 15: federal statues and treaties made pursuant to the Articles of Confederation would be "the supreme law of the respective States ... and ... the Judiciary of the several States shall be bound thereby." It evolved into the Supremacy Clause of the Constitution.[16]

Another issue with implications for the practice of federalism probably frustrated Madison even more. The Virginia Plan had proposed that in a new, bicameral legislature, state representation in the lower house would be "proportioned to the Quotas of contribution, or to the number of free inhabitants, as the one or the other rule may seem best in different cases." Members of the upper house would be selected by the lower house from candidates nominated by the state legislatures, but the Virginia Plan rather archly skirted the issue of representation in what would become the Senate. The idea of basing representation on a state's contribution to the national treasury eventually went by the wayside. Under a modified Virginia Plan, the larger states would probably enjoy an even greater advantage in a new House of Representatives. Madison never clearly explained how his Senate would be composed, but envisioned as a relatively small, deliberative body, it seemed unlikely to offer the small states more than token representation.[17]

They objected vehemently, proposing in the New Jersey Plan to retain the Confederation's unicameral Congress in which each state had one vote, and arguing more realistically elsewhere that in a bicameral legislature, state equality should prevail in at least one house. The conflict deadlocked the convention and complicated the resolution of other issues.[18] Proportional representation favored the large states, and Virginia was the most populous of them all. If securing a political advantage for his home state undoubtedly influenced Madison's thinking, state equality also presented theoretical difficulties. Equal representation in the Senate could only be justified logically if the states were recognized as political entities possessing at least some degree of sovereignty. Oliver Ellsworth of Connecticut, John Dickinson of Delaware, and others favored a system that would be "partly federal and partly national," and they argued that the new Congress ought to embody proportional representation and state equality. They prevailed when the convention approved the Great Compromise on July 16.[19]

The New Jersey delegates David Brearley and William Paterson had illustrated Madison's dilemma when they suggested, presumably as a debating tactic, that the United States be divided into thirteen new states of equal size. "The dissimilarities" Madison replied, "existing in the rules of property, as well as the manners, habits and prejudices of the different States, amounted to a prohibition of the attempt." He was forced to admit the distinctive characteristics of the individual states and the impracticality of making the national government responsible for "all the minute objects which fall under the cognizance of the local jurisdictions." Yet, if it were practical to bypass the state governments, "the people would not be less free as members of one great Republic than as members of thirteen small ones." By the end of June, Madison conceded "the mixed nature" of the government emerging from the debates but "thought too much stress was laid on the rank of the States as political societies." The small states, he argued, had more to fear from a loose confederation that put few restraints on their more powerful neighbors than from "a perfect incorporation" of authority in the central government. They ought, therefore, to support "that form of Govt. which will most approximate the States to the conditions of counties" within the states. He changed no minds.[20]

Shortly before the convention approved the Great Compromise, Madison acknowledged the logic of state equality when the national government acted on the states, but "he called for a single instance in which the Genl. Govt. was not to act on the people individually." In fact, while Madison hoped to establish a government that could function, for the most part, independently of the state governments, he also saw it throughout the convention as a check on the states. In an August 9 speech, for example, he argued successfully for federal oversight of the "time, manner, and mode" of congressional elections.[21]

The convention's decision to allow state legislators to select their state's senators represented another defeat for Madison; he warned it would infuse into the national legislature some of the most pernicious policies of the state assemblies, specifically "schemes of paper money." To be sure, he prevailed on other issues. He thought at least one branch of the national legislature ought to be popularly elected—as the House of Representatives would be—in part to avoid "too great an agency of the State Governments in the General one." The other delegates agreed with his argument that to ensure its supremacy over state law, the Constitution should be ratified by state conventions, not state legislatures. A law violating a popularly ratified constitution, he told them, "would be considered by the Judges as null & void."²²

As the convention neared its end, Madison privately feared "that the plan should it be adopted will neither effectively answer its national object nor prevent the local mischiefs which every where excite disgust against the state governments." After the convention, Madison continued to defend the congressional negative. Once the Constitution became public, he believed initially that Americans were divided between those who thought the convention had done too much and those who thought it had not done enough.²³

Few of the Constitution's critics shared Madison's concerns about the weaknesses of a reformed national government. Generally recognizing the need to strengthen the Confederation Congress, Anti-Federalists alleged the Philadelphia Convention had gone too far, creating a national government that threatened the rights of the states and the liberties of their citizens. And if the new, federal Supreme Court had the responsibility for resolving conflicts between the state and national governments, as an agency of the central government, how impartial could it be? Even Jefferson, Madison's closest political ally, deplored the Constitution's lack of a bill of rights and the president's eligibility for reelection.²⁴

In November 1787, Madison began work on his contributions to the *Federalist* essays, which were written primarily to promote ratification of the Constitution in New York, and he began to adjust his thinking to political reality. He faced a twofold challenge: to convince voters that the nation needed a more energetic central government and to reassure them that the government created by the Constitution was not so strong as to threaten their liberties or the legitimate prerogatives of the states. Several of his essays dealt either directly or indirectly with the issue of federalism. His first and best known, *Federalist* No. 10, laid out the purported advantages of the extended republic, chiefly the tendency of its various factions to neutralize one another, over the states as a guardian of individual rights and the public interest. In *Federalist* No. 14, Madison stressed the impracticality of extending federal jurisdiction beyond certain enumerated objects and the indispensable utility of the state governments. Were the states to be abolished, "the general government would be compelled by the principle of self-preservation, to reinstate them." Appearing in December within a few days of each other, *Federalist* Nos. 18–20 surveyed the history of confederacies from the Achaean League to the Netherlands. Experience, Madison concluded, "emphatically illustrates the tendency of federal bodies, rather to anarchy among the members, than to tyranny in the head."²⁵

In *Federalist* No. 37, Madison addressed what would be a recurrent theme throughout his political life: the obstacles to a proper division of power in a federal system. The Philadelphia Convention had struggled to strike a balance between effective government and liberty. "Not less arduous must have been the task of marking the proper line of partition, between the authority of the general, and that of the State Governments." The delegates had been challenged by the abstract nature of the problem, the feebleness of human intellect, and the limits of language. Political considerations, including the rivalry between large and small states, aggravated their difficulties. The public, in those circumstances, ought not to expect an intellectually elegant solution to the problem of federalism. "The convention must have been compelled to sacrifice theoretical propriety to the force of extraneous considerations." The Great Compromise, for example, might be logically appropriate "in a compound republic partaking both of the national and federal character," but, quoting George Washington, Madison admitted in *Federalist* No. 62 that it was the product "'of a spirit of amity, and that mutual deference and concession which the peculiarity of our political situation rendered indispensable.'"[26]

Madison offered his most elaborate explanation of the partly federal, partly national character of the Constitution in *Federalist* No. 39, which first appeared on January 16, 1788. Madison examined the document's treatment of federal-state relations from a series of different perspectives. "The act . . . establishing the Constitution, will not be a *national* but a *federal* act" because ratification would be "by the people . . . as composing the distinct and independent States" that would be bound by it, and not by a majority of the states or a majority of individual voters.[27]

The process by which officers of the new government were to be selected presented, Madison wrote, "at least as many *federal* as *national* features." Because its members were popularly elected, the House of Representatives was a national assembly, but the equality of the states in the Senate and senators' selection by the state legislatures made it a federal body. A presidential election combined federal and national features. "The immediate election" would be by the states, but each state cast its vote in a "compound ratio" reflecting the state's population plus two additional electoral votes. If no candidate received a majority in the Electoral College, the House would choose the winner—a national feature—while each state, in the federal fashion, would have one vote.[28]

In some cases, especially controversies to which the states were parties, the new government would act in a mixed capacity, but "the operation of the government on the people in their individual capacities, in its ordinary and most essential proceedings," will "on the whole" be national. In the scope of its powers, "the proposed Government cannot be deemed a *national* one; since its jurisdiction extends to certain enumerated objects only, and leaves to the several States a residuary and inviolable sovereignty over all other objects." Before the convention, Madison had rejected the states' inviolable sovereignty; during the ratification debate, he would invoke it frequently. Madison conceded the Supreme Court would decide conflicts between state and national authority, a concession that would often give his federalism a nationalist edge. At the same time, he tried to reassure his readers that "all the usual and most effectual precautions are taken to secure . . . the court's impartiality," although he did not explain what they were. Instead, he made a practical argument: a supreme authority "is clearly essential to prevent an appeal to the sword."[29]

Finally, *Federalist* No. 39 argued that the Constitution's amendment process was neither wholly national, because amendments could not be made by a simple, national majority, nor wholly federal, because they did not require the unanimous consent of the states. The Constitution, Madison concluded, is "neither a national nor a federal constitution; but a composition of both."[30]

In later essays, Madison argued that the states would enjoy a number of advantages in defending their interests against an overreaching federal government, and in a dramatic retreat from the tenor of his "Vices" memorandum, protecting the rights of their citizens. *Federalist* No. 43 cited the ability of the states to call a national convention to consider amending the Constitution as one example. Should Congress abuse its powers under the "necessary and proper" clause of Article I, Section 8, the state legislatures, he wrote in *Federalist* No. 44, "will be ever ready to mark the innovation, to sound the alarm to the people, and to exert their local influence in effecting a change of federal representatives."[31]

Madison's earlier skepticism about the state governments crept out occasionally, as when he claimed the state assemblies were more likely to exercise unchecked power than was Congress. He was, after all, asking voters to support strengthening the national government. In *Federalist* No. 45, he responded to Anti-Federalists who claimed the Constitution would "derogate from the importance" of the state governments, with a rhetorical question: was the American Revolution fought to protect the liberty of the people or the powers of the states?[32]

For the most part, however, Madison stressed the safeguards to state autonomy. The federal government depended on the states for the election of the president and senators, and state officials could influence House elections, presumably by their authority to draw congressional districts. State governments would offer more patronage; Madison anticipated that if Congress imposed internal taxes, they could be collected by agents of the states. The powers of the federal government were few and largely limited to war, diplomacy, and foreign trade. If federal power swelled in wartime, peace would be the norm. By contrast, "the powers reserved to the several States will extend to all the objects, which, in the ordinary course of affairs, concern the lives, liberties and properties of the people; and the internal order, improvement, and prosperity of the State." The separation of legislative, executive, and judicial powers at the national level, coupled with the division of power between the state and national governments, provided "a double security" for "the rights of the people."[33]

People would naturally feel greater loyalty to their local governments, and federal lawmakers would bring their local attachments to Congress. Madison expected they "will probably in all cases have been members, and may even at the very time be members, of the state legislature." The federal government, moreover, would struggle to enforce a law unpopular within a state; reflecting an eighteenth-century attitude, a regular army could never be a match for the state militia and a people, Madison wrote, with "the advantage of being armed."[34]

In June 1788, as a delegate to the Richmond convention called to consider the ratification of the Constitution in Virginia, Madison repeated many of the arguments he had made in his *Federalist* essays.[35] To win ratification, however, Virginia's Federalists agreed to accept a compromise that had originally been negotiated in the Massachusetts convention: they would support amendments, including a bill of rights, after the Constitution took effect. Madison had feared that opening the door to amendments prematurely would derail the tenuous ratification process. But he eventually relented, and as a member of the first Congress to meet under the Constitution, he introduced a set of amendments that became the Bill of Rights. They included a provision no one had proposed: a ban on state interference with the freedom of the press, the right to a jury trial in criminal cases, and freedom of religion. He called it "the most valuable amendment on the whole list." Reflecting Madison's lingering suspicions of state governments, it died in the Senate.[36]

During the ratification debate, Madison had represented the Constitution as creating a central government of limited and enumerated powers. The states, he had said, retained sovereignty over those subjects left to their jurisdiction, although the federal courts would police the boundary between state and national authority. The Tenth Amendment, providing that "the powers not delegated to the United States by the Constitution, nor prohibited by it to the States, are reserved to the States respectively, or to the people," attempted to ratify that understanding.[37]

Madison felt obligated to honor the representations he had made in his *Federalist* essays and at the Virginia ratifying convention. He considered the political system created in 1787 to be unique, and its uniqueness meant it could only be understood by studying its origins. Madison said repeatedly that the Constitution ought to be interpreted as it was understood when it was adopted. He was not perfectly consistent in explaining how that understanding might be discovered, but he generally put the greatest emphasis on the debates of the state ratifying conventions. As he explained during the Jay Treaty debate, "If we were to look . . . for the meaning of the instrument, beyond the face of the instrument, we must look for it not in the general convention, which proposed, but in the state conventions, which accepted and ratified the Constitution." Nevertheless, Madison also realized that in interpreting the Constitution "the consequences" of a particular interpretation should be considered.[38]

Madison has often been accused of inconsistency, allegedly championing states' rights in the 1790s and then returning to his earlier nationalism after the Democratic-Republicans took power in 1801. Madison, for example, opposed the creation of the First Bank of the United States in 1791 and then signed legislation chartering the Second Bank of the United States during his second term as president. Madison denied the charge, but he admitted after leaving the White House that, in 1787, he may have favored a stronger national government than the debate over the Constitution, and later events, proved to be necessary.[39]

By 1791, Madison had become concerned that the excessive "consolidation" of power in the national government might leave Congress with more responsibilities than it could manage. Power would then flow naturally to the president, eventually making the chief executive a virtual monarch. Finding authority to charter a national bank in the Constitution's "necessary and proper clause," as Treasury Secretary Alexander Hamilton had attempted to do, Madison argued, would establish "a precedent of interpretation, levelling all the barriers which limit the powers of the general government, and protect those of the state governments."[40] The difficulty his administration faced in financing the War of 1812 probably played a part in Madison's change of position. He claimed, however, to be yielding to "evidence of the Public Judgment, necessarily superseding individual opinions" about the constitutionality of a national bank. Successive legislatures, with the apparent approval of the people, had supported a bank, and in the interest of predictability, Madison put his reservations aside.[41]

In the Virginia Resolutions of 1798, in which the state assembly declared the notorious Alien and Sedition Acts to be unconstitutional, Madison raised again the dangers of "consolidation" and appeared to challenge the jurisdiction of the Supreme Court to determine the scope of federal power. Madison claimed the states could "interpose [themselves] for arresting the progress of the evil, and for maintaining within their respective limits, the authorities, rights and liberties appertaining to them." The vagueness of "interposition" caused endless confusion. Madison confided to Jefferson that he had been intentionally imprecise. He seemed to assume that a state retained, as a matter of natural law and self-preservation, a right of resistance, but he was unsure the state legislature was the "legitimate organ" to exercise it. In ordinary cases, Madison acknowledged that the Supreme Court had the last word as a matter of law, but a judicial opinion ought not to preclude efforts by a state or by the people to reverse the decision through the political process. That was the goal, he claimed in an 1800 report to the Virginia Assembly, of the Virginia Resolutions, and he had predicted in *The Federalist* that the state assemblies would speak up when the federal government threatened the people's rights. No less a nationalist than Alexander Hamilton had made a similar argument in *Federalist* No. 28; it was hardly the kind of "interposition" advocated by southern segregationists in the 1950s.[42]

A loose construction of the "necessary and proper clause," Madison warned, would jeopardize the capacity of the courts to strike a balance between federal and state prerogatives. If the clause were to be read narrowly, judges would know when Congress exceeded its power. If the clause were to be read broadly, litigation challenging federal statutes would become policy disputes beyond the competency of the courts to resolve. As president, Madison applied a similar logic when he vetoed an internal improvements bill based in part on the Constitution's general welfare clause. Interpreting the clause as an affirmative grant of power to Congress would preclude the federal courts from "guarding the boundary between the legislative powers of the General and State Governments" because questions involving the general welfare raised policy issues not suitable to judicial determination.[43]

In a republic, Madison had long thought, the greatest threat to liberty came from an oppressive majority, although a minority faction, if it seized the reins of government, could be equally dangerous, at least in the short term. Consequently, he came to believe the courts could interpret the Constitution more faithfully than legislators could because judges would be less amenable to public pressure. Yet, as he wrote Jefferson after both men had retired from public office, "the Judiciary career has not corresponded with what was anticipated." Chief Justice John Marshall's opinion in *McCulloch v. Maryland* (1819), upholding the constitutionality of the Bank of the United States, Madison complained, had granted Congress "a Legislative discretion ... to which no practical limit can be assigned." Allowing Congress any reasonable means to achieve a constitutionally enumerated end, as Marshall seemed to do, raised issues "evidently beyond the reach of Judicial cognizance."[44]

Frustrated though he was by the Marshall court, Madison continued to defend the court's right to arbitrate disputes between the state and federal governments. Motivated in part by his fear that the Nullification Crisis, South Carolina's dispute with Congress and President Andrew Jackson over a protective tariff, might lead to disunion or civil war, Madison stressed the need for a peaceful method to resolve jurisdictional conflicts. Only the Supreme Court could ensure the uniform application of federal law, and a tariff would be ineffective if its enforcement varied from state to state. Permitting the states as a group to resolve disputes, as South Carolina's John C. Calhoun had proposed, would be time-consuming and expensive and would "impair the salutary veneration for a system requiring such frequent interpositions." Another alternative, expecting state and federal officials to negotiate their differences, struck Madison as politically unrealistic.[45]

Notwithstanding the Supreme Court's ultimate legal authority, Madison argued that adequate safeguards existed to protect the states and their citizens. Congress would respond to pressure from voters and state legislatures to curb a rogue court, and presidents responded to public opinion as well. Judges who abused their positions could be impeached and removed from office.[46]

He had predicted in *Federalist* No. 39 that the federal courts would maintain the appropriate balance between state and federal power, but privately he had his doubts. Shortly before writing *Federalist* No. 39, Madison had expressed his misgivings about judicial review to Jefferson: it was a slow and costly way to set aside bad laws and could place an intolerable burden on private litigants. A state, moreover, might ignore a federal court order, thus creating a constitutional crisis. The congressional negative allowed federal lawmakers, whom he then deemed more trustworthy, to resolve jurisdictional disputes through the ordinary legislative process. As he told Jefferson, "The impossibility of dividing powers of legislation, in such a manner, as to be free from different constructions by different interests, or even from ambiguity in the judgment of the impartial, requires some such expedient as I contend for." More than thirty years later, after the federal courts had demonstrated more vigor than he had anticipated, his "doubts as to the ultimate & fixed character of a Political Establishment distinguished by so novel & complex a mechanism" as its federal system remained.[47]

As circumstances changed, Madison's thinking about federalism and the courts evolved. The constitutional debates of 1787 and 1788 led him to moderate his earlier nationalism. His preference for a congressional veto gave way in time to a defense of federal judicial review. Less subject to popular passions than was Congress, the Supreme Court struck him as the most convenient and impartial forum for resolving issues involving federalism and for keeping Congress largely tethered to its enumerated powers. Above all, he hoped to preserve the Union. "The advice nearest to my heart and deepest in my convictions," he wrote in his last public statement, "is that the Union of the states be cherished and perpetuated."[48]

Ultimately Madisonian federalism combined a deference to the Supreme Court with a commitment to stability, predictability, and a generally strict construction of the Constitution. Congress's discretion would be limited, but as a practical matter, the national government would be supreme within the federal system. It was a precarious balance, one complicated by Madison himself. Jefferson once observed that the best defense of the states' autonomy was "wise" state government, but after working to reform Virginia's legal code in the mid-1780s, Madison gave little thought to improving the quality of political life in the states. His version of federalism limited the power of the federal government to address the issue of slavery, while his apparent inconsistencies have exposed him to the charge he lacked any fixed theory of constitutional interpretation. In the immediate aftermath of the Constitutional Convention, Madison had predicted "a continual struggle" over national versus state sovereignty, and history proved him right.[49]

NOTES

1. JM to Thomas Jefferson, October 24, 1787, in *Republic of Letters: The Correspondence between Thomas Jefferson and James Madison, 1776–1826* (hereafter *ROL*), 3 vols., ed. James Morton Smith (New York: W. W. Norton, 1995), 1:498; "Government of the United States," *National Gazette*, February 6, 1792, in *James Madison, Writings* (hereafter *JMW*), ed. Jack N. Rakove (New York: Library of America, 1999), 508–9; JM to Spencer Roane, June 29, 1821, *JMW*, 777.

2. JM to William Cabell Rives, March 12, 1833, *JMW*, 863–66; "On Nullification," December 1834, in *Letters and Other Writings of James Madison*, 4 vols. (Philadelphia: J. B. Lippincott, 1867), 4:425.

3. "Of Ancient and Modern Confederacies," ca. 1786, in *The Mind of the Founder: Sources of the Political Thought of James Madison*, rev. ed., ed. Marvin Meyers (Waltham, Mass.: Brandeis University Press, 1981), 47–56; Michael P. Zuckert, "Federalism and the Founding: Toward a Reinterpretation of the Constitutional Convention," *Review of Politics* 48, no. 2 (Spring 1986): 166–210, 172; Colleen A. Sheehan, *The Mind of James Madison: The Legacy of Classical Republicanism* (New York: Cambridge University Press, 2015), 92; Peter S. Onuf, "Federalist Republican: Michael Zuckert's James Madison," *American Political Thought* 8, no. 2 (Spring 2019): 258–70, 263; "Government of the United States," *National Gazette*, February 6, 1792, *JMW*, 509.

4. JM to Thomas Jefferson, April 16, 1781, *ROL*, 1:186–87; *JMW*, 19.

5. JM to James Monroe, August 7, 1785, *JMW*, 36–39.

6. JM to Thomas Jefferson, August 12, 1786, *ROL*, 1:428–33; JM to Thomas Jefferson, December 4, 1786, *ROL*, 1:454–57; JM to George Washington, December 7, 1786, *JMW*, 59–61; Michael J. Klarman, *The Framers' Coup: The Making of the United States Constitution* (New York: Oxford University Press, 2016), 43–46.

7. JM to Thomas Jefferson, July 3, 1784, *ROL*, 1:321–24; JM to Thomas Jefferson, January 9, 1785, *ROL*, 1:355–64; JM to Thomas Jefferson, January 22, 1786, *ROL*, 1:401–8; JM to Thomas Jefferson, August 12, 1786, *ROL*,1:428–33; JM to Thomas Jefferson, December 4, 1786, *ROL*, 1: 454–57; JM to Thomas Jefferson, February 15, 1787, *ROL*, 1:466–68.
8. JM to Edmund Pendleton, February 24, 1787, *JMW*, 61–63.
9. "Vices of the Political System of the United States," April 1787, *JMW*, 69–80.
10. Ibid, 69–76.
11. Ibid, 76–78.
12. Ibid, 78–80. See Douglass Adair, "'That Politics May Be Reduced to a Science:' David Hume, James Madison, and the Tenth Federalist," in *Fame and the Founding Fathers*, ed. Trevor Colbourn (Indianapolis: Liberty Fund, 1974), 132–51.
13. JM to Thomas Jefferson, March 19, 1787, *ROL*, 1:469–74.
14. Ibid., 1:470; Alison L. LaCroix, *The Ideological Origins of American Federalism* (Cambridge, Mass.: Harvard University Press, 2010), 145–46.
15. JM to Edmund Randolph, April 8, 1787, in *Papers of James Madison* (hereafter *PJM*), 17 vols., ed. William T. Hutchinson and William M. E. Rachel (Chicago: University of Chicago Press; Charlottesville: University of Virginia Press, 1962–1991), 9:368–71; JM to George Washington, April 16, 1787, *JMW*, 80–85; Jack N. Rakove, *A Politician Thinking: The Creative Mind of James Madison* (Norman: University of Oklahoma Press, 2017), 51–53.
16. Virginia Plan, May 29, 1787, *JMW*, 90; *Records of the Federal Constitutional Convention of 1787*, 4 vols., ed. Max Farrand (New Haven, Conn.: Yale University Press, 1937), 1:164, 245. See also Charles F. Hobson, "The Negative on State Laws: James Madison, the Constitution and the Crisis of Republican Government," *William and Mary Quarterly*, 36, no. 2 (April 1979): 215–35, 227–28; and Larry D. Kramer, "Madison's Audience," *Harvard Law Review* 112 (January 1999), 611–79. In retirement, Madison conceded the congressional veto had been ill conceived. Rakove, *Politician Thinking*, 52; "A Sketch Never Finished Nor Applied," ca. 1830, *JMW*, 839; *PJM*, 9:322n4.
17. Virginia Plan, May 29, 1787, *JMW*, 89.
18. New Jersey Plan, June 15, 1787, Farrand, *Records*,1:242–45; Klarman, *Framers' Coup*, 153–54; Richard Beeman, *Plain, Honest Men: The Making of the American Constitution* (New York: Random House, 2009), 146–52.
19. Jack N. Rakove, *Original Meanings: Politics and Ideas in the Making of the Constitution* (New York: A. A. Knopf, 1997), 170–71; Forrest McDonald, *Novus Ordo Seclorum: The Intellectual Origins of the Constitution* (Lawrence: University Press of Kansas, 1985), 213–15, 234–35; Farrand, *Records*, 1:474–75, 2:15.
20. Farrand, *Records*, 1:321, 357–58, 449, 463; Noah Feldman, *The Three Lives of James Madison: Genius, Partisan, President* (New York: Random House, 2017), 141.
21. Farrand, *Records*, 2:9, 240–41. The convention ultimately agreed to give the states primary jurisdiction for determining the "Times, Places, and Manner" of congressional elections, subject to federal regulation except for "the Places of chusing Senators." U.S. Constitution, Article I, Section 4.
22. Farrand, *Records*, 1:134, 154, 2:92–93, 109–11.

23. JM to Thomas Jefferson, September 6, 1787, *ROL*, 1:491; JM to Thomas Jefferson, October 24 and November 1, 1787, *ROL*, 1:496–502; JM to Archibald Stuart, October 30, 1787, *PJM*, 10:232–33.

24. Saul Cornell, *Anti-Federalism and the Dissenting Tradition in America, 1788–1828* (Chapel Hill: University of North Carolina Press, 1999), 61–74; Lance Banning, *The Sacred Fire of Liberty: James Madison and the Founding of the Federal Republic* (Ithaca, N.Y.: Cornell University Press, 1995), 241–42; Christopher M. Duncan, *The Anti-Federalists and Early American Political Thought* (DeKalb: Northern Illinois University Press, 1995), 156–72; Jackson Turner Main, *The Anti-Federalists: Critics of the Constitution, 1781–1788* (Chapel Hill: University of North Carolina Press, 1961), 125–26; TJ to John Adams, November 13, 1787, *Thomas Jefferson, Writings*, ed. Merrill D. Peterson (New York: Library of America, 1984), 912–14 (hereafter *TJW*); TJ to JM, December 20, 1787, *ROL*, 1:511–15.

25. Banning, *Sacred Fire of Liberty*, 201; *Federalist* No. 10, in Alexander Hamilton, James Madison, and John Jay, *The Federalist*, ed. Jacob E. Cooke (Middletown, Conn.: Wesleyan University Press, 1961), 56–65 (subsequent citations are to this edition); *Federalist* No. 14, 86; *Federalist* No. 18, 117; *Federalist* No. 19, 117–23; *Federalist* No. 20, 124–29.

26. *Federalist* No. 37, 231–39, 234; *Federalist* No. 62, 416.

27. Rakove, *Original Meanings*, 161–62; Forrest McDonald, *States' Rights and the Union: "Imperium in Imperio," 1776–1876* (Lawrence: University Press of Kansas, 2000), 19–21; *Federalist* No. 39, 254.

28. *Federalist* No. 39, 255.

29. *Federalist* No. 39, 255–56. See *Federalist* No. 40, 262, on the states' "sovereign and independent jurisdiction" in "all unenumerated cases." In *Federalist* No. 43, 296, Madison wrote that the clause in Article V providing "that no State, without its Consent, shall be deprived of its equal Suffrage in the Senate" was "probably meant as a palladium to the residuary sovereignty of the states."

30. *Federalist* No. 39, 257.

31. *Federalist* No. 43, 296; *Federalist* No. 44, 305. See also *Federalist* No. 52, 358–59; *Federalist* No. 55, 376.

32. *Federalist* No. 44, 305; *Federalist* No. 45, 309.

33. *Federalist* No. 45, 313; *Federalist* No. 51, 351.

34. *Federalist* No. 46, 315–23; *Federalist* No. 56, 380.

35. *JMW*, 354–65, 366–79, 393–400.

36. *JMW*, 437–52, 470.

37. To be sure, Madison's successful opposition to Anti-Federalist efforts to insert "expressly" before "delegated" narrowed the scope of the amendment. See Jonathan Gienapp, *The Second Creation: Fixing the American Constitution in the Founding Era* (Cambridge, Mass.: Harvard University Press, 2018), 228–29.

38. *JMW*, 482, 574; Detached Memorandum, ca. 1819, *JMW*, 750–51; JM to Thomas Ritchie, September 15, 1821, in *Papers of James Madison*, Retirement Series, 3 vols., ed. David Mattern et al. (Charlottesville: University of Virginia Press, 2009–), 2:381–82; JM to John G. Jackson, December 28, 1821, *PJM*, 2:241–42; JM to Henry Lee, June, 25, 1824, *JMW*, 803–4; JM to Andrew Stevenson, March 25, 1826, *Founders Online*, National Archives,

accessed April 11, 2019; JM to Daniel Webster, May 27, 1830, *Founders Online,* National Archives, accessed September 29, 2019; JM to Edward Everett, August 28, 1830, *JMW,* 842; JM to William Cabell Rives, March 12, 1833, *JMW,* 863–66.

39. Jeff Broadwater, "James Madison and the Constitution: Reassessing the 'Madison Problem,'" *Virginia Magazine of History and Biography,* 123, no. 3 (2015): 202–35; JM to John G. Jackson, December 28, 1821, *PJM,* Retirement Series, 2:441–42; JM to Nicholas P. Trist, December 1, 1831, in *Writings of James Madison,* 9 vols., ed. Galliard Hunt (New York: G. P. Putnam's Sons, 1900–10), 9:471–77.

40. "Consolidation," *National Gazette,* December 5, 1791, *JMW,* 498–500; "Political Reflections," *Aurora General Advertiser,* February 23, 1799, *JMW,* 606–7; *JMW,* 490.

41. Seventh Annual Message to Congress, December 5, 1815, *JMW,* 714; JM to Charles Jared Ingersoll, June 25, 1831, Meyers, *Mind of the Founder,* 390–93; JM to Nicholas Trist, December 1, 1831, *WJM,* 9:477; Detached Memoranda, ca. 1819, *JMW,* 756.

42. Virginia Resolutions, December 21, 1798, *JMW,* 589; JM to Thomas Jefferson, December 29, 1798, *ROL,* 2:1085; JM to Nicholas P. Trist, December 1, 1831, *WJM,* 9:471–77; Report on the Alien and Sedition Acts, January 7, 1800, *JMW,* 608–62. The Virginia Resolutions did refer to the Constitution as "a compact to which the states are parties" (*JMW,* 589), terminology usually associated, perhaps inaccurately, with an extreme states' rights position. But Madison later said the Virginia Resolutions were simply "expressions of opinion" aimed at "exciting reflection." *JMW,* 659. See JM to Edward Everett, August 28, 1830, *JMW,* 842–52, for a pro-Union definition of "compact." See also Aaron N. Coleman, *The American Revolution, State Sovereignty, and the American Constitutional Settlement, 1765–1800* (Lanham, Md.: Lexington Books, 2016), 223–26; and McDonald, *States' Rights and the Union,* 7–11. On *Federalist* No. 28, see John B. Boles, *Seven Virginians: The Men Who Shaped Our Republic* (Charlottesville: University of Virginia Press, 2023), 176–77.

43. Report on the Alien and Sedition Acts, January 7, 1800, *JMW,* 643–44; Veto Message, March 3, 1817, *JMW,* 719. For more on the general welfare clause, see JM to James Robertson, April 20, 1831, *Founders Online,* National Archives, accessed September 29, 2019.

44. JM to Thomas Jefferson, October 17, 1788, *ROL,* 1:564–65; Drew R. McCoy, *The Last of the Fathers: James Madison and the Republican Legacy* (New York: Cambridge University Press, 1989), 101–2; JM to Spencer Roane, September 2, 1819, *JMW,* 733–37; JM to Thomas Jefferson, June 27, 1823, *ROL,* 3:1869; JM to Spencer Roane, May 6, 1821, *JMW,* 772–77.

45. JM to Edward Everett, August 28, 1830, *JMW,* 842–52, 845. Madison did not insist on uniformity in all cases. He considered the states to be laboratories in which "important experiments" could be undertaken. If successful, they could be adopted elsewhere. If they failed, the damage would be contained. JM to Edward Livingston, July 10, 1822, *JMW,* 786–89.

As did the militantly proslavery Calhoun, Madison could read the Constitution to protect slavery. He effectively neutralized antislavery petitions submitted to the First Congress, and in 1819 he supported Missouri's admission into the Union as a slave state. Yet in light of his initial preference for a more vigorous national government, his philosophical opposition to slavery, his defense of federal judicial review, and his opposition to Calhoun's extreme states' rights views, it seems unlikely that a desire to defend slavery was a primary motive behind his approach to federalism. As Quentin P. Taylor's essay in this volume suggests, Madison's priority was nation building, not the abolition or preservation of slavery. See also Jeff Broadwater, "'Those from Whom I Derive My Public Station': James Madison, the Politics of Race, and the Fate of Slavery in the Western Territories," *Journal of East Tennessee History* 87 (2015): 64–83.

46. JM to Edward Everett, August 28, 1830, *JMW*, 842–52.

47. Rakove, *Original Meanings*, 176; JM to Thomas Jefferson, October 24, 1787, *ROL*, 1:499–500; JM to Spencer Roane, May 6, 1821, *JMW*, 733. See also Jeremy D. Bailey, *James Madison and Constitutional Imperfection* (New York: Cambridge University Press, 2015), 172–74.

48. "Advice to My Country," 1834, *JMW*, 866.

49. Thomas Jefferson to Archibald Stuart, December 23, 1791, *TJW*, 983–84; JM to TJ, October 24, 1787, *ROL*, 1:499; Jay Cost, *James Madison: America's First Politician* (New York: Basic Books, 2021), 284.

The "Stepfather" of the Bill of Rights

Madison and the Problem of Parchment Barriers

PAUL FINKELMAN

In September 1794 James Madison married Dolley Payne Todd, a twenty-six-year-old widowed mother. Madison helped raise her son, John Payne Todd, never fathering children of his own. Madison's family life was a metaphor for his political life. He was a stepfather to John Todd and was in many ways the "stepfather" to his two "political children"—the Constitution and the Bill of Rights.

Madison has often been called the "father" of both documents,[1] but his paternity of the Constitution is exaggerated, and his paternity of the Bill of Rights was both reluctant and unenthusiastic. A key player in organizing the Constitutional Convention, Madison was unhappy with the final product. He thought the government would be dangerously weak. He nevertheless worked hard for ratification, believing that this was the best Constitution the nation was likely to get, and if it failed, the nation was doomed.

At the Constitutional Convention he opposed adding a bill of rights to the proposed frame of government and "never considered" it "essential to the federal constitution." When he proposed what became the Bill of Rights in the first Congress, he never argued with passion or conviction for the amendments. He merely conceded "that in a certain form and to a certain extent, such a provision was neither improper nor altogether useless."[2] It is hard to imagine a legislator being less enthusiastic in introducing monumental legislation. The "Father of the Bill of Rights" was clearly a reluctant stepparent.

To understand why Madison opposed a bill of rights until the moment he tepidly proposed it, I begin with a cursory look at his role in creating the Constitution.

THE STEPFATHER OF THE CONSTITUTION

When the Annapolis Convention collapsed in 1786, Madison and other nationalists generated the call for what became the Constitutional Convention. Madison optimistically believed the convention would create a strong national government to end what his fellow Virginia delegate Edmund Randolph called "the imbecility of the existing confederacy."[3] Madison's extensive notes of the debates became our most important source for what happened in the Constitutional Convention, although we know his notes were often incomplete and that he tampered with them late in life.[4] He worked tirelessly to secure ratification, helping to write *The Federalist Papers,* and spoke forcefully and often at the Virginia ratifying convention.

Despite his hard work to secure ratification, Madison was frustrated by what the convention produced. He opposed the creation of the Senate, which allowed tiny states such as Delaware, Rhode Island, and New Hampshire to have the same number of votes as Virginia, Pennsylvania, or North Carolina. He wanted population-based representation in both houses of Congress. He unsuccessfully argued that Congress should have the power to grant charters of incorporation. He personally favored a direct election of the president by the people of the nation but supported the Electoral College to increase the influence of the slave states in electing the president, by folding the three-fifths clause into the allocation of electors.[5] He despised the slave trade clause that prohibited Congress from banning the African slave trade until *at the earliest* 1808 and undermined Congress's commerce power. He asserted this clause protecting the African trade was "dishonorable to the National character."[6]

Madison worked hard for ratification of the Constitution, not because he loved it, but because he thought without it the nation would collapse into anarchy or tyranny, or a collection of tiny republics to be picked off by Britain, Spain, or France. Despite its many faults, he thought it was a vast improvement over the "imbecility" of the Articles of Confederation. Madison never claimed to be its father; at best he might have been a stepfather. For Madison, an imperfect union was better than none at all. Thus, during the ratification struggle he parried Anti-Federalist arguments when he could and ignored them when he had no persuasive counterarguments.

The Federalist Papers, which he wrote with Alexander Hamilton and John Jay, solidified his place in history. Marrying philosophy, history, political theory, and practical politics, today they are often seen as an "oracle" for the Constitution's meaning. This is clearly a mistake, since the *Federalist* was written for a purely partisan purpose: to persuade New York voters to support ratification.[7] The essays were designed to put a political "spin" on the Constitution, not to provide a theoretical guide to the document. Thus, for example, the *Federalist* never discussed the Fugitive Slave Clause, because no "spin" could have justified it to northerners.[8] Even mentioning it would have undermined support for the Constitution in New York.

Anti-Federalists offered many arguments against ratification, but most focused on fears of a stronger national government. They have been correctly seen as "men of little faith," because of their often weird and paranoid claims that the Constitution would create a dictatorship or oligarchy and because of their religious bigotry.[9] The political scientist Herbert Storing sought to rehabilitate the Anti-Federalists by focusing on their political theories and their very best arguments. But even he admitted that the Anti-Federalists "had the weaker argument" and lost because "they refused to accept, or they accepted only halfheartedly, that the prime need was a government with the capacity to govern."[10]

Anti-Federalists almost universally argued that the Constitution needed a bill of rights to protect the people from arbitrary government and to guarantee due process of law, freedom of the press, and liberty of conscience.[11] But despite the claims of Storing and others, the Anti-Federalists were mostly interested in completely derailing the Constitution and used the demand for a bill of rights as their Trojan horse for destroying the work of the Philadelphia Convention.

Even their demand for a bill or rights was suspect. While allegedly desiring protection of religious liberty, many Anti-Federalists objected to the Constitution's prohibition of religious tests for officeholding. A North Carolina Anti-Federalist worried "that Papists may occupy" the presidency or "Mahometans may take it." In New York, "Curtiopolis" complained that the Constitution allowed officeholders to be "Quakers," "Mahometans, who ridicule the doctrine of the trinity," Deists, and other "abominable wretches." Absurdly, he worried that a Jew would "command" "the whole militia" and "our dear posterity may be ordered to rebuild Jerusalem."[12] One paranoid New Hampshire Anti-Federalist argued, "a Turk, a Jew, a Roman Catholic, and what is worse a Universalist, may be elected President." In Massachusetts, Major Thomas Lusk "shuddered at the idea that Roman Catholics, Papists, and Pagans might be introduced into office."[13] Patrick Henry, the nation's leading Anti-Federalist, had opposed Madison's bill (first drafted by Jefferson) to disestablish the Episcopal Church in Virginia. Thus, it was hard to take seriously Anti-Federalist demands for a bill of rights to protect religious freedom.

Anti-Federalists also found endless other reasons for defeating the Constitution. The historian Saul Cornell listed nine major areas for Anti-Federalists' opposition to the Constitution, with the Bill of Rights listed as number six, illustrating that the issue was somewhat important to most Anti-Federalists, but mostly useful as a battering ram against the new Constitution.[14] Not surprisingly, the Anti-Federalist calls for a bill of rights struck Madison and other Federalists as disingenuous. Patrick Henry simply feared a functional government, asserting the Constitution "has an awful squinting; it squints towards monarchy. . . . Your President may easily become King."[15] Others feared the Senate, the large size of House districts, the creation of a standing army, and tyrannical federal courts. During the ratification struggle Madison and other Federalists offered coherent and often persuasive arguments against these bizarre claims. After ratification most of these structural arguments and religiously bigoted complaints disappeared.

Some southerners, such as Henry, predicted the Constitution would be used to destroy slavery. Southern Federalists, including Madison, easily refuted these claims because it was patently obvious that the Constitution protected slavery. Edmund Randolph, who had refused to sign the Constitution, assured the Virginia ratifying convention that "there was not a member of the Virginia delegation who had *the smallest suspicion of the abolition of slavery.*" Madison pointed out that Virginians would have a right to recover fugitive slaves who escaped to northern states, which they did not currently have. South Carolina's General Charles Cotesworth Pinckney bragged to his legislature, "We have a security that the general government can never emancipate them, for no such authority is granted and it is admitted, on all hands, that the general government has no powers but what are expressly granted by the Constitution, and that all rights not expressed were reserved by the several states."[16]

The question of slavery was more powerful for northern opponents of the Constitution, who objected to the specific protections for the African slave trade, counting slaves for representation, and the obligation of northerners to suppress slave rebellions. Three Massachusetts Anti-Federalists—Consider Arms, Malichi Maynard, and Samuel Field—believed the Constitution's "lust for slavery, [was] portentous of much evil in America, for the cry of innocent blood, . . . hath undoubtedly reached to the Heavens, to which that cry is always directed, and will draw down upon them vengeance adequate to the enormity of the crime." In New York "A Countryman from Dutchess County" thought that Americans might become "a happy and respectable people" if the states were forced into "relinquishing every idea of drenching the bowels of Africa in gore, for the sake of enslaving its free-born innocent inhabitants."[17] The Anti-Federalists understood, far better than the Federalists, the danger of the proslavery compact that had been created in Philadelphia.[18] But their complaints gained little traction in the North and none in the South and did not directly impact the debate over a bill of rights.[19]

Madison and other Federalists downplayed slavery when campaigning for ratification in the North. At best they could argue that the slave trade clause empowered the national government to eventually end the trade, which it could not do under the Articles of Confederation. A few falsely claimed that after 1808

Congress could end slavery or that after Congress ended the trade in 1808 slavery would die out, which was clearly absurd since slavery had been flourishing in the nation without the slave trade since the Revolution began.

Far more important than slavery or the fear of Catholic, Jewish, or "Mahometan" presidents were Anti-Federalist concerns over the lack of a bill of rights. By this time most states had a bill of rights. Anti-Federalists argued the omission of a bill of rights confirmed that the Philadelphia delegates were plotting to undermine American liberty.

In response, Federalists argued against the necessity or even the value of a bill of rights. Derisively calling a bill of rights a useless "parchment barrier," Madison told Jefferson: "Experience proves the inefficacy of a bill of rights on those occasions when its controul is most needed. Repeated violations of these parchment barriers have been committed by overbearing majorities in every state." In Virginia he had "seen the bill of rights violated in every instance where it has been opposed to a popular current." He warned that "restrictions however strongly marked on paper will never be regarded when opposed to the decided sense of the public; and after repeated violations in extraordinary cases, they will lose even their ordinary efficacy."[20]

How then, did Madison go from dismissing "parchment barriers" to drafting the Bill of Rights? How did he become, however reluctantly, the "stepfather" of the Bill of Rights?

THE BILL OF RIGHTS AND THE CONSTITUTIONAL CONVENTION

In the Constitutional Convention various delegates proposed a bill of rights, but the state delegations unanimously rejected this. At the end of the convention Mason, Randolph, and Elbridge Gerry of Massachusetts refused to sign the document. Mason began his explanation with "There is no Declaration of Rights." Mason listed other issues including the commerce power, the protection of the African slave trade, and the presidential pardon power, but the lack of a bill of rights magnified these shortcomings. Mason feared the Senate and the president would combine "to accomplish what usurpations they pleased upon the rights and liberties of the people," while the federal judiciary would "absorb and destroy the judiciaries of the several States." Without a bill of rights, Congress threatened the "security" of "the people for their rights."[21]

Instead of signing, Randolph proposed a second convention to consider amendments, including a bill of rights. Gerry agreed with many of Mason's criticisms, but he could "get over all these" defects "if the rights of the Citizens were not rendered insecure" by the virtually unlimited power of Congress under the necessary and proper clause and the lack of a guarantee of jury trials in civil cases.[22]

While Mason, Randolph, and Gerry argued for explicit protections of liberty, Madison, who spoke on virtually every issue at the convention, remained silent. Why did Madison fail to support his colleagues from Virginia on this major issue? If he opposed a bill of rights, why was he quiet?

Madison's silence suggests his uncharacteristic ambivalence. Madison firmly supported individual rights and personal freedom. In 1774 he had considered "the possibility that a 'Bill of Rights' might be adopted by [the Continental] Congress and confirmed by the King or Parliament" so that America's liberties would be "as firmly fixed and defined as those of England."[23] Later he participated in drafting Virginia's Declaration of Rights. He guided the Virginia Statute for Religious Freedom (1786) through the legislature. As one historian noted, with some exaggeration, "No man of his [Madison's] generation had a broader or deeper commitment to the general principles of civil liberty and procedural justice."[24] Yet even when he later introduced in Congress the amendments that became the Bill of Rights, Madison was ambivalent. In fact, from 1787 until Congress debated the amendments in 1789, Madison consistently argued against a federal bill of rights.

REASONS FOR FEDERALIST OPPOSITION TO A BILL OF RIGHTS

During this period Madison and other Federalists offered five major objections to the addition of a bill of rights.

An Unnecessary Addition to the Constitution

Federalists argued a Bill of Rights was unnecessary because the states were the main guarantors of liberty, and the national government under the Constitution lacked power to interfere with basic rights and liberties.

At the convention James Wilson asserted the states would "preserve the rights of individuals." Oliver Ellsworth explained he looked to the state governments "for the preservation of his rights." Roger Sherman argued that "the State Declarations of Rights are not repealed by this Constitution; and being in force are sufficient." Many of the delegates, including Madison, supported Sherman.[25] Madison maintained that the constitution created a government of limited powers that did not empower the national government to interfere with basic rights, which "are reserved by the manner in which the federal powers are granted."[26]

A Redundant Addition to the Constitution

While asserting the national government had no power over basic rights and thus a bill of rights was unnecessary, Federalists noted clauses that protected individual liberties and rights. These included bans on religious tests for officeholding, multiple officeholding for federal officials, the suspension of the writ of habeas corpus except in time of actual invasion or rebellion, ex post facto laws, writs of attainder, and titles of nobility as well as a guarantee of jury trials in criminal cases and eliminating the oppressive English concepts of treason by requiring two witnesses to an overt act and prohibiting the practice of punishing children for the crimes of their parents.

Other provisions protected many basic liberties and rights. One Madison biographer found "twenty-four elements of a Bill of Rights in a Constitution that is said to contain none."[27] Madison did not make such a careful count, but he extolled the document's protections of liberty.

A Useless Addition to the Constitution

Madison simultaneously argued that a bill of rights—what he derisively called a parchment barrier—was also useless in stopping the government from trampling on the liberties of the people. As noted above, more than a year after the convention Madison told Jefferson that "experience proves the inefficacy of a bill of rights on those occasions when its controul is most needed. Repeated violations of these parchment barriers have been committed by overbearing majorities in every state."[28]

Madison's disdain for "parchment barriers" reflected his contempt for Virginia's "parochial, so illiberal, so small-minded" state legislators who "had no regard for public honor or honesty" and were "reluctant to do anything that might appear unpopular." Such "clods," as historian Gordon Wood called them, could not be expected to respect a bill of rights.[29]

A Dangerous Addition to the Constitution

Madison also argued that a bill of rights was dangerous because a complete enumeration of all rights would be impossible, and any rights not enumerated would have been given up. In *Federalist* No. 84 Alexander Hamilton asserted that a bill of rights "would even be dangerous. They would contain various exceptions to powers not granted; and, on this very account, would afford a colorable pretext to claim more than were granted."[30] Madison agreed, telling Jefferson a bill of rights had to "be so framed as not to imply powers not meant to be included in the enumeration."[31]

Madison also believed a bill of rights would be dangerous because it could not fully secure rights. He assumed New Englanders would oppose a true separation of church and state, and thus the "rights of Conscience" would be "narrowed much more" by a bill of rights than any government would dare do on its own.[32] For Madison an incomplete protection of conscience was worse than none at all.

A Violation of a Republican Constitution

Finally, Federalists argued a bill of rights was unnecessary under a republican form of government. Oliver Ellsworth, writing under the nom de plume "Landowner," argued that a bill of rights was something that the people wrested from the king. This was unnecessary in America "since government is considered as originating from the people," who did not need to give rights to themselves. Similarly, James Wilson argued, "It would have been superfluous and absurd, to have stipulated with a federal body of our own creation, that we should enjoy those privileges, of which we are not divested."[33]

Madison's more sophisticated analysis conceded a republican government might threaten liberty, but such threats would not come from a ruling elite, such as a king taking rights from the people. Rather, identifying what would later be called the tyranny of the majority, Madison believed that in a republic, threats to liberty would emanate from the popularly elected legislature, where a determined majority would simply ignore a "parchment barrier." Diversity would protect liberty, and so religious freedom was secured by "that multiplicity of sects, which pervades America, and which is the best and only security for religious liberty in any society."[34] Madison later told Jefferson: "Wherever the real power in a Government lies, there is the danger of oppression. In our Governments the real power lies in the majority of the Community, and the invasion of private rights is chiefly to be apprehended, not from acts of Government contrary to the sense of its constituents, but from acts in which the Government is the mere instrument of the major number of the constituents."[35] Madison doubted a bill of rights could forestall a determined majority wishing to trample on the rights of a minority.

WORKING FOR RATIFICATION

After the Constitutional Convention Madison was quickly drawn into the debates to secure ratification and prevent a second convention, which he believed would be disastrous.[36] Madison was clearly ambivalent about the Constitution, which did not create the strong government that he wanted. Indeed, the "Constitution Madison expounded and defended as 'Publius' was a pale version of the plan he had carefully worked out before the Philadelphia meeting."[37] But it was a vast improvement over the Articles of Confederation. So he supported it, claiming there was a "blending" of "a proper stability & energy in the Government with the essential characters of the republican Form" while retaining "a proper line of demarcation between the national and State authorities."[38] But this was mostly a political posture and not an accurate reflection of Madison's true beliefs.

Privately Madison argued the government under the Constitution would be too weak, telling Jefferson the Constitution "will neither effectually answer its national object nor prevent the local mischiefs which every where excite disgusts agst. the state governments." In late October he still bemoaned that the convention had not adopted his proposal to give Congress a "constitutional negative on the laws of the States."[39]

Madison told his Virginia allies that amendments would destroy the Constitution's delicate balance between competing interests. Madison thought the new government was already dangerously weak, and any amendments would further weaken it.

Opposition to the Constitution formed once the document became public. The most common Anti-Federalist complaint was the lack of a bill of rights. Thus, in defending the Constitution, Madison had to oppose the call for a bill of rights. Otherwise, he would have had to admit that the Constitution had a major defect. Madison was firmly convinced that ratification was an all-or-nothing proposition, and admitting the need for a bill of rights would undermine ratification.

Madison's first test of the issue came in the Congress, operating under the Articles of Confederation, which received the work of the Constitutional Convention. Madison was one of more than a dozen signers who were also in Congress. Madison and these other "fiery zealots," helped defeat a motion by Virginia's Richard Henry Lee and New York's Melancton Smith to add a bill of rights to the Constitution.[40] Madison focused on the illegitimacy of Congress adding to the work of the Convention,[41] which enabled him to oppose a bill of rights without having to take any position on its merits. Madison and his allies then convinced the Congress to send the Constitution to the states without any changes.

On October 24 Madison sent Jefferson a seventeen-page letter, analyzing the Constitution. His biggest concern was the inability of the national government to veto state legislation. Madison feared state legislatures would destroy the liberties of minorities. He thought this problem could be prevented by giving the national government the power to overrule the states. In an argument later developed in *Federalist* Nos. 10 and 14, Madison declared that "private rights will be more secure under the Guardianship of the General Government than under the State Governments" because the constituency of the national government would be so diverse that no single group would control it.[42]

Madison did not fear a majority in the national government might deny people basic liberties, and so he said nothing about a bill of rights, except to note that George Mason had left Philadelphia "in exceeding ill humour" because he "considers the want of a Bill of Rights as a fatal objection."[43] Madison thought that a stronger national government was necessary to protect the people from their state governments but did not think the people needed to be protected from the national government by a bill of rights.

DEFENDING THE CONSTITUTION, OPPOSING A BILL OF RIGHTS, AND *THE FEDERALIST PAPERS*

In mid-November 1787 Madison joined Alexander Hamilton and John Jay in writing *The Federalist Papers*.[44] As "Publius," Madison anonymously opposed to a bill of rights.

Madison's first contribution, the now-classic *Federalist* No. 10, argued that the greatest danger to liberty in a Republic came from "the violence of faction," which he defined as "a number of citizens, whether amounting to a majority or minority of the whole, who are united and actuated by some common impulse of passion, or of interest, adverse to the rights of other citizens, or to the permanent and aggregated interests of the community." Madison saw no way to eliminate the causes of faction without destroying political liberty itself, but he argued that increasing the size of electoral districts (and increasing the number of voters within them) would reduce the danger from faction because no single interest could obtain a majority. Madison assumed that competing interests would neutralize each other, preventing factions from threatening basic liberties, thus making a bill of rights unnecessary.[45]

In *Federalist* No. 51 Madison argued the Constitution's system of checks and balances combined with the diversity of the people would prevent one faction from taking power and threatening the liberty of its opponents. He famously declared that "if men were angels, no government would be necessary," but, given human nature, some formal controls were necessary. He believed that the people themselves would "no doubt [be] the primary control on the government," but that "auxiliary precautions" were also useful, including the Constitution's aim "to divide and arrange several offices in such a manner that each may be a check on the other." Thus, no single branch of government could threaten liberty while the division between the states and the federal government provided a "double security to the rights of the people."[46]

For Madison, the diversity of the people—not a bill of rights—would protect liberty. As long as the "society itself will be broken into so many parts, interests and classes of citizens, that the rights of individuals or of the minority, will be in little danger from interested combinations of the majority. In a free government, the security for civil rights must be the same as that for religious rights. It consists in one case in the multiplicity of interests, and in the other, in the multiplicity of sects. The degree of security in both cases will depend on the number of interests and sects."[47] Jack Rakove succinctly explains that Madison's theory rested on the notion that "diversity begets jealousy, and jealousy begets security."[48]

In *Federalist* No. 57, Madison argued that the "vigilant and manly spirit which actuates the people of America" would prevent the legislature from usurping its power.[49] Ever attuned to turning private interest to the public good, Madison argued that members of the House of Representatives would never betray the liberties of the people, because if they did, they would not be reelected. In these essays Madison argued that the political process, governmental structures, and demographic diversity would protect liberty.

In *Federalist* No. 38 he casually dismissed calls for a bill of rights because the Anti-Federalists could not all agree on what protections of liberty they wanted.[50] Madison also attacked the call for a bill of rights in *Federalist* Nos. 44, 46, and 48. The most direct rejection of a bill of rights in *The Federalist* came from Hamilton, who argued in *Federalist* No. 84: "Why declare that things shall not be done which there is no power to do? Why, for instance, should it be said that the liberty of the press shall not be restrained, when no power is given by which restrictions may be imposed?" Madison later explained that while the F*ederalist*'s "writers are not mutually answerable for all the ideas of each other," the project was carried out "in concert" between the three authors.[51] "In concert" the authors put together a general outline of the project, which included their unanimous opposition to a bill of rights.

THE PRIVATE MADISON AND THE BILL OF RIGHTS

In his private correspondence Madison consistently opposed a bill of rights, asserting "powerfull reasons that may be urged agt. the adoption of a Bill of Rights."[52] Most Federalists, including Madison, held their opponents in such contempt that they could not seriously consider their demands for a bill of rights. General Henry Knox believed that Anti-Federalists were "Demagogues and vicious characters." Federalists described their opponents as "wicked," "malignant, ignorant, and short-sighted triflers," "fools and knaves" opposed to men "of abilities and virtue" who "wish[ed] Damnation to their Country." A New Hampshire Federalist thought Anti-Federalists were "*fools, blockheads,* and *mad men.*" In New York "Caesar" thought that the demands for a bill of rights were made by "designing croakers" in order "to frighten the people with ideal bugbears."[53]

Madison thought Edmund Randolph and George Mason did "not object to the substance of the Governt. but contend for a few additional Guards in favor of the Rights of the States and of the people," conceding they were "men of intelligence, patriotism, property, and independent circumstances." But he thought most Anti-Federalists were "guided" by the arch-demagogue Patrick Henry, who would "strike at the essence of the System." He believed Henry's followers had "disunion assuredly for its object." Because this was the "real tendency" of Anti-Federalism, Madison saw "no middle ground" between supporters and opponents of the Constitution. He happily noted that outside Virginia the educated elite were "zealously attached to the proposed Constitution." In New England "the men of letters, the principle Off[i]cers of Govt. the Judges & Lawyers, the Clergy, and men of property" almost universally supported the Constitution, while the opposition consisted of "ignorant and jealous men."[54]

Madison believed the proponents of amendments were anti-nationalists, like Henry, who wanted to destroy the Constitution, or people lacking "intelligence, patriotism, property, and independent circumstances"—not men who Madison thought should govern the republic. Because Madison thought those who demanded amendments "threaten shipwreck to our liberty," he could not concede the validity of any of their points.[55]

Echoing *Federalist* No. 38, Madison was also contemptuous of the Anti-Federalists because they could not agree on what they wanted. Their positions were "as heterogeneous as can be imagined."[56] Federalists were also "heterogeneous" on many points, but they all agreed the Constitution should be ratified, so it did not matter if they supported ratification for different reasons.

THE VIRGINIA RATIFYING CONVENTION

In March 1788 Madison returned home to seek election to Virginia's ratifying convention. Growing Anti-Federalism made Madison's presence imperative. By this time the debate over a bill of rights had been altered by the Massachusetts ratifying convention.

When the Massachusetts convention opened in January 1788, an Anti-Federalist victory seemed certain. The convention elected John Hancock, an apparent Anti-Federalist, as its president. Samuel Adams, the old revolutionary hero and perhaps the Commonwealth's most powerful politician, was thoroughly committed to a bill of rights.[57] But after significant debate, the convention's Federalists shrewdly compromised, suggesting ratification with recommended amendments. They persuaded John Hancock to present these amendments and eventually brought Adams on board. A few other Anti-Federalists joined as well, and the Constitution squeaked through, 187 to 168.

The importance of the Massachusetts compromise—ratification with recommended amendments—was not immediately apparent to Madison, who condemned the recommended amendments as "a blemish," even though he conceded they were "in the least Offensive form" and were inconsequential.[58] Madison focused on winning in New Hampshire and Virginia.[59]

When Madison returned to Virginia, he was forced to campaign for office for the first time in his career. He privately met with the influential Baptist minister Rev. John Leland, who feared the Constitution would undermine religious freedom. Madison's long record of supporting religious liberty, and his sincere empathy for Leland's concerns, convinced the minister to support him.[60]

On election day, March 24, Madison overcame his natural shyness in his first public speech to voters. He tried to dispel the "absurd and groundless prejudices against the fœderal Constitution." This brief campaign was successful, as he beat his nearest Anti-Federalist rival by a margin of almost four to one.[61] Madison was pledged to ratify the Constitution as written, with no commitment to prior amendments or any alterations.

Leland's support helped secure Madison's electoral victory and was critical for his eventual support for a bill of rights. Before that meeting Madison had dismissed Anti-Federalist demands for a bill of rights as a smokescreen for defeating the Constitution. Leland, however, supported the Constitution but sincerely wanted a bill of rights to protect religious freedom. Because Leland supported ratification and was not trying to undermine the new plan of government, Madison was forced to take seriously the bill of rights argument, even though he did not agree with it.[62]

The Virginia convention was almost evenly split between Federalists and Anti-Federalists. Madison believed there was a real danger of Virginia conditionally ratifying or, worse, demanding a second convention. Either would have "endangered" both "the Constitution, and the Union." Still opposed to amendments, Madison saw that recommending future amendments, as Massachusetts had done, might blunt Anti-Federalist opposition, thus avoiding conditional ratification or a second convention that would "be fatal."[63] Once a lukewarm supporter of the Constitution, Madison now equated its success with that of the nation itself.

This change reflected Madison's evaluation of Virginia politics, rather than any alteration in his opposition to a bill of rights. Madison feared a second convention would lack the "same spirit of compromise" of the previous summer, and at a second convention it would be "easy also for those who have latent views of disunion, to carry them on under the mask of contending for alterations popular in some but inadmissible in other parts of the U. States."[64] Madison could give no quarter to those who wanted fundamental changes in the Constitution, but he had to blunt the increasingly popular demand for a bill of rights. Recommended amendments—what he called a "blemish" in Massachusetts—looked better all the time.

At the Virginia ratifying convention Madison gave no immediate indication of his new position. He initially stressed his argument articulated in *Federalist* No. 10, that the greatest threat to liberty came from the "majority trampling on the rights of the minority." He mirrored Hamilton's argument in *Federalist* No. 84 that civil liberties were safe in a government of limited powers, reiterating that Congress could not create a national religion because "the government has no jurisdiction over it." Madison also attacked the impracticality of "obtaining previous amendments," explaining that if Virginia added them, they would have to be submitted to all the other states, which might then submit amendments of their own.[65] This would lead to an endless process that would produce nothing.

On June 12 Madison reiterated that paper guarantees were worthless, rhetorically asking: "Is a bill of rights a security for religion? Would the bill of rights in this state exempt the people from paying for the support of one particular sect, if such sect were exclusively established by law? If there were a majority of one sect, a bill of rights would be a poor protection for liberty." He again argued that the "multiplicity of sects, which pervades America," was the "only security for religious liberty in any society." Reminding the convention that he had always "warmly supported religious freedom," Madison argued "a variety of sects," not a bill of rights, was the key to religious freedom.[66]

By mid-June Madison privately predicted the Federalists would narrowly defeat the demand for previous amendments.[67] Confident of success, for the first time Madison argued against the substance of some rights, noting that though the jury trial was "sacred," there were circumstances, such as during an insurrection, when the legislature must have "discretion" in setting the rules for trials.[68]

Now fully expecting to win in the convention, Madison spoke against ratification with amendments, but he finally declared that after ratification he would support "a conciliatory declaration of certain fundamental principles of liberty, in a form not affecting the validity & plenitude of the ratification."[69] If Virginia ratified the Constitution, he would "freely, fairly and dispassionately consider and investigate your propositions, and endeavour to gratify your wishes." He promised to support recommended amendments that were "not objectionable, or unsafe." He still denied the necessity of amendments but promised to consider them "because they can produce no possible danger, and may gratify some gentlemen's wishes."[70] Thus, Madison supported recommended amendments as a matter of political expedience and accommodation, not conviction.

MADISON, JEFFERSON, AND THE BILL OF RIGHTS: THE MYTH OF THE "GREAT COLLABORATION"

While working for ratification and against a bill of rights, Madison carried on a long-distance correspondence with Thomas Jefferson, America's ambassador in Paris. The conventional historical wisdom is that this correspondence was a "Great Collaboration," as Jefferson's "letters persuad[ed] Madison to switch positions" to support the Bill of Rights.[71]

Despite the claims of many distinguished scholars that this "Great Collaboration" changed the course of American history, it is a myth. The timing of when these letters were written, received, and answered made it impossible for Jefferson to affect Madison's thinking. The conventional wisdom is based on Jefferson's well-known letter of December 20, 1787, arguing for a bill of rights and criticizing Madison's opposition.[72] But Madison did not receive this letter until July 1788, which was *after* Virginia had ratified the Constitution and after Madison himself had publicly announced his willingness to support future amendments. Thus, Jefferson's letter had absolutely no influence on Madison's actions or thinking during the ratification process. This chronology shows that it is simply wrong to claim that Jefferson "converted Madison to the cause of adding a Bill of Rights to the new federal Constitution."[73]

This correspondence is very useful for teaching us that Madison truly opposed the adoption of a bill of rights, while Jefferson really wanted one. But the chronology confirms that Madison "converted" to modestly supporting the bill of rights because of political necessity rather than Jefferson's arguments. The "conversion," such as it was, took place before Madison received Jefferson's letters supporting a bill of rights.

George Washington sent Jefferson a copy of the Constitution immediately after the Constitutional Convention, and later Franklin did as well. On October 24, 1787, Madison sent Jefferson a seventeen-page letter in which he was guardedly enthusiastic about the Constitution but thought it did not go far enough in nationalizing power. The letter arrived in Paris in late December. Jefferson's thoughtful response, his famous letter of December 20, 1787, reflected his own quite different concerns about the Constitution.

After detailing what he liked about the Constitution, Jefferson turned to "what I do not like," focusing on "the omission of a bill of rights providing clearly and without the aid of sophisms for freedom of religion, freedom of the press, protection against standing armies, restriction against monopolies, the eternal and unremitting force of the habeas corpus laws, and trials by jury in all matters of fact triable by the laws of the land." Jefferson argued that "a bill of rights is what the people are entitled to against every government on earth, general or particular, and what no just government should refuse, or rest on inference." [74] Advocates of the "Great Collaboration" use this letter to prove their claim.

However, Madison did not receive this letter until July 1788, almost a month after Virginia had ratified the Constitution and Madison had agreed (for tactical reasons) to support recommended amendments. On July 24, Madison answered Jefferson's letter of December 20, 1787. He said nothing about a bill of rights, perhaps because Jefferson's points were already moot.[75] Madison now supported post-ratification amendments, not because he had been convinced of their virtues by Jefferson's arguments, but because of political necessity.

On July 31, 1788, Jefferson wrote Madison once again, "rejoic[ing] at the acceptance of our new constitution by nine states." Jefferson once again expressed hope that "a bill of rights will be formed to guard the people against the federal government, as they are already guarded against their state governments in most instances."[76] This letter arrived in late October, long after Madison, for tactical reaons, was publicly advocating amendments.

In August 1788 Madison sent Jefferson two letters describing the ratification struggles in New York and North Carolina. He conceded that the Constitution was not perfect and that "a trial for one year [of the workings of the Constitution] will probably suggest more real amendments than all the antecedent speculations of our most sagacious politicians."[77] Madison was far more concerned with the mechanics of government under the Constitution than a bill of rights.

In mid-October 1788 Madison finally received Jefferson's letter of July 31, in which he had again strenuously argued for a bill of rights. Madison had never responded to Jefferson's arguments set out in his letter of December 20, 1787. Nor had he responded to Jefferson's public letters, which had continued to "criticize

... the omission of a bill of rights."⁷⁸ Finally, on October 17, 1788, Madison faced the criticism of his friend.

His response emphatically shows Jefferson's strong appeals had no effect on Madison's view that a bill of rights was unnecessary. Madison claimed he had "always been in favor of a bill of rights," but he then repeated the litany of arguments against one, including that (1) it was unnecessary under a government of limited powers; (2) it could not be complete enough, especially because New Englanders would oppose absolute religious freedom; (3) the inherent tension between the states and the federal government made a bill of rights unnecessary; (4) "[r]epeated violations of these parchment barriers" showed that a bill of rights was useless; and (5) a bill of rights was really needed to protect the people against a monarch, which was not a situation the Americans faced.⁷⁹

After detailing why a bill of rights was unnecessary, Madison explained his willingness to support one. He conceded that "political truths declared" in a "solemn manner" would "acquire by degrees the character of fundamental maxims of free Government, and as they become incorporated with the national sentiment, counteract the impulses of interest and passion." While Madison thought the majority would still ignore the bill of rights when convenient, those oppressed might find "a bill of rights will be a good ground for an appeal to the sense of the community." Finally, he conceded a small point to the opposition, noting that perhaps "a succession of artful and ambitious rulers, may by gradual & well-timed advances, finally erect an independent Government on the subversion of liberty," and a bill of rights would be "prudent" "especially when the precaution can do no injury."⁸⁰

Unwilling to concede too much, Madison immediately added that he saw "no tendency in our governments to danger on that side." Writing privately to Jefferson, Madison reasserted his ambivalent opposition to a bill of rights. "Supposing a bill of rights be proper" he wrote, "I am inclined to think that *absolute* restrictions in cases that are doubtful, or where emergencies may overrule them, ought to be avoided." He warned that "restrictions however strongly marked on paper will never be regarded when opposed to the decided sense of the public; and after repeated violations in extraordinary cases, they will lose even their ordinary efficacy." Madison doubted any legislature would obey constitutionally imposed limits. The "clods" in the legislatures, as Gordon Wood described them, whether it be state or federal, would do as they pleased.⁸¹

On November 18, 1788, well before he received Madison's letter of October 17, Jefferson again urged Madison to support a bill of rights, not on ideological or philosophical grounds, but as a matter of practical politics. By the time Madison received this letter, in March 1789, he had already adopted this position and in fact had been elected to Congress because of it.[82] So once again, Jefferson's views had no effect on Madison.

In February 1789 Madison's letter of October 17, 1788, finally reached Jefferson. In his response, on March 15, 1789, Jefferson once more argued for a bill of rights, but Jefferson's thoughts had little effect on Madison's conduct, because he did not receive the letter until the end of May, by which time Madison had been elected to Congress promising to introduce amendments. Madison wrote back that a bill of rights would be introduced into Congress within a week.[83]

MADISON MOVES TOWARD HIS PATERNITY

Until ratification was secured, Madison opposed a bill of rights, because admitting that a bill of rights might be necessary would jeopardize ratification. His claim in his October 17, 1788, letter that he had "always been in favor of a bill of rights" is at best overstated but was not in fact not disingenuous. Even when Madison introduced the amendments that became the Bill of Rights, he was ambivalent. Virginia politics and national politics, not political theory, led him to propose amendments.

Patrick Henry, Virginia's most powerful politician, correctly blamed Madison for his embarrassing defeat at the ratification convention. Thus Henry prevented the Virginia legislature from choosing Madison for the U.S. Senate and then tried to prevent Madison from winning a seat in the House of Representatives by gerrymandering his home county into "a Congressional district otherwise composed of counties considered heavily antifederal."[84] As he had before the ratification convention, Madison was forced to return to Virginia to campaign for office—which he hated doing.

Madison faced a tough campaign against his neighbor and friend, James Monroe, the moderate Anti-Federalist Henry supported.[85] Henry and his allies circulated false rumors that Madison opposed any changes in the Constitution, including an amendment protecting religious freedom. On January 2, 1789, Madison wrote to Rev. George Eve, a leading Baptist minister, to explain his position and his sympathy for sincerely held Baptist fears about religious liberty. In a surprisingly frank letter for a candidate seeking votes, Madison disagreed with Rev. Eve that the Constitution posed "serious dangers" to religious liberty. However, with the Constitution ratified, he was willing to support "amendments, if pursued with a proper moderation" because now they would "be not only safe, but may well serve the double purpose of satisfying the minds of well meaning opponents, and of providing additional guards in favour of liberty." He told Rev.

Eve that future amendments were "the safest mode" of change because Congress would preserve the Constitution while writing the amendments. He warned that a second convention "containing perhaps insidious characters" would "be but too likely to turn every thing into confusion and uncertainty."[86]

In private letters and newspapers Madison gave his "unequivocal pledge" to work for amendments. This counterattack was successful. Rev. Eve defended Madison, reminding other Baptists that Madison had always supported their interests by fighting for full religious freedom in Virginia. Madison debated Monroe in Baptist meetings, German churches, and numerous courthouses, always explaining his willingness to introduce amendments. The campaign ended with "a resounding federalist victory ... in a district 'rigged' against" Madison.[87]

AN AMBIVALENT ADVOCATE

Madison arrived in Congress pledged to propose amendments, but a bill of rights was not high on anyone else's agenda. Some Federalists opposed any changes to the Constitution while Anti-Federalists understood that a bill of rights would undermine their goal of a second convention. After incessantly demanding a bill of rights, the Anti-Federalists viewed it as a "Tub to the Whale," designed to divert attention from more substantive constitutional changes. When Congress passed the amendments, which in theory they wanted, many Anti-Federalists were deeply unhappy, because the proposed changes did not limit congressional taxing power, eviscerate the powers of the executive branch, or prevent a standing army. As Saul Cornell notes, the Anti-Federalists wanted "serious structural change" and were not particularly interested in civil liberties. Aedamus Burke, a disgruntled representative from South Carolina, complained that the proposed amendments did not include "those solid and substantial amendments which the people expect; they are little better than whip-syllabub, and frothy and full of wind, formed only to please the palate, or they are like a tub thrown out to a whale, to secure the freight of the ship and its peaceable voyage."[88]

While Anti-Federalists suddenly were no longer interested in a bill of rights, the Federalist majority was at best ambivalent. Many representatives agreed a bill of rights might be important, but they prioritized establishing executive departments, creating a judiciary, and raising revenue. Others doubtless agreed with Georgia's James Jackson that the Constitution was "like a vessel just launched, and lying at the wharf; she is untried." Amendments should be delayed until this ship of state could be launched, and Congress would be "guided by the experiment."[89]

Madison felt a personal obligation to fulfill his campaign promise to support amendments. He still did not think them necessary to preserve liberty—on that point he had not wavered—but he believed amendments would remove the fears of many Americans, such as his Baptist constituents, while heading off a second convention, which he truly feared.

For Madison the bill of rights was now a question of tactics. As the ghostwriter for George Washington's first address to the Congress, Madison deftly inserted language reminding Congress of its duty to consider amendments to the Constitution that would respond to the "objections which have been urged against the System." Washington made no specific recommendations but placed his "entire confidence" that in its "discernment and pursuit of the public good," Congress would show "a reverence for the characteristic rights of freemen, and a regard for the public harmony."[90]

Madison next proposed that the House formally respond to Washington, "assuring him of their disposition to concur in giving effect to every measure which may tend to secure the liberties, promote the harmony, and advance the happiness and prosperity of their country." Madison drafted this reply, which included a promise that the issue of amendments "will receive all the attention demanded by its importance."[91]

This episode was a magnificent strategic coup for Madison. He put his own views on a bill of rights into Washington's mouth and then persuaded the House to let him answer Washington, when in fact he was answering himself. Robert Rutland claimed Washington was acting "cautiously" in calling for Congress to act in its own "discernment of the public good."[92] However, Madison cleverly had Washington endorse amendments without appearing too heavy-handed and followed this by drafting a resolution supporting the speech that he had written for Washington. Madison's adroit pen put both the president and the House on record supporting amendments.[93]

After unexpected delays, Madison finally proposed amendments on June 8, 1789, declaring he was "bound in honor and in duty" to bring them forward to demonstrate to those who feared the new government that "those who have been friendly to . . . this constitution" were also "sincerely devoted to liberty" and not attempting to "lay the foundation of an aristocracy or despotism." He believed that many Anti-Federalists were now ready "to join their support to the cause of Federalism, if they were satisfied on this one point." Furthermore, he argued amendments might convince North Carolina and Rhode Island to finally ratify the Constitution.[94]

Even while proposing amendments, Madison remained ambivalent about their substance. Madison did not propose a bill of rights as such. Rather, he offered a series of changes to the main body of the Constitution scattered in eight separate places. Madison noted that his proposal "relates to what may be called a bill of rights" but he did not call it that, just as he did not propose it as a unified package.[95]

Madison's arguments lacked passion. Admitting this was an "important subject," and these were "great and important rights," he also reaffirmed that he had "never considered" a bill of rights "essential to the federal constitution." But post-ratification Madison was willing to concede "that in a certain form and to a certain extent, such a provision was neither improper nor altogether useless."[96]

Madison followed with a balanced assessment of the pros and cons of a bill of rights. His most innovative proposal concerned the vexing problem that "by enumerating particular exceptions of the grant of power, it would disparage those rights which were not placed in that enumeration," making them "insecure." He argued that this problem could be "guarded against" with a provision that became the Ninth Amendment.[97]

Madison asked for a special committee to consider the amendments, arguing "we should obtain the confidence of our fellow citizens, in proportion as we fortify the rights of the people against the encroachments of the government." Instead, the House referred the amendments to a committee of the whole, further delaying their adoption.[98]

Madison hoped the amendments would satisfy "a majority of those who have opposed the Constitution," proudly noting that "the structure & stamina of the Govt. are as little touched as possible."[99] Madison had strategically avoided anything of a "controversial nature" because of the "caprice & discord of opinions" of members in the House and Senate, two-thirds of which had to approve the amendments, and in the state legislatures, three-fourths of which had to ratify them. The amendments had a "twofold object of removing the fears of the discontented and of avoiding all such alterations as would either displease the adverse side, or endanger the success of the measure."[100]

On July 21, Madison "begged the House to indulge him in the further consideration of amendments." In no mood for another debate in the committee of the whole, the House finally created a select committee, which Madison chaired. On August 13 the committee reported back to Congress. After eight days of debate, the House adopted the amendments on August 22. Although active in these debates, Madison did not dominate them.[101]

Madison never directly supported the merits of a bill of rights, although he spoke in favor of religious liberty, a free press, and the educational value of what he still called "parchment barriers." Mostly he argued that the amendments would "promote that spirit of urbanity and unanimity which the Government" needed. Madison did not even affirmatively argue for the protection of religious liberty—a cause always dear to his heart. He refused to say "whether" such a provision was "necessary or not," asserting only that it "had been required by some of the State Conventions," which feared that under the Constitution's necessary and proper clause Congress might "infringe the rights of conscience, and establish a national religion." He consistently "appeal[ed] to the gentlemen who have heard the voice of the country" arguing "the amendments now proposed" were "those most strenuously required by the opponents to the constitution."[102]

Only twice did Madison speak with passion, in favor of limiting the powers of the states, rather than limiting the power of the national government. He passionately supported a proposal to prohibit the states from infringing "the equal rights of conscience, . . . the freedom of the press, [and] trial by jury in criminal cases." Madison thought this was "the most valuable amendment in the whole list."[103] Although the House approved this clause, the Senate did not, and thus these rights would not become applicable to the states until after the adoption of the Fourteenth Amendment and its modern development, starting with *Gitlow v. New York*.[104] Similarly, Madison emphatically and successfully opposed adding the word "expressly" to what became the Tenth Amendment. Madison thought this would give the states too much power.[105]

A RELUCTANT PATERNITY AND MODERN INTERPRETATION

Madison did not enjoy these debates—what he called this "nauseous project." Getting the amendments through Congress was "extremely difficult and fatiguing" and "exceedingly wearisome."[106] Madison's ambivalence about the goal surely made the process more nauseous. A few days before the House voted, Madison observed that "we are so deep in them now, that right or wrong some thing must be done." This was hardly the sentiment of an enthusiastic partisan. But Madison had not become one, even as he supported the addition of a bill of rights. With victory in sight, he could only marshal a series of weak or tactical arguments: a bill of rights was "a thing not improper in itself"; without "assurances" of subsequent amendments the Constitution might not have been ratified; "as an honest man," Madison felt "bound" to support amendments after the Virginia convention recommended them; without his promise to support amendments Virginia would likely have elected another Anti-Federalist to Congress, instead of Madison; if Madison had not introduced his amendments, Anti-Federalists would have presented more damaging ones; once the amendments were adopted, they "would kill the opposition every where, and by putting an end to the disaffection to the Govt. itself" the amendments would head off a second convention; and the amendments were necessary to bring North Carolina into the Union.[107]

An understanding of Madison's ambivalence is not of mere antiquarian value. It affects how we think of the Bill of Rights today. In an age when judges, political leaders, lawyers, and a very few trained historians call for a jurisprudence of original intent, Madison's intent, as the "father" of the Bill of Rights, takes on new meaning. Indeed, "arguably, it is all the more important to" understand Madison's intent in our own age as we hear "glib calls to return to a 'jurisprudence of original intention.'" Some three decades ago Jack Rakove noted this issue, but what he wrote then might have been written this year: "Whenever such calls are allowed to rest on crude and fragmentary caricatures of a complex historical reality, we should recognize that it is our own political culture, more than that of 'The Founders,' which is being exposed."[108] Madison's intent was to mollify Anti-Federalists and others who feared the new government. This was an open-ended goal that undermines originalists, who would look for a specific intent of the framers. Madison's specific political intent was to guarantee that the Constitution would succeed by giving the dissenting minority what it demanded: both specific and more general protections of liberty.

This understanding of Madison's intent tells us virtually nothing about where Madison thought the amendments would lead. Much of Madison's original proposal was changed or jettisoned, including his most cherished amendment, to limit the states from abridging freedom of religion, speech, and due process of law. But much also entered the Bill of Rights as Madison penned it. Four of Madison's proposals look almost exactly like the language eventually used in the Fourth, Sixth, Eighth, and Tenth Amendments.[109] Madison proposed much of the language in the other six amendments. Thus, if we were to seek someone's intent, we would begin with Madison's. But Madison, it appears, had no clear substantive intent. Madison's reasons for supporting amendments were political and tactical, not philosophical.

Despite his ambivalence and misgivings, Madison fought hard for the Bill of Rights. Duty to his constituents, duty to himself as an "honest man," and his keen sense of politics kept him going. So did Madison's libertarian values. Whether opposing a bill of rights at the Convention and during the ratification struggle or giving lukewarm support in Congress, Madison never attacked the liberties they were designed to protect. He never denied the value of due process, freedom of expression, and religious liberty. He doubted the efficacy of the amendments, not the values they stood for. That, in the end, enabled him to support the Bill of Rights, even while uncertain if it was either necessary or prudent. He would, in effect, leave that question to future generations.

Madison's ambivalence about the Bill of Rights reminds us that liberty is ultimately protected, not by parchment barriers, but by the "vigilant ... spirit which actuates the people of America."[110] The Bill of Rights articulates the goals of that spirit. But if Madison intended anything specific, it was that the people, in each generation, would find meaning in the words of the amendments, rather than seek the intentions of their authors.

NOTES

1. Irving Brant, *James Madison: Father of The Constitution, 1787–1800* (Indianapolis: Bobbs-Merrill, 1950), 161.
2. *Annals of Congress*, 1st Cong., 1st Sess., 1:453.
3. Max Farrand, ed., *The Records of the Federal Convention of 1787* (New Haven: Yale University Press, 1966), 1:255. James Wilson would say substantially the same thing in the Pennsylvania Convention, talking about "the weakness and imbecility of the existing confederation." Speech of Wilson, November 24, 1787, Farrand, *Records*, 3:142.
4. See Mary Sarah Bilder, *Madison's Hand: Revising the Constitutional Convention* (Cambridge, Mass.: Harvard University Press, 2015).
5. Paul Finkelman, "The Proslavery Origins of the Electoral College," *Cardozo Law Review* 23 (2002): 1145–57.
6. Farrand, *Records*, 2: 414–15. For a discussion of this history, see Paul Finkelman, "The Constitution and the Intentions of the Framers: The Limits of Historical Analysis," *University of Pittsburgh Law Review*, 50 (1989): 349–98. Bilder, *Madison's Hand,* argues that Madison may not have in fact uttered these words. However, like some other Virginians, Madison opposed the continuation of the African trade for a variety of reasons, including public safety, economics, and racism. He had few qualms about owning slaves (he had about one hundred) or about the existence of slavery. In 1789, while sitting in the first federal Congress, he tried to modify the Northwest Ordinance to allow slavery north of the Ohio River. Paul Finkelman, *Slavery and the Founders: Race and Liberty in the Age of Jefferson*, 3rd ed. (New York: Routledge, 2014), 61–62. It is important not to confuse opposition to the trade with opposition to slavery. This is especially true for Virginians, who had a surplus of slaves to sell to the Carolinas and Georgia.
7. As such *The Federalist Papers* were an utter failure. New Yorkers elected an overwhelmingly Anti-Federalist convention. If the New York Anti-Federalist leaders, Governor George Clinton and Melancton Smith, had swiftly called the convention to order and quickly defeated the Constitution, Virginia might have followed suit, and without support from Virginia and New York the Constitution would probably have failed. But Clinton and Smith dallied, New Hampshire and Virginia ratified, and the Anti-Federalist majority in New York caved.
8. On the adoption of the Fugitive Slave Clause see Finkelman, *Slavery and the Founders*, 30–34, 102–8.
9. Cecelia Kenyon, *Men of Little Faith: Selected Writings of Cecelia Kenyon*, ed. Stanley Elkins, Eric McKitrick, and Leo Weinstein (Amherst: University of Massachusetts Press, 2002). For a more sympathetic view of the Anti-Federalists, see Saul Cornell, *The Other*

Founders: Anti-Federalism & the Dissenting Tradition in America, 1788–1828 (Chapel Hill: University of North Carolina Press, 1999). With the emergence of an "Imperial Presidency" under Richard Nixon and the attempted coup by Donald Trump to hold on to the presidency after being decisively defeated in the 2020 election, one might argue that the Anti-Federalists of 1787–88 were prescient. But this seems overdramatic and too cute. The opponents of the Constitution imagined a monarchy or Caesarian-like military dictatorship under the Constitution, which of course never happened. Indeed, without being Pollyannaish, the outcomes in 1974 and 2020–21 suggest that the Constitution, combined with two centuries of government, were stronger than the Anti-Federalists could imagine.

10. "What the Anti-Federalists Were For," in *The Complete Anti-Federalist*, ed. Herbert Storing, 7 vols. (Chicago: University of Chicago Press, 1981), 1:71, 72. In the interest of full disclosure, I should note that Storing was on my dissertation committee.

11. Ibid., 1:64.

12. Jonathan Elliot, ed., *The Debates in the Several State Conventions on the Adoption of the Federal Constitution*, 5 vols. (1987; repr., New York: Burt Franklin, 1988), 2:215; Curtiopolis (January 18, 1788), in *The Documentary History of the Ratification of the Constitution*, ed. John P. Kaminski and Gaspare J. Saladino (Madison: State Historical Society of Wisconsin, 1984), 15:399, 401. Jews did gain substantial political rights under the Constitution and under a few state constitutions in this period, but the miniscule size of the Jewish population in this period made the fear of one being elected president more than absurd. Paul Finkelman and Lance J. Sussman, "The American Revolution and the Emergence of Jewish Legal and Political Equality in the New Nation," *American Jewish Archives Journal* 75 (2023): 1-47.

13. Quoted in Morton Borden, *Jews, Turks, and Infidels* (Chapel Hill: University of North Carolina Press, 1984), 16, 15.

14. Cornell, *Other Founders*, 30–31.

15. "Speeches of Patrick Henry in the Virginia State Ratifying Convention" (speech of June 5, 1788), in Storing, *Complete Anti-Federalist*, 5:224.

16. Elliot, *Debates*, 3:598–99 (Randolph), 4:286 (Pinckney) (emphasis in the original).

17. Consider Arms, Malichi Maynard, and Samuel Field, "Reasons for Dissent" (April 1788), in Storing, *Complete Anti-Federalist* 4:256; "Letters from a Countryman from Dutchess County" (letter of January 22, 1788), in ibid., 6:62.

18. On the proslavery constitution see Paul Finkelman, *Supreme Injustice: Slavery in the Nation's Highest Court* (Cambridge, Mass.: Harvard University Press, 2018) 11–25.

19. Significantly, Storing did not discuss slavery, or antislavery, in his essay "What the Anti-Federalists Were For." A recent book argues that the Second Amendment was designed to protect slavery. Carl Bogus, *Madison's Militia: The Hidden History of the Second Amendment* (New York: Oxford University Press, 2023). Although Bogus provides an excellent example of how the militia worked to suppress slave rebellions, he provides very little evidence that any debates of the Second Amendment were tied to slavery. The proposed amendments from the state ratifying conventions simply do not support such a claim. The most expansive proposed amendments for a right to own weapons came from Anti-Federalists in Pennsylvania, which was the first state in the nation to begin to end slavery. Virginia's convention offered forty amendments to the Constitution, most

dealing with structural changes or limitations on congressional power. Only one, number 31, dealt with the militia, and it simply said that the states could arm and organize their militias if the national government failed to do so. The delegates in the Virginia convention and other southern state conventions talked a lot about slavery, despite Bogus's truly odd claim that it was such "'a delicate subject' that public discussion of it was frowned upon" (68). But none of the debates over the militia were tied to slavery. South Carolina's proposed amendments said nothing about the militia, while Maryland's proposed amendment simply said that the members of the militia would not be subject to "martial law, exception in time of war, invasion or rebellion." See Paul Finkelman, "'A Well Regulated Militia': The Second Amendment in Historical Perspective," *Chicago-Kent Law Review*, 76 (2000): 195, 199–201, 206–13.

20. Madison to Jefferson, October 17, 1788, in *The Papers of James Madison* (hereafter PJM), ed. Robert Rutland (Chicago: University of Chicago Press, 1977), 11:297–99.

21. Farrand, *Records*, 2:637–40.

22. Ibid., 2:632–33; "Hon. Mr. Gerry's Objections to Signing the National Constitution," in Storing, *Complete Anti-Federalist*, 2:6–7.

23. Pauline Maier, *From Resistance to Revolution: Colonial Radicals and the Development of American Opposition to Britain, 1765–1776* (New York: Vintage Books, 1974), 245.

24. Marvin Meyers, ed., *The Mind of the Founder: Sources on the Political Thought of James Madison* (Indianapolis: Bobbs-Merrill, 1973) xxxvii.

25. Farrand, *Records*, 1:354, 1:492, 2:588. In the debate over a specific protection for a free press Sherman again argued that "the power of Congress does not extend to the Press" and thus the proposal was unnecessary (2:618). Here Sherman carried a narrow majority that probably did not include Madison. Oddly, Sherman and Ellsworth came from Connecticut, which had not written a state constitution and did not have a bill of rights.

26. Madison to Jefferson, October 17, 1788, *PJM*, 11: 295–300, quote from 297.

27. Irving Brant, *The Bill of Rights: Its Origin and Meaning* (Indianapolis: Bobbs-Merrill, 1965), 12.

28. Madison to Jefferson, October 17, 1788, *PJM*, 11:297–99.

29. Gordon Wood, "Interests and Disinterestedness in the Making of the Constitution," in *Beyond Confederation: Origins of the Constitution and American National Identity*, ed. Richard Beeman, Stephen Botein, and Edward Carter (Chapel Hill: University of North Carolina Press, 1987) 74.

30. Hamilton, *Federalist* No. 84, in *The Papers of Alexander Hamilton*, ed. Harold C. Syrett (New York: Columbia University Press, 1962), 4:706.

31. Madison to Jefferson, October 17, 1788, *PJM*, 11:297. Madison would eventually solve this problem with the 9th and 10th Amendments.

32. Madison to Jefferson, October 17, 1788, *PJM*, 11:297.

33. "The Landowner," No. 6, reprinted in *Essays on the Constitution of the United States,* ed. Paul Leicester Ford (1892; repr., New York: B. Franklin, 1970), 163; "Substance of an Address by James Wilson," in *Pamphlets on the Constitution of the United States*, ed. Paul L. Ford (Brooklyn, N.Y., 1888), 161.

34. "Madison in the Virginia Ratification Convention," reprinted in *PJM*, 11:130.
35. Madison to Jefferson, October 17, 1788, *PJM*, 11:298.
36. "Editorial Note," *PJM*, 10:259.
37. Charles Hobson, "The Negative on State Laws: James Madison, the Constitution, and the Crisis of Republican Government," *William & Mary Quarterly*, 3rd ser., 36 (1979): 217.
38. Madison to Edmund Pendleton, September 20, 1787, *PJM*, 10:71.
39. Madison to Jefferson, September 6, 1787; *Madison to Jefferson*, October 24, 1787, PJM, 10:212, 163–64.
40. The term "fiery zealots" is Richard Henry Lee's. Brant, *James Madison*, 161.
41. Madison to George Washington, September 30, 1787, *PJM*, 10:179–81.
42. Madison to Thomas Jefferson, October 24, 1787, *PJM*, 10:212. In 1789, when he drafted what became the Bill of Rights, Madison attempted to make certain amendments applicable to the states in one last attempt to secure a federal veto over some state legislation. This provision passed the House, but the Senate rejected it.
43. Madison to Jefferson, October 24, 1787, *PJM*, 10:215.
44. The editors of the *PJM* suggest that Madison was not brought into the project "until the middle of November, perhaps as late as the seventeenth." *PJM*, 10:261. Ralph Ketcham argues the collaboration began just after October 10. Ralph L. Ketcham, *James Madison: A Biography* (New York: Macmillan, 1971), 239.
45. *Federalist* No. 10, *PJM*, 10:264, 269. He had developed these arguments earlier, in "The Vices of the Political System," PJM, 9:350–54.
46. *Federalist* No. 51, *PJM*, 10:477–78.
47. Ibid., 10:478–79.
48. Jack Rakove, "The Madisonian Theory of Rights," *William & Mary Law Review* 31 (1990): 245, at 259.
49. Federalist No. 57, *PJM*, 10:523.
50. Federalist No. 38, *PJM*, 10:367–68.
51. Hamilton, *Federalist* No. 84, in *Hamilton Papers*, 4:706; Madison to Jefferson, August 11, 1788, PJM, 11:227.
52. George Turberville to Madison, April 16, 1788, in *PJM*, 11:23.
53. Robert Rutland, *Ordeal of the Constitution: The Antifederalists and the Ratification Struggle, 1787–1788* (Norman: University of Oklahoma Press, 1966), 34, 73, 269, 216; "Letters of Caesar, II," in Ford, *Essays on the Constitution*, 289. Ford incorrectly identifies the author of this letter as Alexander Hamilton. *Papers of Alexander Hamilton*, 4:278–79.
54. Madison to Jefferson, December 9, 1787, and Madison to Edmund Pendleton, February 21, 1788, *PJM*, 10:312–13, 532–33. Madison conceded that "men equally respectable in every point of character" were on both sides of the issue, but he believed the Virginia Anti-Federalists wanted to "dismember the Union." Madison to Archibald Stuart, December 14, 1787, *PJM*, 10:325–26.

55. Madison to Washington, December 14, 1787, and February 15, 1788, *PJM*, 10:325–27, 510–11.
56. *Federalist* No. 38, PJM, 10:367–70; Madison to Edmund Pendleton, February 21, 1788, *PJM*, 10:367–70, 532–33.
57. Pauline Maier, *The Old Revolutionaries: Political Lives in the Age of Samuel Adams* (New York: Vintage Books, 1982), 25.
58. Madison to Washington, December 14, 1787, and February 15, 1788, *PJM*, 10:325–27, 510–11.
59. Madison to Edmund Randolph, March 3, 1788, *PJM*, 10:554–55; Madison to Washington, February 15, 1788, PJM, 10:510–11.
60. Lyman H. Butterfield, "Elder John Leland, Jeffersonian Itinerant," *Proceedings of the American Antiquarian Society* 62, part 2 (1952): 183–96.
61. Madison to Eliza House Trist, March 25, 1788, *PJM*, 11:5–6; Ketcham, *James Madison*, 251.
62. John Kukla, "A Spectrum of Sentiments: Virginia's Federalists, Antifederalists, and 'Federalists Who Are for Amendments,' 1787–1788," *Virginia Magazine of History and Biography* 96 (1988): 282.
63. Madison to Jefferson, April 23, 1788; Madison to George Nichols, April 8, 1788, *PJM*, 11:28–29, 11–12.
64. Madison to Jefferson, April 23, 1788, *PJM*, 11:28–29.
65. Speech of Madison, June 6, 1788, *PJM*, 11: 79, 84.
66. Speech of Madison, June 12, 1788, *PJM*, 11:130, 131.
67. Madison to Rufus King, June 18, 22, 1788, *PJM*, 11:152, 167. See also, on Madison's confidence, Madison to Hamilton, June 20, 1788, and June 22, 1788, Madison to George Washington, June 23, 1788, and Madison to James Madison Sr., June 20, 1788, *PJM*, 11:157, 166, 168, 157–58.
68. Speech of Madison, June 20, 1788, *PJM*, 11:164.
69. Speech of Madison, June 24, 1788; Madison to Ambrose Madison, June 24, 1788, *PJM*, 11:174–75; 170–71.
70. Speech of Madison, June 24, 1788, *PJM*, 11:177.
71. Adrienne Koch, *Jefferson and Madison: The Great Collaboration* (New York: Oxford University Press, 1950), 3–32; Leonard W. Levy, "The Bill of Rights," in *Encyclopedia of the American Constitution*, ed. Leonard W. Levy, Kenneth Karst, and Dennis Mahoney (New York: Macmillan, 1986) 1:114.
72. Jefferson to Madison, December 20, 1787, in *The Papers of Thomas Jefferson*, ed. Julian P. Boyd (Princeton: Princeton University Press, 1955), 12:438.
73. Leonard W. Levy, *Jefferson and Civil Liberties: The Darker Side* (Cambridge, Mass.: Harvard University Press, 1963) 3.
74. Koch, *Jefferson and Madison*, 39, asserts these men "rushed copies" of the Constitution to Jefferson. This is true for Washington, but not for Franklin and Madison, who sent their letters on October 14 and October 24, respectively. Washington to Jefferson, September 18, 1787, and Franklin to Jefferson, October 14, 1787, in *Papers of Thomas Jefferson*, 12:149,

236, 270; Madison to Jefferson, October 24, 1787, *PJM*, 10:205–20; Jefferson to Madison, December 20, 1787, *Papers of Thomas Jefferson*, 12:438, 441 (acknowledging receipt of Madison's letter of October 24).
75. Madison to Jefferson, July 24, 1788, *PJM*, 11:196–98.
76. Jefferson to Madison, July 31, 1788, *PJM*, 11:212, 213.
77. Madison to Jefferson, August 23, 1788, *PJM*, 11:238–39; see also Madison to Jefferson, August 10, 1788, *PJM*, 11:225. On September 21 and October 8, 1788, Madison again wrote Jefferson but did not discuss the substantive questions of a bill of rights. *PJM*, 11:257–59, 276–77.
78. Madison to Edmund Randolph, August 2, 1788, *PJM*, 11:215.
79. Madison to Jefferson, October 17, 1788, *PJM*, 11:-297–98.
80. Ibid., 11:298–99.
81. Ibid., 11:299 (emphasis in the original); Wood, "Interests and Disinterestedness," 74.
82. Jefferson to Madison, November 18, 1788, *PJM*, 11:353–54; Madison to Jefferson, March 29, 1789, *PJM*, 12:38.
83. Jefferson to Madison, March 15, 1789; Madison to Jefferson, May 27, 1789, *PJM*, 12:13, 186.
84. Ketcham, *James Madison*, 275.
85. Harry Ammon, *James Monroe: The Quest for National Identity* (Charlottesville: University Press of Virginia, 1990), 73–77.
86. Madison to George Eve, January 2, 1789, *PJM*, 11:404–5.
87. Madison to Thomas Mann Randolph, January 13, 1789, published in the *Virginia Independent Chronicle*, January 28, 1789; Madison to "A Resident of Spotsylvania County," January 27, 1789, published in *Virginia Herald*, January 29, 1789; Benjamin Johnson to Madison, January 19, 1789, *PJM*, 11:415–17, 428–29, 423–24; Ketcham, *James Madison*, 276–77.
88. The phrase "Tub to the Whale" comes from Jonathan Swift, "Tale of a Tub" (1704): "Seamen have a custom, when they meet a whale, to fling him out an empty tub by way of amusement, to divert him from laying violent hands upon the ship." Kenneth R. Bowling, "'Tub to the Whale': The Founding Fathers and the Adoption of the Federal Bill of Rights," *Journal of the Early Republic* 8 (1988): 223; Cornell, *Other Founders*, 162.
89. *Annals of Congress*, 1st Cong. 1st Sess., 1:442.
90. Tench Coxe to Madison, March 18 and 24, 1789, Edmund Randolph to Madison, March 26, 1789, "Address of the President to Congress," April 30, 1789, and "Editorial Note," all in *PJM*, 12:12: 21, 27, 31, 123, 120.
91. *Annals of Congress*, 1st Cong., 1st Sess., 1:242 (May 1, 1789); *PJM*, 12:132–34 and 134n; *Annals of Congress*, 1st Cong., 1st Sess., 1:258 (May 5, 1789).
92. Robert Rutland, *The Birth of the Bill of Rights*, 1767–1791 (Chapel Hill: University of North Carolina Press,1955), 198.
93. Later in the debates Madison produced a letter from Washington in which the president declared he saw "nothing exceptionable in the proposed amendments"; some were "im-

portantly necessary," while others, while not essential, were "necessary to quiet the fears of some respectable characters and well meaning Men." Thus, Washington declared his hope they would receive "a favorable reception in both houses" of Congress. Washington to Madison, [ca. 31 May 1789], *PJM*, 12:191.

94. Debate of June 8, 1789, *Annals of Congress*, 1st Cong., 1st. Sess., 1:257, 440–41, 444, 449; Charlene Bangs Bickford and Helen E. Veit, eds., D*ocumentary History of the First Federal Congress of the United States of America: Legislative Histories; Amendments to the Constitution through Foreign Officers Bill* (Baltimore: Johns Hopkins University Press, 1986), 4:3.

95. *Annals of Congress*, 1st Cong., 1st Sess., 1:453.

96. Ibid., 1:453.

97. Ibid., 1:456.

98. Ibid., 1:459.

99. Madison to Jefferson, June 13, 1789, Madison to Edmund Randolph, June 15, 1789, *PJM*, 12:218, 219.

100. Madison to Edmund Pendleton, June 21, 1789, Madison to Edmund Randolph, June 15, 1789, and Madison to Samuel Johnston, June 21, 1789, *PJM*, 12:253, 219.

101. *Annals of Congress*, 1st Cong., 1st Sess. 1:685–92. Madison spoke 23 times during these debates, while Elbridge Gerry spoke 29 times. Nine other men spoke at least 10 times each, for a collective total of 130 times. This is based on a count of speeches in *Annals of Congress*, 1st Cong., 1st Sess. 1:730–808.

102. Ibid., 1:731, 746, 758, 775.

103. Ibid., 1:783–84.

104. *Gitlow v. New York*, 268 U.S. 652 (1925).

105. *Annals of Congress*, 1st Cong., 1st Sess., 1:790.

106. Madison to Richard Peters, August 19, 1789, Madison to Edmund Randolph, August 21, 1789, Madison to Edmund Pendleton, August 21, 1789, *PJM*, 12:346, 348. See also Rakove, "Madisonian Theory of Rights," 245–46.

107. Madison to Richard Peters, August 19, 1789, *PJM*, 12:347.

108. Jack Rakove, "The Madisonian Moment," *University of Chicago Law Review* 55 (1988): 473, at 475–76.

109. Madison proposed in the following order: "Excessive bail shall not be required, nor excessive fines imposed, nor cruel and unusual punishments be imposed"; "The rights of the people to be secured in their persons; their houses, their papers, and their other property, from all unreasonable searches and seizures, shall not be violated by warrants issued without probable cause, supported by oath or affirmation, or not particularly describing the places to be searched, or the persons or things to be seized"; "In all criminal prosecutions, the accused shall enjoy the right to a speedy and public trial, to be informed of the cause and nature of the accusation, to be confronted with his accusers, and the witnesses against him; to have a compulsory process for obtaining witnesses in his favor; and to have the assistance of counsel"; "The powers not delegated by this constitution, nor prohibited by it to the States respectively." Debate of June 8, 1789, *Annals of Congress*, 1st Cong., 1st Sess., 1:452, 453.

110. *Federalist* No. 57, PJM, 10:523.

"Pray of Liberty of Conscience to Revive among Us"

Madison on Freedom of Religion

HOWARD SCHWEBER

Of all the areas of constitutional law that are the subject of current controversy, none has given rise to more fervent disagreements than the question of religious freedom. In recent years the Roberts court has radically upended long-standing understandings in favor of newly minted principles, in response to which justices in the minority have penned vigorous dissenting opinions. And as in so many other areas, both sides of these debates and justices writing in earlier eras all cite James Madison as their inspiration and authority.

The issue of public funding for religious private schools provides a perfect illustration. In *Everson v. Board of Education* (1947), Justice Black wrote: "The 'establishment of religion' clause of the First Amendment means at least this. ... No tax in any amount, large or small, can be levied to support any religious activities or institutions, whatever they may be called, or whatever form they may adopt to teach or practice religion."[1] In support of his position, Black cited Madison's "Memorial and Remonstrance": "In it, [Madison] eloquently argued that a true religion did not need the support of law; that no person, either believer or nonbeliever, should be taxed to support a religious institution of any kind."[2] In 1973, Chief Justice Burger authored an opinion continuing the rule declared in *Everson* that public support could not be directly supplied to fund religious education but permitting funding for secular activities.[3] Justice Douglas dissented on the grounds that Burger had not gone far enough to ensure that no public money would be used to support religious education, quoting "Memorial and Remonstrance" and stating, "From the days of Madison, the issue of subsidy has never been a question of the amount of the subsidy, but rather a principle of no subsidy at all."[4]

Throughout this long period, then, Madison was consistently cited for the proposition that the Establishment Clause requires a strict separation between public funding and religious expression. Fifty years after *Lemon*, however, Chief Justice Roberts cited Madison in support of the proposition that a state is *required* to provide funding to support religious private schools if it funds secular private schools. "Madison objected in part because the Bill provided special support to certain churches and clergy, thereby 'violat[ing] equality by subjecting some to peculiar burdens.'... If anything, excluding religious schools from such programs would appear to impose the "peculiar burdens" feared by Madison."[5] In his dissent, Justice Breyer continued to present the traditional reading by which Madison was understood to argue that "compelling state sponsorship of religion ... [is] 'a signal of persecution' that 'degrades from the equal rank of citizens all those whose opinions in religion do not bend to those of the Legislative authority.'"[6]

Observing these different invocations of Madison, one might conclude that his thoughts on religious liberty were so gnomic or so inconsistent that there is no coherent theory to be found. In fact, this is not the case; there are few other areas of constitutional law and politics regarding which Madison thought as long or as deeply, and his thinking on the topic deserves the careful attention of modern readers.

James Madison's concern for religious liberty can literally be said to be what led him to be involved in thinking about constitutionalism in the first place. At the age of twenty-two he visited Baptist ministers who had been jailed. His response in a letter to his friend William Bradford was furious. "That diabolical Hell conceived principle of persecution rages among some and to their infamy the Clergy can furnish their Quota of Imps for such business." He closed the letter with a lament: "So I leave you to pity me and pray of Liberty of Conscience to revive among us."[7] The event may have changed his life. Madison's thinking evolved over time in many areas, including issues involving church-state relations, but his revulsion at the prospect of the power of government being deployed to prevent expressions of religious conscience remained a constant.

Furthermore, Madison's experiences observing the multiplicity of religious sects in Virginia played an important role in the development of his theory of factions. In his early writings Madison found no clear solution to the problem of religious dominance by a majority. His famous "Memorial and Remonstrance" ends with a statement of a puzzling problem. "True it is that no other rule exists, by which any question which may divide a Society, can be ultimately determined, but the will of the majority; but it is also true that the majority may trespass on the rights of the minority."[8] In *Federalist* No. 10 Madison found a solution to this classic problem in his theory of factions. There is strong evidence to support the idea that he derived this theory by observing the effects of a multiplicity of religious sects in Virginia. In a speech to the Virginia ratifying convention on June 12, 1788, Madison explained: "This freedom [of religion arises from that multiplicity of sects, which pervades America, and which is the best and only security for religious liberty in any society. For where there is such a variety of sects, there cannot be a majority of any one sect to oppress and persecute the rest. . . . A particular State might concur in one religious project.—But the United States abound in such a vast variety of sects, that it is a strong security against religious persecution, and is sufficient to authorise a conclusion, that no one sect will ever be able to out number or depress the rest."[9]

Religious liberty, in other words, can accurately be described as one of the centrally motivating concerns and one of the central models for Madison's thinking. But opposing the imprisonment of Baptists was simple. What should America's Constitution say (and mean) about the relationship between religion/church and politics/the state writ large? Freedom to engage in worship might be a clear requirement, but how far should that freedom extend? To explore these questions, this chapter is divided into four sections: Madison's view of religion generally; Madison's treatment of free exercise and the question of exemptions; Madison's view of the Establishment Clause in relation to public support for religious actors and institutions; and Madison's view of the Establishment Clause with respect to what Justice O'Connor called the "endorsement" problem. The conclusion engages in the ever-popular parlor game of speculating about what Madison would have thought of some recent developments in First Amendment religion clauses.

MADISON'S VIEW OF RELIGION

Was Madison a Religious Believer?

One pair of questions that is often raised is to what degree Madison himself was a religious believer, and to what degree the answer to that question should motivate our understanding of his thinking. Most scholars find the answer to the first question ambiguous. In 1773 Madison had written to a friend suggesting that they both become ministers. Only two months later, however, he switched to a focus in law, and the next year he entered politics as a member of the Orange County Committee of Safety. According to James Hutson, "For the rest of his life there is no mention in his writings of Jesus Christ nor of any of the issues that might concern a practicing Christian. Late in retirement there are a few enigmatic references to religion, but nothing else. With Madison, unlike Jefferson or any of the other principal founding fathers with the possible exception of Washington, one peers into a void when trying to discern evidence of personal religious belief."[10] Jack Rakove finds the same absence of probative evidence. "Was he a Unitarian? Was he a Christian in the orthodox sense of believing in the divinity of Jesus or simply a deist? Did he believe in miracles or divine revelation? To these questions there are no positive answers."[11]

Some of Madison's most prominent biographers such as Irving Brant and Ralph L. Ketcham insist that he was a Jeffersonian Deist.[12] Still others insist that Madison's religious convictions played a greater role in his thinking that is commonly recognized. John Noonan declares that Madison was "a pious Christian" guided by "a faith stupendous in modern eyes"; Joseph Loconte argues that Madison's ideas about channeling ambition and factional interest derived from his belief in the depravity of man as a result of original sin.[13] The latter claim is disputed by Noah Feldman, who points out that while Madison certainly did not view men as "angels," in 1788 in an address to Congress he was equally certain that they could and would display sufficient virtue to act as republican citizens participating in his "filter" model of representation.[14] More generally, claims by Noonan and others largely rest on Madison's rhetoric in two public documents, his "Memorial and Remonstrance" and a 1792 essay entitled "Property."[15] Critics point out that in both instances Madison was engaged in trying to recruit support among religious communities and that his private comments may have been entirely different.[16]

A search for indirect intellectual influences is equally unrevealing. As a young man Madison had considered becoming a minister, and his primary educational influences were religiously inclined men. Yet there is little evidence of direct influence on religious beliefs in the sense of theology or doctrine, as opposed to other intellectual currents. The Rev. James Witherspoon is a case in point. Madison encountered Witherspoon at Princeton. Witherspoon was president of the college, taught the required course in moral philosophy, and became something of a mentor to the young Madison. Madison finished his undergraduate studies in only two years by dint of "hard work and lack of sleep"; apparently exhausted by the endeavor, he remained on campus for a third year studying Hebrew and political philosophy under Witherspoon's tutelage. But Witherspoon's teaching of moral philosophy was heterodox, informed at least as much by Scottish common sense realism as by his own preferred Presbyterian doctrines (although there was substantial overlap between the two). This was consistent with Scottish common sense philosophy, which taught that religion and science could be reconciled, but that in teaching religious elements they should be separated out.[17]

By contrast, at the same time the curriculum at William and Mary included instruction in Anglican theology, leading some biographers to speculate that it was his distaste for religious instruction that attracted Madison to Princeton.[18] There are additional reasons to think that Witherspoon's influence was more philosophical than religious: when Witherspoon published his collected sermons, Madison did not order a copy despite the fact that Witherspoon was by that time an extremely prominent national figure.[19] Feldman, in fact, speculates that as an Anglican at a Presbyterian college, Madison had the experience of being "a dissenter from their dissent."[20]

If Madison's religiosity in college is ambiguous, it becomes no clearer when one turns to his later life. Madison was an intermittent churchgoer—so was Jefferson, for that matter—but in one of the few accounts we have that is a personal dialogue on the subject of religion, Bishop Meade (Anglican bishop of Virginia) wrote, "I was never at Mr. Madison's but once, and then our conversation took such a turn—though not designed on my part—as to call forth some expressions and arguments which left the impression on my mind that his creed was not strictly regulated by the Bible."[21]

In short, the arguments for Madison as a religious believer in any doctrinal sense are thin at best. But that observation by no means exhausts the exploration of Madison's attitudes toward religion. Regardless of his views on the truth of theological doctrines, Madison held a complex and deeply informing set of views about the role of religion in society.

The Political Utility of Religion

Regardless of his personal beliefs, Madison conceived of religion as a useful mechanism for making men more virtuous than they otherwise might be, a classical republican argument that did not depend on personal faith for its validity.[22] At times Madison comes close to describing religion as a kind of noble lie, as in a letter to Jefferson dated October 24, 1787: "However erroneous or ridiculous these grounds of dissention and faction may appear to the enlightened Statesman or the benevolent philosopher, the bulk of mankind, who are neither Statesman nor philosophers, will continue to view them in a different light."[23] In an 1825 letter to Rev. Beasley he diplomatically avoided questions about his own faith by stating, "The belief in a God All Powerful wise and good, is so essential to the moral order of the World and to the happiness of man, that arguments which enforce it cannot be drawn from too many sources."[24]

At the same time, Madison made repeated comments suggesting that religion was something to be feared as well as valued. In his October 24 letter to Jefferson, Madison observed, "Even in its coolest state [religion] has been much oftener a motive to oppression than a restraint from it."[25] Madison emphasized the point again in an address to the Constitutional Convention on June 6, 1787, asserting that not only was "little to be expected" from religion in a positive way, but that it might become "a motive to persecution and oppression."[26]

And even as a socially positive force, religion would not be sufficient to ground the republic in the required degree of virtue. In "Vices of the Political System of the United States" Madison asked whether religious belief could "be a sufficient restraint? It is not pretended to be such on men individually considered. Will its effects be greater on them considered in an aggregate view? quite the reverse."[27] He made the same argument—that energetic government was needed to control men's destructive impulse toward majoritarian tyranny—in *Federalist* No. 10: "We well know that neither moral nor religious motives can be relied on as an adequate control. They are not found to be such on the injustice and violence of individuals and lose their efficiency in proportion to the number combined together."[28]

As with so many things, then, for Madison religion could be a force for good or for ill and had to be integrated with other institutional mechanisms if the new polity was to be a success. The analogy to Madison's discussion of factions is instructive: like factions, religion would be a force for good only if it were brought into service of a republican political order. Religious liberty and pluralism were Madison's radical solution, a rejection of nearly all republican theorists before him.

Religions and Liberty of Conscience: Was Religion a Special Case?

A third question about Madison's ideas has to do with the relationship between religious freedom and freedom of conscience. Did Madison use the two phrases interchangeably, or was religious freedom a special case? Michael W. McConnell, for example, leaves the question as unresolved, arguing that either interpretation supports a set of outcomes concerning religious exemptions.[29]

Here it is useful to look at the public statements that have been used to support the claim that Madison was motivated by religious fervor, starting with his 1785 "Memorial and Remonstrance" challenging a proposed general assessment for the support of religious institutions. The context of the document is important. General assessments were common practice in the states, and the Virginia proposal had strong support. Madison was trying to recruit support from Baptists, Presbyterians, and other non-Anglican religious communities by presenting the assessment as a restoration of the kind of Anglican establishment that had fallen out of favor everywhere after the Revolution. "Who does not see that the same authority which can establish Christianity, in exclusion of all other Religions, may establish with the same ease any particular sect of Christians, in exclusion of all other sects?"[30] Interestingly, Madison insisted on publishing his tract anonymously (George Mason took the lead in presenting it to the public), suggesting that he was concerned to preserve his political position and maneuverability in future controversies in the event the assessment was adopted.

Madison began by declaring the special place of religious faith in a statement most frequently relied on by writers seeking to identify a religious motivation in his political theory.

> The Religion then of every man must be left to the conviction and conscience of every man; and it is the right of every man to exercise it as these may dictate. This right is in its nature an unalienable right. It is unalienable, because the opinions of men, depending only on the evidence contemplated by their own minds cannot follow the dictates of other men: It is unalienable also, because what is here a right towards men, is a duty towards the Creator. It is the duty of every man to render to the Creator such homage and such only as he believes to be acceptable to him. This duty is precedent, both in order of time and in degree of obligation, to the claims of Civil Society.... We maintain therefore that in matters of Religion, no man's right is abridged by the institution of Civil Society and that Religion is wholly exempt from its cognizance.[31]

Vincent Anthony Munoz reads this language in Lockean terms to mean that for Madison religious belief was outside the social contract and thus a matter "wholly exempt from the cognizance" of civil authority.[32] It is worth noting that opposition to Anglican religious establishment had been a key feature of the earliest colonial settlements by the Puritans of New England, whereas in Virginia Anglican establishment had remained in place until the Revolution.[33] Madison was thus making an argument that positioned himself as an outsider from Virginia's elites in a profound way (which may help account for his desire for anonymity).

This argument lies squarely in the realm of liberty of conscience, of which religious faith is presented as an exemplar case. Separately, however, Madison also presented another argument: that government support for religion was unhealthful for the religion being supported. "Experience witnesseth that ecclesiastical establishments, instead of maintaining the purity and efficacy of Religion, have had a contrary operation. During almost fifteen centuries has the legal establishment of Christianity been on trial. What have been its fruits? More or less in all places, pride and indolence in the Clergy, ignorance and servility in the laity, in both, superstition, bigotry and persecution."[34] This was an argument that had no obvious counterpart in any general liberty of conscience. Madison was not protective of the political sentiments of Loyalists during the Revolution, for example. In the Virginia Resolution he articulated a powerful principle of freedom of expression, to be sure, but that argument never extended to prohibiting civil authority from *supporting* a particular viewpoint. The idea that government support corrupts was unique to the case of religion.

The same conclusion emerges from a reading of Madison's essay "Property." "Property" was one of a series of eighteen essays that Madison published leading up to the election of 1792. The essays were intensely political and frequently partisan: in "Parties" Madison abandoned his earlier ideal of nonpartisanship, declaring "in every political society parties are unavoidable"; in "Universal Peace" he praised the French Constitution of 1791, thus siding with Jefferson and against Hamilton; in "Spirit of Governments" he decried "bounties to favorites" as an example of corruption, an undisguised attack on Hamilton's "Report on Manufactures"; and other essays attacked public debt, speculators, and aristocrats. In one of these essays, "A Candid State of Parties," Madison named the Republican Party: "The Republican party, as it may be termed, . . . will naturally find their account . . . in banishing every other distinction than that between enemies and friends to republican government." Irving Brant considered this essay the "political christening" of the phrase "Republican party."[35]

In that politicized context, Madison once again took up his pen to discuss religious liberty in Lockean terms.

> In its larger and juster meaning, it embraces every thing to which a man may attach a value and have a right; and *which leaves to every one else the like advantage*. In the former sense, a man's land, or merchandize, or money is called his property. In the latter sense, a man has property in his opinions and the free communication of them. He has a property of peculiar value in his religious opinions, and in the profession and practice dictated by them. He has property very dear to him in the safety and liberty of his person. He has an equal property in the free use of his faculties and free choice of the objects on which to employ them. In a word, as a man is said to have a right to his property, he may be equally said to have a property in his rights.[36]

Here religious belief appears as an example of general liberty of opinion and expression, but one that is "of peculiar value." The idea of "a property in his rights" speaks volumes about competing republican and liberal conceptions of liberty at play in the political vocabulary of the founding era. When "Property" is read in context with the other essays in the series, one sees that Madison is trying to appeal to liberals for support by separating himself from Adams's Christian republicanism. Tying economic and legal liberty to liberty of conscience both created a bridge of common interest between economically liberal Anglicans and members of minority religious communities while conversely creating a reason for religious minorities to support Madison's preferred economic platforms in his competition with Hamilton. In other words, Madison was crafting a constellation of ideas and interests around which he could build his "Republican Party." Some writers have suggested that in fact the politics of the issue made Madison's position overdetermined.[37] It is equally sensible, however, to conclude that the strength of religious communities' self-identification (the political reality of pluralism) gave a political impetus to a position that fit with Madison's personal commitment to the idea of religion as a special case rather than just another species of property right or expression of conscience.

In his depiction of religious faith as outside the social contract (employing Munoz's formulation) and also as a basis for a destructive form of faction, we see a familiar pair of principles that religion is both specially valuable and vulnerable on the one hand and is a potential source of political corruption (in its broad sense) on the other. Another way of articulating this familiar pair of principles as the idea of religion as a special case: specially valuable and hence inalienable, specially dangerous and hence to be prevented from establishment. The dual clauses securing "free exercise" and "no establishment" appear in the First Amendment as the expression of these dual principles.

MODERN ISSUES IN RELIGIOUS LIBERTY: MADISON'S VIEWS

Public Financial Support for Religious Institutions

Of all the modern constitutional questions that arise under the religion clauses of the First Amendment, Madison's position on the provision of public funds to religious institutions seems the clearest and the one that most defined his position that religion was a special case. In his "Memorial and Remonstrance," Madison laid out the application of his understanding to the provision of public funds to religious institutions in strong if not strident terms. Even a collection of "three pence" to support a church would constitute a religious establishment. Religious establishments, in turn, were toxic both to religion and the civil authority.

> Because experience witnesseth that ecclesiastical establishments, instead of maintaining the purity and efficacy of Religion, have had a contrary operation. During almost fifteen centuries has the legal establishment of Christianity been on trial. What have been its fruits? More or less in all places, pride and indolence in the Clergy, ignorance and servility in the laity, in both, superstition, bigotry and persecution.
>
> What influence in fact have ecclesiastical establishments had on Civil Society? In some instances they have been seen to erect a spiritual tyranny on the ru-

ins of the Civil authority; in many instances they have been seen upholding the thrones of political tyranny: in no instance have they been seen the guardians of the liberties of the people. Rulers who wished to subvert the public liberty, may have found an established Clergy convenient auxiliaries.[38]

It bears reiterating that there is nothing in Madison's writings that takes anything like a similar position with government "establishment" of political or other doctrines; the treatment of religion marks it as a special case outside of and separate from freedom of conscience generally. Even if one is inclined to dismiss this as politically motivated rhetoric, it is unlike the rhetoric Madison deployed in any other context. In fact, Virginia's proposed assessment was liberal even by the standards of the time; Madison's staunch opposition was among the most extreme political positions he ever took, and certainly one of his most consistent. It bears reiterating that Madison had no similar resistance to public funding for a nonreligious viewpoint. Madison was thus propounding the "dual danger" theory exemplified in Chief Justice Burger's opinion: that religion could be a danger to the state and that the state could be a danger to religion. Alternatively, one can think of the same thing in terms of a duality of qualities that made religion a special case: both specially powerful and specially precious.

Some writers have tried to draw distinctions among forms of public support to reach a different conclusion about what Madison would have thought. The Virginia general assessment, after all, was directed toward the direct subsidy of religious institutions. Building on that fact, some authors argue that the case would have been different if the question had involved other forms of support. Robert L. Cord concludes that in Madison's view nondiscriminatory aid—aid available to all churches or religious groups—would be acceptable, an argument he formulated specifically to counteract the "strict separationist" interpretation ascribed to the Founders by the Warren and Burger courts.[39]

As a thesis about popular understandings in the founding era, Cord's thesis may have merit. As a description of Madison's thinking specifically, however, it is difficult to maintain. A key part of the "Memorial and Remonstrance" was Madison's "slippery slope" argument that said that nondiscriminatory support was merely a step toward outright establishment. "Who does not see that the same authority which can establish Christianity, in exclusion of all other Religions, may establish with the same ease any particular sect of Christians, in exclusion of all other sects?"[40] Madison was insistent that in this situation, in sharp contrast to others, even the slightest encroachment on principle was to be resisted. "Because it is proper to take alarm at the first experiment on our liberties. We hold this prudent jealousy to be the first duty of Citizens, and one of the noblest characteristics of the late Revolution." Madison was notably much less eager to see "jealousy" in response to his Virginia Plan or in his responses to Anti-Federalist challenges in *The Federalist Papers*. Once again religion appears as a special case.

Madison's actions suited his words. Two of the seven laws that Madison vetoed as president involved direct institutional subsidy: one was a law providing for the incorporation of a church in the District of Columbia; the other was a law granting land in a new territory to a church.

> The Bill exceeds the rightful authority, to which Governments are limited by the essential distinction between Civil and Religious functions, and violates, in particular, the Article of the Constitution of the United States which declares, that "Congress shall make no law respecting a Religious establishment." The Bill enacts into, and establishes by law, sundry rules and proceedings relative purely to the organization and polity of the Church incorporated.... Because the Bill vests in the said incorporated Church, an authority to provide for the support of the poor, and the education of poor children of the same, an authority, which being altogether superfluous if the provision is to be the result of pious charity, would be a precedent for giving to religious Societies as such, a legal agency in carrying into effect a public and civil duty.[41]

There are three distinct arguments in this passage. First, the bill would involve civil authority in the internal governance of churches; second, the bill would involve civil authority in the *enforcement* of church rules and doctrines; and third, the bill would establish a precedent for granting public support to religious institutions to carry out secular mandates. The latter is yet another point where Madison's views of the Establishment Clause contradict modern understandings, as the Supreme Court has held that so long as a secular purpose such as "support for the poor" is being served, the allocation of public funds to religious institutions is not prohibited.[42] Thus to a far greater degree than the general rhetoric of the "Memorial and Remonstrance," this expression of specific objections demonstrates the contradiction between Madison's views and those of the modern court.

On the same day that he vetoed the incorporation of a church in Virginia, Madison also vetoed a bill proposing to grant territory for the establishment of churches. His argument was succinct: "The bill in reserving a certain parcel of land of the United States for the use of said Baptist Church comprises a principle and precedent for the appropriation of funds of the United States for the use and support of religious societies, contrary to the article of the Constitution which declares that "Congress shall make no law respecting a religious establishment.'"[43]

Comparing these Madisonian positions to modern constitutional doctrine demonstrates clear tensions. It was not merely the specifics of the proposed Virginia assessment that Madison found objectionable; he objected to any use of public funds to support religious institutions regardless of the specific purpose of the support. Public support for private educational alternatives would have appealed to Madison as promotions of freedom of conscience; public support for churches to provide education, on the other hand, would run afoul of the treatment of religion as a special case.

On the other hand, his comments about the political utility of religion can be read to suggest the possibility of a distinction between actors and institutions. That is, Madison might have accepted public support for religious schools so long as they were not attached to churches. It is true that Madison expressed his greatest concerns about the dangers of religious establishment in the context of ecclesiastical institutions. His concern was not only with direct provision of financial support; late in his life Madison became deeply concerned about the implications of permitting churches to have the same kinds of legal privileges that attached to secular actors. In England and elsewhere in Europe the established churches had become immensely wealthy and hence immensely powerful. Shakespeare's *Henry V*, for example, opens with a discussion of the king's need for funding from the Anglican Church to prepare for a possible war with France. It was in response to this reality that the founders of Massachusetts had in fact favored public funding for churches, to prevent them from becoming possessors of private wealth. Madison had led the charge to prevent public funding; now he was reckoning with the consequences of allowing religious institutions to become powerful civil societal actors. Incorporation was a critical concern; quite apart from permitting churches to gather wealth, incorporation meant the civil authorities providing legal privileges that would serve that end, wrapping them in legal protections and prerogatives unavailable to mere associations or partnerships among persons.

Around 1817 Madison wrote his "Detached Memoranda."[44] Never published nor intended for publication, these memoranda contain Madison's private thoughts. Among his specific points of concern, Madison expressed the fear that churches were becoming wealthy and thus powerful institutions, a fear that went with his general distrust of corporations, banks, and other institutions of speculation. "The danger of silent accumulations & encroachments by Ecclesiastical Bodies have not sufficiently engaged attention in the U. S. . . . [B]esides the danger of a direct mixture of Religion & civil Government, there is an evil which ought to be guarded [against] in the indefinite accumulation of property from the capacity of holding it in perpetuity by ecclesiastical corporations. The power of all corporations, ought to be limited in this respect. . . . The excessive wealth of ecclesiastical Corporations and the misuse of it in many Countries of Europe has long been a topic of complaint. In some of them the Church has amassed half perhaps the property of the nation."[45]

The reference to European experience takes Madison's comments out of the area of a general concern about concentrations of wealth in his reference to "the power of all corporations." The increasing reliance on corporations to carry out public functions was a cause for concern, but religious corporations raised unique concerns of their own separate from any general theory of economics; once again Madison was treating religion as a special case.

Madison made his concern more explicit in a letter to Jefferson dated December 31, 1824, writing that charters would permit "a creed however absurd or contrary to that of a more enlightened Age" to be perpetuated indefinitely.[46] There is an element of a Holmesian "marketplace of ideas" metaphor here, as Madison seemed to think that without the special legal privileges that permitted corporations to accumulate and hold wealth indefinitely the doctrines of at least some religious sects would fall by the wayside; in this way an unwholesome combination of free religious conscience and state-granted prerogative resulted in a perversion of religious doctrine of an entirely different kind than that mentioned in the "dual danger" idea. Madison's comment lends further support to the idea that while he viewed "religion" as something valuable, that did not extend to favor it for particular or traditional doctrine, and indeed that he viewed religion as *sometimes* positive and sometimes not.

But the general idea that if civil authorities support the promulgation of any set of ideas, it must support the promulgation of religious ideas in equal measure flies in the face of a consistent and unbroken record. So, too, does the idea that it is appropriate to grant public funds to churches or equivalent institutions to carry out secular public goods or that the use of tax dollars to evangelize on behalf of a religion can ever be justified. Madison's views were not those of all the members of his generation, to be sure, but insofar as Madison himself is the focus and the issue is the use of public moneys, his attachment to a strict separationist position seems both clear and consistent.

THE PROBLEM OF GOVERNMENT ENDORSEMENT

Providing money and legal privileges is not the only way in which civil authority can support religion. In 1984 Justice O'Connor coined the term "endorsement" to describe what she saw as impermissible expression of support for religion by government actors. "Endorsement sends a message to non-adherents that they are outsiders, not full members of the political community, and an accompanying message to adherents that they are insiders, favored members of the political community. Disapproval sends the opposite message."[47] Public displays, official statements, and other expressions of approval (or disapproval) for religious practices risk running afoul of the anti-endorsement principle. Recent cases, however, have drawn the lines around what constitutes endorsement narrowly. The use of sectarian public prayers before legislative sessions was upheld in 2014; in 2019 Justice Alito declared the anti-endorsement principle to be inoperative in the context of a public monument in the form of a forty-foot-high cross.[48]

Madison's views on the question are potentially ambiguous. In his Detached Memoranda Madison expressed his objections to the use of public chaplains and public declaration of days of thanksgiving. "Is the appointment of Chaplains to the two Houses of Congress consistent with the Constitution, and with the pure principle of religious freedom? In strictness the answer on both points must be in the negative. The Constitution of the U. S. forbids everything like an establishment of a national religion. The law appointing Chaplains establishes a religious worship for the national representatives, to be performed by Ministers of religion, elected by a majority of them; and these are to be paid out of the national taxes." Madison was specifically concerned with the exclusionary message that O'Connor had identified and that the majority in *Galloway* declined to consider. "The establishment of the chaplainship to Congs is a palpable violation of equal rights, as well as of Constitutional principles: The tenets of the chaplains elected [by the majority] shut the door of worship agst the members whose creeds & consciences forbid a participation in that of the majority."[49]

As for proclamations of days of thanksgiving, Madison's private thoughts expressed in the memoranda was even more strongly stated.

> The objections to them are 1. that Govts ought not to interpose in relation to those subject to their authority but in cases where they can do it with effect. An *advisory* Govt is a contradiction in terms. 2. The members of a Govt as such can in no sense, be regarded as possessing an advisory trust from their Constituents in their religious capacities. . . . 3. They seem to imply and certainly nourish the erroneous idea of a *national* religion. The idea just as it related to the Jewish nation under a theocracy, having been improperly adopted by so many nations which have embraced Xnity, is too apt to lurk in the bosoms even of Americans, who in general are aware of the distinction between religious & political societies. The idea also of a union of all to form one nation under one Govt in acts of devotion to the God of all is an imposing idea."[50]

These statements were not the first time Madison had taken a position. In 1786 Madison scolded Christian conservatives for trying to insert the words "Jesus

Christ" into the preamble to the Virginia Statute of Religious Freedom. In the Detached Memoranda Madison recalls the debate over the statute thirty-five years earlier. "The opponents of the amendment having turned the feeling as well as judgment of the House agst it, by successfully contending that the better proof of reverence for that holy name wd be not to profane it by making it a topic of legisl. discussion, & particularly by making his religion the means of abridging the natural and equal rights of all men, in defiance of his own declaration that his Kingdom was not of this world."[51]

Madison in 1817 was thus declaring a position that he was and had always been opposed to religious endorsements. But how can these statements be squared with Madison's apparently firm and unwavering belief in the utility (if not the sufficiency) of religions teaching for promoting civic virtue? Furthermore, how do these sentiments relate to Madison's actions in declaring four separate days of national thanksgiving while he was president? Nor were those the only instances of Madison's participation in thanksgiving exercises. During the Revolution he had supported and participated in drafting declarations of thanksgiving. In 1799 Madison presented a bill, drafted by Jefferson, providing for declarations of days of thanksgiving in Virginia.[52]

As always, one explanation is that Madison simply changed his mind (and perhaps that his recollection of the Virginia debate was inaccurate). A different explanation, however, points to an important dimension of Madison's general theory of constitutional authority. In a speech to the Fourth Congress in April 1796, Madison declared his commitment to a principle of popular constitutionalism. "Whatever veneration might be entertained for the body of men who formed our Constitution, the sense of that body could never be regarded as the oracular guide in expounding the Constitution. As the instrument came from them it was nothing more than the draft of a plan, nothing but a dead letter, until life and validity were breathed into it by the voices of the people, speaking through the several State Conventions. If we were to look, therefore, for the meaning of the instrument beyond the face of the instrument, we must look for it, not in the General Convention, which proposed, but in the State Conventions, which accepted and ratified the Constitution."[53]

Madison's comments articulate a principle of popular constitutional construction that permitted him to sign into law a bill establishing the Second Bank of the United States in 1816, even though he had opposed the First Bank as unconstitutional earlier: the conviction that long-settled use established a precedent that legitimized a practice. In 1811 as a member of Congress, Madison had argued strenuously against the constitutionality of the bank (as he had also done in 1791). In 1815 he vetoed a bill to revive the bank under a new charter on policy grounds but explicitly eschewed any constitutional objections. "Waiving the question of the constitutional authority of the Legislature to establish an incorporated bank as being precluded in my judgment ... by indications, in different modes, of a concurrence of the general will of the nation, the proposed bank does not appear to be calculated to answer the purposes of reviving the public credit."[54] In 1816, under continuing pressure, Madison signed the Second Bank Bill. Explaining his actions, he later wrote in correspondence that "the inconsistency is apparent only not real. . . . [M]y abstract opinion of the text of the Constitution is not changed, and the assent was given in pursuance of my early and unchanged opinion, that in the case of a Constitution, as of a law, a course of authoritative expositions sufficiently deliberate, uniform, and settled, was an evidence of the Public Will necessarily overruling individual opinions."[55] This position was consistent with Madison's declaration in a letter in 1826: "My construction of the Constitution on this point is not changed. But ... I did not feel myself, as a public man, at liberty, to sacrifice all these public considerations to my private opinion."[56] As H. Jefferson Powell concludes, "However strongly he might have fought constitutional error when it first appeared, for Madison there could be no return to the unadorned text from interpretations that had received the approbation of the people. The Constitution is a public document, and its interpretation, for Madison, was in the end a public process."[57]

Thus, Madison's comments on the Second Bank suggest that his popular constitutionalism extended beyond reference to the understandings of ratifying conventions to a general principle of constitutional meaning determined by constitutional politics. The suggestive possibility is that Madison took the same view on the use of public chaplains and the declaration of days of thanksgiving. In his own view these practices represented religious establishments, but he recognized a contrary and longstanding public understanding as a valid source of constitutional authority binding on his actions as president even though the actions contradicted his personal constitutional convictions expressed in the Detached Memoranda.[58]

What is clear, however, is that in his own mind Madison found a version of O'Connor's "endorsement" theory to be deeply concerning. The message of unequal citizenship was precisely the kind of intrusion of religious factions into republican citizenship that was one-half of the dual danger model; the attachment of state voices to the support of religious adherence was the other. Madison's concerns were not unusual: as president, Jefferson refused to issue proclamations of thanksgiving, and late in his life Washington expressed regret for having done so. Anti-Federalists had warned that "the exclusion of religious tests is by many thought dangerous and impolitic. They suppose ... pagans, deists, and

Mahometans might obtain offices among us." Others referred to "a Papist, an Infidel," "Jews and heathens."[59] Madison no less than his friend Jefferson understood the inequality among citizens that would result from a government that aligned itself with religion for its claims to the loyalty of its supporters.

THE QUESTION OF RELIGIOUS EXEMPTIONS AND LEGAL PRIVILEGES

Among current controversies over questions of religious liberty, none gets more attention than the claim that religious believers should be constitutionally entitled to exemption from the operation of generally applicable laws. The U.S. Supreme Court disavowed this position in *Employment Division, Oregon Dept. of Human Services v. Smith* (1990). As Justice Scalia put it in his majority opinion, "It may fairly be said that leaving accommodation to the political process will place at a relative disadvantage those religious practices that are not widely engaged in; but that unavoidable consequence of democratic government must be preferred to a system in which each conscience is a law unto itself or in which judges weigh the social importance of all laws against the centrality of all religious beliefs."[60] In response, however, both Congress and numerous state legislatures adopted "religious freedom restoration acts" designed to secure a right to exemptions by acts of legislation. The problems arise when these statutes are in tension with others, as when employers assert a right to be exempted from antidiscrimination statutes based on their religious commitments. As a matter of rhetoric, it is difficult to imagine anything less Madisonian than Scalia's dismissal of concerns for religious minorities. But in the context of arguments about a constitutional right to exemption from the operation of generally applicable laws—and leaving the rhetoric aside—the issue is much more complicated.

Michael W. McConnell argues that while there is evidence for different positions, the best conclusion is that the framers in general would favor a range of exemptions. With respect to Madison specifically, however, McConnell's conclusions are much more equivocal. Citing the language in the "Memorial and Remonstrance" where Madison speaks of religious duties as "precedent . . . to the claims of Civil Society," McConnell observes: "This striking passage illuminates the radical foundations of Madison's writings on religious liberty. While it does not prove that Madison supported free exercise exemptions, it suggests an approach toward religious liberty consonant with them."[61] McConnell acknowledges the existence of other passages in which Madison complained of "peculiar exemptions" granted to Quakers and Mennonites "provides some support for the no-exemptions view, since it describes the 'peculiar exemptions' in the bill as 'extraordinary privileges' that violate the principle of religious equality. However, the meaning of the passage is ambiguous."[62] Anthony Munoz, drawing on the same language, finds an absolute right to exemption from civil regulation but only as to the exercise of gathering to engage in prayer.[63]

McConnell also points to Madison's role in drafting Virginia's Statute of Religious Freedom. George Mason's original draft had provided an exception to the exercise of religious liberty where "under color of religion any man disturb the peace, the happiness, or safety of society." Madison proposed instead that free exercise be protected "unless under color of religion the preservation of equal liberty and the existence of the State are manifestly endangered." As McConnell argues, "The "preservation of equal liberty" and "manifest endangerment of the existence of the State . . . is a standard that only the most critical acts of government can satisfy."[64] Noah Feldman makes if anything a stronger case, relying on the language of Madison's fourth proposed amendment to the Constitution. Madison's original text read, "The civil rights of none shall be abridged on account of religious belief or worship, nor shall any national religion be established, nor shall the full and equal rights of conscience be in any manner, or on any pretext, infringed." Feldman reads the last phrase as a guarantee of religious exemptions: "The right of conscience—the right not to be coerced to act against one's beliefs—would be protected absolutely."[65]

One difficulty with drawing conclusions from McConell's and Feldman's arguments on this point is that we must understand what Madison meant by the "free exercise of religion" that he was protecting. If that free exercise extends only to acts of worship and prayer, then there is no basis for a general principle of an entitlement to exemptions in other areas of conduct. It is noteworthy that Madison also offered an amendment that would have stripped ministers of "peculiar emoluments or privileges"; an exemption from the operation of ordinary law, as McConnell observed, can certainly be understood as a "privilege," and if Madison did not intend this privilege to extend to ministers, it seems unlikely that he would have wanted it extended to congregants.

Another potential difficulty with the broad pro-exemption readings of Madison's views is that they do not adequately distinguish between a view of religious freedom that would *permit* religions exemptions and one that would *require* such exemptions—the distinction relied upon by the modern Supreme Court. Numerous writers have noted that Madison believed strongly in the necessity of protecting religious freedom in constitutional text rather than leaving the matter to legislatures, but that observation does not resolve the scope of the freedom to be protected.[66] Jack Rakove argues that the issues simply did not arise, so that debates in the 1780s provide little guidance for modern understanding. "No one then was imagining the ambit of the modern regulatory state or the multiple points where its reach would intersect or conflict with private religious conviction. The general assessment bill traveled well-trodden ground, and so did Madison."[67]

There is also the question that was raised earlier about the relationship between freedom of religion and a more general liberty of conscience. Certainly, there is no argument that Madison believed that every individual was entitled to be exempted from state coercion—that is, the enforcement of the law—in any way that offended his or her individual conscience. Rakove suggests that establishing freedom of religious conscience was a step toward abandoning the idea of anti-sedition laws: "In Jefferson's imagination and Madison's, the expression of religious opinions was a harbinger for a broader enlightenment. Once blasphemy became a problematic legal concept—an offense that was rarely prosecuted even as freethinkers were multiplying—could the erosion of seditions libel be far behind?"[68] But as Rakove also notes, in his original draft of the religious liberty provision of the Virginia Constitution, Jefferson had included a clause permitting prosecution for "seditious behavior" or "seditions preaching or conversation against the authority of the civil government."[69] If Madison disagreed with his friend on this point, that fact does not appear to be recorded in their public debates or private correspondence.

There is one case in which Madison's pro-exemption position is clear, the case of exemption from military service. In his proposed amendment describing the role of the militias, Madison included the statement "no person religiously scrupulous of bearing arms shall be compelled to render military service in person."[70] As soon as we move beyond that specific example, however, the case becomes much more difficult to make, as Madison himself acknowledged in a letter in 1833. "I must admit . . . that it may not be easy, in every possible case, to trace the line of separation between the rights of religion and the Civil authority with such distinctness to avoid collisions and doubts on unessential points. . . . By an entire abstinence of the Gov't from interference in any way whatsoever, beyond the necessity of preserving public order and protecting each sect agst. trespasses on its legal rights by others."[71] That letter, of course, was written long after the debates in the Virginia legislature and the Constitutional Convention, but it repeats the "necessity of preserving public order" idea of Madison's revisions to Virginia's Statute of Religious Freedom. What is not clear, moreover, is whether Madison is saying that government may only interfere in the practices of religious worship based on "the necessity of preserving public order" or whether that standard is intended to describe the scope of exemptions for individuals from the operation of civil law.

In some cases it appears that Madison was less protective of religiously motivated conduct than we might expect. As noted earlier, in 1799 Jefferson drafted and Madison submitted a bill for the declaration of days of thanksgiving in Virginia. That bill stated: "Every minister of the gospel shall on each day so to be appointed, attend and perform divine service and preach a sermon, or discourse, suited to the occasion, in his church, on pain of forfeiting fifty pounds for every failure, not having a reasonable excuse."[72] That was less than a year before the debates over the Virginia Statute for Religious Freedom. Was Madison's rhetoric in drafting that statute unduly absolutist, or had he changed his views in the intervening months? Madison also joined with Jefferson in supporting civil penalties for Sabbath breaking as an example of a threat to civil order, suggesting that the "necessity of preserving public order" might not be as narrow a standard as it at first appears even if the exception was intended to apply to laws outside the scope of practices of worship.

Another place to look for guidance might be the succession of drafts of what became the religion clauses of the First Amendment. Madison's original proposed draft, presented on June 8, 1789, read, "The civil rights of none shall be abridged on account of religious belief or worship, nor shall any national religion be established, nor shall the full and equal rights of conscience by in any manner, or on any pretext infringed." The Senate's version read, "Congress shall make no law establishing articles of faith, or a mode of worship, or prohibiting the free exercise of religion." The House rejected the Senate version and appointed Madison to a committee to propose a revision; that committee's version became the modern First Amendment.[73] The repeated emphasis on worship casts doubt on the idea that the "free exercise of religion" was understood to extend to, say, employment practices or immunity from insurance requirements. It is true, as Rakove observes, statutes mandating those kinds of requirements were far in the future. But the common-law tradition bestowed enormous (and by modern standards intrusive) power on local authorities to regulate social and economic life; it would not have been difficult to imagine potential points of conflict beyond the question of militia service. Considering again Madison's comments about special privileges for Quakers and Mennonites, it is difficult to credit the idea that his implication was that no one should be required to pay any taxes—as opposed to assessments for the support of churches—if doing so contradicted an article of their faith. Certainly there is nothing that authors have pointed to in Madison's writings to support such an extreme reading.

The question, though, remains: can we intuit anything about Madison's likely attitudes about exemption questions other than that he rejected both the idea of total subordination of religious duties to civil authority and, by surmise, that he would have equally rejected the opposite extreme proposition if it had been suggested? Ultimately, the most informative observation may be that as late as the 1833 letter cited earlier he wrote, "it may not be easy, in every possible case, to trace the line of separation" on "unessential points." The term "unessential" may be the key. With respect to acts of worship there is little doubt that Madison would have staked out a nearly absolutist position. With respect to militia service, he felt that specific provisions were required. Other cases were likely "unessential," matters that could be left to the constitutional politics of popular interpretation that were discussed in the last section. It is important to recall that Madison's idea of factions drew its initial inspiration from the problem of conflicts among religious sects; Madison likely would have relied on the structural element of plurality to resolve "unessential" conflicts despite the special status of religion, if only because after more than fifty years of contemplation he remained unable to articulate a more specific standard.

CONCLUSION

Religious liberty was at the core of Madison's conception of constitutional rights protections. Regarding issues that he characterized as "unessential," he was willing to rely on popular constitutionalism and structural solutions. Where core principles of religious freedom were concerned, however, his positions were the most absolute of any he articulated in his speeches and writings. Above all, Madison insisted on treating religion as a special case: a special and especially crucial case of freedom of conscience, and a special and especially dangerous case of political faction. To the extent that modern legal thinkers move away from this core principle they are wrong to assert that they are reasoning in Madisonian terms.

NOTES

1. *Everson v. Board of Education*, 330 U.S. 1, 15–16 (1947).
2. *Id.* at 12.
3. *Lemon v. Kurtzman*, 411 U.S. 192 (1973).
4. *Id.* at 209–10.
5. *Espinoza v. Montana Dept. of Revenue*, 591 U.S. ___ (2020), 18–1195 slip op. at 15 (2020) (Roberts, C. J.).
6. *Id.* slip op. at 8 (Breyer, J., dissenting).

7. James Madison, letter to William Bradford January 22, 1774, quoted in Noah Feldman, *The Three Lives of James Madison: Genius, Partisan, President* (London: Picador Press, 2020), 12–14.

8. James Madison, "Memorial and Remonstrance against Religious Assessments, [ca. 20 June] 1785," Founders Online, National Archives, https://founders.archives.gov/documents/Madison/01-08-02-0163.

9. James Madison, speech of June 12, 1788, in *The Documentary History of the Ratification of the Constitution Digital Edition*, ed. John P. Kaminski, Gaspare J. Saladino, Richard Leffler, Charles H. Schoenleber, and Margaret A. Hogan, vol. 10 (Charlottesville: University of Virginia Press, 2009), https://rotunda.upress.virginia.edu/founders/default.xqy?keys=RNCN-print-02-10-02-0002-0002.

10. James Hutson, "James Madison and the Social Utility of Religion: Risks v. Rewards" (paper presented at Library of Congress, September 19, 2017), https://www.loc.gov/loc/madison/hutson-paper.html#:~:text=Madison%20on%20the%20subject%20of,not%20kneel%20himself%20at%20prayers.

11. Jack Rakove, *Beyond Belief, Beyond Conscience: The Radical Significance of the Free Exercise of Religion* (New York: Oxford University Press, 2020), 71.

12. Irving Brant, *James Madison*, vol. 3, *Father of the Constitution, 1787–1800* (Indianapolis: Bobbs-Merrill, 1951); Ralph L. Ketcham, "James Madison and Religion: A New Hypothesis," *Journal of the Presbyterian Historical Society* 38 (1960): 65–90.

13. John Noonan, *The Lustre of Our Country: The American Experience of Religious Freedom* (Berkeley: University of California Press, 1998); Joseph Loconte, "Faith and the Founding: The Influence of Religion on the Politics of James Madison," *Journal of Church and State* 45 (2003): 699–715.

14. Feldman, *Three Lives of James Madison*, 237.

15. Madison, "Memorial and Remonstrance"; Madison, March 29, 1792, "Property," *The Writings of James Madison*, vol. 6, *1790–1802*, https://oll.libertyfund.org/titles/madison-the-writings-vol-6-1790-1802.

16. Thomas Lindsay, "James Madison on Religion and Politics: Rhetoric and Reality," *Journal of Church and State* 85 (1991): 1321–37; Donald L. Drakeman, "Religion and the Republic: James Madison and the First Amendment," *Journal of Church and State* 25 (1983): 427–45.

17. On the importance of Scottish common sense philosophy to the founding generation and Jefferson in particular see Garry Wills, *Inventing America: Jefferson's Declaration of Independence* (Garden City, N.Y.: Doubleday, 1978); for contrary arguments see Ronald Hamowy, "Jefferson and the Scottish Enlightenment: A Critique of Garry Wills's *Inventing America: Jefferson's Declaration of Independence*," *William and Mary Quarterly*, 3rd ser., 36 (1979): 503–23; Joseph J. Ellis, American Sphinx: The Character of Thomas Jefferson (New York: Random House Digital, 1998). Some historians have questioned the relevance of formal political thought for the founding generation, emphasizing their need to arrive at practical solutions through political compromise. See Pauline Maier, *American Scripture: Making the Declaration of Independence* (New York: Vintage Press, 1998); Jack N. Rakove, *Original Meanings: Politics and Ideas in the Making of the Constitution* (New York: Vintage Press, 1997).

18. "Correspondence of Ezra Stiles, President of Yale College, and James Madison, President of William and Mary College, 1780," *William and Mary Quarterly* 7 (1927): 292–96, 294.
19. Hutson, "James Madison."
20. Feldman, *Three Lives of James Madison*, 12.
21. Bishop Mead, quoted in Hutson, "James Madison."
22. Loconte, "Faith and the Founding," 704; James H. Hutson, *Religion and the Founding of the American Republic* (Washington, D.C.: Library of Congress, 1998), 63. This idea of religious instruction as useful for civic purposes appears in an interesting way in discussions of education in the new territories. In the Land Ordinance of 1784, written by Jefferson, there is no mention of religion or education; that statute was supplemented by the Land Ordinance of 1785, which specified that newly created townships should set aside lots for public schools but did not mention religion; finally the Northwest Ordinance of July 13, 1787, declared in Article 3, "Religion, morality, and knowledge being necessary to good government and the happiness of mankind, schools and the means of education shall forever be encouraged." Avalon Project, Lillian Goldman Law Library, Yale Law School, https://avalon.law.yale.edu/18th_century/nworder.asp.
23. James Madison, *The Writings of James Madison*, ed. William T. Hutchinson (Chicago: University of Chicago Press 1962), 10:213–14.
24. Ibid., 10:230–31.
25. Jack N. Rakove, ed., *Madison: Writings* (New York: Library of America, 1999), 142–58.
26. Ibid., 94.
27. James Madison, "Vices of the Political System of the United States," April 30, 1787, Founders Online, National Archives, https://founders.archives.gov/documents/Madison/01-09-02-0187.
28. James Madison, *Federalist* No. 10, November 12, 1787, Avalon Project, https://avalon.law.yale.edu/18th_century/fed10.asp.
29. Michael W. McConnell, "The Origins and Historical Understanding of Free Exercise of Religion," *Harvard Law Review* 103 (1990): 1409–517.
30. Madison, "Memorial and Remonstrance."
31. Ibid.
32. Vincent Anthony Munoz, "James Madison's Principle of Religious Liberty," *American Political Science Review* 97 (2003): 17–32.
33. The *Massachusetts Body of Liberties* of 1641 prohibits civil authorities from interfering in religious teachings in the churches, while a 1646 statute prohibited punishment for holding heterodox beliefs, both limited by the distinction between heresy and blasphemy (the latter was not tolerated). The same document bans public religious celebrations, church weddings, and civil interventions by civil authorities into the individual teachings and practices of churches. This is the earliest case of a government in power giving legal force to a principle of antiestablishmentarianism of which we are aware.
34. Madison, "Memorial and Remonstrance."
35. Brant, *James Madison*, 3:348; for copies of all of Madison's essays see *The Writings of James*

Madison, ed. Gallard Hunt, Online Library of Liberty, https://oll.libertyfund.org/title/madison-the-writings-of-james-madison-9-vols.

36. Madison, "Property."
37. Feldman, Three Lives of James Madison, 233.
38. Madison, "Memorial and Remonstrance."
39. Robert L. Cord, *Separation of Church and State: Historical Fact and Current Fiction* (New York: Lambeth Press, 1982).
40. Madison, "Memorial and Remonstrance."
41. Madison, Veto Message re "An Act incorporating the protestant Episcopal Church in the Town of Alexandria in the District of Columbia," February 21, 1811, Miller Center, University of Virginia, https://millercenter.org/the-presidency/presidential-speeches/february-21-1811-veto-act-incorporating-alexandria-protestant.
42. See, e.g., *Bowen v. Kendrick*, 487 U.S. 589 (1988); *Agostini v. Felton* 521 U.S. 203 (1997).
43. Madison, Veto Message re "An act for the relief of . . . the Baptist Church at Salem Meeting House, in the Mississippi Territory," February 28, 1811, American Presidency Project, University of California, Santa Barbara, https://www.presidency.ucsb.edu/documents/veto-message-167.
44. The Detached Memoranda are variously dated "circa 1817" and "circa 1820." Compare "Detached Memoranda," *William & Mary Quarterly*, 3d ser., 3 (1946): 554–60 (which dated the memoranda as 1817), and "Detached Memoranda, ca. 31 January 1820," Founders Online, National Archives, https://founders.archives.gov/documents/Madison/04-01-02-0549. The contents of the two versions are identical.
45. "Detached Memoranda," *William & Mary Quarterly*, 554, 555–56.
46. "From James Madison to Thomas Jefferson, 31 December 1824," Founders Online, National Archives, https://founders.archives.gov/documents/Madison/04-03-02-0453.
47. *Lynch v. Donnelly*, 465 U.S. 668, 688 (1984).
48. *Town of Greece v. Galloway*, 572 U.S. 565 (2014); *American Legion v. American Humanist Ass'n*. 588 U.S. ____, 139 S. Ct. 2067 (2019). Curiously, in the latter case Justice Alito cited a different version of the anti-endorsement principle in support of his position, one that focused on the danger of a perception of endorsement of an anti-religious message. "A government that roams the land, tearing down monuments with religious symbolism and scrubbing away any reference to the divine will strike many as aggressively hostile to religion." American Legion, Nos. 17–1717 and 17–1818, slip op. at 20 (Alito, J.) Alito provided no explanation as to why endorsement of anti-religion is problematic while endorsement of religion is not.
49. Madison, "Detached Memoranda," *William & Mary Quarterly*, 557.
50. Ibid., 558.
51. Ibid., 556–57.
52. "A Bill for Appointing Days of Public Fasting and Thanksgiving," June 18, 1779, Founders Online, National Archives, https://founders.archives.gov/documents/Jefferson/01-02-02-0132-0004-0085.

53. *Debates and Proceedings in the Congress of the United States*, vol. 5, 4th Cong., 1st Sess., 1776, Library of Congress, https://webarchive.loc.gov/all/20211104211716/https://memory.loc.gov/cgi-bin/ampage?collId=llac&fileName=005/llac005.db&recNum=59.
54. Madison, "Message to the Senate Returning Without Approval 'An Act to Incorporate the Subscribers to the Bank of the United States of America,'" January 30, 1815, American Presidency Project, University of California, Santa Barbara, https://www.presidency.ucsb.edu/documents/message-the-senate-returning-without-approval-act-incorporate-the-subscribers-the-bank-the.
55. Madison, Letter to Charles E. Haynes, February 25, 1831, Founders Early Access, University of Virginia Press, https://rotunda.upress.virginia.edu/founders/default.xqy?keys=FOEA-print-02-02-02-2286.
56. Madison, Letter to Marquis de Lafayette, November 1826, Founders Early Access, University of Virginia Press, https://rotunda.upress.virginia.edu/founders/default.xqy?keys=FOEA-search-1-2&expandNote=on.
57. H. Jefferson Powell, "The Original Understanding of Original Intent," *Harvard Law Review* 98 (1985): 885–948, 944.
58. A separate possibility is that Madison made exceptions for periods of war; all his presidential proclamations took place during the War of 1812, and he had similarly supported and participated in drafting such proclamations during the Revolution. Hutson, "James Madison." This explanation, however, does not appear to figure in Madison's writings.
59. Isaac Kramnick, "The Great National Discussion: The Discourse of Politics in 1787, *William and Mary Quarterly* 45 (1988): 3–32, 10.
60. *Employment Division, Oregon Dept. of Human Services v. Smith*, 494 U.S. 872 (1990), 980.
61. McConnell, "Origins and Historical Understanding," 1453n231.
62. Ibid., 235.
63. Munoz, "James Madison's Principle," 29.
64. McConnell, "Origins and Historical Understanding," 1462–63.
65. Feldman, *Three Lives of James Madison*, 268.
66. See, e.g., McConnell, "Origins and Historical Understanding," 1444–45.
67. Rakove, *Beyond Belief*, 83–84.10.
68. Ibid., 88.
69. Ibid., 73.
70. Feldman, *Three Lives of James Madison*, 269.
71. Madison, Letter to Rev. Jasper Adams, September 1833, Founders Early Access, University of Virginia Press, https://rotunda.upress.virginia.edu/founders/default.xqy?keys=FOEA-search-1-1&expandNote=on.
72. Madison, "Detached Memoranda," *William & Mary Quarterly*.
73. Rakove, *Beyond Belief*, 95–96.

Madison and the Logic of Republican Government

GEORGE THOMAS

The American Constitution begins as an act of "We the People," but the idea of popular sovereignty was left to implication. In *Federalist* No. 40, James Madison made this clear: the proposed constitution was "to be of no more consequence than the paper on which it is written, unless it be stamped with the approbation of those to whom it is addressed."[1] It was only with popular ratification that the Constitution would be legitimate. And, indeed, *The Federalist* framed the debate over the Constitution as a debate over the very possibility of establishing popular government.

Yet even while defending America's republican experiment as a form of popular government, *The Federalist* spoke powerfully to the vices of popular government, deeply concerned about the "popular arts," where the people might be "stimulated by some irregular passion" or where the people might be "misled by the artful misrepresentations of interested men."[2] Madison in particular made a crucial distinction between two "species" of popular government: in a pure democracy, "the people meet and exercise the government in person; in a republic they assemble and administer it by their representatives and agents."[3] Madison argued for the clear superiority of a republic over a democracy as the most defensible species of popular government. Madison did not find democracy superior but impractical. Nor did he think that a republican government should simply mirror the voice of the people. For Madison, republican government was not a subsite for democracy, but a superior form of government.[4]

Although Madison began from the premise that the will of the people ought to ultimately govern us, he insisted that political institutions and intermediary civic institutions were essential in cultivating the "cool and deliberate sense of the community."[5] This is the essence of Madison's republicanism. By way of representation and other devices, Madison sought to put distance between the government and the people to better secure the public good. But, just as surely, Madison ultimately wanted the government accountable to the people. How to strike this balance? The seminal texts of Madison's republican vision, *Federalist* Nos. 10 and 51, speak to this balance, even while they do not represent the whole of his thinking. *Federalist* No. 10 argues for a large republic with a diversity of interests and representation, giving us a republican cure to the perils of a potentially unvirtuous people. The separation of powers articulated in Federalist No. 51 rests on this foundation, reflecting the diversity of interests in the large republic by way of political institutions, but also structuring institutions in a manner that contains overly ambitious government officers.

Madison's republican vision consistently sought to strike this balance between cultivating a true sense of the public good by way of representation and institutional design and keeping representatives and the government responsible to the people over time. These sentiments find expression in his early and late thinking, even if the tone and emphasis are markedly different. Crucial, too, is the balance between what are often described as the liberal and republican elements of Madison's thought. Madison's republican vision was distinctly liberal, limiting the sort of things popular majorities could decide, thus protecting individual rights and minorities from overbearing majorities. If Madison did not rely on a virtuous citizenry dedicated to the public good, his republicanism nevertheless sought to shape and educate the public mind to foster knowledgeable citizens prepared for republican self-government

This chapter first takes up Madison's argument as a "votary" of republican government rooted in representation as superior to pure democracy. It then turns to Madison's analysis of representation within political institutions as refining popular will and constructing the public good. Madison's republicanism highlights the benefits of representation and the direct exclusion of the people from the government. But even here there is a balance between civil society and political institutions, as well as nods to shaping the public mind. These latter elements in Madison's republicanism come out much more fully in the 1790s as he turned to the importance of politics "out-of-doors" in defending the emergence of political parties and other elements of civil society as crucial features of republican government.[6] The final section of this chapter focuses on the threat to republicanism from an abusive government attempting to silence its critics with the Sedition Act of 1798. Examining Madison's thinking during both a moment of creating republican government and a moment of securing republican government is a helpful reminder that Madison is not only a democratic and constitutional theorist, but a leading political actor and statesman who brought theory and practice together in a singular manner. At different moments in time, depending on the circumstances he faced, he played up different elements of his republican vision and refined his understanding based on experience.

REPUBLICAN GOVERNMENT AND THE SUPERIORITY OF REPRESENTATION

In *The Federalist*, Madison pointed to representation as the crucial distinction between a republic and a democracy. While arguing that the "people alone" are the "ultimate authority," Madison nevertheless insisted, "the public voice, pronounced by the representatives of the people, will be more consonant to the public good than if pronounced by the people themselves."[7] Madison divided popular government into two forms. In a democracy—which he often called a "pure" democracy—the people are directly engaged in the administration of government. Today, we usually call this direct democracy. In a republic a "scheme of representation takes place," removing the people from the direct administration of government.[8] Today, we usually call this representative democracy. Both, again, are forms of popular government. Contrary to the now fashionable insistence in some circles that "America is a republic, not a democracy," Madison did not mean to empower minority rule. Rather, Madison argued for a complex form of majority rule that would both protect individual rights and bring out the public good.[9] In this, Madison sought to secure representatives who were "fit characters" with "enlightened views and virtuous sentiments."[10] Representatives were not to be the mere mouthpiece of the people, but were to reflect on their own as they deliberated about public issues.[11]

Madison made the comparison between a popular representative government and popular democratic government explicit in *Federalist* No. 10, where he identified the problem of faction as the central problem of popular government, and where he situated representation as a crucial republican solution to this problem. I do not rehash the whole of Madison's argument regarding faction as it is taken up in another chapter, except insofar as it illuminates the nature of republican government and its superiority to *pure* democracy. Madison argues that the crucial distinction is, first, that in a republic the government is delegated to a small number of citizens elected by the rest and, second, that this increases the size of the political community. These two features provide a cure to the ills of popular government. Representation acts to "refine and enlarge the public views," by way of having them engaged by a representative body. Public ideas and issues are better engaged within a representative body because they must pass through "a temperate and respectable body of citizens."[12] This connects several elements of Madison's thinking. Madison argued that the representatives themselves, selected by citizens, were much more likely to be knowledgeable and informed; their "wisdom" made them more likely to "discern the true interests of their county" and less likely to "sacrifice" it to "temporary or partial considerations."[13] Consider that Madison's great fear with popular government was that a "faction"—that is, a self-interested group "adverse to the rights of other citizens, or to the permanent and aggregate interest of the community"—would more easily prevail in a pure democracy or a small republic. In both cases, because of the small size of the country, a faction that included most of the population could prevail by simple numbers. Small size made it more likely that overbearing majorities with similar interests could easily form, acting in ways that harm minorities and "invade the rights of other citizens."[14]

While this was true of both a small republic and a pure democracy, a pure democracy was even more susceptible to the ills of faction because the people were more likely to be driven by passion and more likely to act on ignorance absent distance between the people's immediate thoughts and governmental action. Pointing to the classical example of pure democracy, Madison insisted: "Had every Athenian citizen been a Socrates; every Athenian assembly would still have been a mob."[15] Madison's point was overwrought, but it made clear his prioritizing constitutional design and his suspicion of relying on virtue. How should the legislature be structured to nurture "the benefits of free consultation and discussion?" If it were too small, it would open itself to "an easy combination for improper purposes." Yet in assemblies that were too large, "passion never fails to wrest the sceptre from reason."[16] Madison picked up this theme in *Federalist* No. 58, arguing that in ancient republics "where the whole body of the people assembled in person, a single orator, or an artful statesman, was generally seen to rule with as complete a sway as if a sceptre had been placed in his single hand."[17] The irony was that a large assembly open to the people may look "more democratic," but "the soul that animates it will be more oligarchic."[18]

In just this way, pure democracy was more open to demagogues—men of "factious tempers," "local prejudices," and "sinister designs"—who would betray the interests of the people.[19] In the ancient polity where pure democracies prevailed as the predominate form of popular government, the "scheme of representation" was "imperfectly known."[20] The small republic was less prone to these shortcomings because it rested on the principle of representation, which allowed it to be relatively larger than a pure democracy. Yet even the small republic, which knew and utilized the representative principle, was prone to these weaknesses.

Madison's argument drew on historical experience in its criticism of both pure democracy and the small republic, challenging the inherited wisdom of Western thought regarding popular government.[21] Democracies and republics, which had up to this point been small republics, had a turbulent history. Madison's own experience in Virginia in the 1780s—and his survey of politics within the states—reinforced his conclusions. He witnessed the problems of deliberation within the legislature, as well as the problem of overbearing majorities disregarding the rights of minorities. Indeed, Madison's argument for a large republic had roots in his "Memorial and Remonstrance," which argued for religious liberty in Virginia against efforts to, in his view, establish religion.[22] Within the confines of a smaller republic, where one single religious sect was likely to have a majority, Madison worried that an overbearing majority could intrude on the rights of religious minorities. The smaller the society, the more likely that a single religious sect dominates. Yet as the scope of the country was extended, the number of religious sects increased, making it less likely that a single religious group could prevail over the others. A wider sphere would naturally bring a diversity of religious interests, making it likely that no single sect could dominate. Given this, religious liberty and tolerance would be in the self-interest of different religious sects.

In a similar fashion, by increasing the size of the republic, a diversity of ideas and interests would naturally follow, making it much more difficult for any single group to form a majority. In the "Memorial and Remonstrance" Madison was worried about religion, but in *Federalist* No. 10 Madison extended his concern to a much wider range of interests and opinions. Madison highlighted the unequal division of property as the "most durable" source of faction.[23] But the essential logic was the same. Madison did not assume benevolence—faction, after all, was sown into the nature of man—but the larger sphere would make it difficult for any single faction to dominate. If the small republic turned on a homogenous people closely linked to the government, Madison turned this logic on its head: a diversity of interests would provide the republican cure to the disease of republican government. The extended sphere, Madison argued, was also likely to increase the quality of representatives. Not only would the large republic increase the likelihood of "fit characters" for office, but the larger the number of citizens engaged in selecting "established characters" would make it more difficult for "unworthy candidates" to "practice with success the vicious arts."[24] There is a tension in the logic of the extended republic. On the one hand, in Robert D. Putnam's wonderfully provocative phrasing, Madisonian design seeks "to make democracy safe for the unvirtuous."[25] On the other hand, it partly does so by seeking to elevate those with virtue to public office. Putnam certainly captures Madison's reluctance to rely on a virtuous people committed to the ideal of a civic community. Yet Putnam also adds an important wrinkle that complements the general thrust of Madison's republicanism even if it does not confirm its particulars. The empirical evidence suggests that civic engagement and participation are more prevalent in modern liberal societies—where self-interest and conflict remain features of political life—than they are in the closed civic community that is taken to exemplify civic virtue.[26]

Madison's large republic was rooted in a wide variety of interests that would conflict, even while seeking to nurture representatives that had "wisdom" and "virtue" to act for the common good.[27] The extended republic made it more likely that representatives would act for the common good—not simply by bargaining among diverse factions and interests that would be represented in Congress (though this would occur), but by filtering the public views by passing them through the legislature.[28] Enlightened representation would allow Congress to act for the permanent interests of the community.[29] And the key to enlightened representation was placing distance between the people and the government.[30] This also comes out in Madison's discussion of the separation of powers, which at least partly works as it does in his eyes because it rests on the extended republic. Yet before turning to the institutions of government, we should pause to note a deep problem of which Madison was acutely aware: the problem of slavery in a republican government. But it's a problem that Madison largely ducked. He did work at the Constitutional Convention to remove any explicit reference to "property in man," but he also supported the Constitution's three-fifths clause, which counted enslaved human beings—even if it only referred to them obliquely—as three-fifths of a person for the *purposes of representation*. But there was no consideration that they would be represented as part of the people.[31]

POLITICAL INSTITUTIONS, REPRESENTATION, AND CONSTRUCTING THE PUBLIC GOOD

In accord with the large republic—the primary way to create "equilibrium in the interests and passions of the Society itself"—American political institutions were crafted to be responsive to the people over time but put space between the people and their representatives.[32] As Madison put it in *Federalist* No. 57, "The aim of every political constitution is, or ought to be, first to obtain for rulers men who possess most wisdom to discern, and most virtue to pursue, the common good of society; and in the next place, to take the most effectual precautions for keeping them virtuous whilst they continue to hold their public trust." Elected political officials, who held their office as a public trust, were not merely to act as a mouthpiece of the citizenry, but to see farther than ordinary citizens: "to refine and enlarge the public views," to have the wisdom to "discern the true interest of their country," and to do so against "temporary or partial consideration."[33] And yet such leaders were to remain dependent on the people. How dependent the different political offices were—and to which version of the people—varied within the separation of powers. The result was a complex system of representation that provided for varying degrees of independence from the people, allowing for representatives with "sound judgement and a certain degree of knowledge" to work for the public good.[34] Within the separation of powers, the various and conflicted interests of a diverse and extended republic get voiced.

The dynamic—and potentially contentious—interaction between the branches of government is similarly designed to achieve the public good by channeling, shaping, and refining popular opinions. We associate Madison first and foremost with checks and balances, with the idea that the government must be limited and contained, but even the separation of powers is designed to refine popular understandings within the large republic. Indeed, Madison's most famous discussion of the separation of powers in *Federalist* No. 51—where "ambition must be made to counteract ambition"—concludes with a discussion of the large republic: "In the extended republic of the United States, and among the great variety of interests, parties, and sects which it embraces, a coalition of a majority of the whole society could seldom take place on any other principles than those of justice and the general good."[35] *Federalist* No. 51, the seminal paper on the separation of powers, echoes *Federalist* No. 10 and the logic of the extended republic. What is crucial for Madison is that the public good is constructed from the "many parts, interests, and classes of citizens" that come from civil society. The separation of powers, representing these different parts, interests, and citizens, passes these views "through the medium of a chosen body of citizens, whose wisdom may best discern the true interests of their country."[36] This is from *Federalist* No. 10, which points to the institutions of government—the medium— where representatives refine popular understandings. Madison repeats this argument in his defense of the Senate, when clashing with the House, as a "temperate and respectful body of citizens" that can correct the "public mind."[37]

Consider that the institutions of the national government represent different versions of the people. The people are not represented as a single entity but are broken into different versions, each represented in our national institutions. Members of the House represent small districts that are likely to have similar interests and opinions, though drawn together in a way that speaks to the "great theatre of the United States."[38] Senators represent the whole people of their respective states, which necessarily broadens the range of interests and views represented, giving it a "due sense of national character."[39] The president does represent the people as a whole, but not in a national plebiscite, though as Jeremy D. Bailey notes, Madison did in time come to see the president as representative of national will in a way that balanced against the Congress representing a complex version of the public.[40] And the federal judiciary, by way of the appointment process and life tenure, is distant from the people.

Even the terms of national offices, staggered as they are, were designed to give voice to the people in different capacities, as well as to shape that voice. The two-year term of representatives keeps them close to the people and allows for an immediate expression of popular understandings based on a range and variety of opinions reflected in the variety of House districts. A six-year term in the Senate, on the other hand, allows for a longer-range vision, which can resist popular passions for "enlightened policy" and an "attachment to the public good."[41] The four-year term of the presidency similarly allows for resistance to "every sudden breeze of passion" or "every transient impulse" of the people, while also broadening to the whole people, diluting the more impassioned voices, to strike a balance among the multitude of interests and voices across the nation.[42] By way of the clash of different interests and ideas, nourished by institutional design, the Madisonian vision seeks the refinement and enlargement of the public mind. As Madison said, particularly in a large country, it is often difficult for the public's "real opinion to be ascertained."[43] Public opinion is not a simple given; nor, even if it can be "ascertained," is it necessarily reflective of the public good. When Madison spoke of the "permanent and aggregate interests" of the community or the public good, he had something in mind that was more objective than interest group bargaining.[44] At the same time, this was something constructed within political institutions relying on civil society, as he rejected the idea of a "will independent of the society itself."[45] For Madison, the multiplicity of interests did not preclude a genuine common interest.[46] Yet this is just where institutional design could help provide for political leadership even while Madison knew that statesmen would not always be at the helm; indeed, precisely because they would not, institutions could help facilitate the construction of a common good. The Madisonian vision sought to force this recognition by requiring the building of complex political majorities made necessary by the large republic and a system of separated power.

Much of Madison's argument about the large republic was speculative—and has only partially been confirmed in the two hundred plus years of representative democracy in America. The separation of powers has not wholly worked out as Madison envisioned. And while he wrote eloquently about the passions of the public sitting in judgment rather than its reason, it is not at all clear that representatives in our contemporary politics are more enlightened than the average voter. Our republican institutions look more like the direct democracy that Madison feared—partly because of political reforms, such as presidential primaries, that make our system more democratic. Madison resisted the popular impulse not simply because he knew that "men were not angels"—which applies just as powerfully to those in power—but because he worried that in the ordinary course of things the public might be inflamed or misled. Although this positions Madison as a critic of pure democracy, he was nevertheless a defender of *popular government* (even if his vision was limited by eighteenth-century understandings that fall acutely short of our view). Madison attempted to design American political institutions to overcome the weaknesses of popular government. Yet this required shaping the public mind, which Madison would come to comprehend more fully in the battles of 1790—particularly over the issue of freedom of speech—as those in power became the crucial threat to the future of republican government.

INTERMEDIARY INSTITUTIONS AND THE PUBLIC MIND

In the debates over the framing and ratification of the Constitution, Madison played up the importance of the government controlling the governed by way of institutional design and enlightened representation.[47] In the 1790s Madison's defense of republican government was more deeply concerned with those in power. To be sure, Madison repeatedly voiced this concern in his defense of the Constitution.[48] Yet with deep divisions on foundational constitutional questions throughout the 1790s—questions of war and peace, the reach of national power, and freedom of speech—Madison came to defend extra-constitutional means of organizing and shaping the public mind. This included political parties—or at least proto-political parties—along with newspapers and educational institutions as essential to making representative democracy work under the Constitution. Madison's initial efforts during this period included his essays for the party press, where he came to articulate a Republican vision at odds with the Federalists. Madison, of course, was a leading Federalist—indeed, one of two key authors of *The Federalist*—when it came to defending and ratifying the Constitution. Yet he would break with his coauthor Alexander Hamilton on key issues, concerned that Federalists were, in fact, pushing against republican government. The Alien and Sedition Acts of 1798 brought this out just before the election of 1800.

There is an important and long-standing scholarly debate over Madison's consistency. I am not concerned with that debate except to say that scholars tend to treat Madison as a philosophical thinker rather than a political actor. Madison was a deep political thinker, but he was also an imperfect political actor who was engaged in bringing his political understandings and principles to life in the conflicted world of late eighteenth- and early nineteenth-century America. It is best to understand his writings and his actions in the 1790s as wrestling with constitutional development in the early years of the Republic where he was attempting to secure the promise of republican government just as he was doing in the 1780s by writing as Publius. Madison's tone certainly changed as he learned from events, but on the essentials of republican government (if not all the particulars) Madison's arguments were largely consistent.

Colleen Sheehan has focused on his "party press" essays and "Notes on Government" to illuminate Madison's republicanism as preoccupied by shaping, mobilizing, and guiding public opinion as the animating spirit of self-government. Sheehan overstates her case (especially in downplaying the liberal features of Madison's thought), but she is persuasive in illustrating how the themes evident in these later essays are evident in his essays as Publius in *The Federalist* as well—even in the vaunted *Federalist* No. 10. As Sheehan argues, "Public opinion is not the sum of ephemeral passions and narrow interests; it is not an aggregate of uninformed minds and wills."[49] Rather, it is something to be refined and constructed—within political institutions to be sure—but also by way of political parties, newspapers, and educational institutions.

I turn to Madison's arguments about free speech in challenging the constitutionality of the Sedition Act of 1798 because they are often overlooked in highlighting his republican understandings. The Sedition Act allowed the government to prosecute its critics for seditious libel, effectively criminalizing criticism of the government.[50] Purportedly concerned about being drawn into war, preoccupied by the makeup of recent immigrants, and worried about agitation against the government, Congress passed the Alien and Sedition Acts together to empower the government to preserve itself against such agitation. The Sedition Act made it a crime to write or speak "false, scandalous and malicious" things against the government with the intent to defame it or bring it into contempt or disrepute.

Madison's critique of the Sedition Act deepened his understanding of republican government and helped forge a crucial constitutional development during this period: legitimating organized opposition to the party in power.[51] The debate around the Sedition Act was inextricably linked to the development of two political parties vying for control of the government. If there was agreement in 1787–88 on ratification of the Constitution—where a Madison and a Hamilton could unite—there was profound disagreement in the 1790s over the meaning of the new Constitution. The development of America's political parties stemmed from these disagreements. Yet if Madison's analysis of republican politics in *The Federalist* focused largely on political institutions, his actions in the 1790s focused more on politics "out-of-doors."[52] Madison's actions and writings criticizing the Sedition Act were a way to mobilize and educate the public to preserve the Constitution against representatives—indeed, a president—who were threatening popular government itself. Before turning to Madison's arguments, we might pause to note that while Madison is frequently invoked as a leading advocate of original meaning—the idea that the Constitution should be interpreted as it was understood by those who ratified it—Madison is perhaps better understood as constructing constitutional meaning here. That is, is not clear that the public who ratified the Constitution thought much about what freedom of speech and the press entailed. Thus, working from underlying principles and understandings of republican government, Madison sought to construct constitutional meaning in a way that was consistent with the nature of republican government.[53] In this, events drove constitutional meaning as they forced foundational questions onto the polity.

To better understand Madison's argument and its deep link to popular government, let me begin with the defense of the Sedition Act by leading Federalists who followed the common-law jurist William Blackstone to gloss the meaning of the freedom of speech and the press. Federalists argued that punishing seditious libel was entirely consistent with freedom of speech: given that free republican government was more dependent on the "good opinion of the people" than other forms of government, it was imperative that such a government be able to punish false speech. As Supreme Court justice Samuel Chase put it, a licentious press was particularly harmful to the republican form of government because it could "corrupt the public opinion ... and destroy the morals of the people."[54]

In contrast, Madison argued that republican government requires "the right of freely examining public characters and measures." This was crucial, in a republican government, "to the just exercise of [the peoples'] electoral rights." Madison went so far as to insist that free communication among the people in evaluating public issues and public characters with the intent of influencing fellow citizens and pressuring the government is "justly deemed the only effectual guardian of every other right."[55] Federalists rejected this understanding of public debate. While they acknowledged the importance of elections to republican government, leading Federalists insisted that once the government was in power, the minority must "surrender up their judgment." Only those whom the nation has chosen by way of elections may weigh in on such questions. Many Federalists doubted it was the place of an ordinary citizen to venture public criticism of the sitting government. Once elections had occurred, "private opinion must give way to public judgment, or there must be the end of government."[56] At the trial of Thomas Cooper, who was an able defender of freedom of speech and the press, the prosecutor reflected this mindset: "It is no less than to call into decision whether Thomas Cooper, the defendant, or the President of the United States, to whom this country has thought proper to confide its most important interests, is best qualified to judge whether the measures adopted by our government are calculated to preserve the peace and promote the happiness of America."[57] Cooper, in short, was in no position to second-guess President Adams because Adams had been elected. In publicly criticizing Adams for his public deeds, Cooper was found guilty of seditious libel. He was fined $400 and sent to prison for six months for voicing these criticisms.

Madison categorically rejected this understanding of freedom of speech as at odds with the republican government. In the American system, power flows from the people, which requires a robust conception of freedom of speech, allowing the people—the popular sovereign—to criticize the government, which is bound by the Constitution. The

> nature of governments elective, limited, and responsible, in all their branches, may well be supposed to require a greater freedom of animadversion than might be tolerated by the genius of such a government as that of Great Britain. In the latter, it is a maxim that the King, an hereditary, not a responsible magistrate, can do no wrong, and that the Legislature, which in two-thirds of its composition, is also hereditary, not responsible, can do what it pleases. In the United States the executive magistrates are not held to be infallible, nor the Legislatures to be omnipotent; and both elective, are both responsible. Is it not natural and necessary, under such different circumstances, that a different degree of freedom in the use of the press should be contemplated?[58]

A popular government of the sort the Constitution brought into being demands that citizens and the press have freedom in canvassing "the merits and measures of public men." In fact, Madison went so far as to argue "it is natural and proper, that, according to the cause and degree of their faults, they should be brought into contempt and disrepute, and incur the hatred of the people."[59] Whether the government deserves praise or contempt "can only be determined by a free examination" and "free communication among the people."[60] Not only would this require criticism of public officials and public policy, it would allow criticism rooted in differing political opinions. Holding the government accountable requires information and debate that speaks to the "merits and demerits" of public officials and their policies.[61] If the party in power can use governmental power to silence opponents, to criminalize differences of political opinion, the political processes is undermined, and republican government is corroded. Public officials cannot be held to be infallible.

Madison made this argument in helping pass the Virginia Resolutions in the state legislature, which were then published and sent to the other states and to Congress to persuade these bodies that the Sedition Act was unconstitutional and ought to be repealed. Madison further took to the newspapers to defend the Democratic-Republican Party in its fight against the Sedition Act and the Adams administration more generally. His defense of the Virginia Resolutions in the Virginia Report was written to influence the election of 1800. The arguments over the Sedition Act were part of the creation of political parties and the development of a distinction between the government and political parties, which would necessarily allow for what we now think of as the loyal opposition: parties that are loyal to the government and the constitutional scheme, but disagree, often profoundly, with the party in power. To put this in perspective, consider that the election of 1800, when Adams stepped down and Jefferson stepped into the presidency, is often regarded as the first peaceful transition of power between opposing political parties within a constitutional scheme. It was an essential step in securing republican government. Yet the concerns that animated Madison's critique of the Sedition Act, and pushed him to articulate a robust understanding of freedom of speech in a republican government, were long-standing. They were evident in his first foray into politics with the "Memorial and Remonstrance," which argued for "the equal freedom" of individuals to follow the dictates of their conscience regarding religion. This required, much as with freedom of speech and the press, the government to allow the flourishing of different opinions within civil society. This argument, as I have noted, presaged the argument of Federalist No. 10. In the Virginia Report, Madison similarly insisted on rights of conscience and freedom of speech—insisting the individual mind must be free to reach judgments, whether about religion or politics, on its own accord. In each instance, Madison took up his pen to persuade his fellow citizens and bring pressure on those in power. The "Memorial and Remonstrance" was written to stop a bill in the Virginia House of Delegates that he viewed as akin to an establishment of religion that harmed religious liberty. In successfully halting the assessment bill, he then helped secure passage of the Virginia Statute on Religious Freedom. In a similar fashion, the Virginia Resolution was written to fellow citizens and the representatives of various states legislatures to persuade Congress to repeal the Sedition Act of 1798. More ambitiously, the lengthy Virginia Report was written to influence the election of 1800.

Madison was engaged in shaping the public mind on such issues—highlighting the relationship between civil society and formal institutions. When it came to shaping American's understanding of freedom of speech and the press in a republican government, this was a continuation of Madison's work in framing the Bill of Rights. In a famous letter to Jefferson, Madison argued that a bill of rights could be most useful in educating the public: "The political truths declared in that solemn manner acquire by degrees the character of fundamental maxims of free Government, and as they become incorporated with the national sentiment, counteract the impulses of interest and passion."[62] It is also important to recall that in defending freedom of speech, Madison had initially included a provision in what would become the Bill of Rights that protected both speech and religion against the states: "No state shall violate the equal rights of conscience, or the freedom of the press."[63] Introduced in 1789, this proposed amendment to the Constitution never made it out of Congress. Madison echoed these concerns throughout his life. Writing on the importance of public education in the 1820s, he insisted: "Learned institutions ought to be the favorite objects with every free people. They throw that light over the public mind which is the best security against crafty and dangerous encroachments on the public liberty."[64]

Madison defended republicanism as a form of popular government when popular government was novel and much in need of a defense. To be sure, Madison only set in motion a republican form of government that required two centuries of struggle to make genuinely republican. And just as surely, America's constitutional scheme has not worked fully in accord with a Madisonian vision, though a Madisonian mindset would have us learn from experience rather than be beholden to the past. But Madison's worries about the "popular arts" where the people might be "misled by the artful misrepresentations of interested men" remains an enduring problem of popular government.[65] So too does his worry that government might become abusive of its power or disconnected from the people it is meant to serve. Striking the right balance between the government and the people—the degree of dependence and independence between them— may be the enduring question of republican government. It was Madison's central preoccupation as constitutional thinker and political actor.

NOTES

1. Madison, *Federalist* No. 40, in Alexander Hamilton, James Madison, and John Jay, *The Federalist Papers*, ed. Ian Shapiro (New Haven: Yale University Press, 2009), 202 (subsequent citations are to this edition).
2. Madison, *Federalist* No. 63, 320.
3. Madison, *Federalist* No. 14, 67.
4. The insistence by some politicians today that "America is a republic, not a democracy," misses how these terms have changed. As I note, when Madison speaks of democracy, he is usually speaking of direct democracy. When we speak of democracy today, we usually mean representative democracy in the manner that Madison spoke of republicanism. For a more detailed critique see George Thomas, "'America Is a Republic, Not a Democracy' Is a Dangerous—and Wrong—Argument" *The Atlantic*, November 2, 2020, https://www.theatlantic.com/ideas/archive/2020/11/yes-constitution-democracy/616949/.

5. Madison, *Federalist* No. 63, 320.
6. Jack N. Rakove, "Politics Indoors and Out-of-Doors: A Fault Line in Madison's Thinking," in *The Cambridge Companion to "The Federalist,"* ed. Jack N. Rakove and Colleen A. Sheehan (New York: Cambridge University Press, 2020), 370–99.
7. Madison, *Federalist* No. 46, 239; *Federalist* No. 10, 51.
8. Madison, *Federalist* No. 10, 51.
9. See Thomas, "'America Is a Republic."
10. Madison, *Federalist* No. 10, 51.
11. Madison, *Federalist* No. 63, 320–21.
12. Ibid., 320.
13. Madison, *Federalist* No. 10, 51.
14. Ibid., 52.
15. Madison, *Federalist* No. 55, 283.
16. Ibid., 283.
17. Madison, *Federalist* No. 58, 299.
18. Ibid.
19. Madison, *Federalist* 10, 51.
20. Ibid.
21. Jack N. Rakove, *A Politician Thinking: The Creative Mind of James Madison* (Norman: University of Oklahoma Press, 2017), 67, 73.
22. James Madison, "The Memorial and Remonstrance against Religious Assessments," in *The Mind of the Founder: Sources of the Political Thought of James Madison*, ed. Marvin Meyers (Hanover, N.H.: Brandeis University Press, 1981), 11. See George Thomas, *The Founders and the Idea of a National University: Constituting the American Mind* (New York: Cambridge University Press, 2015), 103.
23. Madison, *Federalist* No. 10, 49.
24. Ibid., 52.
25. Robert D. Putnam, *Making Democracy Work: Civic Traditions in Modern Italy* (Princeton: Princeton University Press, 1993), 87.
26. Ibid., 114–15.
27. Madison, *Federalist* No. 57, 290.
28. Alan Gibson, "Madison's Republican Remedy," in Rakove and Sheehan, *Cambridge Companion to "The Federalist,"* 295.
29. Jeremy D. Bailey gives us good reason to be skeptical of the idea that Madison thought representation would be quite so virtuous. Bailey, *James Madison and Constitutional Imperfection* (New York: Cambridge University Press, 2015), 52–56.
30. If this might sound aristocratic, in *Federalist* Nos. 55 and 63 Madison noted how important it was that both suffrage and political offices be open to all and not concentrate along class divisions.
31. In *Federalist* No. 54, Madison gave the three-fifths clause a perverse, if somewhat tepid,

defense of the different sorts of interests that could be represented. Madison, *Federalist* No. 54, 281. For Madison on this issue, see Noah Feldman, *The Three Lives of James Madison: Genius, Partisan, President* (New York: Random House, 2017), 155–59.

32. Rakove, "Politics Indoors and Out-of-Doors," 371.
33. Madison, *Federalist* No. 57, 290.
34. Madison, *Federalist* No. 53, 274.
35. Madison, *Federalist* No. 51, 266.
36. Madison, *Federalist* No. 10, 51.
37. Madison, *Federalist* No. 63, 320.
38. Madison, *Federalist* No. 53, 274.
39. Madison, *Federalist* No. 63, 318.
40. Bailey, *James Madison and Constitutional Imperfection*, 66.
41. Madison, *Federalist* No. 63, 325.
42. Hamilton, *Federalist* No. 70, 362.
43. Madison, "Public Opinion," *National Gazette*, December 19, 1791.
44. Madison, *Federalist* No. 10, 48.
45. Madison, *Federalist* No. 51, 266.
46. Gibson, "Madison's Republican Remedy," 267.
47. Madison, *Federalist* No. 51, 264.
48. Madison, *Federalist* No. 55, 285, in which he notes that republican government depends more on virtuous characteristics than other forms of government.
49. Colleen A. Sheehan, *James Madison and the Spirit of Republican Self-Government* (New York: Cambridge University Press, 2009), 79.
50. Terri Diane Halperin, *The Alien and Sedition Acts of 1798* (Baltimore: Johns Hopkins University Press, 2016), 29.
51. Bailey, *James Madison and Constitutional Imperfection*, 105, 107. See also Gerald Leonard and Saul Cornell, *The Partisan Republic: Democracy, Exclusion, and the Fall of the Founders' Constitution, 1780s–1830s* (New York: Cambridge University Press, 2019).
52. Rakove, "Politics Indoors and Out-of-Doors," 373.
53. For an extended analysis of this point, see George Thomas, *The (Un)Written Constitution* (New York: Oxford University Press, 2021), 64–79.
54. Wendell Bird, *Press and Speech under Assault: The Early Supreme Court Justices, the Sedition Act of 1798, and the Campaign against Dissent* (New York: Oxford University Press, 2016), 397.
55. Madison, "Report of the Virginia Resolutions," in *Founders' Constitution*, ed. Philip B. Kurland and Ralph Lerner (Indianapolis: Liberty Fund, 1987), 5:144–45.
56. Bird, *Press and Speech under Assault*, 297.
57. Thomas Cooper, *An Account of the Trial of Thomas Cooper, of Northumberland; on a Charge of Libel against the President of the United States* (Philadelphia: J. Bloren, 1800), 35.
58. Madison, "Report on the Virginia Resolutions," 142.

59. Ibid., 144.
60. Ibid.
61. Ibid., 145.
62. Madison to Thomas Jefferson, October 17, 1788, Founders Online, National Archives, https://founders.archives.gov/documents/Madison/01-11-02-0218.
63. Helen E. Veit, Kenneth R. Bowling, and Charlene Bangs Bickford, eds., *Creating the Bill of Rights: The Documentary Record from the First Federal Congress* (Baltimore: Johns Hopkins University Press, 1991), 13.
64. Madison to William T. Barry, August 4, 1822, Founders Online, National Archives, https://founders.archives.gov/documents/Madison/04-02-02-0480.
65. Madison, *Federalist* No. 63, 320.

Beyond Mandate Talk

*Madisonian Constitutionalism
and Democratic Discourse*

ZACHARY K. GERMAN

"Mandate talk" is a common part of American political rhetoric and commentary, especially in the immediate aftermath of elections, both presidential and midterm.[1] Political scientists have long observed this phenomenon, remarking, for example, that the "search for mandates" is "a recurrent feature of the interpretation of elections—particularly of landslides," that "the discussion of presidential mandates is as certain as a presidential election itself," that "partisan victors in nearly every election claim to have received a mandate to govern from the public," that "mandates are a central democratic myth," even that mandate talk amounts to a "postelection routine."[2] The concept of a mandate is frequently deployed both as a conceptual device for understanding the policy implications of any given electoral outcome and as a rhetorical device for advocating certain policies as the consequences of the American people's electoral choices.

While there is not a single definition of an electoral mandate, the common understanding is fairly straightforward, denoting when an electoral outcome indicates definitive support for principles, priorities, and policies, and thus, when the electoral success of a candidate or a political party is essentially a popular endorsement of an idea or a set of ideas. Put differently, a mandate claim contends that the electorate has issued "authoritative commands" or "policy directives" to elected officials or has granted a "right" to the victors "to implement a specific set of policies," not merely because they obtained power legitimately but because they did so with a "policy mandate" in tow.[3] To oppose the implementation of these policies would appear to defy the will of the people, insofar as a mandate implies a "right against others . . . not to obstruct" and imposes a "duty to defer" on elected officials who might otherwise resist such policies.[4]

Scholars have expressed much skepticism of the existence and discoverability of electoral mandates in American politics, both in general and in concrete cases.[5] If they do exist, even only as social constructions, some stress that they rarely occur.[6] Nevertheless, regardless of whether mandates exist or how frequently they may happen, mandate talk is a standard and recurring feature of our political discourse. This phenomenon may seem to be a benign and even useful facet of

American political rhetoric, as members of different branches and parties make and respond to competing claims that they represent the will of the American people.[7] However, in this essay, I examine the concept of mandates in the context of Madison's constitutional thought, particularly as he developed that thought in the 1780s, when he was most intensively engaged in the work of constitutional design. I argue that a Madisonian understanding of constitutionalism leads us to question whether mandate talk is healthy for political discourse or consistent with the constitutional features that Madison thought were vitally important.[8]

From a Madisonian perspective, mandate talk promotes a faulty conception of the significance of electoral outcomes and the implications that they should have. Madison's analyses of the extended republic, federalism, representation, and the separation of powers each indicate that the Constitution was not designed to produce or implement electoral mandates in the straightforward way that elected officials and political commentators frequently suggest. Thus, on the one hand, when mandate rhetoric is effective in persuading elected officials to act upon a perceived mandate from the people—or in persuading voters that they should hold those officials accountable for their degree of fidelity to that claimed mandate—it may tend toward undermining key benefits of the framers' institutional design.[9] On the other hand, when mandate rhetoric is unable to achieve policy aims, as it often is, its prevalence may cultivate a concern among the American people that constitutional institutions are defective, proving insufficiently responsive to the people's will. In contrast, Madison's constitutional thought highlights the complexity of public opinion in a diverse republic, along with the need for political institutions and elected officials to account for, channel, and refine public opinion in a manner compatible with the qualities of good government.

MANDATES AND MADISON'S EXTENDED REPUBLIC

The invocation of an electoral mandate is, in part, an agenda-setting mechanism. The case for a mandate typically rests on the premise that a recent campaign and election determined (or demonstrated) what the electorate wants political leaders to prioritize and how the electorate wants those leaders to act upon those priorities. In many cases, mandate claims fizzle without much in the way of policy consequences. However, when effective, appeals to mandates have the capacity to promote government action and efficiency, by decreasing conflict (and thus delay) over what the agenda will be and how agenda items will be resolved. Widespread perceptions of the existence of a mandate seem to correspond to significant legislative accomplishments.[10] What we should note here is that Madison's famous argument for the advantages of an extended republic in *Federalist* No. 10 is contingent upon the condition that the American people will be limited in what they directly determine at the ballot box in terms of agenda setting and policymaking. As Madison understands it, this is vital to the extended republic's role in defusing the danger of majority faction.[11]

Madison's definition of "faction" draws out this point: "By a faction, I understand a number of citizens, whether amounting to a majority or minority of the whole, who are united and actuated by some common impulse of passion, or of interest, adverse to the rights of other citizens, or to the permanent and aggregate interests of the community."[12] While Madison's definition does not entail that every political majority is factious in nature, it does make clear that a faction may be what someone claiming a mandate might call—with less precision but more rhetorical force—"the American people" themselves. Madison's aspiration for the extended republic is that it will "break and control the violence of faction," especially that of majority factions, in a manner consistent with republican principles, rather than effectuating their will.[13]

The state governments, Madison notes, were distinguished by the fact that they "are too unstable; that the public good is disregarded in the conflicts of rival parties; and that measures are too often decided, not according to the rules of justice, and the rights of the minor party, but by the superior force of an interested and overbearing majority."[14] They were not failing to implement the wishes of majorities; they were failing insofar as they were acting upon those wishes to the detriment of other goods toward which government should aim—stability, the public good, justice, and the protection of individual rights.[15] Majority rule is not merely an insufficient criterion of good government; historically, it has consistently been at odds with good government, as "the friend of popular governments, never finds himself so much alarmed for their character and fate, as when he contemplates their propensity to this dangerous vice [of faction]."[16] The task of institutional design, then, is to render popular government more conducive to the reliable production of these other governmental goods. Such a task requires regulation of how the people's will is reflected in policymaking.

Madison predicts that the diversity of interests subsumed within the extended republic, functioning through the "scheme of representation" absent in "pure democracies," will achieve this aim of constitutionalism.[17] He expects that the federal government will integrate so many interests and opinions that elected officials will generally be unable to discover a factious "common impulse" among their colleagues to provide the basis for quick collective action. Without that common impulse, they will have no choice but to work to find common ground upon which to craft laws. That common ground could be found in no other way than through compromise, deliberation, and a little dose of public-spiritedness. Or so Madison says in *Federalist* No. 51: "In the extended republic of the United States, and among the great variety of interests, parties, and sects, which it embraces, a coalition of a majority of the whole society could seldom take place upon any other principles, than those of justice and the general good."[18] Madison anticipates that shifting away from conflict between few partial interests to deliberation and compromise among many partial interests will, generally speaking, tend toward the approximation of justice and the common good.

In light of our increasingly polarized two-party system today, we might suspect that the interaction of many interests in Madison's extended republic has largely been supplanted by a conflict between only two polarized parties—that the "greater variety" that Madison describes has been consolidated into the two parties' "common impulses." Certainly, the barriers to coordination among members of a faction are no longer what Madison perceived them to be. While he does not reject Madison's extended republic analysis as a whole, Cass R. Sunstein suggests that it warrants "serious qualifications" in the light of our contemporary experience. For example, he notes that, even as the nation has grown, it "is in important respects far smaller than it once was, among other things because it is so easy to communicate and organize across geographical barriers that were once formidable."[19] The combination of polarization, communication, and organization makes it at least plausible to say in the wake of some elections that a natural majority (as opposed to a constructed or coalitional one)—and thus potentially a faction—has taken the reins of government.[20]

A discussion of the nature and degree of polarization in the contemporary United States goes beyond the scope of this essay, but we should note that the logic of the extended republic depends upon the existence of diverse interests and the significance of that diversity to political activity. Thus, it is worth considering the extent to which an array of opinions, passions, and interests may be sorted into the two major parties today. Each party must strive to capture at least a plurality of the politically active electorate within an electoral district. Even with a growing emphasis on turnout, on "getting out the base," the parties must, therefore, make a broad enough appeal to win elections. It is for this reason that we continue to see "wings" and "caucuses" within each party, with party leaders tasked with the responsibility of arbitrating intraparty disagreements. Moreover, elections are determined by a variety of factors, including partisanship, negative partisanship, candidate characteristics, retrospective voting, and local circumstances, in addition to commitment to party principles and positions on national policy issues. So, while our contemporary political circumstances generate reasonable concerns about the ongoing efficacy of the extended republic, we should not be too quick to conclude that it no longer mitigates the dangers of faction.

Nevertheless, mandate talk may work against this benefit of the extended republic by declaring that an election has exhibited a natural or preexisting majority among the American voting public regarding policies or partisan priorities. Madison, however, hoped that the extended republic would be defined by the construction of majorities through, first, the multiplicity of elections and, second, the interaction of interests in Congress.[21] Thus, when mandate talk is rhetorically successful by prompting elected officials to act upon a simple, homogeneous interpretation of the meaning and implications of the most recent election, such rhetoric may have the effect of diminishing the safeguard that Madison intended for the extended republic to provide against faction. When, however, mandate claims are unable to bring about policy change, due in part to the operation of the extended republic, appeals to mandates foster a concern that the constitutional system is obstructing the majority's will. While some will view the rejection of a particular mandate claim as salutary, others will interpret such a rejection as flouting the rule of the people, thereby depleting public confidence in constitutional institutions.

MANDATES AND MADISON'S "PARTLY FEDERAL, PARTLY NATIONAL" SYSTEM

In *Federalist* No. 51, Madison states that "experience has taught mankind the necessity of auxiliary precautions" beyond the accountability of the government to the people.[22] The plural character of that term, "auxiliary precautions," is essential for Madison. He did not rest political liberty on any one of those precautions (e.g., the extended republic, federalism, the separation of powers), but on the combination of all of them. In this section, I turn to the auxiliary precaution of federalism, which Madison describes as providing, in tandem with the separation of powers, "a double security ... to the rights of the people."[23]

While the Constitution constrains what elected officials are permitted to do in various ways, Madison's conception of the Constitution's "partly federal, and partly national" character highlights an important way in which rhetorical appeals to "the will of the people" may be constitutionally misleading.[24] When one invokes the existence of an electoral mandate, one is generally claiming that "the American people have spoken" on a given issue. However, Madison's understanding of the federal system entails that the American people are not the relevant constituency for some political matters. In fact, through the Constitution, the

American people have limited their own collective jurisdiction, allocating the authority to make some political decisions to the people within each state.

As Madison puts it in *Federalist* No. 39, the American people make up one political community "united for particular purposes."[25] The federal government's "jurisdiction extends to certain enumerated objects only," while the state governments retain "a residuary and inviolable sovereignty over all other objects."[26] "The powers delegated by the proposed constitution to the federal government, are few and defined," he reiterates in *Federalist* No. 45. "Those which are to remain in the state governments, are numerous and indefinite."[27] The Constitution acknowledges the importance of states as political communities distinct from the nation as an overarching political community. Because the state governments are not merely administrative units of the federal government, some political issues are not subject to decisions by the American people as a whole, save through a constitutional amendment.

During the debates over the creation and ratification of the Constitution, Madison was deeply critical of the state governments and in favor of empowering a general government, which has led to his reputation both as a nationalist and as inconsistent between the 1780s and 1790s. Yet Madison did not endorse a fully consolidated government in the 1780s; even then, he viewed such a consolidation as inadvisable. He affirmed that some powers should belong to the federal government while others should be retained by the states.[28] Admittedly, his proposal for a congressional negative on state laws would have been a much more expansive supervisory power for the federal government than the Constitution ultimately contained, but it would have been negative or corrective in character.[29] By implication, a significant portion of governing authority would be in the hands of the people of the individual states. The will of the American people would thereby be largely inoperable with respect to those political matters. In the absence of Madison's congressional negative, this is even more so the case.

S. Adam Seagrave's analysis of Madison's conception of "layered social compacts" helpfully illuminates this point: "The 'people' ... take on a double character: (1) '*as* individuals composing one entire nation'; and (2) '*as* composing the distinct and independent States to which they respectively belong.'"[30] Put differently, "The same individuals are conceived as belonging simultaneously to two different 'peoples,' in the social compact sense of a political community that collectively possesses 'supreme authority' over its government." As Seagrave points out, "The national-level sovereign people ... holds the right of judgment regarding the division of power between the two levels of government as codified in the Constitution."[31] Nonetheless, that right of judgment should be exercised as a way of settling what is codified within the Constitution; the division of power is not subject to reallocation through ordinary lawmaking.

Invocations of electoral mandates do not necessarily violate Madison's conception of federalism, just as they do not necessarily violate any provision of the Constitution. Mandate claims may pertain to what Madison would have considered issues constitutionally assigned to the national government. But mandate talk has the potential to run afoul of Madison's federal system in the following way: When someone claims that there is a mandate to address a political problem at the national level, the assumed premise often seems to be that the American people, on an election-by-election basis, get to decide what qualifies, under the Constitution, as a national issue. Mandate talk often takes the form of asserting that "the people have spoken," that elected officials are "doing what [they were] elected to do," that the victorious party is pursuing the preferences of "the people who sent us here."[32] However, Madison's understanding of the federal character of the Constitution maintains that the American people have drawn a constitutional line between national and state issues. For Madison, constitutional self-government includes the right of the people of the states to govern themselves, subject only to specified constitutional constraints, with respect to the issues that the Constitution leaves within the purview of the states.[33] The American people may redraw the line between federal and state jurisdiction through the constitutional mode that they have provided for themselves, but until they have done so, that line represents a fundamental expression of their will that, according to Madison, ordinary elections cannot supersede.[34]

MANDATES, REPRESENTATION, AND THE SEPARATION OF POWERS

As we have just seen, Madison viewed the federal structure of the United States as institutionalizing the principle that, for some political issues, the American people, taken as a whole, are not the relevant constituency—and thus any claimed mandate is subject to the more fundamental mandate implemented in the Constitution. Madison's analysis of the separation of powers draws out the fact that, even for national purposes, the Constitution does not treat the American people as a singular constituency expressing their will through a single type of elected official. Instead, the Constitution channels the expressions of the people's will in different ways for different purposes, in a manner that is intended both to promote good governance and to preserve liberty.

In *Federalist* No. 37, Madison explains that a good government consists of several ingredients that are difficult to obtain simultaneously: "Among the difficulties encountered by the convention, a very important one must have lain, in combining the requisite stability and energy in government, with the inviolable attention due to liberty, and to the republican form."[35] He goes on to illustrate the difficulty of this task. Republican liberty calls for short terms and large bodies of representatives; stability, in contrast, is promoted by lengthier terms; and energy is served by both lengthier terms and "the execution of [power] by a single hand."[36] Wisdom and responsibility for the general welfare, unmentioned in *Federalist* No. 37 but present in later essays, require both long terms and select bodies.

A complex government, embodied in the separation of powers, is Madison's solution for overcoming these tensions in designing a good government.[37] Because it is impossible to craft a single institution that yields all the ingredients of good governance, Madison turned to several institutions, each particularly responsible for providing one or more—but not all—of those ingredients. Thus, we might say that each part of the government is designed with a constitutional mandate. Madison anticipated that each institution would primarily embody the attributes of good government for which it is suited: republican liberty in the House; stability and wisdom in the Senate; energy in the executive.[38]

The House of Representatives presents the most direct reflection of the voting public, due to its representation based on population, short terms, and direct elections. It is the home of republican accountability in Madison's system, although even here the fundamental aim of the institutional design of the House is "to obtain for rulers men who possess most wisdom to discern, and most virtue to pursue, the common good of the society" and to ensure that those representatives remain virtuous while they are in office.[39] Popular accountability is key to that end, but responsiveness to public opinion is not the primary or exclusive end in itself.[40] To the contrary, an important advantage of a republic over "a pure democracy" is that a republic enables the "substitution of representatives, whose enlightened views and virtuous sentiments render them superior to local prejudices, and to schemes of injustice."[41] Representation in the extended republic holds out the prospect of representatives who would "refine and enlarge the public views," rather than merely reflecting them.[42]

Moreover, members of the House could not be expected simply to embody the will of the American people, but rather the separate wills of different subsets of the people. It was, in part, for this reason that Madison feared that partial interests, rather than a commitment to the general welfare of the nation, would sometimes drive representatives' behavior: "A local spirit will infallibly prevail much more in the members of the congress, than a national spirit will prevail in the legislatures of the particular states."[43] Madison hoped that members of Congress would be better equipped to act with a "national spirit," but he also thought that the extended republic would turn the presence of local interests to the advantage of the nation, as it hindered the formation of majority factions and forced the construction of majorities through deliberation and compromise. As previously mentioned, by simplifying the significance of an electoral outcome, mandate talk suggests that "the people" of the extended republic have voiced their will. Yet each biennial election of Congress involves many outcomes, rather than a single one that expresses a unified popular will.[44] For Madison, it is only through the coordination of these electoral outcomes, through constitutional institutions, that the people's will may be approximated in a manner consistent with the ends of government.

This function of the House is also the reason why Madison saw a limit to the size of any legislative body. The Anti-Federalists advocated a much smaller ratio of representation and thus a significantly larger legislature to reflect the people more closely; as Brutus would say, "The very term, representative, implies, that the person or body chosen for this purpose, should resemble those who appoint them. . . . It ought to be so constituted, that a person, who is a stranger to the country, might be able to form a just idea of their character, by knowing that of their representatives."[45] For Brutus, representatives under the Constitution would represent far too many constituents to serve this purpose. Today proposals to expand the House of Representatives echo his concerns.[46]

Madison understood the importance of congresspeople meaningfully representing their constituents. Yet he insisted, "In all very numerous assemblies, of whatever characters composed, passion never fails to wrest the sceptre from reason. Had every Athenian citizen been a Socrates, every Athenian assembly would still have been a mob."[47] The preconditions of deliberation set limits to how many representatives could serve in a legislative assembly, even the legislative assembly that was intended to be closest to the people.

Madison evidently considered the limited size of a deliberative legislative body to be such an important consideration that he addressed it in his proposal for amendments in the First Congress. As Madison alludes in his speech in the House, many Anti-Federalists criticized the clause of the Constitution that "declares, that the number of representatives shall not exceed the proportion of one for every thirty thousand persons, and allows one representative to every state which rates below that proportion."[48] The Anti-Federalists objected to how small the House would be, and to how Congress could constitutionally decrease the number further. In addressing these concerns, Madison attempted to seize the opportunity to set not only a floor, but also a ceiling, to the number of representatives in the House, so that the number could never be increased "to a very unwieldy degree."[49]

The institutional mandate of the Senate is further removed from responsiveness to the people. Much of the focus on the Senate during the Convention and ratification debates dwelled upon state equality and state representation, the former of which is an ongoing source of criticism of the Senate today. For instance, Sanford Levinson refers to "the totally unjustifiable power given small, usually rural, states in the Senate."[50] Due to equal state representation, in addition to the historical development of the filibuster, some object that the Senate has become indefensibly obstructionist to the majority's will.

Madison had his own criticisms of the Senate's equal state representation and relationship to the states.[51] What he did not have reservations about was the Senate's role as a stabilizing institution within a popular government, an institution where statesmen could take responsibility for the good of the nation rather than being immediately responsive to the opinions of the people—indeed, that they could resist the "occasional impetuosities of the more numerous branch."[52] That was a recurring theme of his analysis of senates as republican institutions.[53]

Some may accuse Madison's case for the Senate as smacking of elitism. Even if we do not find it objectionable in principle, we might doubt whether senators today are qualified or even willing to play the role that Madison assigns to them. Madison, however, saw no incompatibility between the purpose of a senate and popular government, and he projected that senators would have the character and wisdom to warrant their elevated position. In *Federalist* No. 63, he makes an important distinction between the settled "sense" of the people and their immediate demands: "As the cool and deliberate sense of the community ought, in all governments, and actually will, in all free governments, ultimately prevail over the views of its rulers: so there are particular moments in public affairs, when the people, stimulated by some irregular passion, or some illicit advantage, or misled by the artful misrepresentations of interested men, may call for measures which they themselves will afterwards be the most ready to lament and condemn."[54] Madison does not lay out the criteria for determining what constitutes the "cool and deliberate sense" of the people, but he affirms that the people's sense, conceived in this fashion, should prevail. He insists only that it is the duty of statesmen, especially within the Senate, to resist the demands of the people when they are characterized by "temporary errors and delusions."[55]

Given the role that Madison envisioned for the Senate, of discerning and acting upon the "cool and deliberate sense of the community" while not feeling bound by the unsettled passions and opinions of the people, it is worth noting a few characteristics of how mandate talk functions in practice. First, some scholars argue that mandate talk tends to be most persuasive in the public mind and among elected officials when election results are surprising.[56] Surprising results demand an explanation that the assertion of a mandate readily provides. Yet if an electoral outcome is unexpected by pundits, political scientists, and political leaders, it must be the case either that those observers had misconstrued the state of public opinion or that public opinion had undergone a significant shift recently. In either case, the element of "surprise" should introduce a healthy degree of skepticism regarding whether one's interpretation of an electoral outcome accurately grasps "the cool and deliberate sense of the community," or even whether the most recent election had exhibited that sense, as opposed to a more transient impulse.

Second, mandate talk seems to be amplified by landslide elections.[57] Yet Madison intended for the staggered electoral cycles and lengthy terms of senators to provide stability by limiting the ramifications of a single electoral event. Writing to Jefferson in 1786, Madison remarks on the Maryland Senate that "the whole body is unluckily by their constitution to be chosen at once," which meant that it was regrettably "probable" that the senate would pose no barrier to the people's inflamed passions for paper money.[58] A well-designed senate, Madison suggests, should moderate the consequences of an unusually one-sided election. When lopsided electoral results diverge from recent trends, senators should be able to question whether those results reliably indicate "the cool and deliberate sense of the community."

Finally, mandate talk peaks in both prevalence and influence immediately after elections and at the beginning of new administrations and legislative sessions, before the fervor of the election has subsided and the losing parties can begin to project a different outcome in the next election. Mandate rhetoric is wielded to get things done *quickly*, while political momentum is on the side of those claiming the mandate. There is some evidence that it can be effective in that respect.[59] As Madison conceives of it, however, the institutional position of senators, with their lengthy terms, should enable them to resist the calls for immediate action, under the banner of a mandate from the people, until they have had the opportunity to reflect sufficiently on the implications of the most recent election.

Senators would have all the more reason to depart from the opinions of the people on certain occasions insofar as, according to Madison, they would ostensibly have expertise on "the laws, the affairs, and the comprehensive interests of their country," as well as a special sensitivity to global opinions and the nation's international reputation.[60] These are the reasons why Madison finds it favorable both that the number of senators is small and that senatorial terms are fairly lengthy. Due to these institutional provisions, Madison posits that senators will possess and act upon "a knowledge of the means by which [the happiness of the people] can best be attained" that the people do not always possess themselves.[61]

Because of the structure of both the House and the Senate, the president of the United States seems to have a distinctive claim to being the sole representative of the entire nation. Woodrow Wilson makes this point repeatedly in *Constitutional Government in the United States*. "We have grown more and more inclined from generation to generation," he writes, "to look to the President as the unifying force in our complex system, the leader both of his party and of the nation." The president is "the only party nominee for whom the whole nation votes." That is to say, "No one else represents the people as a whole, exercising a national choice." This means that "his is the only national voice in affairs" and that "he is undoubtedly the only spokesman of the whole people."[62] Put differently, Wilson suggests that it is necessary and salutary for the president to claim a mandate from the people.[63]

Madison was confident that the presidential office would regularly be filled by fit characters.[64] He also noted that the president is, in contrast to members of institutions such as the Senate, responsible in some sense to the American people as a whole.[65] But this acknowledgment does not entail that the president is capable of representing the American people in a way that could override the pretensions of Congress to do the same. Moreover, Wilson's understanding of presidential representation misses Madison's crucial point that the various institutions of the federal government are designed with particular functions or ends in mind. The sole executive is primarily designed to promote the energetic execution of the laws and protection of the nation, not deliberation and compromise among the diverse interests of the United States in the process of lawmaking. Thus, while the president may have a national constituency that no other single elected official has, Madison's constitutional thought does not privilege that voice in determining the course of national policy.

In addition to facilitating the fulfillment of their distinctive functions, Madison explains the other main purpose of the separation of powers in *Federalist* No. 47, where he states that it is an "essential precaution in favour of liberty."[66] It is indispensable because "the accumulation of all powers, legislative, executive, and judiciary, in the same hands, whether of one, a few, or many, and whether hereditary, self-appointed, or elective, may justly be pronounced the very definition of tyranny."[67] Madison learned this insight, most directly, from Montesquieu, whom he describes as "the oracle" of the separation of powers.[68]

That "oracle" also pointed to an essential precondition of the separation of powers. In his discussion of English liberty, Montesquieu emphasizes that the various powers must derive from genuinely distinct sources. If powers are formally separated but all drawn from the same body of people, the separation will lack much of its liberty-preserving potential. Montesquieu illustrates this point with the example of Venice: "Thus, in Venice, the *Great Council* has legislation; the *Pregadi*, execution; *Quarantia*, the power of judging. But the ill is that these different tribunals are formed of magistrates taken from the same body; this makes them nearly a single power."[69] Luckily for England, the branches of the government stem from meaningfully different social sources.

Madison opposed the mixed English system on principle; it was, after all, antithetical to "the fundamental principles of the revolution."[70] But that only impressed upon him the necessity of coming up with a wholly republican alternative to the English system. Drawing the members of the different branches from the American people in different ways and giving them different institutional incentives were key pieces of that alternative. As Michael Zuckert explains, "To decree separate powers was easy enough, but to make them genuinely separate was much more difficult under the constraint imposed by the all-republican rule. Madison's first answer was to attempt to derive the different powers so far as possible from different constituencies, or to make them responsible in different ways to the same constituency."[71] Seen in that light, mandate talk conflicts with this precondition for the separation of powers, insofar as it tends to give the impression that elected officials and citizens more generally should think of the House, Senate, and executive as responsible to the same constituency in the same ways.

PUBLIC OPINION, DEMOCRATIC DISCOURSE, AND THE PERPETUATION OF MADISONIAN CONSTITUTIONALISM

To the extent that the rhetoric of mandates is in tension with key features of Madison's constitutional design, the prevalence of mandate talk renders it more doubtful that Americans will maintain an appreciation for those constitutional features, and the occasional efficacy of mandate talk calls into question whether those features will consistently achieve their purposes. Granted, Madison intended constitutional structures to be more robust than what he sometimes called mere "parchment barriers"—the term he used to characterize various ineffective separation-of-powers systems in the state constitutions, as well as declarations of rights.[72] For this reason, it would be easy to conclude that the practice of mandate-claiming is a harmless or even ultimately productive exercise of political maneuvering within our constitutional system. However, Madison's thought draws our attention to the important relationship between public discourse, public opinion, and the functioning of a constitutional government.

Mandate talk teaches citizens to expect both too much, in one sense, and too little, in another, from the form of government under which they live. In teaching them to expect *too much*, mandate talk suggests that there should be a rather direct relationship between electoral outcomes and policy outcomes. Since the Constitution was not designed to facilitate that relationship, the frequent failure of mandate claims to yield satisfactory policy achievements may promote frustration, disenchantment, and cynicism regarding our political system. Divided government is thus particularly frustrating when it results in gridlock, while unified government is perhaps even more infuriating for partisans of the party in power—and the grounds for scoffing by the opposition party. The growing evidence of Americans' discontent with their political institutions may be partly driven by this disjunction between the expectations and the realities of the consequences of elections.

Mandate talk may even exacerbate the problems of gridlock and polarization. The rhetoric of mandates conveys to voters that the people have spoken, that elected officials are aware of what the people have expressed through their votes, and that the only appropriate response is for those officials to enact the people's mandate. On such an understanding, why should voters support an approach of deliberation and compromise with those allegedly standing in the way of the people's will? That approach would seem to involve abandoning the majority's wishes in favor of capitulating to a recalcitrant minority. In contrast to that understanding, while Madison wanted the Constitution to result in governmental action, not paralysis, he recognized that the constitutional process would nevertheless be complicated, coordinating the diverse interests of the members of the various branches and the constituents to which they are accountable. Moreover, he acknowledged that some slowness and friction in lawmaking are beneficial.[73]

If, in one sense, the rhetoric of mandates teaches citizens to expect too much, it may also incline them to expect *too little*. It encourages citizens to consider what Herbert J. Storing would call "simplistic democracy," rather than complex constitutionalism, to be the defining characteristic of their political system.[74] Madison's constitutionalism seeks to preserve liberty, to protect individual rights, to promote good government, to provide for self-government by citizens who are members of multiple political communities simultaneously, and to pursue the public good of the nation. For Madison, the accountability of the government to the people is an essential condition of good government, on both principled and practical grounds. But it is not a sufficient condition. The people's views need to be structured, channeled, and refined appropriately through the mechanisms of the extended republic, federalism, representation, and the separation of powers.

Consequently, when mandate talk proves persuasive, thereby convincing elected officials to submit to a claimed mandate out of a consideration of electoral repercussions, it threatens to detract from the advantages that Madison anticipated from these constitutional features.

In our present political circumstances, we may be tempted to believe that mandate talk is "simply necessary" to overcome the gridlock that our constitutional system makes possible—that is, to carry out the will of the people in spite of the obstacles that the Constitution places in the way.[75] However, rather than thinking of our constitutional institutions as barriers to the realization of the people's will, Madison's thought directs our attention to the possibility that mandate talk may be a barrier to the attainment of the goods that the Constitution is designed to produce. Without a sufficient appreciation for that design, we may expect our leaders and institutions to continue to fall short of the high aspirations of Madison's Constitution.

NOTES

I am grateful to Eric T. Kasper and Howard Schweber for their feedback and editorial guidance of this volume. I am also appreciative of the comments and questions I received when I presented a version of this project at the New England Political Science Association's Annual Meeting.

1. For a sampling from recent elections, see Brian Wingfield, "A Clear Mandate for Obama," *Forbes*, November 5, 2008; Kate Zernike, "Tea Party Comes to Power on an Unclear Mandate," *New York Times*, November 2, 2010; Alan Greenblatt, "For Obama, Vindication, but Not a Mandate," *NPR*, November 7, 2012; John Nichols, "This President Can—and Must—Claim a Mandate to Govern," *The Nation*, January 20, 2013; Doyle McManus, "A New GOP Mandate?" *Los Angeles Times*, November 4, 2014; Bradford Richardson, "Donald Trump Campaign Says It Has a 'Mandate,'" *Washington Times*, November 14, 2016; Jesse Ferguson, "Donald Trump and the Republicans Have No Mandate," *Time*, December 21, 2016; Robert Pear, "Democrats Won a Mandate on Health Care. How Will They Use It?," *New York Times*, November 10, 2018; "Joe Biden's Non-Mandate," *Wall Street Journal*, November 5, 2020; Jennifer Epstein, "Biden Has 'Clear Mandate,' Aides Say as Electoral College Votes," *Bloomberg*, December 14, 2020.

2. Stanley Kelley, *Interpreting Elections* (Princeton: Princeton University Press, 1983), 126; Lawrence J. Grossback, David A. M. Peterson, and James A. Stimson, "Comparing Competing Theories on the Causes of Mandate Perceptions," *American Journal of Political Science* 49, no. 2 (2005): 406; Paul E. Rutledge, "Mandate," in *Encyclopedia of U.S. Campaigns, Elections, and Electoral Behavior*, ed. Kenneth F. Warren (Thousand Oaks, Calif.: SAGE, 2008), 391; Marjorie Randon Hershey, "The Meaning of a Mandate: Interpretations of 'Mandate' in 1984 Presidential Election Coverage," *Polity* 27, no. 2 (1994): 232; Jeffrey S. Peake, "Review: *Mandate Politics*," *Journal of Politics* 69, no. 3 (2007): 891. See also Julia R. Azari, "Institutional Change and the Presidential Mandate," *Social Science History* 37, no. 4 (2013): 483–84; Jeremy D. Bailey, *The Idea of Presidential Representa-*

tion: An Intellectual and Political History (Lawrence: University Press of Kansas, 2019), 3; Patricia Heidotting Conley, *Presidential Mandates: How Elections Shape the National Agenda* (Chicago: University of Chicago Press, 2001), xi.

3. Kelley, *Interpreting Elections*, 127; Lawrence J. Grossback, David A. M. Peterson, and James A. Stimson, *Mandate Politics* (Cambridge: Cambridge University Press, 2006), 17; Robert E. Goodin and Michael Saward, "Dog Whistles and Democratic Mandates," *Political Quarterly* 76, no. 4 (2005): 472. For various conceptions of electoral mandates, see Azari, "Institutional Change," 485–89; Hershey, "Meaning of a Mandate," 228–31.

4. Goodin and Saward, "Dog Whistles and Democratic Mandates," 472–73.

5. For references to or discussions of this skepticism, see Azari, "Institutional Change," 483–84; Conley, *Presidential Mandates*, 1–2, 4–5; Robert A. Dahl, "Myth of the Presidential Mandate," *Political Science Quarterly* 105, no. 3 (1990): 355–72; Goodin and Saward, "Dog Whistles and Democratic Mandates"; Grossback, Peterson, and Stimson, *Mandate Politics*, 14, 17, 28–29; Hershey, "Meaning of a Mandate," 231, 253; Kelley, *Interpreting Elections*, 133–37; Peake, "Review: *Mandate Politics*," 891; Rutledge, "Mandate," 391; Wayne P. Steger, "The Occurrence and Consequences of Electoral Mandates in Historical Context," *Congress & the Presidency: A Journal of Capital Studies* 27, no. 2 (2000): 121, 123–24; Raymond E. Wolfinger, "Dealignment, Realignment, and Mandates in the 1984 Election," in *The American Elections of 1984*, ed. Austin Ranney (Washington, D.C.: Duke University Press, 1985), 293.

6. See, e.g., Grossback, Peterson, and Stimson, *Mandate Politics*, i, 24; Kelley, *Interpreting Elections*, 140; Rutledge, "Mandate."

7. While not specifically analyzing the concept of mandates, Bruce Ackerman is a notable proponent of this type of position. See, e.g., Ackerman, "The Storrs Lectures: Discovering the Constitution," *Yale University Law Journal* 93, no. 6 (1984): 1028–29, 1031, 1055–56.

8. For other discussions of normative concerns about electoral mandates, see Julia R. Azari, *Delivering the People's Message: The Changing Politics of the Presidential Mandate* (Ithaca: Cornell University Press, 2014), 171–73; Dahl, "Myth of the Presidential Mandate"; Kelley, *Interpreting Elections*, 129–33; Steger, "Occurrence and Consequences," 123.

9. I do not mean to suggest that the perception of a mandate is the primary or exclusive motivation of elected officials when they claim to be following a mandate; clearly, an appeal to the will of the people is a convenient justification for the pursuit of policy goals that one may hold for other reasons. However, insofar as elected officials are motivated by concerns about reelection, a mandate claim may influence the behavior of officials who would otherwise not be inclined to support the policies entailed by that claim.

10. See Grossback, Peterson, and Stimson, *Mandate Politics*, 17, 24, 28, 109, 193; Conley, *Presidential Mandates*, 73–76.

11. For a thoughtful recent treatment of Madison's argument for the extended republic, see Alan Gibson, "Madison's Republican Remedy: The Tenth *Federalist* and the Creation of an Impartial Republic," in *The Cambridge Companion to "The Federalist*,*"* ed. Jack N. Rakove and Colleen A. Sheehan (Cambridge: Cambridge University Press, 2020), 263–301.

12. James Madison, *Federalist* No. 10, in Alexander Hamilton, John Jay, and James Madison, *The Federalist*, ed. George W. Carey and James McClellan, Gideon ed. (Indianapolis: Liberty Fund, 2001), 43 (subsequent citations are to this edition).

13. Ibid., 42.
14. Ibid.
15. See also, e.g., Madison, "Property," in *James Madison: Writings*, ed. Jack N. Rakove (New York: Library of America, 1999), 515.
16. Madison, *Federalist* No. 10, 42.
17. Ibid., 45–48.
18. Madison, *Federalist* No. 51, 271.
19. Cass R. Sunstein, *This Is Not Normal: The Politics of Everyday Expectations* (New Haven: Yale University Press, 2021), 82.
20. Due to factors such as plurality voting, the Electoral College, and equal state representation in the Senate, it is also possible for candidates and parties to have electoral success without the support of a national majority. On "natural majorities" versus "constructed majorities" in Madison's thought, see Michael Zuckert, "James Madison in *The Federalist*: Elucidating 'The Particular Structure of This Government,'" in A *Companion to James Madison and James Monroe*, ed. Stuart E. Leibiger (Malden, Mass.: Wiley-Blackwell, 2013), 106–7.
21. This argument for the diversity of American interests and opinions must be reconciled with (or distinguished from) Madison's case for a certain type of consolidated opinion in his essay "Consolidation," in *Madison: Writings*, 498–500.
22. Madison, *Federalist* No. 51, 269.
23. Ibid., 270.
24. Madison, *Federalist* No. 39, 199.
25. Ibid., 198.
26. Ibid. See also Madison, *Federalist* No. 14, 65.
27. Madison, *Federalist* No. 45, 241. See also Madison, *Federalist* No. 46, 243.
28. Madison to George Washington, April 16, 1787, in *Madison: Writings*, 80–81; Madison to Thomas Jefferson, October 24, 1787, in *Madison: Writings*, 144; Madison, "Speech in the Virginia Ratifying Convention in Defense of the Constitution," in *Madison: Writings*, 362–63; Madison, *Federalist* No. 10, 47; and Madison, *Federalist* No. 14, 65.
29. Madison's opposition in the 1780s to rendering all political questions national is too often overlooked, due in part to a neglect of his reasoning behind his proposal for a congressional negative on state laws. See Michael P. Zuckert, "Federalism and the Founding: Toward a Reinterpretation of the Constitutional Convention," *Review of Politics* 48, no. 2 (1986): 166–210.
30. S. Adam Seagrave, "Madison's Tightrope: The Federal Union and the Madisonian Foundations of Legitimate Government," *Polity* 47, no. 2 (2015): 259 (emphasis in original).
31. Ibid., 269.
32. Azari, *Delivering the People's Message*, 4, 23.
33. I should note that the persuasiveness of this point against mandate talk will hinge on whether one thinks that Madison has a correct view of the federal character of the Constitution, which method of constitutional interpretation one adopts, and how well one thinks that a Madisonian federal system is capable of serving the national interest today.

34. Madison's shift on the national bank raises an important question regarding whether he would concede that the American people may effectively reallocate the distribution of federal and state powers over a considerable period, without resorting to a constitutional amendment. However, his position on the bank does not entail that one election, or even consecutive elections, could authorize such a reallocation.
35. Madison, *Federalist* No. 37, 181.
36. Ibid., 182.
37. This solution of complex government involves what are sometimes called "veto points," which increase the difficulty of passing legislation, even with popular support. Sanford Levinson argues that the presidential veto and "a wide range of other veto points in our legislative system ... make it extremely difficult for the national government to pass legislation that is, in the language of the Constitution, 'necessary and proper' to achieve the great aims set out by the Preamble, including 'establishing justice' and 'providing for the general welfare.'" Levinson also doubts whether the separation of powers even serves its aims effectively today. Sanford Levinson and Jack M. Balkin, *Democracy and Dysfunction* (Chicago: University of Chicago Press, 2019), 13, 50, 86. For the Anti-Federalists' concerns with the Federalist solution of complex government, see Herbert J. Storing, *What the Anti-Federalists Were For* (Chicago: University of Chicago Press, 1981), 53–63.
38. Madison does not appear to allude to the judiciary in *Federalist* No. 37. For Madison's complex position on the judiciary, see Michael P. Zuckert, "Judicial Review and the Incomplete Constitution: A Madisonian Perspective on the Supreme Court and the Idea of Constitutionalism," in *The Supreme Court and the Idea of Constitutionalism*, ed. Steven Kautz, Arthur Melzer, Jerry Weinberger, and M. Richard Zinman (Philadelphia: University of Pennsylvania Press, 2009), 53–77.
39. Madison, *Federalist* No. 57, 295. See also James Madison, *Debates in the Federal Convention of 1787*, ed. Gordon Lloyd (Ashland, Ohio: Ashbrook Center, 2014), 132.
40. Thus, Madison rejected the popular axiom "that where annual elections end, tyranny begins," in favor of biennial elections in the House. Indeed, he initially supported three-year terms for a less responsive but more stable and knowledgeable House. Madison, *Federalist* No. 53, 276–77; Madison, *Debates in the Federal Convention*, 72–73.
41. Madison, *Federalist* No. 10, 46, 48.
42. Ibid., 46.
43. Madison, *Federalist* No. 46, 244.
44. No provision in the Constitution necessitates either the precise number of members in the House or the use of single-member districts, whereby a single candidate is elected from a single congressional district. Prior to 1842, some states employed statewide, "general-ticket" elections, which generally resulted in unified party delegations. The Apportionment Act of 1842 required states to implement the single-member district mode instead of the general-ticket method. However, even if Congress allowed states to return to a statewide system, and even if some or all state governments elected to do so, there would still be numerous outcomes in any congressional election. See "The Apportionment Act of 1842: 'In All Cases, by District,'" United States House of Representatives, History, Art & Archives, April 16, 2019, https://history.house.gov/Blog/2019/April/4-16-Apportionment-1/.

45. *Brutus*, "No. 3," in *The Anti-Federalist Writings of the Melancton Smith Circle*, ed. Michael P. Zuckert and Derek A. Webb (Indianapolis: Liberty Fund, 2009), 188.
46. See, e.g., Larry J. Sabato, *A More Perfect Constitution: Why the Constitution Must Be Revised: Ideas to Inspire a New Generation* (New York: Walker, 2008), 37–40.
47. Madison, *Federalist* No. 55, 288.
48. Madison, "Speech in Congress Proposing Constitutional Amendments," in *Madison: Writings*, 449.
49. Ibid., 450.
50. Levinson and Balkin, *Democracy and Dysfunction*, 11. See also 13.
51. See, e.g., Madison, "Remarks in the Federal Convention on the Senate, June 7, 1787," in *Madison: Writings*, 98–99. However, see Madison's balanced appraisal of the Senate's features, albeit incentivized by the rhetorical context, in *Federalist* No. 62, 320–21.
52. Madison, "Observations on the 'Draught of a Constitution for Virginia,' c. October 15, 1788," in *Madison: Writings*, 409.
53. See Madison to Caleb Wallace, August 23, 1785, in *Madison: Writings*, 40; Madison to Thomas Jefferson, August 12, 1786, in *Madison: Writings*, 54; Madison, "Remarks in the Federal Convention on the Senate, June 7, 1787," in *Madison: Writings*, 98; Madison, "Speech in the Federal Convention on the Senate, June 26, 1787," in *Madison: Writings*, 110–11; and Madison, *Debates in the Federal Convention*, 39, 76, 149.
54. Madison, *Federalist* No. 63, 327.
55. For more on the "cool and deliberate sense" of the people, see Greg Weiner, "'The Cool and Deliberate Sense of the Community': *The Federalist* on Congress," in Rakove and Sheehan, *Cambridge Companion to "The Federalist,"* 400–425; Greg Weiner, *Madison's Metronome: The Constitution, Majority Rule, and the Tempo of American Politics* (Lawrence: University Press of Kansas, 2012). Madison also distinguishes between the "passions" and "reason" of the people in *Federalist* No. 49, 264, and *Federalist* No. 50, 266.
56. Grossback, Peterson, and Stimson, *Mandate Politics*, 16, 35, 40, 188–89; Conley, *Presidential Mandates*, 33, 39–41, 168.
57. Kelley, *Interpreting Elections*, 126, 128; Grossback, Peterson, and Stimson, *Mandate Politics*, 35–36; Conley, *Presidential Mandates*, 41–42, 168.
58. Madison to Jefferson, August 12, 1786, in *Madison: Writings*, 54.
59. Grossback, Peterson, and Stimson, *Mandate Politics*, 17, 24, 28, 109, 193; Conley, *Presidential Mandates*, 73–76.
60. Madison, *Federalist* No. 62, 322; *Federalist* No. 63, 325.
61. Madison, *Federalist* No. 62, 322.
62. Woodrow Wilson, *Constitutional Government in the United States* (New Brunswick, N.J.: Transaction, 2002), 60, 67, 68, 73.
63. Wilson receives a lot of attention in accounts of the development of presidential representation, but other prominent figures, at earlier stages of American constitutional development, include Andrew Jackson and Thomas Jefferson. See Stephen F. Knott, *The Lost Soul of the American Presidency: The Decline into Demagoguery and the Prospects for*

Renewal (Lawrence: University Press of Kansas, 2019); Bailey, *Idea of Presidential Representation*.

64. Madison, "Speech in Congress on Presidential Removal Power," in *Madison: Writings,* 453–54, 460.
65. Ibid., 463.
66. Madison, *Federalist* No. 47, 249.
67. Ibid.
68. Ibid., 250.
69. Montesquieu, *The Spirit of the Laws*, trans. and ed. Anne M. Cohler, Basia Carolyn Miller, and Harold Samuel Stone (Cambridge: Cambridge University Press, 1989), Book 11, Chapter 6 (emphasis in original).
70. Madison, *Federalist* No. 39, 194.
71. Michael P. Zuckert, "The Political Science of James Madison," in *History of American Political Thought*, ed. Bryan-Paul Frost and Jeffrey Sikkenga (Lanham, Md.: Lexington Books, 2003), 160.
72. On parchment or paper barriers, see Madison, *Federalist* No. 48, 256; Madison, *Debates in the Federal Convention,* 271; Madison to Thomas Jefferson, October 17, 1788, in *Madison: Writings,* 420; Madison, "Speech in Congress Proposing Constitutional Amendments," 446–47.
73. Madison, *Federalist* No. 62, 321.
74. Herbert J. Storing, "In Defense of the Electoral College," in *Toward a More Perfect Union: Writings of Herbert J. Storing*, ed. Joseph M. Bessette (Washington, D.C.: AEI Press, 1995), 395.
75. Grossback, Peterson, and Stimson, *Mandate Politics,* 193.

CONTRIBUTORS

JEFF BROADWATER is professor emeritus of history at Barton College. His publications include *Jefferson, Madison, and the Making of the Constitution* (2019); *James Madison, A Son of Virginia and a Founder of the Nation* (2012); and *George Mason, Forgotten Founder* (2006). He has written numerous articles, essays, and reviews, and he coedited, with Troy L. Kickler, *North Carolina's Revolutionary Founders* (2019). He holds a PhD from Vanderbilt and a law degree from the University of Arkansas.

PAUL FINKELMAN earned his PhD in history at the University of Chicago and was a fellow in law and humanities at Harvard Law School. He has published more than 225 scholarly articles and more than 50 books. The U.S. Supreme Court has cited his work in six cases as have many other courts. He has published pieces in the *New York Times, Washington Post, The Atlantic, Washington Monthly, Huffington Post, Los Angeles Review of Books, TheRoot.com,* and *USA Today*. He was an expert witness in the lawsuits over the ownership of Barry Bonds's seventy-third home run ball and in the Alabama Ten Commandments Monument case. He is currently distinguished professor of law at the University of Cincinnati College of Law.

ZACHARY K. GERMAN is an assistant professor in the School of Civic and Economic Thought and Leadership at Arizona State University, where he teaches courses on political thought, constitutionalism, and leadership. Focused primarily on American political and constitutional thought and early modern thought, his research addresses questions of statesmanship, political culture and civic character, civic education, politics and religion, and constitutional design. His work has appeared in such publications as *American Political Thought,* the *Political Science Reviewer, Lincoln and Democratic Statesmanship* (2020), and *Trump and Political Philosophy: Patriotism, Cosmopolitanism, and Civic Virtue* (2018).

ALAN R. GIBSON is a senior fellow at the Kinder Institute on Constitutional Democracy at the University of Missouri. His research interests are focused on the political thought of the American Founders, especially James Madison. He is the author of several articles on Madison's political thought and two books on the historiography of the American founding, *Interpreting the Founding: Guide to the Enduring Debates over the Origins and Foundations of the American Republic* (2010) and *Understanding the Founding: The Crucial Questions* (2007). He is currently working on book-length studies of Madison's political thought and his record of the debates in the Federal Convention.

ERIC T. KASPER is a professor of political science at the University of Wisconsin–Eau Claire, where he also serves as the director of the Menard Center for Constitutional Studies. His research is mostly focused on the U.S. Supreme Court and the U.S. Constitution, particularly the First Amendment. He has previously authored or edited seven books, including *To Secure the Liberty of the People: James Madison's Bill of Rights and the Supreme Court's Interpretation* (2010). His most recent book, coauthored with Troy A. Kozma, is *The Supreme Court and the Philosopher: How John Stuart Mill Shaped U.S. Free Speech Protections* (2024).

JACK N. RAKOVE is the William Robertson Coe Professor of History and American Studies and professor of political science emeritus at Stanford University. He is the author of eight books, including *Original Meanings: Politics and Ideas in the Making of the Constitution* (1996), which won the Pulitzer Prize for History; *Revolutionaries: A New History of the Invention of America* (2010), which was a finalist for the George Washington Book Prize; and *A Politician Thinking: The Creative Mind of James Madison* (2017).

HOWARD SCHWEBER is a professor emeritus in the Department of Political Science and was an affiliate faculty member in the law school, legal studies, and integrated liberal studies programs at University of Wisconsin–Madison. Professor Schweber was a practicing lawyer before receiving his PhD in political science. Over the past twenty years he has taught various courses on constitutional law, the Supreme Court, and constitutional and democratic theory. He is the author of four books and coeditor of a fifth, as well as the author of more than forty articles and book chapters.

DAVID J. SIEMERS is Distinguished Professor of Political Science at the University of Wisconsin–Oshkosh. He has written four books, including most recently the *Myth of Coequal Branches: Restoring the Constitution's Separation of Functions* (2018). His work focuses on the American founding, constitutional development, and interbranch relations. His current research examines calumny, the use of lying and innuendo for political effect. He lives in Oshkosh, Wisconsin, with his wife, who is an economist, and his dog, who is a corgi.

QUENTIN P. TAYLOR is professor of history and political science at Rogers State University. He has published a number of articles and chapters on James Madison and *The Federalist Papers* over the last two decades.

GEORGE THOMAS is Wohlford Professor of American Political Institutions and director of the Salvatori Center at Claremont McKenna College. He is the author of *The (Un)Written Constitution* (2021), *The Founders and the Idea of a*

National University: Constituting the American Mind (2015), and The Madisonian Constitution (2008). In addition to scholarly articles, his work also has appeared in *The Atlantic, The Bulwark*, and the Washington Post.

LYNN UZZELL is associate professor of political science at Bethel University and the founding director of the Summer Civics Institute at the University of Virginia. For four years she was also the scholar in residence at the Center for the Constitution at James Madison's Montpelier. She specializes in the Constitutional Convention of 1787 and the political thought of James Madison. Her current projects include studies in the integrity of Madison's Notes of the Constitutional Convention, Madison's understanding of the Free Exercise clause, and his antislavery constitutionalism.

MICHAEL P. ZUCKERT is Dreux Professor emeritus at the University of Notre Dame. He currently is a clinical professor for the School of Civic and Economic Thought and Leadership at Arizona State University. He is now preparing a study called *The Constitution's Madison*.

INDEX

accountability, 241, 244
Ackerman, Bruce, 252n7
Act of 1782, 87
Adams, John, 48–49, 230–32
Adams, John Quincy, 135, 136
Adams, Samuel, 177
age requirements, 61
Alien and Sedition Acts (1798), 3, 116–17, 157, 213, 229–32; Hamilton on, 228; Madison on, 229–32; Thomas on, 13
Alito, Samuel A., Jr., 218n48
Allen, W. G., 103n23
Amar, Akhil Reed, 57, 66
Anglicanism, 198–99
Annapolis Convention (1786), 25, 87, 103n25, 165
Anti-Federalists, 10–11, 153, 188n7; on Bill of Rights, 21–22, 29, 32, 167, 169, 177; on civil liberties, 183; complaints about Constitution by, 173; on "instruction" model of representation, 6–7, 14; Knox on, 176; Montesquieu and, 126; on religious freedom, 167; on representation, 70; on separation of powers, 143n13; on Virginia Plan, 73
Apportionment Act (1842), 254n44
Arms, Consider, 168
Articles of Confederation, 23–25; diplomacy under, 130, 149; "imbecility" of, 166; separation of powers in, 130; slavery under, 168; state legislatures and, 125–26; taxation under, 148; three-fifths proposal for, 20, 87

Bacon's Rebellion, 97, 105n56
Bailey, Jeremy D., 17n31, 124, 226, 234n29
Banning, Lance, 57, 144n33
Barry, Richard, 40
Beard, Charles A, 33, 55
Benson, Egbert, 133
Berkin, Carol, 17n31
Bilder, Mary Sarah, 27, 104n35
Bill of Rights, 10, 11, 107, 156, 169–72; Anti-Federalists on, 21–22, 29, 32, 167, 169, 177; Federalist opposition to, 170–72; Finkelman on, 165–88; Hamilton on, 171–72, 175; Jefferson on, 153, 179–82; plebiscites and, 71; ratification of, 176–77, 185; Roosevelt on, 50; "stepfather" of, 165, 186–88. See also Constitutional Amendments; religious freedom
Black, Hugo, 195
Blackstone, William, 230
blasphemy, 213, 217n33
Bogus, Carl, 189n19
Bork, Robert, 11
Bradford, William, 196
Brant, Irving, 16n31, 198
Brearley, David, 152
Breyer, Stephen, 196
Broadwater, Jeff, 9–10, 21, 147–60
Brookhiser, Richard, 22, 39, 40, 41, 124
Burger, Warren E., 195, 204
Burke, Aedamus, 183

Calhoun, John C., 10, 117–18, 159, 163n45
California Gold Rush, 48
Catholics, 167, 169, 211
Chase, Samuel, 230
checks and balances, 8, 150; factionalism and, 174–75; majority rule and, 55–56, 140; separation of powers and, 111, 114, 123–24, 226
Cheney, Lynne, 22, 124
church-state separation, 12, 195, 197, 205
civic education, 57, 224
civil liberties, 170, 178, 183
Claiborne, William C. C., 136–37, 146n63
Clark, Abraham, 25
Clinton, George, 188n7
Cogswell, William, 42
Collier, Christopher, 39
Collier, James Lincoln, 39
Confederation Congress (1780–83), 86
Connelly, William F., Jr., 124
consistency debate about Madison, 123, 135–38, 142, 228
Constitution (U.S.): Article I of, 107, 155; Article II of, 107; Article III of, 107, 117; criticisms of, 55–56, 173; generational views of, 49–51; institutional design of, 116, 123–27, 132–35; Jefferson on, 180; "paternity" of, 5–6, 18, 38–47, 165–69, 182; ratification of, 18–19, 172–74, 176–80, 229; slavery in, 84–100; Supremacy Clause of, 151. See also three-fifths clause

261

Constitutional Amendments, 155, 187; First, 12–13, 214, 230–31, 233; Second, 156, 189n19; Ninth, 11, 185, 190n31; Tenth, 156, 186, 187, 190n31; Thirteenth, 4, 49; Fourteenth, 49, 81n60, 186; Fifteenth, 49. *See also* Bill of Rights; religious freedom
constitutionalism, 1–2, 5, 237–51; antislavery, 97–98, 105n56; judicial review in, 121n13; ongoing, 141–42; popular, 12–14, 209, 210, 215; separation of powers and, 8–9, 125, 143n13
Cooper, Thomas, 230–31
Cord, Robert L., 204
Cornell, Saul, 167, 183
Corwin, Edward S., 39, 126
cosmopolitan elites, 56
Council of Censors, 131
Council of Revision (proposed), 8, 9, 113–15, 121n13, 143–44n19
coverture laws, 60
Crowninshield, Jacob, 136

Darwinism, 50
Davis, David Brion, 103n28
debtor relief laws, 56, 64–65, 149
Declaration of Rights (Va.), 170
Declaratory Act (1766), 150
deism, 167, 198, 210–11. *See also* religion
democracy, 220–24; Athenian, 153, 223; direct, 222; egalitarianism and, 56, 58; "pure," 239; republicanism versus, 55–59, 71–72, 220, 221–23, 233n4; "simplistic," 250
Democratic Party, 34
Democratic-Republican Party, 3, 157, 231
Detached Memoranda (Madison), 206–10
Diamond, Martin, 56–57
Dickinson, John, 18, 25, 152
diplomacy, 130, 138, 149
"dirty compromise," 93, 100, 104n37
diversity, 58–65, 172, 175, 220
domestic violence clause, 88, 96, 105nn55–56
Douglas, William O., 195
Dred Scott decision, 21
Duane, James, 23
Dunmore, Lord, 86

egalitarianism, 56, 58, 65–68, 73, 151–52
Electoral College, 6, 66, 69, 76; creation of, 154; Great Compromise on, 92; opposition to, 166; slavery and, 103n34; supporters of, 7
electoral mandates, 13–14, 237–38, 243–51

elitism, 62, 246
Elkins, Stanley, 140
Elliot, James, 136
Elliott, William S., 40
Ellis, Joseph, 19
Ellsworth, Oliver, 93, 151–52, 170, 172, 190n25
Employment Division, Oregon Dept. of Human Services v. Smith, 211
enslaved persons: disenfranchisement of, 56; emancipation of, 85, 87; free Blacks versus, 7, 56, 59, 60, 86; Revolutionary War and, 86; tax on, 92, 93, 99, 104n41. *See also* slavery
Establishment Clause, 12, 195, 197, 205
Eve, George, 182–83

factionalism, 89, 174, 196–97, 204–5, 239; demagogues and, 223; popular government and, 222–23; sources of, 33
federalism: critics of, 176–77, 184; evolution of, 147–60; Madison's approach to, 123–24, 153–55, 160, 164n45, 238, 241; mandates and, 14, 251; "new," 10; separation of powers and, 2–4, 7, 20–21, 29, 252
Federalist Papers, 18, 166, 174; (No. 14), 153; (No. 28), 158; (No. 38), 175, 176; (No. 40), 220; (No. 42), 129, 130; (No. 43), 97, 155, 162n29; (No. 44), 155, 175; (No. 45), 9–10, 18, 155, 242; (No. 46), 18, 175; (No. 47), 137, 248; (No. 48), 143n14, 175; (No. 49), 9, 30, 31–32, 141; (No. 50), 30, 31–32, 129, 131; (No. 53), 254n40; (No. 54), 20, 99, 234n31; (No. 55), 234n30; (No. 57), 62, 175, 225; (No. 58), 223; (No. 62), 9, 35, 154; (No. 63), 13, 234n30, 246; (No. 84), 171–72, 178
—(No. 10), 2, 6, 18, 153; on diversity, 220, 221; on electoral candidates, 74; on factionalism, 33, 89, 174, 196, 222–23; on freedom of speech, 232; on minority rights, 178; on policymaking, 239; on property rights, 224; on religious beliefs, 200; on separation of powers, 226; Sheehan on, 229; Thomas on, 13
—(No. 37), 18, 133, 153–54; on good government, 243–44; on judiciary, 254n38; on separation of power, 128–29
—(No. 39), 9, 18, 21, 154; on Constitutional amendments, 155; on definition of republic, 96, 115; on elections, 69, 118; on judicial review, 159; on political community, 242
—(No. 51), 2, 33, 141; on accountability, 241; on checks and balances, 111, 174–75, 220–21; on

INDEX

majority rule, 240; on separation of powers, 18, 111, 226
Feldman, Noah, 17n31, 22, 198, 199, 212
Field, Samuel, 168
Fifth Provincial Convention (1776), 31
filibuster, 246
Finkelman, Paul, 10–11, 18, 165–88; on Bill of Rights, 22; on "dirty compromise," 104n37; on three-fifths clause, 103n34
First Bank of the United States, 157, 209–10
FitzSimons, Thomas, 24
Founders' Constitution, 78n1; anti-dynastic features of, 57; complexity of, 73–77; democratic concerns with, 55–59, 71–72; electoral districts of, 63; political equality in, 65–68, 73; universal suffrage and, 60
"Framers' Coup," 32
free Blacks, 7, 56, 59, 60, 86
freedom of conscience, 200–203. *See also* religious freedom
freedom of speech, 3, 12–13, 190n25, 230–31, 233
Fugitive Slave Acts, 21, 104n45
fugitive slave clause, 11; Finkelman on, 104n46, 166, 168; Rutledge on, 94–95

Gallatin, Albert, 135
George III (Great Britain), 138
German, Zachary K., 13–14, 237–51
Gerry, Elbridge, 14, 27, 114, 169–70
Gibson, Alan R., 6–7, 20, 41, 55–77, 123
Gitlow v. New York (1925), 186
"Great Collaboration," 11, 17n31, 179–85
"Great Compromise," 9, 35, 92, 152, 154
Gutzman, Kevin R. C., 40

Haitian Revolution, 97
Hamburger, Philip, 107–9, 110, 115
Hamilton, Alexander, 18, 228; on Bill of Rights, 171–72, 175; on Constitution's ratification, 229; on emancipation, 86; Harper on, 23; Robert Morris and, 24; on national bank, 119, 157; Washington and, 23
Hancock, John, 177
Harper, John Lamberton, 23
Henry, Patrick, 99; on Bill of Rights, 176; on Constitution, 167–68, 182
Holmes, Oliver Wendell, Jr., 207
Holton, Woody, 33, 56, 63–64
Hutson, James, 197

inclusiveness. *See* diversity

Indigenous peoples, 60; disenfranchisement of, 56; Madison on, 84
individual rights, 170; Constitutional provisions for, 174; majority rule versus, 57, 73–74; public good and, 149, 153, 175
Ingersoll, Charles Jared, 44–45, 46, 47–48, 50, 51
institutions, 246; Constitutional, 123–27, 132–35; intermediary, 228–33; political, 225–28
interest groups, 222

Jackson, Andrew, 34, 159
Jackson, James, 184
Jay-Gardoqui negotiations, 24
Jay Treaty, 9, 125, 138–40, 142, 157
Jefferson, Thomas: on Bill of Rights, 153, 179–82; collaboration with Madison of, 11, 17n3, 179–85; on Constitution, 180; deism of, 198; on Louisiana Purchase, 135; Madison and, 3, 19; *Notes on the State of Virginia*, 85, 108; on religious freedom, 22, 148; removal plan of, 85
Jewish citizens, 167, 169, 189n12, 208
Jones, Charles O., 127
Jones, Joseph, 86
"judicial ideals," 107
judicial review, 8, 107–20; Hamburger on, 107–9; Madison's alternative to, 112–15

Kasper, Eric T., 1–15, 19
Kauffmann, Bruce G., 40
Kentuckian constitution, 8–9, 108, 114, 141
Kernell, Samuel, 17n31
Ketcham, Ralph L., 135, 136, 144n33, 198
King, Rufus, 92–93, 105n55
Klarman, Michael, 28, 29, 32, 33, 105n46
Knox, Henry, 176
Kramnick, Isaac, 15n2

land speculators, 65
Lee, Richard Henry, 173
"legislative vortex," 112–13, 125–28
legitimacy debates of Constitution, 55
Leland, John, 177
Lemon v. Kurtzman (1973), 195
Levinson, Sanford V., 41, 246, 254n37
Lincoln, Abraham, 49
Lind, Michael, 50
List, Friedrich, 44
Locke, John, 111–12, 137
Loconte, Joseph, 198
"long leash" theory, 6

INDEX

Louisiana Purchase, 125, 135–38, 142, 145n56
Lusk, Thomas, 167

Machiavellianism, 23, 102n20
Madison, James: consistency debate about, 123, 135–38, 142, 228; family of, 19, 165; as "father of Constitution," 5–6, 18, 38–47, 165–69, 182; on free Blacks, 7; on Native Americans, 7; pen name of, 33, 174; as political strategist, 5, 18–36; religious beliefs of, 197–99; on slavery, 4, 7, 20, 84–100, 163n45, 188n6
—works of: Detached Memoranda, 206–10; "Memorial and Remonstrance Against Religious Assessments," 22, 195, 198, 203–4, 223–24, 232; *Notes of the Convention*, 40; "Notes on Ancient and Modern Confederacies," 26; "Notes on Government," 228–29; "Property," 198; *Report on the Virginia Resolutions*, 13. *See also* "Vices of the Political System"
"Madisonian moment," 89, 102n20
Madison's paradox, 108–12
Maier, Pauline, 25–26
majority rule, 81n58; consequences of, 67–68, 73–74; individual rights versus, 57; tyranny of, 89
mandates, 13–14, 237–38, 243–51
manumission laws, 85, 86, 90
Marshall, John, 158
Martin, Luther, 94
Marxism, 56
Mason, George, 93, 99; on Bill of Rights, 174, 176; on religious freedom, 212
Mason, Matthew, 105n49, 169–70
Massachusetts Constitution, 28
Matthews, Richard K., 102n23
Maynard, Malichi, 168
McConnell, Michael W., 211–12
McCulloch v. Maryland (1819), 158
McDonald, Forrest, 39, 42, 43, 46–47; on republicanism, 102n16, 105n52
McKitrick, Eric, 140
"Memorial and Remonstrance Against Religious Assessments" (Madison), 22, 195, 198, 203–4, 223–24, 232
military service, 12, 213–14
militias, 156, 189n19
Miller, William Lee, 41
minority rights, 71–72, 150, 173–74; *Federalist* No. 10 on, 178, 239; of religious sects, 167, 169, 211, 224

Missouri Crisis (1819), 100
Monroe, James, 25, 183
Montesquieu, 110–12, 126, 150, 248–49
Morris, Gouverneur, 18, 40, 59, 92–94
Morris, Robert, 23, 24, 144n33
Muhlenberg, Frederick Augustus, 139
Munoz, Anthony, 212
Muslims, 167, 169, 211

national bank, 158; Hamilton on, 119, 157; Madison on, 119–20, 136, 137, 157
nationalism, 157, 159–60
Native Americans. *See* Indigenous peoples
naturalization requirements, 59
natural law, 85, 98
Nedelsky, Jennifer, 56, 63–64
Netherlands, 153
Neustadt, Richard E., 126, 134
New Federalism, 10
New Jersey Plan (1787), 151
New Left, 56
New Orleans, 67–68, 145n56, 148
Nixon, Richard, 189n9
Noonan, John, 198
Northwest Ordinance (1787), 94, 188n6, 217n22
Northwest Territory, 138
Notes of the Convention (Madison), 40
"Notes on Ancient and Modern Confederacies" (Madison), 26
"Notes on Government" (Madison), 228–29
Nullification Crisis (1832), 10, 118, 159

O'Connor, Sandra Day, 197, 207–8, 210
oligarchy, 88, 89, 96, 97; federal representatives and, 62, 72, 223; religious bigotry and, 167
originalists, 1–2, 187

paper money, 148, 149, 152, 247; debtor relief and, 56, 64, 65
"parchment barriers," 171, 172, 185
Paris, Treaty of (1783), 148
Paterson, William, 18, 152
Pennsylvanian Constitution, 131
Pinckney, Charles, 25, 40, 168
Pitkin, Hanna, 6
Pleasants, Robert, 90
plebiscite, 226
political parties, 13, 139–40, 141–42, 229–30
"political science," 129
Powell, H. Jefferson, 210
Presbyterianism, 198–99
presidential term, 227

INDEX

private rights. *See* individual rights
Privy Council (UK), 150
Progressive Party, 55–56, 72, 77
"Property" (Madison), 198
property qualifications for voting, 55–56, 59, 63, 64, 89–90
Protestant work ethic, 15n2
public good, 184, 221; compromises for, 138–42; individual rights and, 149, 153, 175; political institutions and, 225–28
public opinion, 57, 225–27, 244
Putnam, Robert D., 224

Quakers, 167, 211, 214
quos leges posterios priores . . ., 28

Rakove, Jack N., 2, 102n20; on diversity, 175; on jurisprudence of original intention, 187; on Madison's career, 16n31; on Madison's religious beliefs, 197–98; on Madison's strategies, 5, 18–36; on religious freedom, 212–13
Randolph, Edmund, 25, 27, 29–32, 74, 165; on Bill of Rights, 169–70, 176; on slavery, 168
Randolph, John, 136
religion, 61; deistic, 167, 198, 210–11; political utility of, 199–200; public support of, 203–7
religious freedom, 10, 195–215; Anti-Federalists on, 167; Congressional chaplains and, 208; diversity and, 30, 150, 172; Finkelman on, 177, 178, 185; freedom of conscience and, 200–203; Jefferson on, 22, 148; "Memorial and Remonstrance" on, 22, 195, 198, 203–4, 223–24; opponents of, 181; Rakove on, 212–13; Virginia Statute for, 206, 212, 214. *See also* Bill of Rights
removal plans: for Blacks, 84–87; for Native Americans, 7
Report on the Virginia Resolutions (Madison), 13
representation, 220; Anti-Federalists on, 70; electoral mandates and, 243–49; "filter" model of, 198; political institutions and, 225–28; proportional, 65–68, 81n51. *See also* three-fifths clause
republicanism, 228, 233; characteristics of, 57–58; complexity of, 73–77; definition of, 78n1, 96, 102n16, 115; democracy versus, 55–59, 71–72, 220, 221–23, 233n4; "gappy," 69; logic of, 220–33; meritocratic, 58; political equality in, 65–68, 73; power dynamics in, 128; responsiveness of, 68–73; slavery and, 87–88

residency requirements, 61
Revolutionary War, 85, 86; financing of, 144n33, 148; slave trade during, 169
Roane, Spencer, 147
Robert, Robert G., Jr., 195–96
Roosevelt, Franklin Delano, 50
Rossiter, Clinton, 39
Rutland, Robert, 184
Rutledge, John, 40–41, 94–95

Saint Domingue (Haiti), 97
Scalia, Antonin, 17n33, 211
Schweber, Howard, 1–15, 19, 22
Scottish common sense philosophy, 198, 216n17
Seagrave, S. Adam, 242
Second Bank of the United States, 157, 209–10, 254n34
Sedgwick, Theodore, 133
Sedition Act (1798), 229–32. *See also* Alien and Sedition Acts
Senate, 35, 166, 246–47; election to, 68–69, 154
separation of powers, 2, 69, 110–12, 123–42; Anti-Federalists on, 143n13; checks and balances and, 111, 114, 123–24, 226; constitutionalism and, 8–9, 125, 143n13; Council of Revision and, 113; electoral mandates and, 243–49; federalism and, 2–4, 7, 20–21, 29, 252; Montesquieu on, 111–12; "pure doctrine" of, 126; "sacred principle" of, 131, 141
Shakespeare, William, 206
Shays, Daniel, 88
Shays' Rebellion, 25, 96, 148–49
Sheehan, Colleen A., 57, 102n23, 228–29
Sherman, Roger, 18, 93, 94, 170, 190n25
Siemers, David J., 8–9, 20–21, 123–42
Signer, Michael, 22
slave insurrections, 86, 96, 105nn55–56
slavery, 4, 7, 26–27; under Articles of Confederation, 168; Constitutional Convention and, 90–93, 103n25; Henry on, 168; Lincoln on, 49; Taylor on, 20, 84–100; in U.S. territories, 145. *See also* enslaved persons; three-fifths clause
slave trade, 93, 95, 100; end of, 168–69; Madison on, 166, 188n6; George Mason on, 99
Smith, Elisha, 46
Smith, James Allen, 55
Smith, Melancton, 173, 188n7
Smith, Rogers, 56
Socrates, 38–39, 223
sovereignty, popular, 220

state authority, 118, 147–60; Constitutional safeguards of, 155; "continual struggle" over, 160; Madison on, 170–71
state legislatures, 125–28, 143n10
Stone, Michael Jenifer, 133
Storing, Herbert, 167, 250
Strong, Caleb, 27
suffrage, 53, 56, 59, 60, 88; Madison on, 62, 89–90, 234n30
Sunstein, Cass R., 240
Supreme Court, 153, 155; jurisdiction of, 157–58, 159. *See also specific cases*
Swift, Jonathan, 193n88

"tandem institutions" model, 127
Taylor, Quentin P., 7, 20, 84–100, 164n45
territories, 130; administration of, 135–38, 148; in Northwest, 94, 138, 188n6, 217n22; slavery in, 145n59
thanksgiving proclamations, 208–10, 214
Thomas, George, 10, 12–13, 20, 116, 220–33; on "agonistic" Madisonian Constitution, 123, 126
three-fifths clause, 6, 7, 20, 87, 98–99; Constitutional Convention and, 91–93; Finkelman on, 103n34; in Founders' Constitution, 65–68, 73; Thomas on, 225. *See also* Constitution; slavery
Thurber, James A., 126
Tocqueville, Alexis de, 1, 40–41
Todd, Dolley Payne, 165
Todd, John Payne, 165
Town of Greece v. Galloway (2014), 208
Treasury Department, 132–33
Trump, Donald, 32, 189n9

Ulmer, Sidney, 40
Unitarianism, 197
Uzzell, Lynn, 5–6, 18, 38–51

veneration norm, 20, 30, 32, 37n20
veto power, 150, 159, 173–74; Levinson on, 254n37; over state legislation, 191n42

"Vices of the Political System" (Madison), 20, 26, 87; on Articles of Confederation, 23; on minority rights, 71–72; on religious beliefs, 200; on separation of powers, 125, 127–28; on states' authority, 149
Vile, John R., 41, 46
Vile, M. J. C., 126
Virginia Plan (1787), 72, 151; for popular representation, 90; Rakove on, 1, 9, 23, 26
Virginia ratifying convention (1788), 176–79
Virginia Resolutions (1798), 10, 116–19, 157, 158, 231–32

War of 1812, 157
Warren, Charles, 39
wartime powers, 155–56
Washington, George, 154; Congressional address of, 184; on emancipation, 86–87; Hamilton and, 23; on Jay Treaty, 138; Maier on, 25–26; on thanksgiving proclamations, 210
Weaver, Richard, 38
Weiner, Greg, 40, 146n72
Wilentz, Sean, 104n34, 104n41
Williamson, Hugh, 92
Wilson, James, 18, 24, 40, 94; on Articles of Confederation, 188n3; on Bill of Rights, 170, 172
Wilson, Woodrow, 50, 248, 255n63
Wirt, William, 84
Witherspoon, James, 198–99
women: coverture laws of, 60; disenfranchisement of, 56, 59, 60
Wood, Gordon S., 1, 123, 171, 181

Zuckert, Michael P., 7–8, 20; on "gappy" republicanism, 69; on judicial review, 107–20; on separation of powers, 123, 249

www.ingramcontent.com/pod-product-compliance
Lightning Source LLC
Chambersburg PA
CBHW031128060226
39204CB00058B/156